THE PEACE TRADITION
IN THE CATHOLIC CHURCH

GARLAND REFERENCE LIBRARY
OF SOCIAL SCIENCE
(VOL. 339)

THE PEACE TRADITION
IN THE CATHOLIC CHURCH
An Annotated Bibliography

compiled by
Ronald G. Musto

BĪP - 9C

GARLAND PUBLISHING, INC.
NEW YORK & LONDON
1987

Library of Congress Cataloging-in-Publication Data

Musto, Ronald G.
The peace tradition in the Catholic Church.

(Garland reference library of social science ; v. 339)
Companion volume to: The Catholic peace tradition.
Includes indexes.
1. Peace—Religious aspects—Catholic Church—
Bibliography.   2. Catholic Church—Doctrines—
Bibliography.   I. Title.   II. Series.
Z7838.P54M87   1987   [BX1795.P43]   016.2618'73   86-31950
ISBN 0-8240-8584-1 (alk. paper)

Printed on acid-free, 250-year-life paper
Manufactured in the United States of America

To Eileen

CONTENTS

* *
*

PREFACE

The following book is the second in a three-part study that hopes
to document the history of the peace tradition in the Roman
Catholic church from the Gospels to the twentieth century. Its
purpose is to show that there truly is a continuing, unbroken, and
self-sustaining stream within Catholicism that bridges the gap
between the martyrs and pacifists of the early church and the work
of John XXIII and the peacemakers of our own time. This series
of studies hopes to reach the teacher, student, or general reader
who might want a basic introduction to the Catholic peace tradition,
those who seek readings in a course on Church or peace history,
and scholars who want an introduction to the materials and issues
involved in the research on this field.

The first part of this study, *The Catholic Peace Tradition* (Orbis
Books, 1986) is a narrative history ranging from the biblical
antecedents of our concepts of peace through the Gospels and early
church, the peace movements of the Middle Ages, the Humanist
tradition of peacemaking, and the problems and promise of peace
in the early modern world, from the missionary pacifists of Latin
America to the papacy's work for international peace. In the
twentieth century the book covers the issues of the world wars and
the role of Catholics in furthering war or peace, the revolution in
church life accomplished by Pope John XXIII and the Second
Vatican Council, and peace movements today in Europe, the Third
World, and the United States. This book was accompanied by
extensive annotation and a complete bibliography, but the limits
imposed by the size of the study and its purpose as an introductory
survey precluded discursive notes and lengthy comments on
citations. The second volume is the present annotated bibliography.

The third, projected volume, is one of readings in Catholic
peace history that will include selections from the primary sources

xiii

used in both *The Catholic Peace Tradition* and cited in this *Annotated Bibliography*. This will include selections from the Bible, writings of the early Fathers, canon law and penitential texts, the lives and sayings of the saints, histories of popular peace movements, monastic texts on the meaning and practice of peace, missionary accounts and plans for nonviolent conversion, Humanist tracts, accounts of individual witnesses for peace, episcopal and papal letters, and the decrees of church synods and councils.

The purposes of the present volume are several: the first is to update the research on the *Catholic Peace Tradition* from November 1984, when research for that book was completed, to November 1986, when research on the present volume was finished. Most of the entries in the present work have already been cited in the first book, but here they are accompanied by appropriate commentary. The second purpose, really an expansion of the first, is to provide the researcher with a detailed analysis of all these and more recent works as the basis both for detailed study of the first book and as a guide for further research in this field. The third purpose is to arrange these materials by topic and period, so that the student will have a framework for study and reading

Research on this project has been an educational one for me, a process that has been full of surprises, and one whose richness of findings has deepened my own understanding of the issues involved and my own faith in the existence of this unique Catholic tradition and its importance as a source of hope and strength for all peacemakers. At the same time it has also convinced me of the high standards of research in, of the questions posed by, and of the controversies engendered by the study of this peace tradition. While peace research courses and curricula have existed for decades on campuses and in schools across the United States, specifically Christian, Catholic and historical studies are yet to be fully provided with a basic set of research materials, questions, and goals. It is my hope that this collection of studies will take a major step toward providing a basis for these endeavors.

I would like to thank those who helped make this project

possible. The research facilities and staffs of the New York Public Library and of the Columbia and of Fordham University Libraries have been indispensable resources. Gary Kuris, Senior Editor; and Pamela Chergotis, Managing Editor, at Garland Publishing have both offered professional, and patient, help in seeing the manuscript of this book to press. Dr. Eileen Gardiner's learning and good sense have informed my judgment and my words.

Finally, let me say that these studies are intended less to provide categorical answers, but — first and foremost — to raise the essential *questions* about the Catholic peace tradition. My hope is that these books will cause others to question, research, and modify existing findings — including my own — and in the process make the Catholic peace tradition, its popular discussion, and its professional study far more widely known, understood, and alive.

* *
*

INTRODUCTION

It is no coincidence — though it may surprise many — that over the last ten years five of the winners of the Nobel Peace Prize have been Roman Catholics (Mairead Corrigan, Betty Williams, Mother Teresa of Calcutta, Adolfo Pérez Esquivel, and Lech Walesa), while numerous others (including Oscar Romero, Dom Helder Camara, Danilo Dolci, Cesar Chavez and Dolores Huerta) have been nominated for the prize in recent years. All have demonstrated the indisputable truth that as never before religious motivations and personal faith are affecting and defining the most important issues of public policy and life facing us today: peace and justice. They have demonstrated that their faith, *as Christians and Catholics*, is a living, active, and important element in the world today and that this faith is based on, and grows vitally from and within, a living Catholic tradition of peacemaking.

WHAT IS CATHOLIC PEACEMAKING?

While its terms and limits are always evolving and growing, this tradition has always defined peace as something active: not passive or acquiescent, not flattering to evil or retreating into indifference or silence, but activist, struggling for justice and motivated by Christian charity. The Catholic tradition sees peace as a force that must confront evil, but at the same time must love the evildoer and convert that evil to good. For the Catholic "turning the other cheek" is not the answer to violence, but only the question that confronts violence at its roots with the reality of peace. From there it seeks to find new answers, to actively solve problems in new ways. While the Catholic tradition has often been equated — unjustly — almost solely with the just war, even this perversion of Christian principle has retained a kernel of this truth: that the Catholic, or any Christian, cannot passively acquiesce to evil, that he or she owes duty and service to the human community, and that this service must go beyond a simple "no" and involve self-sacrifice and struggle.

As the materials in this bibliography will show, many Catholics throughout the church's history have understood this truth; but only recently, in the twentieth century and in the wake of its holocausts, has the church seriously begun to question its own assumptions about the nature of this struggle and about this sacrifice and service. Thus in recent decades the term "pacifism" has begun to be replaced by "peacemaking" as the definition of Catholic action — not that "pacifism" has been rejected, but that our understanding of its meaning has taken on all the fullness and activism of the Christian meaning of "peace" as a force of love and justice in the world. At the same time, especially since Pope John XXIII, the church as a whole has begun to explicitly reject the just-war tradition as a theology, and to see it as a secular idolization of war. Today, therefore, we talk of "nonviolence" and active resistance instead of "passive resistance." We can describe nonviolent revolutions and "people's power" because we have actually seen them at work, and when we discuss resistance to war, we fully realize that this is only one part of an active and positive embrace of justice and love for the victims as well as the agents of violence and exploitation. The examples of the many individuals in the following selections will show, if nothing else, that there is certainly nothing "passive" about the life of the peacemaker.

THE SCOPE OF THIS WORK

The following bibliography, then, is a guide to the literature on this peace tradition in the Catholic church. It covers material ranging from ancient Greek, Roman and biblical concepts of peace, through the message of peacemaking in the Gospels, the early church, the peace movments of the Middle Ages, the Humanist peacemakers of the Renaissance and early modern Europe, the missionary pacifists of the age of discovery, and Catholic plans for world peace and international law from the Middle Ages to the twentieth century. In this century it includes materials on the crisis of conscience and complicity faced by Catholics during the world wars, the revolutionary impact of Pope John XXIII and the Second Vatican Council, and contemporary Catholic peacemaking in Europe, the Third World, and in the United States.

Topics covered include all forms of Catholic peacemaking: pacifism in the traditional sense; key elements of the just-war tradition that include attempts to limit war, to define the justness of conflicts, and to clarify the role and rights of conscience; the place of international law in Catholic thought; theologies of peace, liberation, and social justice; and well as those mystical, apocalyptic, and even contemplative elements of Catholicism that have contributed to our understanding and practice of peace.

This bibliography hopes to be as comprehensive as possible, and therefore includes a wide variety of materials. Primary sources include theological and philosophical works, canon law, penitential literature, the lives of the saints, the tracts of pacifist missionaries, of Humanists and Catholic internationalists, accounts of popular peace movements from the Middle Ages to the present, selections from church councils throughout Catholic history, including key texts in Latin American Liberation Theology, modern papal bulls, including *Pacem in Terris* and *Populorum Progressio,* and the writings of contemporary Catholic peacemakers around the world.

Secondary sources include a wide range of materials. Since Catholic peace history is a relatively new field and will be approached by many with limited historical background to its issues and personalities, I have chosen to include a fair number of general, and more specialized, historical surveys of the periods covered. For certain eras, for example that of the Roman Empire and early church whose culture, social life and religious assumptions were so different from our own, I have had to include a large amount of secondary studies that attempt to establish the social ethos, the prevailing value system, of the age. In such cases only by understanding the social and moral milieu in which Christianity grew can one really understand the nature of its efforts at making peace. Such secondary works are thus intended to both ground the study in its historical reality and to provide ready reference to either the general student or the professional specialist. Because my definition of peace follows contemporary Catholic practice, the works listed here are often not restricted simply to narrowly defined peace movements or statements: they also include works on the Catholic monastic tradition, on nonviolent missionary work, on the work of the church for social justice. While the church's teaching on economic justice certainly forms a part of this teaching on social justice, this is really a topic that belongs to another special field of research and is not included here.

Directly relevant secondary materials include surveys of peace concepts and movements, studies of key thinkers from the early church through the twentieth century, monographs on special aspects and individuals, specialized scholarly articles and more general encyclopedia articles, specialized philological dictionaries, and — especially for the twentieth century — articles from magazines, newspapers, and newsletters on the activities of individual peacemakers, groups, and movements. In all areas published books, articles, and available dissertations are included. Unpublished papers and archives are not.

The materials assembled here cover the literature, both secondary and primary, in English, French, German, Italian, Spanish, Portuguese, and Latin. I have aimed to be as comprehensive as possible when dealing specifically with the Catholic peace tradition as discussed above, but have been more selective with historical background materials, with the tangential literature on the just war, and with the most recent periodical literature of current events. When comprehensive bibliographies on particular topics already exist, as for example on Thomas

Merton, Dorothy Day or the Berrigans, I have generally cited only these but have also included those materials, whether listed in these bibliographies or not, that I have found particularly worthy of mention.

THE ENTRIES

This bibliography includes materials up to November 1986. In many cases studies that were written in the nineteenth century or in the first two decades of this century and incorporated into later research have not been included, since their findings or their usefulness as research resources have been superceded. The entries themselves are arranged by chronological topic, and then alphabetically by author or by title where there is no author. All entries are numbered consecutively, and cross references are by number entry, marked in boldface. Entries that occur in more than one section or chapter generally contain a shortened author and title entry, along with a cross reference to the original citation.

The number and division of chapters in this book has been designed to follow as closely as possible the sequence in my narrative account, *The Catholic Peace Tradition*. This is so that the user of the bibliography can have an easy frame of reference to this narrative history, and that the reader of the narrative can easily assemble the research materials used for any particular topic or period. Only one chapter in this book, "Introductory," does not follow this pattern. This chapter, instead, contains materials that are of a general use for the study of peace, or materials that occur in more than one chapter and for which an initial reference here, without annotation, has proven more useful and convenient. The length of my comments varies, of course, with the importance or difficulty of the interpretation of the material. In occasional entries I have also included personal comments on the importance of the materials or taken issue with interpretations. In some cases I have listed materials that I have not seen, but I have so noted all these instances. In cases of subsequent editions of works cited, I have found it sufficient simply to note this in the main entry.

I have also included indexes by author name and an index of proper names not already listed in author or title indexes. The book's division by period and topic itself provides a fully adequate index to subject matter.

AN OVERVIEW OF THE DATA

The reader might well ask if this divergent material presents any coherent image of Catholic peacemaking or any patterns in the way this peace history has been treated. While any comments we make here are preliminary and subject to longer and more careful study, in general we can see two patterns emerging: one is a development of interpretation over time, the other a variation by historical methodology.

Historical Development

In keeping with the church's hierarchical and authoritarian tone from the beginning of the twentieth century into the 1930s, peace studies for the Catholic tradition seem to have been confined to the study of papal pronouncements and of the church's internationalist stance. Such studies include the works of de la Brière (**7**); Eppstein (**828**); and Lange (**654, 655**). With the carnage of World War I the research published during the 1920s and 1930s seems to reflect a new emphasis on a sentimental, internationalist type of pacifism. This saw hope for humanity in international disarmament, international peace societies, and a profound, yet almost naive, trust in governments to bring about this peace. It also produced several works on peace history that idealized any attempts to establish order, even that won by the gun, as "pacifist." Examples include Duval's *De la paix de Dieu à la paix de fer* (**358**); the works of Alfred Vanderpol (**618**); and Constantinescu-Bagdat's *Études d'histoire pacifique* (**813**).

Yet this period also produced several very carefully drawn accounts of the peace tradition that fully acknowledged the reality and force of peacemaking in history. These seem to have been influenced both by the horror of the first world war and by the new emphasis on a "populist" type of history writing. Examples range from the appearance in 1917 of Mary Wood's *Spirit of Protest in Old French Literature* (572); Strattmann's *The Church and War* (54); Bonnaud-Delamare's *L'idée de paix à l'époque carolingienne* (326), John McNeill's "Asceticism versus Militarism" (338); MacKinney's "The People and Public Opinion in the Eleventh-Century Peace Movement." (401); to Palmer Throop's *Criticism of the Crusades* (569) of 1940 and Elizabeth Suleiman's *Vision of World Peace* (815) of 1941.

Research into the peace tradition conducted in the 1940s and 1950s, as for example sections in Lebreton and Zeiller's *History of the Primitive Church* (169), tended to reflect the deep patriotism and cold-war policies of the Catholic church in most Western democracies during the period. Internationalism predominates (e.g., Flannery, 26; Guerry, 894; and Koenig, 896); while pacifism is seen as heterodox in the very least, dangerous, selfish and evasive, shirking social responsibility, and — if existent at all — the province of a small group of elitist intellectuals. This attitude survives into the 1960s in such works as Fontaine's "Christians and Military Service" (224) and forms the normative influence of the *New Catholic Encyclopedia* 1967 edition, in which pacifism as a Catholic option is dismissed outright (See McReavy, 61). At the same time works that did maintain the existence of a Christian peace tradition tended to rely on the presentation of the works of such great thinkers as Erasmus. See, for example, Chapiro's *Erasmus and Our Struggle for Peace* (687) or Mayer's *Pacifist Conscience* (36); or even the excellent and close textual analysis of Adam's *Better Part of Valor* (648).

With the late 1960s a new literature of peace emerges, perhaps in response to Vietnam and Vatican II, and grows stronger through the 1970s and into the early 1980s. Many examples could be cited, among the best are the volumes of the *Receuils...Jean Bodin* (46-48), actually published since the early 1950s; Zampaglione's *Idea of Peace in Antiquity* (58); McSorley's *New Testament Basis of*

Peacemaking (**136**); the writings of Thomas Merton (**40, 933-936, 1309-1323**) Gordon Zahn (chapters 12, 15), Haines (**334**), Renna (**340**), Cowdrey (**354**), E.R. Daniel (**455**), Webb (**497**); Brachin (**684**); Tracy (**735**); and many others.

Too much should not be made of these rather artificial periodizations, yet we can conclude that in the early 1980s, in the United States at least, a change in the outlook and interest of mainstream historical writing on war and peace seems to have abandoned peace studies in favor of an increasing interest in the technology, organization, psychology, and rules of war. At the same time, however, there has been a great increase in the number of books and articles published by "alternative" journals and presses and by journals devoted especially to peace research. This in part simply reflects the explosion of Catholic peace activities in the late twentieth century, and in part a new determination among Catholics that peace studies must again become part of the intellectual mainstream.

This last development has been matched by a new emphasis on the Third World and its practicing peacemakers. Orbis Books of the Maryknoll Order, for example, has set the lead in both addressing itself to the problems of the Third World and actively seeking out and translating the works of Third-World authors intimately involved with this process. Paulist Press has begun to address the issues of war and peace, but from an American perspective. Pax Christi has also begun to publish a steady stream of pamphlets and studies on individual Catholic peacemakers. Recent years have seen a renewed interest in the life of Dorothy Day, the Catholic Worker, the Berrigans, and Thomas Merton (see Chapter 15) among even the mainstream media that has helped "relegitimize" the Catholic peace tradition. The enormous impact of the 1983 U.S. bishops' pastoral, *The Challenge of Peace* (**1457-1485**) has not yet been fully felt, but it seems safe to say that this, and similar statements, will spur a great deal more of Catholic peace research in the United States. A large body of studies of all types has been maintained in Europe, but this area might better be surveyed in the discussion of methodology that follows.

Methodology

The second major pattern is that of methodological differences. This, of course, often coincides with the changing fashion in historical writing over time. Throughout the nineteenth century and the early decades of this century historical emphasis has been on great man: the king, hero, diplomat, pope or bishop, on the great intellectual, internationalist, or famous missionary. Thus studies of papal peace ideas, of Erasmus, or Bartolomé de las Casas characterized the impetus of peace research into the 1940s and 1950s. Since World War II, however, the emergence of the "new history" and its emphasis on social movements, popular spirituality, the "secondary" biography of the "typical" man or women, and of the ideas and mores of the vast majority of people have had a definite impact on peace research. It has resulted in a new interest in popular peace movements from the Middle Ages to the present, on the role of women, the analysis of class and economic factors in determining the success or failure of peace movements, the impact of cultural conflict and exchange, the role of the media in forming and disseminating the message of peace. Examples of this new interpretive method can be found in the work of Georges Duby (**389, 390**), the collection *La pace nel...trecento* (**449**), Fumigalli (**478**), or Gennaro (**493, 501, 502**). While born and still flourishing in Europe, this methodology has taken particularly strong root in Latin America, where theory and theology are intimately linked to praxis in descriptions of the daily lives and ideas of the continent's simple and oppressed as, for example, in the work of Gustavo Gutierrez (**1158-1160**) or Adolfo Pérez Esquivel (**1201-1212**).

These studies seem to have less impact on the way American or British scholars study the historical peace tradition. This remains largely confined to the Holy Biography or the Great Work within the limitations of intellectual history, to the exclusion of social or economic strains. Those who do touch on "peace" topics seem to be dominated by a sociological, institutional framework that all too easily fits into the narrow confines of legal history (e.g., the canonical school of Johnson, **612**; Russell, **50**; and Siberry, **567, 568**) that sees war and peace as matters of law and order. In their emphasis on the written text, its transmission, and transmutation, these excellent scholars offer important and profound insights, but they seem to ignore the profoundly religious, very often mystical and transcendental, character of Catholic peace movements. Such studies have also, it seems, failed to synthesize their interpretation of texts with a contextual outlook that considers not only the words but also the existential situation of their writer — whether this be Francis of Assisi, Ramon Lull, or Bartolomé de las Casas — and to take account of the fact that these people *lived* lives of peacemaking, no matter how ambiguously we might read their written texts. By and large historians of whatever methodological school have also ignored the role of women in peace work, and this, unfortunately, is reflected in the paucity of information for all but medieval and the most recent Catholic history.

Finally, I should note several areas covered in this bibliography that were only partially treated or not dealt with at all in *The Catholic Peace Tradition*. Primarily these include the revolutionary situation in Central America, including Nicaragua; the martyrdom of the American churchwomen in El Salvador, and the Sanctuary Movement in the United States. Since the narrative history could not possibly encompass every group or individual in the history of Catholic peacemaking, it had to select cases that spoke for a region or a period as a whole. In this bibliography I have tried to amplify this treatment. I hope that I have not, but suspect I still have, omitted many peacemakers that I invite readers to bring to my attention through criticism and suggestions for revisions.

* *
*

ABBREVIATIONS

BS

Bibliotheca Sanctorum. Istituto Giovanni XXII della Pontificia Università Lateranense. 12 vols. Rome: Società Grafica Romana, 1961-1970.

Butler

Alban Butler. *Butler's Lives of the Saints.* 4 vols. Donald Attwater and Herbert Thurston, eds. New York: Kennedy, 1956.

CAH

Cambridge Ancient History. 12 vols. 2nd., revised ed. in progress. New York: Cambridge University Press, 1923-.

CCSL

Corpus Christianorum. Series Latina. Turnhout, Paris: Brepols, 1953-.

CMH

The Cambridge Medieval History. 8 vols. New York: Cambridge University Press, 1913-1967.

CPG

Clavis Patrum Graecorum. Maurice Geerard, ed. Turnhout: Brepols, 1974-.

CPL

Clavis Patrum Latinorum. Eligius Dekkers, ed. Steinberg: St. Peter's Abbey, 1951-.

CSEL

Corpus Scriptorum Ecclesiasticorum Latinorum. 60 vols. Vienna: Akademie der Wissenschaften, 866-1913.

DACL
Dictionnaire d'archéologie chrétienne et de liturgie. Fernand Cabrol, Henri Leclercq, and Henri Marrou, eds. 15 vols. Paris: Letouzey et Ané, 1907-1953.

DMA
Dictionary of the Middle Ages. Joseph R. Strayer, ed. New York: Charles Scribner's, 1982-.

DSAM
Dictionnaire de spiritualité, ascetique, et mystique, doctrine et histoire. 10 vols. Paris: Mythe, 1937-.

DTC
Dictionnaire de théologie catholique. A. Vancant, E. Mangenot, and E. Amann, eds. 15 vols. in 23, with supplements. Paris: Letouzey et Ané, 1903-1972.

EC
Enciclopedia Cattolica. 12 vols. Vatican City: Ente per l'Enciclopedia Cattolica, 1949-1954.

LCC
Library of Christian Classics. J. Baille, J.T. MacNeill, H.P. van Dusen, eds. Philadelphia: Westminster, 1953-.

MGH
Monumenta Germaniae Historiae. Hanover: Gesellachaft fur altere deutsche Geschichtskunde, 1826-.

NCE
The New Catholic Encyclopedia. 15 vols. Washington, D.C.: Publisher's Guild, and New York: McGraw-Hill, 1967.

NCMH
The New Cambridge Modern History. 14 vols. New York: Cambridge University Press, 1964-1970.

NCR

National Catholic Reporter

NOP

In the Name of Peace: Collective Statements of the United States Catholic Bishops on War and Peace 1919-1980. Washington, D.C.: U.S. Conference of Bishops, 1983.

Omnibus

Habig, Marion A., O.F.M., ed. *St. Francis of Assisi, Writings and Early Biographies. English Omnibus of the Sources for the Life of St. Francis.* Chicago: Franciscan Herald Press, 1973.

PG

Patrologia Cursus Completus. Series Greca. Jacques-Paul Migne *et al.*, eds. 161 vols. Paris: Migne, 1857-1934.

PL

Patrologia Cursus Completus. Series Latina. Jacques-Paul Migne *et al.*, eds. 221 vols. Paris: Migne, 1843-1890.

Previté-Orton

C.W. Previté-Orton, *The Shorter Cambridge Medieval History.* 2 vols. Cambridge: Cambridge University Press, 1966.

Recueils...
  Jean Bodin

Paix. Recueils de la Société Jean Bodin. Vols. 14 & 15 (1961).

THE PEACE TRADITION
IN THE CATHOLIC CHURCH
An Annotated Bibliography

INTRODUCTORY: *General and Multiperiod Books on the Christian Peace Tradition*

1   Attwater, Donald. *The Penguin Dictionary of Saints*. New York: Penguin Books, 1976.

Attwater, an editor of *Butler's Lives* (9), and a member of the British chapter of Pax Christi, fills this handy collection of saints' lives with unusual aspects, including the pacifism of many official Catholic saints usually overlooked in other collections.

2   Bainton, Roland H. *Christian Attitudes Toward War and Peace*. Knoxville, TN: Abingdon Press, 1960.

3   Baldwin, Marshall, ed. *Christianity Through the Thirteenth Century*. New York: Harper & Row, 1970.

4   *Bibliotheca Sanctorum*. Istituto Giovanni XXIII della Pontificia Università Lateranense, 12 vols. & index. Rome: Società Grafica Romana, 1961-70.

The most complete collection of saints lives available, including iconography, copiously illustrated with excellent, signed articles and bibliography.

5   Bokenkotter, Thomas. *A Concise History of the Catholic Church*. Rev. ed. Garden City, NY: Doubleday, 1979.

6   Bosc, Robert. *Évangile, violence et paix.* Paris: Le
       Centurion, 1975.

       Modern theological reflections on terms, the attitudes
       of the various churches toward violence, the just-war
       theory, and various Christian traditions from the just war
       to Liberation Theology. Peace can be pursued on various
       levels: the search for methods, in politics, the evangelical
       life, and that of political morality.

7   Brière, Yves, de la. *L'église et paix.* Paris: Flammarion,
       1932.

8   Brock, Peter. *The Roots of War Resistance. Pacifism
       from the Early Church to Tolstoy.* Nyack, NY:
       Fellowship of Reconciliation, 1981.

9   Butler, Alban. *Lives of the Saints.* Donald Attwater and
       Herbert Thurston, eds. 4 vols. New York: Kennedy,
       1956.

       The best collection available in English.

10   *The Cambridge Medieval History (CMH).*

       The standard research and reference history for the
       period, edited and written by a series of distinguished
       historians. Excellent background for the chronology,
       personalities, institutions, and cultural life of the period
       300 to 1500.

11   Carroll, Berenice, and Clinton Fink. *Peace and War:
       Guide to Bibliographies.* War-Peace Bibliographies
       Series, vol. 16. New York: ABC-Clio, 1982.

12   Clotfelter, J. "Why Peace Movements Fail," *Christian*

Century 99, 24 (July 21-28, 1982): 790-93.

A theoretical piece focusing on the modern period but having general application. Movements fail because they do not reflect the basic values of their societies; they identify too widely with national symbols and themes, or alternately, with symbols hostile to it; they focus on the past, present, or distant future, not on the immediate future; they are unwilling to convince their audience of the social costs of war; they fail to bridge class and ideological divisions; they are identified with appeasement of the enemy. Specifically Christian movements define peace too narrowly and dwell more on fear than on hope.

13   Comblin, Joseph. *Théologie de la paix.* 2 vols. Paris: Éditions universitaires, 1963.

14   Coste, René. *L'église et la paix.* Paris: Desclée, 1979.

Modern meditations on the choice between Mars or Jesus. Examines the face of war, the logic and the ethic of war, the Gospel message of peace, violence and nonviolence, the Bomb, strategies of survival, the arms industry and the merchants of death, and various reactions. These include prophetism, realism, and terrorism. The church is essentially linked to peace, however. Concludes with some suggestions for action.

15   Delaney, John J. *Pocket Dictionary of Saints.* Abridged ed. of *Dictionary of Saints.* New York: Doubleday, 1983.

16   *Dictionnaire d'archéologie chrétienne et de liturgie (DACL).* Ferdinand Cabrol, Henri Leclercq, and Henri-I. Marrou, eds. 15 vols. Paris, 1907-1953.

4 General and Multiperiod Books

17   Dictionary of the Middle Ages (DMA). Joseph R. Strayer,
      ed. New York: Charles Scribner's, 1982-.

18   Douglas, James W. The Non-Violent Cross. A Theology
      of Revolution and Peace. New York: Macmillan,
      1968.

19   Du Cange, Charles Du Fresne. "Pax," Glossarium Mediae
      et Infimae Latinitatis. 10 vols. Paris: Osmont, 1937-
      38. 2: 228-31.

20   Egan, Eileen. "The Beatitudes, the Works of Mercy, and
      Pacifism." See 51, 169-87.

21   Erdmann, C. The Origins of the Idea of Crusade.
      Marshall W. Baldwin and Walter Goffart, transls.
      Princeton: Princeton University Press, 1977.

22   Fahey, Joseph J. "Pax Christi." See 51, 59-71.

23   ——."Peace, International," NCE 17: 494-6.

24   ——.Peace, War and the Christian Conscience. New York:
      The Christophers, 1982.

      Designed as a brief introduction to the topic, this
      booklet traces the peace tradition from Gospel pacifism
      and the Early Church, through just-war and holy-war
      traditions of the Middle Ages and the Renaissance-
      Reformation periods to statements of modern popes,
      councils, and U.S. bishops.

25   Ferguson, John. War and Peace in the World's Religions.
      Nyack, NY: Fellowship of Reconciliation, 1977.

A world-wide survey of the peace traditions in ten of the world's major religions.

26   Flannery, Harry W., ed. *Pattern for Peace: Catholic Statements on International Order.* Westminster, MD: Newman, 1962.

27   Fliche, A., and V. Martin, eds. *Histoire de l'église depuis les origines jusqu'à nos jours.* Paris: Bloud & Gay, 1934-.

A scholarly and authoritative history covering all of church history and institutions. Still in progress.

28   Guinan, Edward, ed. *Peace and Nonviolence: Basic Writings.* New York: Paulist Press, 1973.

Includes pieces by the Berrigans, Helder Camara, Cesar Chavez, Thomas Cornell, Dorothy Day, Danilo Dolci, Erasmus, Franz Jaegerstaetter, Thomas Merton, and various popes, bishops, and councils. Short bibliographies after each section.

29   Hehir, J. Bryan. "The Just-War Ethic and Catholic Theology: Dynamics of Change and Continuity." See **51,** 15-39.

30   Holmes, Arthur F. *War and Christian Ethics.* Grand Rapids, MI: Baker Book House, 1975.

A collection of primary source readings, primarily on the just-war tradition. Pacifism takes a secondary place. Lacks bibliography.

31   "Irenics: The Study of Peace," *America* 125 (Oct. 30,
           1971): 336.

           Describes the general field of peace studies, as it is
        emerging in the United States and in Catholic circles, as a
        legitimate field of research.

32   Klassen, Walter. "The Doctrine of the Just War in the
           West: A Summary," *Peace Research Reviews* VII-6
           (1978).

           A brief but useful survey, covering all periods from
        antiquity to the modern age.

33   Lammers, Stephen E. "Roman Catholic Social Ethics and
           Pacifism." See **51**, 93-103.

34   Lawler, F.X. "Mystical Body of Christ," *NCE* 10: 166-
           70.

           Useful background for the dialogue within the
        Catholic, and Christian, traditions that forms a model for
        the process of peacemaking.

35   Macquarrie, John. *The Concept of Peace*. New York:
           Harper & Row, 1973.

           A modern, theological, ethical reflection on peace as
        more than simply the absence of war. Peace is a whole-
        ness, a restoration of the "fractured areas" of our lives and
        the world. Peace is more than a concept but a technique.

36   McCormick, R.A. "War, Morality of," *NCE* 14: 802-7.

37   McGinn, Bernard, ed. and transl. *Apocalyptic Spirituality*.
           New York: Paulist Press, 1979.

38   ——.*Visions of the End. Apocalyptic Traditions in the Middle Ages.* New York: Columbia University Press, 1979.

Short selections from a wide variety of apocalyptic writings. Excellent bibliography.

39   Mayer, Peter. *The Pacifist Conscience.* Harmondsworth: Penguin Books, 1966.

40   Merton, Thomas. *The Nonviolent Alternative.* Revised edition of *Thomas Merton on Peace.* Gordon Zahn, ed. New York: Farrar, Straus Giroux, 1980.

41   Neill, Stephen. *A History of Christian Missions.* Baltimore: Penguin Books, 1964.

42   O'Brien, David J., and Thomas A. Shannon, eds. *Renewing the Earth. Catholic Documents on Peace, Justice and Liberation.* Garden City, NY: Doubleday, 1977.

43   *Peace and Change: A Journal of Peace Research.* Conference on Peace Research in History. Consortium on Peace Research.

A typescript quarterly covering a full range of articles on historical topics, contemporary politics, diplomatic history, women's studies, prisoners of conscience, peace research and teaching, book reviews, etc. Articles by noted peace historians, including Elise Boulding, Peter Brock, Sandi Cooper.

44   *Peace Spirituality for Peacemakers.* Antwerp: Pax Christi
        International, 1983.

        An excellent collection of modern reflections on
        peacemaking by some of the world's most prominent
        peacemakers and theorists, including Dom Helder Camara,
        Edward Schillebeeckx, Joseph Comblin, Donal
        O'Mahoney, and others.

45   Powers, R.T., and H.A. Freeman. "Conscientious
        Objectors," *NCE* 4: 204-6.

        Ranges over the entire history of Catholic
        peacemaking, concluding that the Catholic church has
        never condoned pacifism. Simply put: "as a general rule,
        a Christian living in the world does not have the objective
        right to adopt an attitude of total nonviolence as the basis
        for a refusal to fulfill his lawful duties as a citizen." Until
        John XXIII many Catholic writers continued to hold that
        Catholics were bound to obey human law above God's.

46   *Recueils de la Société Jean Bodin* 9 (1958).

47   *Recueils de la Société Jean Bodin* 14 (1961).

48   *Recueils de la Société Jean Bodin* 15 (1961).

49   Roemer, William F., and John Tracy Ellis. *The Catholic
        Church and Peace Efforts.* Washington, DC: CAIP,
        1934.

        This short pamphlet is an historical survey covering
        the Christian philosophy of peace, the church's influence
        in the Roman Empire, the contribution of the church to the
        law of nations, the Peace and Truce of God, Vitoria, papal
        arbitration and peacemaking, and the efforts of the

Franciscans, Dominicans, and Third Orders.

50   Russell, Frederick H. *The Just War in the Middle Ages.* New York: Cambridge University Press, 1975.

51   Shannon, Thomas A., ed. *War or Peace? The Search for New Answers.* Maryknoll, NY: Orbis Books, 1982.

52   ——.*What Are They Saying About Peace and War?* New York: Paulist Press, 1983.

Includes discussions of the development of the just-war tradition in the world's major religions, an historical survey of Roman Catholic teachings on war and peace from the early church to John Paul II. American reflections include major pastorals, the writings of John Ford, Gerald Kelly, John Courtney Murray, Paul Hanley Furfey, Dorothy Day, Thomas Merton, Daniel Berrigan, J. Bryan Hehir, Charles Curran, and Gordon Zahn, reflecting the full spectrum of Catholic thought and action. Shannon then surveys contemporary developments in the thought of American bishops individually and as a group, including the Bishop's Pastoral (**1457** to **1485**). He then examines the current state of the question of war and peace in Catholic thought and action and demonstrates how American Catholics have begun to move away from a theology of war to one of peacemaking.

53   Shiels, W.J., ed. *The Church and War.* Papers of the Twenty-First and Twenty-Second Meetings of the Ecclesiastical History Society. *Studies in Church History* 20. Oxford: Basil Blackwell, New York: Harper & Row, 1983.

This is a regrettable collection, not on the peace

tradition within Christianity, but on the church's embrace of war. The essays, by notable British scholars, cover the full range of Christian history from the early church to World War II, but they are remarkably unified in outlook and intent. While strenuously denying that the collection of essays was in any way affected by the full flush of Great Britain's first military victory in a generation, in the Falklands ("the military actions in the South Atlantic" as the editor euphemistically puts it), he does admit with surprise that the theme of the collection was "unexpectedly topical." This came about, not from the author's intention for a collection on war and religion to be topical, but "in light of . . .the debate about the precise form of the national service of thanksgiving and remembrance which subsequently took place."

Without doubt, religion and scholarship serve the state. While the tone is modern, often sardonic and sarcastic, the approach is outdated. The terms "peace," "pacifism," and others often at the center of discussion are never defined. In only one case, Peter Biller's "Medieval Waldensian Abhorrence of Killing Pre-1400" (pp. 129-46) is medieval pacifism discussed, and this in the old equation with heresy.

54   Strattmann, Franziscus. *The Church and War, A Catholic Study*. New York: Kennedy, 1928.

Traces the emergence of Catholic theories on war and peace, pacifism, just war, and holy war. Takes the Erasmian notion of the church as the mystical body, with Christ as the head, and concludes that war is a tragedy that rends this body and pits one part against another.

55   Vanderhaar, Gerard. *Nonviolence in Christian Tradition*. Erie, PA: Pax Christi, 1983.

A review from the New Testament, to early Christian pacifism, St. Augustine, and the barbarization of Christianity in the Middle Ages. While the Middle Ages gave birth to the Crusades, it also saw St. Francis of Assisi and such pacifist groups as the heretical Waldensians, forced to hide in the hills. From Erasmus and the Reformation the trail leads straight to the Quakers. In the modern world nonviolence may almost have succeeded in making the American colonies independent of Great Britain. In the twentieth century Gandhi has inspired peacemakers as diverse as Martin Luther King, Cesar Chavez, and Danilo Dolci. The question remains, however: can nonviolence succeed in today's world?

56   Woito, Robert *To End War: An Introduction — Ideas, Books, Organizations, Work That Can Help.* Sixth ed. Berkeley: World Without War Council, 1982.

Surveys all aspects of the apparatus of peacemaking: ideas, contexts, and actions. Realms of action include politics, arms control, internationalism, economics, human rights, the environment, and world organizations. There are also sections for personal reflection, analysis, and planning.

Chapters 15, "Religious and Ethical Thought on War (pp. 382-415); 16, "Social Change: Nonviolent Approaches (pp. 416-33); and 17, "Peace Research" (434-60) are especially relevant to Catholic peace history. Good bibliographies. Excellent list of organizations and publications.

57   Zahn, Gordon. *War, Conscience and Dissent.* New York: Hawthorne, 1967.

58   Zampaglione, Gerardo. *The Idea of Peace in Antiquity.*
        Richard Dunn, transl. Notre Dame, IN: University of
        Notre Dame Press, 1973.

                        * *
                         *

CHAPTER 1: *A Catholic Definition of Peace.*
The Meaning of Peacemaking

Some Dictionary Definitions

59   Curran, P.C. "Peace," *NCE* 11 (1967): 37.

        A standard pre-Vatican II definition: peace is untroubled peace of mind, composure of soul, or tranquility between persons. Peace postulates order and harmony. Charity, however, is the basis of peace.

60   McKenzie, John L., S.J. "Peace," *Dictionary of the Bible.* Milwaukee: Bruce Publishing, 1965, 651-52.

        A brief review of its meanings using biblical citations. Lacks bibliography.

61   McReavy, L.L. "Pacifism," *NCE* 10: 855-57.

        An historical survey in the pre-Vatican II mold, emphasizing the incompatibility of pacifism with the Catholic tradition. The early Fathers avoided the problem of war by avoiding public life. Augustine justified war. Covers 1000 years of the Middle Ages in six lines. Only heretics, or Protestants, were ever pacifists. In the modern world no Catholic can possibly be a pacifist. Fills out the last part of the article with a lengthy discussion of the just war, including nuclear pacifism, and Catholics' duty to repel "godless tyranny."

13

62   *The Compact Edition of the Oxford English Dictionary*
Oxford: Oxford University Press, 1971, 2: 2105 (P:
581-84).

All the English meanings of peace: freedom from war
civil disorder and violence, a cessation of hostilities,
personal peace and quiet, peace of mind, friendliness,
stillness and quiet, public order, reconciliation. The
peacemaker is one who brings all this about.

63   *Webster's New Collegiate Dictionary.* Springfield, MA:
G. & C. Merriam Co., 1981, 815, 831, 835.

Contemporary American meanings and derivations for
pacific, pacifism, pacifist, passive, peace, peaceable, and
peacemaker. Offers a few surprises in the strict dictionary
meanings of words often confused in popular usage.

Peace in the Classical World

64   Den Boer, Willem. *Private Morality in Greece and Rome.*
Leiden: Brill, 1979.

A good summary of recent scholarship. Den Boer is
skeptical of attempts to read too many Christian overtones
of human solidarity into *eirene*, an essentially social or
political term. Other terms like *filia* (love of neighbor),
homonoia (unity or concord), and *galene* (inner calm) more
expressed the Christian content of peace.

65   Grant, Michael. *History of Rome.* New York: Charles
Scribner's, 1978.

A general introduction written by an acknowledged
master. Covers many topics of importance, including the
Roman state, imperialism, the army, and Roman religion.

Emphasizes the essentially public, and not ethical, character of Roman religion and, subsequently, of Roman concepts of peace.

66   Harris, William V. *War and Imperialism in Republican Rome 327-70 BC*. Oxford: Clarendon Press, 1979.

Presents the thesis that throughout its long history of essentially aggressive and imperialistic wars, Rome was motivated primarily by the ethos of the warrior elite. While it made war almost every year in the period examined, Rome was always careful to maintain at least the pretext of a defensive and "just" war supported by the proper religious sanctions. In fact, "the Romans seem to have conceived of *pax* as a condition that could only result from successful war." No successful opposition to war ever existed within Roman society in this period.

67   Hopkins, Keith. *Conquerors and Slaves: Sociological Studies in Roman History* 1. New York: Cambridge University Press, 1977.

Rome conquered the entire Mediterranean basin in two centuries and spent more of its years at war than any other pre-industrial society. "Right down to the end of the Republic Rome is best seen as a warrior state." While the rhetoric of peace masked their aggressions, accounts of war, slaughter, conquest and enslavement fascinated the Romans. Excellent background for the social ethos that Christian peacemakers confronted in the first centuries C.E.

68   MacMullen, Ramsay. *Paganism in the Roman Empire*. New Haven: Yale University Press, 1981.

Pages 50-57 provide valuable discussion of the goals

of Roman religion and its contrast to Judaeo-Christian concepts of peace. To the Romans peace meant the benefits gainable through public action: health, beauty, financial gain, safety. Material benefits followed service to the gods. Salvation meant health and prosperity.

69   Melko, Matthew, and Richard D. Weigel. *Peace in the Ancient World.* Jefferson, NC: McFarland, 1981.

The *Pax Romana* is paradigmatic. This book describes peace as that of imperial order and the absence of physical conflict in space and time. The authors follow it fortunes in the various Egyptian kingdoms, Phoenicia, Athens, Corinth, under the Achaemenids and Ptolemies, in the Roman Republic, Empire, and in Iberia. The study ranges from 2000 B.C.E. to 400 C.E.

70   Préaux, Claire. "La paix a l'époque hellenistique." See **47**, 227-301.

Good introduction to peace as a rare commodity in the Greek world. Details the frequency of wars and the aspirations for peace, including the social peace within city-states, peace between cities, the king's peace, and procedures for obtaining peace agreements.

71   Zampaglione. *Idea of Peace.* See **58**.

This is the best and most comprehensive book on the topic, the place to begin any study. The meanings of peace as *pax* for the Romans, *eirene* for the Greeks, and *salom* for the Hebrews is given careful and detailed discussion, paying close attention to etymologies, ancient (including biblical) sources where the terms appear, the intellectual framework of the concept's development, and modern scholarly opinion. Good bibliography.

The Meaning of *eirene*

72. Beck, H., and Colin Brown. "Peace," *New International Dictionary of New Testament Theology*. Grand Rapids, MI: Zondervan, 1978, 2: 776-83.

The etymology of *eirene* from Homer through Plato and Epictetus to the Septuagint. Generally for the pagan Greeks peace meant the absence of war and the state of law and order that gives rise to prosperity. With Plato peace also meant peaceful conduct in an external sense, and only with the Stoics a spiritual peace. With the Septuagint Greek picked up the meanings of *salom* and is used almost invariably to translate that word. Extensive use of biblical citations.

73 Foerster, W., et al. "*Eirene*," *Theological Dictionary of the New Testament*. Gerhard Kittel, ed.; Geoffrey W. Bromley, transl. and ed. Grand Rapids, MI: Eerdmans, 1976, 2: 400-420.

Traces the meanings of *eirene* from its Greek origins, compares it with Roman *pax*, and shows how the concept was transformed when used to translate Hebrew *salom* in the Septuagint. An excellent introduction to the etymological study of our Biblical concepts of peace. Extensive use of biblical citations.

The Meaning of *pax*

74 Imbert, Jean. "Pax Romana." See **47**, 303-19.

For the Romans peace was essentially the absence of armed struggle and was based on treaties between states. Both war and peace had their basis in law.

75   *Oxford Latin Dictionary.* Charlton T. Lewis and Charles
        Short, eds. Oxford: Clarendon Press, 1966, 1320.

        Derivations and meaning of *pax* as peace, a treaty of
        peace, tranquility, the absence of war, peace of mind, the
        rest of sleep or death, a favor, permission, or a dominion
        or empire. Hence the irony of the *Pax Romana.*

76   Roscher, Wilhelm Heinrich. "Pax," in *Ausführliches
        Lexicon der griechischen und romischen Mythologie.*
        6 vols. Leipzig, 1884-1937; reprint Hildesheim: Olms,
        1965. 3, 2: 1719-22.

        Surveys the Latin meanings of peace.

77   Waddy, L.H. *Pax Romana and World Peace.* New York:
        Norton, 1954.

        This frankly apologetic work bears all the marks of the
        Cold War and begs comparisons to the post-war *Pax
        Americana.* Peace is the international stability of order
        gained through constant vigilance and the readiness to
        defend it militarily. Its benefits are political, economic,
        and cultural.

Peace in the Old Testament

78   Albright, William Foxwell. *From the Stone Age to
        Christianity.* 2nd ed. New York: Doubleday, 1957.

        Valuable and accessible introduction to the history of
        the ancient Israelites.

79   Anderson, Bernhard W. *Understanding the Old Testament*. Englewood Cliffs, NJ: Prentice Hall, 1975.

A good general history, with a definite political approach. The role of suffering in creating both the discipline of Jewish history and of the Jewish nation is stressed.

80   Baron, Salo Wittmayer. *A Social and Religious History of the Jews*. 17 vols. New York: Columbia University Press, 1952-1976.

This is the standard historical reference on the history of the Jews. Volume 1 offers good background for the Old Testament. Volume 2 covers the period that witnessed the rise of Christianity.

81   *Cambridge Ancient History*. 12 vols. New York: Cambridge University Press, 1923-1939.

Revised and updated. The standard history of the ancient world. Classic articles by recognized authorities. In process of revision.

82   Cook, Stanley A. "Israel and the Neighboring States." See **81**, 3 (1965): 354-87.

From the ninth century B.C.E. to the fall of Ephraim.

83   ——."Israel Before the Prophets." See **81**, 3: 416-57.

On primitive Hebrew religious belief, Jahwism, and the prophets' evolution toward an ethical theism.

84   Noth, Martin. *The Old Testament World.* Victor I. Gruhn,
            transl. Philadelphia: Fortress Press, 1964.

            An excellent introduction to the period. While political
            history is given only a brief synopsis, the book reviews
            the text of the Old Testament and its development.

85   Peebles, B.M. "Bible, IV, 13: Latin Versions," *NCE* 2:
            436-57.

            Excellent background introduction to the Old Latin,
            Vulgate, and later versions.

The Meaning of *salom*

86   Beck, H., and Colin Brown. "Peace." See **72.**

            In the Old Testament *salom* meant material well-being
            and the summation of all other goods, but it was bound
            with the social and political aspirations of Israel and
            involved all the gifts of Yahweh. With the Prophets it took
            on the meanings of salvation. Extensive use of biblical
            citations.

87   Gross, Heinrich. "Peace," *An Encyclopedia of Biblical
            Theology. The Complete Sacramentum Verbi.*
            Johannes Baptist Bauer, ed. 3 vols. New York:
            Herder & Herder, 1970, 648-51.

            Follows the development of *salom* from its Semitic
            roots in Sumerian *silim* and Akkadian *salamu*, meaning
            whole or uninjured, through the Old Testament concepts of
            harmony, success, even cooperation in battle. The
            Prophetic and eschatological traditions deepened the
            meanings of *salom* to both inner peace and the peace of
            those who share in the Covenant: the result of inner

conversion in seeking justice. The use of Greek *eirene* to translate *salom* in the Septuagint brought new dimensions to the Greek word. Extensive use of biblical citations.

88   Hanson, Paul D. "War and Peace in the Hebrew Bible," *Interpretation* (Richmond) 38, 4 (1984): 341-62.

Discusses the problem of war in the Old Testament and Yahweh's nature as a warrior God. There have historically been several responses: to deny any connection between Christianity and the Old Testament, to reject biblical religion as a source of peacemaking, and to fall into Marionism, that is, to see the Old Testament as a mere shadow, either as allegory or as false image.

While the Old Testament teaching on war and peace has long been regarded as offensive to many Christians, it has much to teach, most especially on its interpretation of *salom*. This is the state of harmony given by God, embodying righteousness and compassion in communal life and in a universe that is essentially moral. In the Old Testament we often see the disruption of this peace by royal ideology and its reassertion by the prophets.

89   Harris, James Douglas. *Shalom: The Biblical Concept of Peace*. Grand Rapids, MI: Baker Book House, 1970.

A good synthesis of a great deal of research. Meanings range from a source of community, inner peace, health and prosperity, the covenant, and salvation itself. God is the giver of *salom*, and the term also carries eschatological extensions. Also examines pre-New Testament connections, with *eirene* in Greek literature, and then explores New Testament meanings in the mission of Jesus and in the Pauline texts. The study concludes with some modern reflections.

90   La Barbera, Robert. "The Man of War and the Man of God: Social Satire in 2 Kings 6:8-7:20," *Catholic Biblical Quarterly* 46, 4 (1984): 637-51.

Traces the conflicts within the northern kingdom among the ruling elite: between kings armies, chariots and weapons that prove ineffective and the military victories brought by Yahweh through the word of the man of God, Elisha.

91   Léon-Dufour, Xavier. "Peace," *Dictionary of Biblical Theology*. P. Joseph Cahill, ed.; E.M. Stewart, transl. New York: Seabury Press, 1973, 411-14.

Surveys the multiple meanings of peace for the ancient Hebrews from its Semitic roots. *Salom*'s meaning evolved from security, good health, and well being to mutual trust, communion with God, and peace as the result of prayer and of justice. Peace is not achieved through states or politics but through God's eschatological restoration. Peace, finally, is the result of justice. Extensive use of biblical citations.

92   Luz, Ulrich, et al., eds. *Eschatologie und Friedens-handeln: Exegetische Beitrage zur Frage Christlicher Friedensverantwortung*. Stuttgart: Verlag Katholisches Bibelwerk, 1981.

An interdisciplinary look at biblical concepts of eschatology and peace, in the prophetic tradition of Micha, Isaias, and Deutero-Isaias. It also examines the apocalyptic tradition. Essays range from the Old Testament to Paul.

93   Rodriquez, M. "Peace (in the Bible)," *NCE* 11: 37-38.

Surveys the meanings of *salom* in the Old Testament
from success and safety, prosperity and general well-being
and its merging with the meanings of Greek *eirene* in the
Septuagint to take on meanings of freedom from war and
security. The Prophetic texts transform the meaning of
salom from earthly to spiritual good, as the essence of
God's kingdom. Extensive use of biblical citations.

94   Skehan, P.W. "Bible, IV, 5: Septuagint," *NCE* 2: 425-29.

Useful introduction to the Greek version of the Old
Testament where the Hebrew meanings of *salom* merged
with the Greek *eirene*.

95   Van der Ploeg, J., O.P. "Peace, I, In the Old Testament,"
       Encyclopedic Dictionary of the Bible. Louis F.
       Hartman, C.SS.R., transl. and ed. New York:
       McGraw-Hill, 1963, 1782-84.

Traces the twenty-five meanings of *salom* in the Old
Testament from success in war to completeness, living
well, prosperity and health, to good relations among
individuals and groups, to God's gift in the Covenant and
the salvation brought by the Messiah and the Prince of
Peace. Extensive use of biblical citations.

*   *
*

CHAPTER 2: *The Context and Message of Peace in the New Testament*

The *Pax Romana*

96   Benario, Herbert W. *An Introduction to Tacitus.* Athens, GA: University of Georgia Press, 1975.

Pages 123-34 provide useful introduction to Tacitus as the moral writer and social critic of Rome and its wars of expansion.

97   Petit, Paul. *Pax Romana.* James Willis, transl. Berkeley: University of California Press, 1976.

Covers the period from 31 B.C.E. to 193 C.E. Studies the Roman army, defenses, frontiers, and the imperial succession, all basic elements of the Roman concept of peace. Religious life, society, and civilization are also treated.

98   Waddy. *Pax Romana.* See **77.**

Praises the benefits of Rome's military domination of the Mediterranean world in much the same terms that a Roman noble of the day might have.

99   Zampaglione. *Idea of Peace.* See **58.**

Examines the philosophical underpinings of the Roman theory in Stoic concepts of world order, the reality of Roman repression in such episodes as the British revolt of 85 C.E., and the real benefits to the empire of centralized authority. On the other hand, the *Pax Romana* never really shaped a unified theory of government, which relied on ad hoc arrangements and local autonomy.

Roman Virtue

100   Den Boer. *Private Morality.* See **64**.

Essential background reading to understand the Sermon on the Mount for classical Greek and Roman notions of "neighbor," "outsider," and "enemy." In the classical world "neighbor" had no Hebrew sense of companion in the covenant, but of one who physically stands beside another. No notions of love or spiritual equality were implied. For Aristotle and the classical tradition outsiders, "barbarians," were natural slaves and inferiors, really not even human. The poor, slaves, and women, all the weak, could never be considered "blessed." Highlights the revolutionary content of the Sermon and the social impact of peacemaking.

101   Earl, Donald C. *The Moral and Political Tradition of Rome.* Ithaca: Cornell University Press, 1967.

Good background for a study of *virtus*, the ethic of the Roman nobility. For the Roman virtue consisted of winning personal preeminence and glory in the commission of great deeds in service to the Roman state. War was the highest stage for such deeds.

102   Finley, Moses I. *Ancient Slavery and Modern Ideology.* New York: Penguin Books, 1983.

In addition to its background information on Roman and Greek attitudes to the outsider and the powerless, this provides an excellent introduction to the historiographical issues involved in the study of Roman and Greek slavery and modern uses and abuses of historical evidence to serve ideological ends. A useful warning to those who seek to understand Roman concepts of freedom and humanity in the context of Christian teachings on peace and justice. Excellent bibliography.

103   Grant, Frederick C. *Ancient Roman Religion.* New York: Liberal Arts Press, 1957.

A collection of source readings and introductory essays on the progress of Roman religion from agricultural cult concerned with security and prosperity, to the mystery and philosophical influences of the East, to the Imperial cult. Religious policy under the empire, the the growth of Christianity, the Roman reaction, and eventual conversion are all included. Useful readings for understanding the peace message of the New Testament in the context of the official demands of the Roman state cult.

104   Lewis, Naphtali, and Meyer Reinhold. *Roman Civilization. Sourcebook II: The Empire.* New York: Harper & Row, 1966.

An excellent collection of primary sources on Roman religion, law, and imperialism, and their confrontation with Christianity.

105   MacMullen, Ramsay. *Roman Social Relations 50 B.C. to A.D. 284.* New Haven: Yale University Press, 1974.

The discussion of "class" on pages 88-120 is especially helpful for the context of Chritianity's message.

106   Nock, A.D. "Religious Developments from the Close of

the Republic to the Death of Nero," *CAH* 10: 465-511.

Sets the context for the Christian conflict with the Roman religion and state. "Roman religion is in its essence a matter of cult acts. What results has little to do with the emotion or imagination or speculation of the individual." Useful background for understanding how Christianity's call to individual conscience and conversion and its ideas of peacemaking were thus totally alien to official Roman religious sensibility.

107   Sherwin-White, Adrian N. *Roman Society and Roman Law in the New Testament.* Oxford: Clarendon, 1963.

Examines the powers of the Roman imperial system and its effects on provincial life in the first century C.E., its *coercitio, cognitio,* and *imperium,* including the legal basis for the trial of Christ. Sets the legal context for the Christian message of love of enemy and obedience to God above man in such instances as the tribute coin and the centurion at Capernaum.

108   Wiedemann, Thomas. *Greek and Roman Slavery.* Baltimore: Johns Hopkins University Press, 1981.

Examines both the legal and ontological status of the slave and the Greek and Roman concept that all foreign subjects were slaves and the moral inferiors of their masters. Necessary background for the revolutionary claims of Christians that all humans were moral equals.

Gentile and Jew

109   Allegro, John Marco. *The Chosen People. A Study of Jewish History from the Time of the Exile Until the*

Revolt of Bar Kocheba. London: Hodder and
Stoughton, 1971.

A good, general introduction to the historical elements
of the Roman occupation of Palestine, its tightened grip on
the life of Israel, the political elements among the Jews,
their differing attitudes to Rome, and the context of the
Christian message of love of enemies.

110   Barrett, Charles Kingsley. *The New Testament Background.* New York: Harper & Row, 1961.

A collection of documents illustrating the life of the
Roman Empire that dominated the life of the New
Testament, including religious, philosophical and political
tracts, and Jewish historical, rabbinical, and scriptural
selections.

111   Bruce, F.F. *New Testament History.* New York:
Doubleday, 1971.

A good historical account of Judaism from Cyrus to
Augustus and of New Testament Judaism, ranging from
the Essenes to the Zealots.   Christ, the Gospels, the
primitive church, Paul, and the spread of Christianity to
Rome are all placed in the historic context of the Roman
Empire.

112   Bultmann, Rudolf. *Primitive Christianity in its Contemporary Setting.* New York: Meridien, 1956.

Examines the intellectual background to both the
Hellenistic and Judaic traditions in conflict in Palestine at
the time of Christ. Christ and his teachings were both tied
to a definite intellectual, social and political context.

113   Foerster, W. *From the Exile to Christ: A Historical Introduction to Palestinian Judaism.* Gordon E. Harris, transl. Philadelphia: Fortress Press, 1964.

Part II covers the Palestine of Jesus' day. Good bibliography.

114   Lohse, Eduard. *The New Testament Environment.* John E. Steely, transl. Nashville: Abingdon Press, 1976.

A very good general survey of the historical background to Christ's message: Judaism in the Hellenistic world, New Testament Judaism, the politics and society of the Roman Empire, its religious and philosophical movements. The bibliography is limited.

115   Stevenson, G., and Arnaldo Momigliano. "Rebellion within the Empire," *CAH* 10 (1966): 840-65.

Good background for Jewish-Roman relations in the Christian era, relations marked primarily by hate for the Romans among the conquered Jews and contempt and repression by the Romans for their subject people.

The Meaning of Peace in the New Testament

116   Bauer, W. *A Greek-English Lexicon of the New Testament.* Chicago: University of Chicago Press, 1979, 331, 687.

For the Greek New Testament meanings of the words *ecthros* for personal enemy and enemy in battle, and *pleision* for neighbor. Necessary background for understanding Christ's call for love of neighbor and enemy.

117   Beck and Brown. "Peace." See **72**.

Examines the New Testament meanings of *eirene*. The Christian concept of peace is all embracing, and the New Testament is the "gospel of peace." Peace is associated with *agape* (love), *charis* (grace), and *zoe* (life); and Christ is the mediator of that peace, bringing the kingdom of God and reconciliation to the world. Christ himself is peace, as is the kingdom of God. Peace is both the gift and challenge to his followers. The *eirenopoios* (peacemaker) is not the one who imposes peace, as in classical Greek, but the one who brings this *salom*, the ethical person. Extensive use of biblical citations.

118   Brock. *Roots*. See **8**.

Christ's Sermon on the Mount is truly pacifist, but it has been variously explained away by Catholics as counsels to perfection; by Lutherans, including Niebuhr, as being personal and individual; and by Augustine and the just-war tradition, which sees killing as a form of love. Christ was nonviolent, even in his most vehement criticism of the rich and powerful and in his prophesies of future divisions. His message of peace was cumulative, not specific to a few isolated texts. His message of nonviolent suffering, forgiveness, and love of enemy are hard to square with the use of violence or war.

119   Cadoux, Cecil J. *The Early Church and the World.* Edinburgh: Clark, 1955.

Ranging from Christ to Constantine, provides an excellent and specific treatment of attitudes to war and peace, the state, and the individual peacemaker in the first centuries. Essential background reading.

120   Curran. "Peace." See **59**.

Implicit in the Beatitudes in the Sermon on the Mount
is the notion that peace is only imperfect in this life. A
pre-Vatican II interpretation.

121   ——."Epikeia," *NCE* 5: 476-77.

Essential to the Christian meaning of peace, *epikeia*
means reasonableness in one's dealings with other people,
a "restrictive interpretation of positive law" that leads one
above the limits of human law to the higher law of God.

122   Egan, Eileen. "The Beatitudes, The Works of Mercy, and
Pacifism." See **51**, 169-87.

A reflection on the Sermon on the Mount, the loss of
early Christian pacifism, the distortion of Christian virtues
in the contemporary world, and a call to return to these
Gospel virtues.

123   Foerster. "Eirene." See **73**.

Examines the meanings of *eirene* in the New
Testament from that of greeting and farewell, to salvation
and fulfillment, to an inner commitment to God that can
lead to bitter enmity with those who do not share it. *Eirene*
is not merely inner peace and harmony of the soul; that is
charis. The peacemaker, *eirenopoios*, is one who establishes peace and concord between people.

124   Frend, W.H.C. *Martyrdom and Persecution in the Early
Church.* Grand Rapids, MI: Baker House, 1981.

The definitive study, with much useful background

information for the Old and New Testament traditions. Christ rejected the messianic violence of the Maccabean tradition in favor of the cross, the suffering servant and prophet. Martyrdom was accepted from the time of Paul on as a perfect imitation of Christ in nonviolent witness to his truth.

125   Fuller, R.H., and I Fuller, eds. *Essays on the Love Commandment*. Philadelphia: Fortress Press, 1978.

       Not seen.

126   Furnish, Victor Paul. *The Love Command in the New Testament*. Nashville: Abingdon Press 1972.

       Focuses on the text of Matthew 5:38-48, related texts, and the forms and history of interpretation.

127   ——."War and Peace in the New Testament," *Interpretation* 38, 4 (1984): 363-79.

       Reviews the political world of the New Testament and Christ's ministry and word. The world of the New Testament was one at peace, in which Christian believers did not hold power, and of which Christians did not believe themselves a part. Nevertheless, the message of both Jesus and Paul was one of nonviolence. Even their imagry, while sometimes violent is meant to illustrate spiritual points about the kingdom and its approach.
       While war and peace are not specifically part of Christ's message, war is never seen as part of God's purpose, and obedience to God always held above that to Caesar. The early church fully understood this non-violence. Reviews many key texts often used to support war and rejects war interpretations.

128   Gross. "Peace." See **87.**

       Peace is both a gift and a task to constantly seek peace. While it is a gift of the Son, it is also a commitment by his disciples to the kingdom of God. Extensive use of biblical citations.

129   Kissinger, Warren S. *The Sermon on the Mount: A History of Interpretations and Bibliography.* Metuchen, NJ: ATLA Bibliography Series, vol. 3, 1975.

       A comprehensive history of interpretations from the Ante-Nicene Fathers to the present followed by an immense bibliography. Kissinger's afterword concludes: "The Sermon on the Mount's radical demands cannot be evaded by understanding them as a summons to repentance and as a preparation for the word of grace. They are not an interim ethic...."

130   Kittel, Gerhard. *Theological Dictionary of the New Testament.* Geoffrey W. Bromley, transl. and ed. Grand Rapids, MI: Eerdmans, 1976.

       A valuable resource.

131   Lassere, Jean. *War and the Gospel.* Oliver Coburn, transl. Scottsdale, PA: Herald Press, 1962, reissued 1974.

       An unabashedly pacifist interpretation of the New Testament that has received much criticism for its admitted "critical insight." While pagan empires are long dead, the values of antiquity live on in the modern love of war and the cult of the state. In the Protestant sectarian tradition, Lassere attempts to uncover the true pacifism of the

Christian church before its supposed lapse into barbarism
with Constantine and the Catholic Middle Ages. Nevertheless, his close attention to the classic biblical texts and
his refutation of standard misinterpretations of these texts
to bolster the crusade and the just war make this essential
reading. For Lassere pacifism is too narrow a term, often
confused with passivism. Nonviolence and active struggle
are more in keeping with the Gospel sense.

132   Léon-Dufour. "Peace." See **91**.

Examines the meanings of *eirene* and *pax* in the New
Testament. In the Gospels peace is not calm but division.
Christ is the prince of peace announced by the angels and
hailed on his entry into Jerusalem. He retains the powers
of peace contained in the Old Testament word: healing,
forgiveness of sins, restoration to life. John's Gospel
stresses the challenge and promise of peace in Christ's
commission to his disciples. Paul's epistles tie peace inextricably to love of God and of fellow humans. The
Mystical Body is the chief agency of this peace. The
Apocalypse makes the New Jerusalem the vision of peace
that Christians pursue relentlessly.

133   Liddell, Henry George, and Robert Scott. *A Greek-
       English Lexicon.* Oxford: Clarendon Press, 1968,
       647.

For the meaning of *pleision*, one's neighbor. See **114**.

134   MacGregor, C.H.C. *The New Testament Basis of
       Pacifism.* Nyack, NY: Fellowship of Reconciliation,
       1968.

Even though some of the issues MacGregor confronts
now seem outdated, this is an excellent introduction to the

texts and basic principles of the Gospels and Epistles. He
rejects objections that the Sermon on the Mount was meant
as an interim ethic, for particular individuals, as Semitic
hyperbole, or as counsels to perfection. It is basic to
understanding Christ's message. While Christ's kingdom
is not of this world, that does not mean it is not for this
world. Truth, love, and peace are Christ's message.
Active nonviolence are its methods, and its context is fully
political, fully in keeping with Jewish, and Christ's own,
concepts of the Messiah. The Christian message of the
New Testament is definitely aimed to undercut Rome and
its prevailing ethos.

Yet Christ's rejection of Messianic war lead to
immediate abandonment by his followers and to his cross.
Christ's followers must imitate this cross, not for the
suffering but the witness to the truth that it is not the
individual Christian, but God's truth that triumphs. Presents a helpful assemblage of important texts on peace,
selflessness, love, forgiveness, love of enemy, suffering,
and reconciliation.

135   Makarewicz, S. "Epikeia (in the Bible)," *NCE* 5: 476-77.

An essential part of Christian peacemaking is *epikeia*,
or forebearance, akin to the equity that a judge exercises to
rise above the letter of the law in order to reach justice. It
is the opposite of strict justice, the *lex talionis*, "an eye for
an eye." In imitating Christ's own forebearance and
gentleness, which mistakenly appears to some as a passive
meekness, Christians will later share in the splendor of
Christ as the glorified judge.

136   McSorley, Richard, S.J. *New Testament Basis of*
        Peacemaking. Washington: Georgetown University
        Center for Peace Studies, 1979.

A fundamental book for the Catholic peace tradition, this covers much the same ground as MacGregor. See 134. It deals with basic principles of the New Testament. These include the priority of love of God and our neighbor, as well as love of our enemies. Such love is not passive, however, but is active peacemaking. Love can never support killing or the use of force in war. Police action should not be confused with war. The pacifist is not against nonlethal, limited force applied in accordance with law. Other principles include God's parentage of all people, our love for them as brothers and sisters, and the infinite value of the human person. The end of love is equal to the means, thus we must reject temptations to power and force and imitate Christ.

The book also covers the classic texts that support nonviolence and rebuts their use to support militarism. It then surveys the peace tradition in the early church and the just-war theory and answers objections to the pacifist position. The book's outlook is activist, it aims at an audience seeking the scriptural foundations for action.

137   Merton, Thomas. "Blessed Are the Meek: The Christian Roots of Nonviolence." See 40, 208-18.

Focuses on Christ's call in the Sermon on the Mount for true Christian humility, its true meaning, not passive meekness or tameness, but a selflessness, a desire not to win but to witness God's truth, thus avoiding moral aggression. True peace is based on the unity, not the division, of humanity. True humility, the weakness of Christ, is like the mustard seed, a slow, secret growth of the hidden power of God that is manifest in one's person. This power is not the desire to prove the other wrong, but it aims at real conversion of both the other and of the self. Nonviolence must be shown as a desirable alternative, not a moral cudgel. This meekness is not a flattering attempt to please one's enemy but a trust in the goodness of other people and a refusal to despair.

138   ——."Peace: Christian Duties and Perspectives." See **40**, 12-19.

Christ is the prince of peace. The Christian is the peacemaker, the true child of God. Moral passivity is the worst danger for the Christian. The just war is impossible.

139   "Paix," *Dictionnaire de théologie catholique. Tables générales.* 2: 3407-9.

Christ as the author of true, not simply, exterior, peace.

140   Perkins, Pheme. *Love Commandments in the New Testament.* New York: Paulist Press, 1982.

This excellent study guide covers the problem of the New Testament ethic, the double love command (Mt. 22:34-40, etc.), the love of enemies, modern interpretive metaphors, the parables of the prodigal son and the good Samaritan, love and Christian conscience, love as Christian freedom, as the fulfillment of the law, love of enemies as witness to God's truth, love of enemies and submission to authority, and God as love. Good selected bibliography, incorporating much recent scholarship.

141   Piper, John. *'Love Your Enemies': Jesus' Love Command in the Synoptic Gospels and in the Early Christian Paraenesis.* Cambridge: Cambridge University Press, 1979.

A remarkable textual study with thoroughgoing notes and bibliography that demonstrates both the genuineness of Jesus' love command and its living tradition in the early church. Surveys the Stoic, Scribal and Rabbinical traditions to show the originality of Christ's message. Even the Old Testament calls to love one's neighbor and sojourners in the land, to reject inner as well as outer grudges, cannot be seen as the sources for the New Testament teaching to love one's enemies voiced by Jesus and repeated by Paul. Christ has rejected the *lex talionis*, "an eye for an eye." Even the institutionalization of Christ's message in the early church could not blunt the force of this command.

It is the act itself that shows Christ's true followers, it is not a prerequisite to becoming the children of God. The way to the goal, the kingdom of God, thus becomes the goal itself. Love of enemy is also a paradox resolved by political context. For while love of enemy rejects violent resistance, it does not forego all resistance, nor does it ignore evil: it aims to convert the enemy over to the truth.

142   Rodriquez. "Peace." See **93**.

In the New Testament *eirene* conflated both the Hebrew and the Greek meanings of peace. Objectively it meant eschatological salvation and cessation of divine wrath, right relations among peoples. Subjectively it meant serenity and tranquility of soul in the awareness of reconciliation with God. In the Gospels it appears as the gift of Christ, the Messianic peace possessed by the Christian even in the present world. In the Epistles it coexists even with the most active conflict as the consequence of justification. It is the fruit and effect of God's grace. In the early church it is also the term used to describe their flourishing condition. Extensive use of biblical citations.

143   Schroeder, F. "Paul, Apostle, St.," *NCE* 11: 1-12.

       A good review of his life, teachings, and writings.

144   Sider, Ronald J. *Christ and Violence.* Nyack, NY:
       Fellowship of Reconciliation.

       Not seen.

145   van der Ploeg. "Peace." See **95**.

       The New Testament continues Old Testament
       meanings of peace, using *eirene* to covey all the meanings
       of *salom.* Peace is a Messianic promise, a gift of Christ, a
       condition of strife with the world, and the flourishing
       condition of the primitive church. For Paul peace is also
       the reconciliation between Gentile and Jew that Christ has
       brought. Extensive use of biblical citations.

The Politics of the Gospels

146   Bammel, Ernst, and C.F.D. Moule, eds. *Jesus and the
       Politics of His Day.* New York: Cambridge University
       Press, 1985.

       A collection of essays that sets out to examine the
       thesis that Jesus was somehow allied with the Zealot
       movement of armed resistance to Rome. Topics discussed
       range from Jesus' relations to the Zealots, his religious
       opposition to Judaism, the sources for the trial of Christ,
       the revolt of 70 C.E. in Christian tradition, Jesus' reputa-
       tion as a brigand in the anti-Christian polemics of the
       pagans, the question of the tribute coin, Jesus' claim to
       bring "no peace but a sword," the question of the two
       swords brought by the apostles just before his arrest, the

political charges against Jesus, and his trial. The over-riding conclusion of the collection is that Jesus was announcing a new order that went beyond political aims but that inevitably brought him and his followers into conflict with the established order. Well annotated with an excellent index to biblical citations.

147   Cassidy, Richard J. *Jesus, Politics and Society. A Study of Luke's Gospel.* Maryknoll, NY: Orbis Books, 1983.

While Jesus and the Zealots were on opposite poles of the world of action and ideas, Jesus' teachings were still powerfully revolutionary, and he was considered dangerous to the Roman Empire. Cassidy examines Luke as a historian, Jesus' social teachings, his attitudes toward political rulers, his trial and execution, the political situation in Israel at the time, social and economic factors, and the various political factions vying for supremacy within Judaism. Well annotated, with an excellent bibliography.

148   Daube, David. *Civil Disobedience in Antiquity.* Edinburgh: Edinburgh University Press, 1972.

Includes many groups: women in the Bible and in Greece and Rome, children and slaves, prophets and philosophers, religious minorities, and liberation movements. Christians are excluded since Christ resorted to violence at a key moment: the cleansing of the Temple. The Sermon on the Mount was in no way nonviolent.

149   Ferguson, John. *The Politics of Love: The New Testament and Nonviolent Revolution*. Nyack, NY: Fellowship of Reconciliation, 1979.

This is essential and basic reading for an understanding of the meaning of Christian peacemaking from the New Testament to Constantine. While it is unfair to extract individual biblical texts either to support or to refute pacifism, current biblical scholarship seeks the overall context of Jesus' words. Such an examination leads one to conclude that the Sermon on the Mount contains Christ's true teaching. His command to love your enemy is not a temporary ethic, it is political and social, not merely personal; and it is a command, not a counsel to perfection. Paul's letters, written down before the Gospels, fully share in Jesus' call to peacemaking. Examines all the key texts in the New Testament, along with problem passages that have traditionally been used to support the warmaker and those supposedly supporting the just-war tradition.

150   Grant, Robert M. *Early Christianity and Society. Seven Studies*. San Francisco: Harper & Row, 1977.

A good survey of Christian attitudes to patriotism, taxes, work, occupation, property, the state, and the *Pax Romana*. Discusses the conflict inherent in the classic dichotomy between Romans 13 and Apocalypse 13, of Rome as God-given authority, or Rome as the persecuting beast.

151   Niebuhr, Reinhold. *Moral Man and Immoral Society*. New York: Charles Scribner's, 1960.

The classic statement of the position that the individual Christian's morality and the Gospel call to perfection has nothing to do with the morality of politics or the secular world, and that the Christian message is at heart non-political. A major objection to any definition of peace as active and engaged with social justice.

152   Troeltsch, Ernst. *The Social Teaching of the Christian Churches*. Olive Wyon, transl. New York: Harper & Row, 1960.

An historical survey of the development of Christian ethics, stemming from the same tradition as Niebuhr's (**151**), that saw Christian ethics as essentially quietist.

153   Zampaglione. *Idea of Peace*. See **58**.

It is difficult to justify even the just war from an exegesis of the Sermon on the Mount, the heart of the Gospel. Imagery of violence is either allegorical or used in parables. Yet, Zampaglione's interpretation of peace in the New Testament is a quietist one. Christ's peace was internal and promised for the future. Love of enemy is merely the means to some future, and individualistic, salvation. Christ's message of peace as interpreted by the early church was essentially otherworldly. No attempt was made to change the present world, and expectations of peace were apocalyptic. Pacifism was simply one element needed to free the downtrodden from frustration and a sense of inferiority. Paul called for obedience and accommodation to political reality.

* *
*

CHAPTER 3: *Peacemaking in the Early Church. From Paul to Constantine*

The Christian Background

154   Altaner, Berthold. *Patrology*. Hilda C. Graff, transl. Westminster, MD: Herder & Herder, 1960.

Essential introduction to the writings of the early Christian peacemakers, arranged by individuals, providing a listing of works, translations, and scholarship.

155   Attwater. *Saints*. See **1.**

Biographies of many of the early peacemakers and martyrs. Selected suggested reading.

156   Bainton, Roland H. *Early Christianity*. New York: Van Nostrand, 1960.

A collection of primary sources in translation, along with historical introduction. Good sources for early Christian antimilitarism and peacemaking. See **190.**

157   Baus, Karl. *From the Apostolic Community to Constantine*. Vol. 1 in Hubert Jedin and John Dolan. *Handbook of Church History (History of the Church)*. New York: Herder & Herder, Seabury Press, 1965-.

Excellent background for Christianity from its Judaic roots, the life of Jesus, the Greco-Roman world, and the post-Apostolic age. Excellent bibliography.

158   Brown, Peter R.L. *The Cult of the Saints: Its Rise and
        Function in Latin Christianity.* Chicago: University of
        Chicago Press, 1981.

        Excellent introduction to the study of individual
        Christian saints and martyrs, the first peacemakers.
        Rejects the theory that popular saints venerated from the
        time of the early church represented a less pure form of
        Christianity or culture.

159   Butler. *Lives.* See **9**.

        The most comprehensive collection available in
        English for the lives of the early peacemakers.

160   Chadwick, Henry. *The Early Church.* Baltimore: Penguin
        Books, 1967.

        Excellent, brief introduction to the historical period.
        The church's growth, its encounter with Rome, the
        development of its institutions, and an examination of its
        major thinkers. In general, while the church tolerated
        existing Roman institutions, including slavery, its em-
        phasis on a new society of equals held deep social and
        political potential.

161   Cohn, Norman. *The Pursuit of the Millennium.* New
        York: Harper & Row, 1961, rev. ed., New York:
        Oxford University Press, 1970.

        Early pages trace the origins of Christian apocalyptic
        from the Jewish tradition through John's *Revelation* and
        into Lactantius and the age of Constantine. Cohn has been
        widely criticized for equating the Christian apocalyptic
        tradition too exclusively with violent social revolt and class
        struggle, reading the totalitarian upheavals of the twentieth

century back into history.

162   Delaney. *Dictionary.* See **15.**

163   *Fathers of the Church. A New Translation.* 68 vols. New
       York: Cima, 1947-.

       Good English editions.

164   Frend, W.H.C. *The Early Church.* Philadelphia: Fortress
       Press, 1982.

       A good, general history of Christianity from the New
       Testament to Constantine. Good chapter bibliographies.

165   Grant, Robert M. *Augustus to Constantine. The Thrust of
       the Christian Movement into the Roman World.* New
       York: Harper & Row, 1970.

       A good general introduction, with an excellent
       bibliography. Follows Cadoux (**193**) in characterizing
       Christian attitudes to war. While the imperial just war was
       conceivable, prayer was the Christian's method of
       defending the empire.

166   ——.*Early Christianity.* See **150.**

       Christian attitudes to the *Pax Romana* were mixed,
       ranging from the support of the stability it provided to
       opposition to Roman tyranny. Taken as a whole,
       however, the Christians, and the Romans themselves,
       considered the church as "a state within a state" con-
       sciously set up to create a new society.

167   Halton, Thomas P., and Robert D. Sider. "A Decade of
        Patristic Scholarship 1970-1970," *Classical World*
        (Nov.-Dec., 1982): 67-127.

        Supplements such works as Altaner (**154**) and
        Quasten (**175**) in locating the lives and works of the early
        church writers.

168   Harnack, Adolf. *The Mission and Expansion of
        Christianity in the First Three Centuries.* James
        Moffatt, transl. and ed. New York: Harper & Row,
        1962.

        The remarkable success of Christianity was due
        largely to its message of salvation, its ethical teaching, and
        its sacramentalism; yet its gospel of love and charity
        "became a social message" that showed that goodness was
        not an "impotent claim or pale ideal" but an active power
        that won over many. See also **226**.

169   Lebreton, Jules, S.J., and Jacques Zeiller. *History of the
        Primitive Church.* Ernest C. Messinger, transl. 3 vols.
        New York: Macmillan, 1944-48.

        Excellent introduction to the period and to the
        questions debated by historians, including the martyrs,
        their numbers and effect, the life of Christians in the early
        Church, and the question of military service. See **243**.

170   *Library of Christian Classics.* J. Baille, J.T. MacNeill,
        and H.P. van Dusen, eds. Philadelphia: Westminster
        Press, 1953-.

        English translations of early Christian writings,
        including those of the peacemakers.

171 Markus, Robert A. *Christianity in the Roman World.* New York: Charles Scribner's, 1974.

A popular, general account of the early church, with fairly good bibliography.

172 McGinn. *Apocalyptic Spirituality.* See **37**.

Using the *Divine Institutes* of Lactantius as his example, McGinn notes that early Christian apocalyptic was fundamentally political in its call to resist evil and in consoling the good. Though activist, it was opposed to violence.

173 ——.*Visions.* See **38**.

Short selections from a wide variety of apocalyptic writings. Useful for the early church.

174 Meeks, Wayne A. *The First Urban Christians. The Social World of the Apostle Paul.* New Haven: Yale University Press, 1983.

A well received analysis of the origins, lives, organization and attitudes of the early Christians. Informative background reading.

175 Quasten, Johannes. *Patrologia.* 3 vols. Westminster, MD: Newman Publishing, 1960.

Like Altaner (**154**) provides useful introduction to the lives, writings of, and scholarship on, the early Christian peacemakers.

176   *A Select Library of Nicene and Post-Nicene Fathers of the Christian Church.* Philip Schaff and Henry Wall, gen. eds. 28 vols. New York: Christian Literature, 1886-1890; reprint, Grand Rapids, MI: Eerdmans, 1952-56.

Source materials for the early Christian intellectual tradition, including nonviolence.

177   Siegman, E.F. "Apocalypse, Book of," *NCE* 1: 654-59.

General introduction to the book and its study.

178   Stevenson, James. *A New Eusebius. Documents Illustrative of the History of the Church to A.D. 337.* London: S.P.C.K., 1960.

Source readings.

179   Von Hefele, Karl Joseph. *A History of the Councils of the Church.* 5 vols. Edinburgh: Clark Publishers, 1883-96; reprint, New York: AMS, 1972.

Basic collection of primary source materials for church councils, including the controversial one of Arles in 314, which some scholars believe legitimized military service for Christians.

180   Wright, Frederick Adam, ed. *Fathers of the Church: Tertullian, Cyprian, Arnobius, Lactantius, Ambrose, Jerome, Augustine.* New York: Dutton, 1929.

Primary source readings.

Christianity and Rome

181   Brown, Peter R.L. *The World of Late Antiquity.* New
         York: Harcourt Brace, 1971.

         Excellent background to the spiritual and intellectual
         world that witnessed the struggle and triumph of
         Christianity, including the imperial cult and its political
         obligations, the militarization of society from c. 250 C.E.,
         the very real social revolution that Christianity offered.

182   Cochrane, Charles N. *Christianity and Classical Culture.*
         A Study of Thought and Action from Augustus to
         Augustine. New York: Oxford University Press,
         1957.

         Traces the transformation of *Romanitas* from a pagan
         to a Christian ideal, including the meanings of the *Pax*
         Romana.

183   Cunningham, Agnes, S.S.C.M. *The Early Church and the*
         State. Philadelphia: Fortress Press, 1982.

         A collection of source readings, with historical
         introduction, including Pliny's description of the legal
         basis for the persecutions and Tertullian's *Apology.*

184   Dörries, Hermann. *Constantine the Great.* Roland H.
         Bainton, transl. New York: Harper & Row, 1972.

         Excellent biography of the Roman emperor converted
         to Christianity, who for many historians of the Christian
         peace tradition marks the end of early church pacifism, the
         beginnings of the Christian alliance of power, and the just-
         and holy-war traditions of the Catholic Middle Ages.
         Includes an analysis of the canons of the controversial

council of Arles summoned by Constantine in 314, which many interpret as legitimizing Christian military service.

185   Ferguson, John. *The Religions of the Roman Empire.* Ithaca, NY: Cornell University Press, 1970.

The nature of Roman religion, the Roman imperial cult, and its essentially political character, and the Christian reluctance to compromise led to inevitable confrontation. Both the monotheism and the nonviolence of Christianity were seen as inimical to the Roman Empire, and the Christian religion was viewed as a subversive movement. One cannot ignore the essentially political character of Christianity. Good bibliography and notes.

186   Jones, A.H.M. "The Social Background of the Struggle Between Paganism and Christianity." See **187**, 17-37.

Useful background information, including the classes, occupations, intellectual and cultural levels of the early Christians, who were generally from the lower and middle ranges and reached prominence only with Constantine's reorganizations in the fourth century. See also **232**.

187   Momigliano, Arnaldo. *The Conflict Between Paganism and Christianity in the Fourth Century.* Oxford: Clarendon Press, 1963.

In his "Christianity and the Decline of the Roman Empire," pp. 1-16, Momigliano states that the rise of Christianity was the single most important factor in the transformation of the Roman world. He notes, however, that this is "not...a simple return to Gibbon. Christianity produced a new style of life, created new loyalties, gave people new ambitions and new satisfactions."

Peacemaking in the Early Church

188   Amaldi, Maria Turriani. "Pax," in *Latinitatis Italicae Medii Aevi unde ab A. CDLXXVI usque ad A. MXXII lexicon imperfectum.* Brussels: Union Academique Internationale, 1936. 2: 219.

    Ranges over the meanings of the Latin word for peace from the early Christian to the medieval.

189   Bainton. *Christian Attitudes.* See **2**.

    Pacifism was the chief attitude of the early church. It was heavily influenced by Stoicism but included an abhorrence to war as murder and the birth of conscientious objection. With the Middle Ages this pacifism shifted to the just-war theory and the holy war or crusade. This too pat distinction has been criticized by J. Bryan Hehir in **29**.

190   ———.*Early Christianity.* See **156**.

    Ancient society knew no modern distinction between Church and State. Religion, politics, and culture were all inextricably linked. Therefore Christian opposition to paganism was essentially political as well as religious. Christian pacifism took several forms but condemned participation in war.

191   ———."The Early Church and War," *Harvard Theological Review* 39 (1946): 189-213.

    Summarizes the historiography of the problem and the evidence for Christians in Roman ranks. While attitudes to Rome varied from approval to outright hostility, Christian

pacifism was not the result of heresy but fully in the
mainstream. See **218**.

192   Brock. *Roots*. See **8**.

The early church marked the high point of Christian
pacifism. Provides selections from the best known early
Christian pacifists, including Ignatius, Origen, Tertullian,
Justin Martyr, and Lactantius. With the coming of the
Middle Ages, Brock asserts, "Christian pacifism is submerged for nearly a millennium" and "the barbarians
militarized Christianity." Typical of the Protestant
interpretation of Church history. See also **221**.

193   Cadoux, C. John. *Early Christian Attitudes to War: A
        Contribution to the History of Christian Ethics*.
        London: Headley, 1919; reprint, New York: Seabury
        Press, 1982.

The book is divided into three main sections: on
Jesus' own teachings, Christian attitudes against war, and
Christian attitudes accepting war. Cadoux holds that
Christ taught nonviolence and love; those texts marshaled
to show his approval of violence or the military do not
really support that conclusion. Christian disapproval of
war covers many topics, including condemnation of war in
the abstract, Christianity's essential pacifism, Christian
refusal to participate in war, and the witness of Christian
conscientious objectors. On the other hand, Christians
used military terminology, accepted the state, and did,
rarely, serve in the army. Christian pacifism remained
strong into the fourth century. An extremely important
and well balanced history. See **222**.

194   Cahill, Lisa Sowle. "Nonresistance, Defense, Violence,
        and the Kingdom in Christian Tradition,"

Interpretation 38, 4 (1984): 380-97.

Using Roland Bainton (2) as a basis, provides an overview of Christian attitudes toward pacifism and "nonresistance." How do pacifists deal with injustice, biblical violence, and Jesus' nonviolence? Surveys Christian thought from Tertullian through Augustine, Aquinas, Luther, the Quakers, Calvin and the Puritans, and Hugo Grotius.

195   Caspary, Gerard E. *Politics and Exegesis: Origen and the Two Swords*. Berkeley and London: University of California Press, 1979.

This is part of a larger study on the evolution of the theory of the two swords in Western political and social thought. This important volume, however, deals with the origin of the idea in the biblical passages of Christ's passion in which the disciples offer him two swords in Gethsemane (Lk 22:36-38) and in which Peter cuts off the servant's ear (Mt 26:52). In both, Christ's rejection of violence and of Zealot revolt seems clear, and this is how Origen interpreted them.

Origen's nonviolent interpretation was key to the West's understanding of these texts and in an allegorical reading of the violence of the Old Testament. Later on, however, the theme was to be transformed into the foundation of Peter's temporal power, as Origen's pacifism was lost on a later age.

Excellent thematic discussions, with superb indexes of biblical and early Christian uses of these texts.

196   Du Cange. "Pax." See **19**, 2: 228-31.

Reviews the medieval meanings of the word. The early Church expanded the meanings of the word in the

New Testament. *Pax* also came to mean the tranquility and order established by the church with its triumph over paganism, a Christian *Pax Romana*, the forgiveness granted sinners by a priest, that gained by the martyrs and confessors, and the greeting of a bishop to his congregation.

197   Egan. "The Beatitudes." See **122**.

Discusses the pacifism of the early church, basing it not on an aversion to idolatry or an unjust state, or apocalyptism, but on the positive Gospel call to make peace. Includes the examples of Maximilian, Lactantius, and Origen.

198   Fenwick, C.G. "Peace, International," *NCE* 11: 38-41.

The historical position of the church is identified with the just-war tradition, from Augustine to the Crusades and Aquinas. Papal internationalism dominates later history. Despite its pre-Vatican II limitations, this serves as good introduction to Catholic definitions.

199   Ferguson. *Politics of Love.* See **149**.

The basic Christian attitude toward Rome during the early church was nonviolent opposition. The Romans accused the Christians not on the basis of specific breaches of the law but of a general attitude. Cites selections from many early peacemakers, including Tarachus, Justin Martyr, Clement of Alexandria, Tatian, Athenagoras, Origen, Tertullian, Cyprian of Carthage, Municius Felix Lactantius, the *Canons of Hippolytus,* and Pope Damasus I. An important survey of early Christian peacemaking.

200   Frend. *Martyrdom.* See **124.**

The story of the Christian martyrs is the "story of the successful Christian revolution against the Roman Empire." This revolution was accomplished through nonviolence, the active witness of thousands of Christians to the truth of the Sermon on the Mount, who convinced the Romans that the people they had previously despised and feared were truly heroic. In the end the pagans grew tired of killing the just; persecution only quickened the pace of conversion.

Traces the tradition of martyrdom from its Jewish roots in Maccabees, Messianic liberation and revolutionary apocalypticism and notes its stark contrast to the Stoics' emphasis on individual rather than community salvation. The Christians' struggle was less against Rome on a purely political plane than against the world of force that it represented. The struggle was waged on the level of religious loyalties and the entire political and cultural sphere that this represented. The struggle at times focused on the Christians' refusal to participate in the state cult, but it went far beyond this.

Frend's scope is comprehensive, tracing the history of the persecutions from the reign of Nero through that of Diocletian. The issues he raises go far beyond that of martyrdom, including the Roman legal basis for the persecutions and selections from the early Fathers explaining the nature of their struggle with Rome. This book presents the best account of Christian nonviolence in action in the early church. See also **248.**

201   Grant, Robert M. "War — Just, Holy, Unjust — in Hellentistic and Early Christian Thought," *Augustinianum* 20 (1980): 173-89.

Traces and evaluates ideas on war in early

Christianity, with special emphasis on the "rules of war."
The pacifism of the synoptic Gospels and early Christian
theologians are too well known to warrant discussion here.
Instead Grant focuses on the transmission of Hellenistic
ideas of the laws and usages of war from Cicero through
Augustine. He stresses, however, that Christian attacks
on Roman morality and religion are largely based on
Roman conduct in war.

202   Hornus, Jean-Michel. *It Is Not Lawful for Me to Fight,
        Early Christian Attitudes Toward War.* Scottsdale, PA:
        Herald Press, 1980.

        Presents a wide variety of selections to demonstrate
that early Christian attitudes to the *Pax Romana* and the
Roman state were mixed. Nevertheless, Hornus shows
that attempts to dismiss early Christian pacifism as the
mood of a small elite, a late development of an intellectual
minority, or an aversion to idolatry are not supported by
the evidence. Christian peacemaking was positive, informed by a reverence for life, and opposed all forms of
killing and violence. Antimilitarism was a definite and
strong current, and even opposition to the imperial cult
was based not on a specific abhorrence to idolatry but on a
general opposition to the Roman state. Includes a very
helpful "Systematic Table of Primary Sources" for
Christian peacemaking. See also **231.**

203   Leclercq, Henri. "Paix," *DACL* 3, 1: 465-83.

        A general introduction to early Christian concepts of
the meaning of peace, using inscriptions and other
funerary motifs as evidence. For the early church *pax* also
meant unity, orthodoxy, or eventually even the physical
object that replaced the kiss of peace during the mass.

204   ——."Paix de l'Église," *DACL* 3, 1: 483-99.

With the conversion of Constantine and the triumph of Christianity, the *pax ecclesiae* (peace of the church) replaced the *Pax Romana* to connote an entire range of meanings involved with the final accommodation between the Christian religion and the empire, at first and primarily a treaty of peace.

205   Le Saint, W. "Tertullian," *NCE* 13: 1019-22.

An introduction to the life and thought of this vigorous early Christian pacifist and opponent of the Roman order. This model of nonviolence has remained controversial to this day. According to Le Saint, "he cannot be recommended without reserve to Christian readers or honored with a place among the Fathers of the Church."

206   MacGregor. *New Testament Basis*. See **134**.

The early Christian outlook was essentially political. While they rendered to Caesar and opposed violent rebellion, they also acknowledged that the oppressor was the oppressor and gave loyalty to God first. Paul's juxtaposition of Romans 12:17-21 to Romans 13:1-7 sums this up. Do not rise up violently against authority, but do not acquiesce to evil. Nonviolent opposition was the basic Christian approach in the early centuries.

207   Swift, Louis J. "War and the Christian Conscience I: The Early Years." *Aufsteig und Niedergang der römischen Welt* 11.23.1 (New York, 1979): 835-68.

On the pre-Constantinian era. Traces the issues of government coercion and authority, conscience and the

Gospel of peace. Traces the scriptural foundations of the early Christian message and its development through Tertullian and Cyprian, Clement and Origen, Arnobius and Lactantius. Draws on both literary evidence and practice.

No one interpretation can be offered to explain why Christians refused military service. Aversion to bloodshed, idolatry, military life, and oath taking all played their part. Swift's work is an excellent broadening of the question away from the narrow issues of "pacifism" toward larger ones of "peacemaking." As he puts it: "the real issue for those Christian writers who dealt with the problem of war at any length was not idolatry or eschatology or antagonism to the empire but simply the notion that killing and love were incompatible."

208   Windass, Stanley. *Christianity Versus Violence: A Social and Historical Study of War and Christianity*. London: Sheed and Ward, 1964.

Until the onset of the Catholic Middle Ages the early Christians were opposed to war. With the end of the early church came a "consecration of violence." Follows the lines of Protestant peace historiography.

209   ——."The Early Christian Attitude to War," *Irish Theological Quarterly* 29 (1962): 235-45.

Not seen.

210   Zampaglione. *Idea of Peace*. See **58**.

Early Christianity was quietist in its attitudes to war and the state. Christians endured martyrdom out of apocalyptic expectation and concern for their own souls. No thought was given to the social dimensions of their acts. In general Christians sought accommodation to the empire and opposed Rome only over the idolatry involved in the imperial cult. Antimilitarism was quickly accommodated to the needs of the state. By the second century only the most extreme fringe groups were still pacifist, while the Sermon on the Mount was imitated only by fanatics, clairvoyants and "those most easily receptive to the immediate intuitions of feeling." Despite this approach, Zampaglione provides abundant selections for the pacifist positions of many writers of the early church.

Roman Religious Reaction

211   Benko, Stephen. *Pagan Rome and the Early Christians.* Bloomington, IN: Indiana University Press, 1984.

Examines Roman attitudes to the early Christians and the consistent charges leveled against them. Problems discussed include the *nomen* or name of Christian and its implications to the Romans, a portrait of an early Christian, charges of immorality and cannibalism, the Christian kiss and charges of licentiousness, magic and Christian practices, and pagan criticism of Christian theology and ethics.

On the whole, Benko demonstrates, the Romans had some good grounds for their charges and suspicions. A good corrective for those who consider all in the early church saintly martyrs.

212   Cumont, Franz. *The Oriental Religions in Roman Paganism.* Grant Showerman, intro. New York: Dover Books, 1956.

The rapid spread of eastern cults, including Christianity, may be explained by their contrast to the unsatisfying official Roman cult and the emotional, personal, and ethical appeal of the mystery cults. Good background.

213   Dodds, E.R. *Pagan and Christian in An Age of Anxiety.* New York: Norton, 1965.

In the end "Christianity...was judged to be worth living for because it was worth dying for." The appeal of the martyrs' nonviolent witness finally overcame Roman paganism.

214   MacMullen, Ramsay. *Christianizing the Roman Empire A.D. 100-400.* New Haven: Yale University Press, 1984.

While many pagans in the late Empire were converted, the question remains: to what extent was their conversion genuine? To what extent did these new, essentially "bedouin," Christians simply adopt a religious subculture, barely touched by true Christian doctrine and ethics? MacMullen stresses that these issues may be unimportant. They seem to have been to the ancients themselves, and this is the criterion that we should keep in mind.

Surveys pagan beliefs, their view of Christianity, the role of Constantine's conversion and its effect on conversion to Christianity for nonreligious motives, and forced conversion. Yet there is evidence of conscious Christian evangelization, for example by Gregory the Wonder Worker or Martin of Tours, who brought many to Christianity as much by their dramatic actions as by their preaching. Conversion of the intellectuals came last of all, and their numbers were insignificant. A good reminder that Christian ethics, and the message of peace, played only one part in the total process of converting the Roman Empire.

215   Nock, A.D. *Conversion. The Old and the New in Religion
        from Alexander the Great to Augustine of Hippo.* New
        York: Oxford University Press, 1965.

        A groundbreaking work tracing the process of con-
        version. Christianity's basic emphasis, one it shared with
        many Eastern cults, was individual and oriented to
        personal salvation. Yet the Roman world had precedents
        in its own religion, philosophy, and literature for the
        personal drama of conversion and martyrdom that it saw
        played out by the Christians. This preparation permitted
        the Romans to understand the Christian struggle and
        finally to change their own hearts and join it.

216   Smith, John Holland. *The Death of Classical Paganism.*
        New York: Charles Scribner's, 1976.

        Traces the progress of the Christianization of the
        empire from Diocletian to Isidore of Seville and the early
        Middle Ages. Includes such topics as the imperial cult, the
        essential link between politics and religion in the late
        antique world, and the suspicion cast on Christians as
        potential traitors, a potential that drove Diocletian to begin
        purging them from the army when the probability of war
        on the frontiers approached.

217   Ste.-Croix, G. de. "Why Were the Early Christians
        Persecuted?" *Past and Present* 26 (1963): 6-38.

        Rejects theories that their refusal to sacrifice out of
        aversion to idolatry was the main cause. They were
        persecuted for the *nomen* (name), the very fact of being
        Christian, never for any particular act. The central issue,
        as revealed by Pliny, was that of religious, and thus of
        political, loyalty to the empire. Underscores the essentially
        political stance of Christianity and of Christian

nonviolence as a revolutionary power.

Christians and the Roman Army

218   Bainton. "Early Church." See **191**.

Christian opposition to service in the Roman army was based primarily on Christ's love command in the Sermon on the Mount. Apocalyptic and purely political motives played a minor role, as did the Christian aversion to idolatry involved in soldiers' sacrificing to the emperor. While army service was not condemned outright, fighting in wars was. There were no Christians known in the Roman army before 170 C.E., and no Christian approved of war prior to the age of Constantine. Police work, serving in the army during the tranquil years of the *Pax Romana,* was acceptable to Christians.

219   Berchem, Andreas. *Le martyre de la Légion Thébaine.* Basel: Schweizerische Beitrage zur Altertumswissenschaft 8, 1968.

Not seen.

220   Brand, Clarence R. *Roman Military Law.* Austin, TX: University of Texas Press, 1968.

A very tidy delineation of all aspects of the topic, including religion and discipline" (pp. 83-98) and offenses and punishments (pp. 99-109).

221   Brock. *Roots.* See **8**.

Draws the distinction between a soldier's military and his police duties, which most often involved little violence during the tranquil years of the *Pax Romana.* Those

Christians in Roman ranks are better known for their conscientious objection than for their military service. Maximilianus is an example.

222   Cadoux. *Early Christian Attitudes*. See **193**.

No evidence exists for Christians in the military before 170 C.E. Episodes, such as the Christian Thundering Legion, are based on faulty and later sources and must be dismissed. Also reviews Tertullian's ideas opposing military service and recounts evidence for Christian soldiers who refused to obey war orders.

223   Davies, R.W. "Police Work in Roman Times," *History Today* 18 (1968): 700-707.

Even according to Christian witnesses like Tertullian, the majority of Roman military work was actually peacekeeping within the empire, tracking down brigands, maintaining general law and order, investigating missing persons and arson cases, and policing the larger cities. Roman soldiers also acted as frontier guards, traffic controllers, and secret police. An important study that may help explain the fact that while Christians might find many of these tasks repugnant, they were, nevertheless, essentially nonmilitary. This may explain the small numbers of Christians who were found in Roman military ranks before Constantine.

224   Fontaine, J. "Christians and Military Service in the Early Church." T. Westow, transl. *Concilium* 7 (1965): 107-119.

Reviews the historiography on the topic and concludes that the entire interest in early Christian pacifism is "dangerous." The evidence on both sides of the debate is

fragmentary and emotional. While his advice on partisan-
ship is certainly worth heeding, one cannot prevent the
historian from attempting to make sense of controversial,
even "dangerous" problems.

225   Gero, Stephen. "'Miles gloriosus,' The Church and
             Military Service According to Tertullian," *Church
             History* 39 (1970): 285-98.

Tertullian's works provide an index to the changing
Christian attitudes to armed service. Before the second
century there is no evidence of Christians in the army.
From 170-80 there was a rapid shift under the Severan
emperors as society became increasingly militarized, and
the new attractiveness of the army began to draw
Christians. Tertullian's condemnations of military service
thus represent an attempt to stem back this tide, and his
works grow stronger in their attacks. Violence and not
idolatry was the stumbling block to Christian participation.
Gero's method argues from known Christian polemics
against the military to Christian enlistment "perhaps in
large numbers," but he fails to provide any but this rather
indirect, and essentially negative, evidence.

226   Harnack. *Mission.* See **168**.

Christian objection to military service stemmed from a
variety of motives. These included opposition to blood
shed, army discipline that involved the use of the death
penalty and other duties opposed to Christians' duty to
God, the cult of the emperor essential to military life,
pagan symbolism used by the military, and the normal
immorality of camp life. A well balanced treatment.

227   Helgeland, John. "Christians and the Roman Army, A.D
             173-337," *Church History* 43 (1974): 149-63, 200.

Interpretations of the early Christian attitude to military service have generally followed sectarian lines. Catholics have stressed Christian loyalty to the state, attributing opposition to service to an aversion to the idolatry involved in soldier's military oaths; Protestant sectaries and pacifists stress the priority of the Sermon on the Mount; while Lutherans and mainline Protestants trace a progress of gradual support for the state. On the whole, however, military service was not really a hot issue in the early church; only a handful of writers voiced concern over it, and no evidence of military service exists before 173 C.E.

While "generally speaking, the Fathers abhorred violence...the evidence gathered from all the Church Fathers of the first three centuries proves that there was no such thing as an early church pacifism." Helgeland accepts such stories as the Christian Thundering Legion and the Theban Legion as accurate evidence of Christian military service. He asserts that Marinus, Maximilianus, Marcellus and other soldier martyrs were executed for breaches of military discipline when they refused to fight. He states that only seven tombstones prior to Constantine can be attributed to Christian soldiers; but that "more are undoubtedly from the time, but it is not possible to say which ones are."

228   ⸺,"Christians and the Roman Army from Marcus Aurelius to Constantine." *Austeig und Niedergang der Römischen Welt* 11.23.1 (1979): 724-834.

An excellent and important introduction to the data and problems, despite Helgeland's all too obvious opinion that opposition to service was based solely on aversion to idolatry and his sometimes overzealous attempt to dispute all other possible interpretations. Helgeland may be too categorical in his dismissal of interpretations comparing the early church's peacemaking to "modern pacifism" as tearing quotations out of context. He, in fact, never defines what he means by this "pacifism" but apparently dismisses it a priori.

Topics include war, violence and military service in the thought of the early church, a very valuable review of the historiography, a review of the problem of Christians in the Roman army, the sources and interpretations, and the issue of military service in the age of Constantine. Excellent bibliography.

229   ——."Roman Army Religion," *Austeig und Niedergang der romischen Welt* II.16.1. Berlin and New York: Walter de Gruyter, 1978.

This "official cult" was highly liturgical and external. Inner belief was not necessary for the participant since external devotions guaranteed the link between the rites performed and the favor of the Gods on the empire, crops, and prosperity.

230   ——.Robert J. Daly, S.J. and J. Robert Burns. *Christians and the Military: The Early Experience.* Philadelphia: Fortress Press, 1985.

This handy, short book discusses and presents essential texts for most of the major issues in the debate over Christian participation in the Roman army and Christian attitudes to it. Topics include the political and ethical background of Jesus' message and the New Testament, the love command and nonviolence; the early church's use of military metaphors to describe the struggle of the Christian, the testimony of Tertullian, the *Apostolic Tradition* of Hippolytus, and Origen on Christian pacifism. The authors also present analyses of evidence for Christian violence and military service: the Apocryphal Gospels, the story of the Thundering Legion, the the Christian military martyrs, and the Canons of the council of Arles. Eusebius, Ambrose and Augustine all saw a divine mission for Christian soldiers. The authors tend to the view that if Christians did resist military service and its violence, it was from an aversion to idolatry, not to any Christian principle of nonviolence based on the Gospels.

231   Hornus. *It Is Not Lawful.* See **202**.

While there were soldiers in the Roman army, the evidence put forth is exaggerated. No evidence exists for the first two centuries; Leclercq's (**234**) evidence of 11 Christian soldiers out of 4700 inscriptions is scanty, but nonetheless significant. Literary evidence, Tertullian's opposition, stories of soldier martyrs, apocryphal legends of military saints, and the Christian soldiers who died during Diocletian's purge all point to an overwhelming Christian pacifism.

232   Jones. "Social Background." See **186**.

Examines the social origins of the Roman army and demonstrates that well into the fourth century it remained peasant, barbarian, within the families of former soldiers, and "overwhelmingly pagan." There is no evidence of large-scale Christian enlistment. This remained exceptional throughout the early church.

233   Klein, Richard. "Tertullian und das römische Reich,"
        Bibliothek der Klassischen Altertumswissenshaften
        n.f. 2 Reihe, Bd. 22. Heidelberg: C. Winter, 1968.

        Not seen.

234   Leclercq, Henri. "Militarisme," *DACL* 11: 1108-81.

        Using epigraphical evidence the author finds eleven
        tombs, out of 4,700 extant, to show that Christians served
        as soldiers. Yet the significance of these inscriptions is
        still much in debate.

235   MacMullen, Ramsay. *Soldier and Civilian in the Later
        Roman Empire.* Harvard Historical Monographs 52,
        Cambridge, MA: Harvard University Press, 1963.

        Roman military service at the height of the empire
        consisted mainly of peaceful police work. Military life
        was largely confined to the camps along the border or in
        provinces and consisted of settling quarrels, calming riots,
        overseeing customs, and pursuing bandits and other
        criminals. It was rarely military duty in the strict sense.

236   Munier, C., ed. *Concilia Galliae A. 314-A. 506. CCSL*
        148, Turnholt: Brepols, 1963.

        For the Council of Arles in 314, which some his-
        torians say appears to have approved Christian military
        service.

237   Powers and Freeman. "Conscientious Objectors." See **45**.

        Pacifism has never been a viable alternative for the
        Catholic or Christian. Any professed opposition to mili-
        tary service in the early church was based on resistance to

idolatry, and Christians were always loyal citizens.
Conscientious objection then, as now, is a selfish escape.
A pre-Vatican II view.

238   Ruyter, Knut Willem, O.F.M. "Pacifism and Military
        Service in the Early Church." *Cross Currents* 32
        (1982): 54-70.

Disputes the categorical dismissal of John Cardinal
O'Connor, then U.S. Military Vicar, that whatever the
early church may have believed about pacifism is irrelevant
to today's situation. The witness of the early church is
important for us today, as the lives and words of the
Berrigans and Plowshares demonstrate.

There is little doubt that the early church rejected
military service. The years 170 to 180, however, did
witness a true moral dilemma for the church as Christians
began to appear in Roman army lists. There were few
Christian volunteers, however, and those few Christian
soldiers were probably converts already in the service.
Ensuing Christian objection to service involved several
factors: violence, the immorality of military life, and
emperor worship.

While pacifism was not normative in later centuries, it
did exist; and even the just war was a Christian attempt to
limit the brutality of war. Today pacifism may well grow
with the change of the church from an institution into a
flock.

239   Ryan, E.A., S.J. "The Rejection of Military Service by
        Christians," *Theological Studies* 13 (1952): 1-32.

Christian opposition to military service, when it
existed was not based on pacifism, but from an abhorrence
to idolatry. Christians, on the whole, were loyal subjects
of the empire.

240   Swift, Louis J. *The Early Fathers on War and Military
        Service.* Wilmington, DE: Michael Glazier, 1983.

        An excellent, brief introduction to the issues facing the
        early Christians that are still relevant today. The New
        Testament pacifist tradition survived well into the third
        century, but did lessen with time. Christian motives for
        opposing war and military service were varied from the
        very start, ranging from this pacifism, to an aversion to
        idolatry, to taking oaths, to the vices of military life. No
        clear consensus ever emerged in the early church, and by
        the fourth century there was clearly a shift toward the just
        war. The primary sources reflect this variety. Good
        bibliography.

241   Tanzarella, Sergio. "I cristiani e il servizio militare nella
        chiesa antica. Il problema dalle origine alla fine del II
        secolo." *Asprenas* 31 (1984): 75-87.

        Not seen.

242   Von Campenhausen, Hans. "Christians and Military
        Service in the Early Church," in *Tradition and Life in
        the Church.* Philadelphia: Fortress Press, 1968.

        While Christians approached military service with
        many different attitudes, the basic Christian attitude was
        one of neutrality toward the passing, non-Christian world
        and never condemned war.

243   Watson, G.R. "Conscription and Voluntary Enlistment in
        the Roman Army," *Proceedings of the African
        Classical Association* 16 (1982): 191-209.

        While conscription was the rule in the fourth century,

military service was voluntary in the late Republic. When precisely can we mark the shift? Watson concludes that it is impossible to tell, and that conditions varied with period. Before the first century C.E., for example, conscription was used frequently, but under the Severans, in the second and third centuries military recruits were mostly volunteers.

Interesting, if inconclusive, evidence for the background of Christian military service.

244   Zeiller, Jacques. "The Question of Military Service." See **169**, 2: 1155-59.

The early Christians were "more truly citizens of the earthly fatherland than has sometimes been thought." Conscientious objection was the province of an intellectual elite, which did not affect "ordinary life." Even Tertullian's opposition was "from an already heretical mouth." Official church teachings stressing pacifism, like the Canons of Hippolytus, were ignored or resisted by the "good sense of the people." Argues backwards from the purges of Christians from the Roman army under Diocletian as "the best proof that from the end of the second to that of the third century...'a conscientious objection' was not felt by the majority." Zeiller's approach is typical of Catholicism smarting from its various *Kulturkampfen* and eager to prove its alliance with the mainstream and the official line.

Soldier Saints

245   Delehaye, Hippolyte. *Les légendes grecques de saints militaires*. Paris: A. Picard, 1909.

Many of our favorite Christian warrior saints, including Trophimus, Sabbatinus, Procopius, and George, are pure fabrications of a later age or simply translations of pagan myths.

246   ——.*The Legends of the Saints*. Donald Attwater, transl. New York: Fordham University Press, 1962.

A general introduction to reading and understanding saints lives and legends according to the literary and religious conventions of the day. Important background to understanding how legends of Christian warriors were produced.

247   Erdmann. *Idea of Crusade*. See **21**.

The fame of many Christian military saints, such as George, Maurice, Sebastian, and Martin rests not on their military exploits but on their Christian virtues.

248   Frend. *Martyrdom*. See **200**.

Examines the issue of Christians in the Roman army during the persecutions of the early fourth century. Such stories as that of the mostly Christian Theban or the Thundering Legion are based on pagan legends or faulty later sources and have little basis in fact. Soldiers known to be Christian are more likely in reality to have been conscientious objectors.

249   Merton, Thomas. "Saint Maximus the Confessor on Nonviolence." See **40**, 172-77.

A modern reflection on the ancient martyr. The message of Maximus is that our materialism ties us down to violence and injustice. Nonviolence is not passive acceptance of injustice. We are to resist not the evildoer but evil, since our resistance to hate vanquishes hate.

250   Musurillo, Herbert A., S.J. *The Acts of the Christian Martyrs.* Oxford: Clarendon Press, 1972.

The lives and deeds of twenty-eight early Christian martyrs, including the soldiers Marinus, Maximilianus, and Marcellus.

251   Siniscalco, Paolo. *Massimiliano: Un obiettore di coscienza del tardo impero. Studi sulla "Passio S. Maximiliani."* Turin: Paravia, 1974.

Not seen.

* *
*

CHAPTER 4: *Christian Peace and the Barbarians.*
Constantine to Charlemagne, 300-800

Introduction: Christian Empire and Imperial Church

252   Bark, William Carroll. *Origins of the Medieval World.*
        Stanford: Stanford University Press, 1966.

        A good, brief, introduction to the period. Topics
        discussed include a review of historiography, the political
        and socio-economic changes in late Roman and early
        medieval society, changes in "moods of thought and ex-
        pression," and the Christianization of the barbarian world.
        Well annotated, with good bibliography.

253   Barnes, Timothy D. *Constantine and Eusebius.*
        Cambridge, MA: Harvard University Press, 1981.

        An interpretative essay on the period, using these key
        figures as paradigms. Extensive bibliography.

254   Baus, Karl. *The Imperial Church from Constantine to the
        Early Middle Ages.* Anselm Biggs, transl. See **157**,
        vol. 2. New York: Seabury Press, 1980.

        An excellent survey of the period.

255   Brown, Peter R.L. "Aspects of the Christianization of the
        Aristocracy." See **256**, 161-82.

        A review of the historiography around the conversion
        of the "Romans of Rome" to Christianity toward the end

of the fifth century, examining the forms of conversion and their motivations.

256 —*Religion and Society in the Age of St. Augustine.* London: Faber & Faber, 1972.

Includes **255** and **269**.

257 *Cambridge Medieval History* 1: *The Christian Roman Empire and the Foundation of the Teutonic Kingdoms.* Cambridge: Cambridge University Press, 1957.

Still the best general introduction to the period, with articles by experts in each field.

258 Chadwick. *Early Church.* See **160**.

Excellent, brief introduction to the period, including discussions of the early church in the West, the origins of monasticism, Augustine, and the church and the barbarians.

259 Cochrane. *Christianity.* See **182**.

Discusses the *New Republic* of Eusebius and his attempt to create a political theory of the Imperial Church and the Christian Empire. This work is an important milestone in what many historians consider the shift from the pure pacifism of the early church to the barbarization of Christianity during the Middle Ages.

260 Dörries. *Constantine.* See **184**.

Examines the impact of the *pax ecclesiae*, the alliance between Christian church and Roman empire, on the spread of the church and on its attitudes toward the state, including a detailed discussion of the canons of the Council of Arles in 314 concerning police and other military duty performed by Christians.

261   Kidd, Beresford J. *Documents Illustrative of the Early Church.* 2 vols. New York: Macmillan, 1920-23.

       A good source collection in English.

262   Moss, H.St.L.B. *The Birth of the Middle Ages.* New York: Oxford University Press, 1961.

       An excellent survey covering the late Roman Empire and the structures of its life, the barbarian world, the clash of the two cultures, the life of the Byzantine Empire, the coming of Islam and the age of Charlemagne.

263   Setton, Kenneth M. *Christian Attitudes Towards the Emperor in the Fourth Century.* New York: Columbia University Press, 1941.

       Good general background for the range of Christian attitudes, from Eusebius' eager praises to Athanasius' condemnations of imperial tyranny.

264   Smith, Michael Auckland. *The Church Under Siege.* Downers Grove, IL: Inter-Varsity Press, 1976.

       A general history of the church from Constantine to Charlemagne, covering the fourth through the eighth century.

265   Stevenson, James. *Creeds, Councils, and Controversies. Documents Illustrative of the History of the Church*

AD 337-461. London: S.P.C.K., 1966.

Many useful documents, including selections from
Basil the Great, Athanasius, Ambrose of Milan, the *Codex
Theodosianus,* Salvian of Marseilles, St. Patrick, and
Prosper of Aquitaine, many of which underscore a
continuing tradition of nonviolence and peacemaking.

Peacemaking in the Roman West: Ambrose and Augustine

266   Augustine. *The City of God.* Henry Bettenson, transl.,
        David Knowles, ed. New York: Pelican, 1977.

While many historians and political thinkers have used
Augustine as the starting point of the Christian just-war
tradition, the *City of God*'s thoughts on war are far more
complex and subtle. The City of God is itself the
apocalyptic city, the New Jerusalem, the "Vision of
Peace." While peace in one sense is the duly ordered
harmony of all elements from the microcosm of the
physical body to the universe as a whole, Christian peace
is far from static order. Tranquility implies the proper
position of each being in its own place in the universe, but
this order is maintained by justice. An order imposed by
tyranny or the "lust for domination," which characterizes
the imposed peace of the Roman Empire, is not true peace
any more than a body hanging upside down is true
posture.

States that live for, and on, war are nothing better than
bands of pirates. "If justice is left out, what are kingdoms
except great robber bands?" The peace of the just war
smacks of the pride that is a perverted imitation of God's
order. "Even just wars, if considered by the wise man
seem lamentable. Consequently there would be no wars
for a wise man." Love of God and of neighbor are the
true principles of world justice and order. Peace is

impossible without this form of justice. Such love implies to "do no harm to anyone, and second, to help everyone whenever possible."

267   Bainton. *Attitudes*. See **2**.

Ambrose's and Augustine's chief contribution to the Christian attitude to war was the development of the just-war theory. As has been said, Bainton tends to caricature the Catholic tradition with this oversimplification.

268   Brown, Peter R.L. *Augustine of Hippo*. London: Faber & Faber, 1967.

The best biography of the man and his world available.

269   ——. "St. Augustine's Attitude to Religious Coercion." See **256**, 260-78.

Traces the halting and ambivalent progress of Augustine's ideas that force can be used against religious dissenters. An important factor in evaluating any of Augustine's ideas about peace. He surely seems to have believed that one could kill the body of one's earthly neighbor in an act of love for his or her soul.

270   Egan. "Beatitudes." See **20**.

While Augustine might rightly be identified with the just-war tradition, his sources were in Cicero and the Roman pagan tradition, not in the Gospels. He maintained the personal nonviolence of the individual Christian by his insistence on an inner disposition of love. Martin of Tours exemplifies this continuing tradition.

271   Ferguson. *Politics*. See **149**.

   While Ambrose stressed that God's servants rely on spiritual, not material, weapons; Augustine represents a shift from early Christian pacifism to the just-war tradition. Constantine marks the great betrayal of Christianity, a pagan, like Satan, tempting the church to accept earthly power. However useful this book is to a study of the New Testament peacemaking, its treatment of the Middle Ages is blurred by a Protestant historiography of decline into barbarity after Constantine.

272   Finn, James. "Pacifism and Justifiable War." See **51**, 3-14.

   The just-war tradition so well established by Augustine has been the dominant tradition of the Catholic church until the last part of the twentieth century.

273   Hehir. "Just-War Ethic." See **29**.

   The just war has a historical, not a doctrinal association with the Catholic church. Its roots and teachings are not solely Christian or Catholic. Despite this, Augustine must be seen as seminal in the theory's development, fusing notions of internal intention, Christian charity, and public order that would allow war in public morality if not in private. Roland Bainton, Hehir maintains, connects the just-war tradition far too exclusively to Catholicism.

274   Ladner, Gerhart B. *The Idea of Reform. Its Impact on Christian Thought and Action in the Age of the Fathers*. Rev. ed. New York: Harper & Row, 1967.

   For Augustine the City of God was inextricably bound

to the Heavenly Jerusalem, the *visio pacis* (vision of peace) of the Apocalypse. While this identification had firm root in early Christian thought and appears, for example, in Origen, for Augustine it took on a political as well as a religious meaning. His City of God is the conscious antithesis of Virgil's Rome, the city that has usurped the powers of God and is dominated by the lust for power. Earthly power is of no avail in God's city, and the true city of God is bound together not by force but by the conversion and reform of individuals to Christian love.

275   McGuire, M.R.P. "Ambrose, St.," *NCE* 1: 372-75.

       A basic introduction.

276   Markus, Robert A. Saeculum: *History and Society in the Theology of St. Augustine.* Cambridge: Cambridge University Press, 1970.

       Not seen.

277   ——."Saint Augustine's Views on the 'Just War'" See 53, 1-13.

       Even though his ideas on other topics might change, Augustine wrote consistently that the Christian could fight if the cause were just and the war carried out justly. By the age of Augustine there were very few pacifists left. Eusebius, Ambrose and Athanasius had made the convincing arguments against it.

278   Merton, Thomas. "The Christian in World Crisis,

Reflections on the Moral Climate of the 1960s." See **40**, 20-62.

Augustine is the father of all modern Christian ideas on war, and in a way the root of the medieval Crusades and Inquisition. His stress on the "tranquility of order" as peace is basically naive as to the good that can be achieved by violence even if combined with good intentions. All later Christian history is witness to the ridiculous attempts to justify war using these criteria. Augustine's theory belongs on the junk pile. Merton uses Bainton (2) as his primary source for the Catholic peace tradition, thus equating the Catholic tradition exclusively with the just war, and inevitably comes to some rather negative conclusions about the peace tradition in his own church.

279   Regout, Robert. *La doctrine de la guerre juste de saint Augustine à nos jours, d'après les théologiens et les canonistes catholiques.* Paris: A. Pedone, 1934; reprint, Aalen: Scientia, 1974.

A survey from Augustine to the twentieth century. Regout first distinguishes the *jus ad bellum* or the just-war criteria for entering a war, from the *jus in bello* or the rules governing its proper conduct. His aim is to discuss the former. Study examines just-war theory from the fourth century through Isidore of Seville, Gratian and the canonists and theologians of the thirteenth to the fifteenth centuries. In the sixteenth and seventeenth century he examines the late scholastics, including Soto, Suarez, and Vitoria.

In our own age the theory has come upon problems of consistency and doctrine, often used as a justification for wars of aggression and confronted by the problems of proportionality that Augustine, supposedly, did not have to face.

280   Russell. *Just War*. See **50**.

Chapter 1, pp. 16-39, examines Augustine's ideas on the just war. The bishop reconciled early Christian pacifism with Roman ideas of just war, making the sin of war an inner attitude, not the external violent act. As such he represents a Christian empire faced with the barbarian threat. Augustine's roots are in Cicero and late imperial ideas of authority as deriving from God. Wars are therefore fought with divine authority to punish wrongdoers. The individual is absolved from any responsibility through his obedience to authority.

281   Swift. Louis J. "St. Ambrose on Violence and War." *Transactions and Proceedings of the American Philological Association*. 101 (1970): 533-43.

Ambrose's thought reflects the Christian situation of the fourth century, as older ideas of peace and forebearance had to be integrated into the larger scope of social justice and order within a Christian empire. The older answers of Tertullian or Eusebius were now too simple. The Roman influence on Ambrose's ideas of peace are strong and evident. While he praises the role of the military in the empire, he clearly distinguishes between just and unjust wars; and Christian principles are at the heart of his distinctions.

While fully a loyal citizen in matters of the empire's defense, in matters of personal violence Ambrose remains a pacifist: self-defense is never acceptable for the Christian. However, when a third party is involved, the use of force is just, since the Christian is then acting out of love. This means not simply nonviolent defense but force.

Ambrose was never really able to reconcile these conflicting loyalties and ideas, and his one work in lavish

praise of the emperor's wars saw Valens crushing defeat
by the Goths. Subsequently Ambrose never spoke in
praise of Roman arms, and in fact opposed both
Theodosius' punishment of rioters and urged nonviolent
defense of church rights in Milan.

282   Synan, Edward A. "Augustine of Hippo, Saint." See **17**,
       1: 646-59.

       A good introduction.

283   Toporoski, Richard. "Ambrose, St." See **17**, 1: 230-32.

       A good introduction.

284   Zampaglione. *Idea of Peace.* See **58**.

       The *City of God* is a pacifist essay, condemning the
Roman Empire and all earthly states built on violence and
suffering. Augustine's just-war theory is only a defensive
answer to attacks on his pacifism following the sack of
Rome. Analyzes the basis of Augustine's theory and the
limits he imposes on violence. In his *Contra Faustum*
Augustine summons up Old Testament origins for the just
war. He could, at times, even defend the *Pax Romana* that
he seems to condemn in the *City of God.* See **343**.

Christian Peacemakers and the Barbarians: Monks and Missions

285   Attwater. *Saints.* See **1**.

       Includes biographies of such early medieval peace-
makers as Adamnan, Amand of Maastricht, Queen

Bathild, Boniface of Crediton, Caesarius of Arles, Columba, Comgall, Geneviève of Paris, Germanus of Auxerre, Germanus of Paris, Pope Gregory the Great, the two Hewalds, Honoratus of Arles, Lambert of Maastricht, Ludger, Lupus of Troyes, Martin of Braga, Martin of Tours, Nicetius of Trier, Patrick, Paulinus of Aquileia, Philibert, Sulpicius, Telemachus, and Victricius.

286   Bainton. *Early Christianity.* See **156**.

Early monasticism's birth was a direct criticism of the imperial church and the marriage of Christianity to political power.

287   Baus, Karl. "Early Christian Monasticism: Development and Expansion in the East." See **288**, 337-73.

Discusses the religious and historical background and first development in Egypt under Anthony and Pachomius, in Nitria and Scete, and surveys the forms of anchoritism and cenobitism, developments in Palestine and in Syria, in Asia Minor, and in Constantinople. Concludes with some of the more extreme forms, including Messalianism.

288   ——.*Imperial Church.* See **254**.

An excellent synthesis covering the church's development under the Roman imperial system, the theological disputes of the fifth century, the spiritual development, including missionary work, the growth of the institutional church, of the clergy, the liturgy, preaching and piety, and of monasticism. Then examines social issues and surveys the growth of the Byzantine and Western churches.

289   ——."Latin Monasticism from the Mid-Fifth Century to the End of the Seventh Century." See **288**, 690-707.

Developments in Italy, Merovingian France, Spain, and North Africa.

290   ——."The Monasticism of the Latin West." See **288**, 374-92.

Developments in Rome and Italy, Gaul, Spain, North Africa. Then analyzes St. Augustine's role in the growth of monasticism, and traces antimonastic sentiment in the West.

291   ——.with Eugen Ewig. "Missionary Activity of the Church." See **288**, 181-230.

Early monasticism in the West was indistinguishable from missionary work. Monks acted as the vanguard of the process of nonviolent confrontation with, and conversion of, the barbarian warrior. Only with Gregory the Great was a coordinated effort begun at conversion outside the old Roman world.

292   *Bibliotheca Sanctorum.* See **4**.

Detailed biographies of such early medieval peacemakers as Adamnan, Amand of Maastricht, Boniface of Crediton, Caesarius of Arles, Columban, Comgall, Germanus of Auxerre, Germanus of Paris, Pope Gregory the Great, Gregory of Tours, Hilary of Poitiers, Pope Leo the Great, Ludger, Martin of Braga, Martin of Tours, Niceta of Remesiana, Nicetius of Trier, Pachomius, Patrick, Paulinus of Aquileia, Paulinus of Nola, Philibert of Nourmoutier, Severinus of Noricum, and Victricius of Rouen.

293   Brown. *World.* See **181**.

Christian monasticism had many roots, in Christian and pagan asceticism, in the popular spirituality of the simple folk of the provinces, the desire for a literal imitation of Christ, in social revolt from the tyranny of imperial society, in the revolt from the violence of the Roman army. Whatever its roots, Eastern monasticism was a revolt from the Roman world, and it expressed for the first time the aspirations of the downtrodden. It was also an offensive against the Roman world, a revolution whose goals were freedom of the body as well as the soul. The monk, the archetypal holy man and woman, thus became one of the few in the late empire capable of challenging the tyranny of the emperors and their administrators. In so doing they took on the prophetic roles of teaching and denunciation of injustice.

Brown's remarks on Western monasticism are more negative. In the West, monasticism tended to be snobbish and self-conscious, antibourgeois and aristocratic, more concerned with the rural ideal of books and dinner parties than with real political, moral, and religious issues. By disdaining the Roman political process and the army, this aristocracy unwittingly led to their collapse but soon learned that they could do without both. Brown asserts that the Western monks shunned the barbarians. Christian pacifism during the period was nothing more than sassy, disguised snobbery, turned off to both the soldier and the citizen.

294   Butler. *Lives.* See **9**, 3-7.

The best source in English for most of the early

medieval peacemakers mentioned in **285** and **292** above.

295   Chitty, Derwas J. *The Desert a City*. Oxford: Basil
        Blackwell, 1966.

        Probably the best introduction available to the early
        monasticism of the Egyptian hermits, including sections
        on Anthony the Hermit and Pachomius.

296   Comblin. *Théologie de la paix*. See **13**.

        The prophetic protest of the early church was
        preserved during the early Middle Ages by the monastic
        movement and the clergy, who did not fear to speak out
        for peace and justice against both imperial tyranny and
        barbarian violence.

297   Courtois, C. "L'évolution du monachisme en Gaule de St
        Martin à St. Columban," *Il monachesimo nell'alto
        medioevo e la formazione della civiltà occidentale*
        Vol. 4 in *Settimane di studi*. Spoleto: Centro italiano d
        studi sull'alto medioevo, 1957, 47-72.

        A good collection of recent research.

298   Duckett, Eleanor Shipley. *Gateway to the Middle Ages.
        Monasticism*. Ann Arbor: University of Michigan
        Press, 1971.

        An excellent introduction to the period and the
        institution, using anecdotal and narrative sources that
        enliven by example. Useful background for the lives of
        Severinus of Noricum and Columban, based closely on
        the original texts.

299   Frazee, Charles A. "Late Roman and Byzantine

Legislation on the Monastic Life from the Fourth to the Eight Centuries," *Church History* 51 (September 1982): 263-79.

While monasticism was a major force of nonviolent social change and conversion of the barbarians, this article should remind us that, like all human institutions, monasticism also often represented the forces of violence.

300   Frend. *Martyrdom.* See **124**, 3-47.

Monasticism's flight from the urban world of the Roman Empire represented a social protest against injustice and shared much of the spirit of the martyrs. It came predominantly from the lower classes and reflected popular spirituality. Anthony the Hermit — nondoctrinal, nonhierarchical, and nonintellectual — was archetypal. The monks set up their own, ideal, Christian social and economic system that replaced oppression and compulsion with nonviolence and cooperation. In Egypt under Pachomius this life attracted tens of thousands.

301   Hillgarth, J.N. *The Conversion of Western Europe 300-750.* Englewood Cliffs, NJ: Prentice-Hall, 1969. Revised as *Christianity and Paganism, 350-750. The Conversion of Western Europe.* Philadelphia: University of Pennsylvania Press, 1986.

A collection of primary sources covering the process of conversion from the late Roman Empire to the barbarian successor states. Selections touch on the history of monasticism and attempts to convert the pagan hinterlands by Victricius of Rouen, monasticism as a form of social revolt, the effects of the barbarian invasions on the process of conversion, and the consciously nonviolent methods used to convert them, even in the face of persecution. On the other hand, the church hierarchy took over many of the practices of the Roman imperial administration, preferring to treat only with the leadership of the barbarian peoples. In the process it assimilated much of the ethos of both empire and barbarian. The revised edition has new sections on Ireland and the seventh-century Frankish church.

302   Knöpfer, J. "Die Akkommodation im altchristlichen Missionswesen," *Zeitschrift für Missionswissenschaft* 1 (1911).

For early medieval attempts at peaceful conversion, including Gregory the Great's attitudes and missions.

303   Knowles, David. *Christian Monasticism*. New York: McGraw-Hill, 1969.

A good general introduction to the subject. Richly illustrated, with a helpful bibliography. Topics include the Egyptian origins under Anthony and Pachomius, its spread and development in the West, the role of monks as missionaries, and the growth of Benedictine monasticism.

304   McDermott, William C. *Monks, Bishops, and Pagans.* Edward Peters, ed. Philadelphia: University of Pennsylvania Press, 1981.

Collection of primary sources, including the works of Gregory the Great, Jonas' *Life of St. Columbanus,* and selections from the *History of the Franks* by Gregory of Tours.

305   Momigliano. "Christianity and Decline." See **187**.

Monasticism was both a revolt against Roman society

and its spiritual evil and a constructive force that built a new political and economic system based on self-government. Unlike pagan society, which resisted or greeted the barbarians with horror and contempt, the new Christian communities welcomed them and began to convert them. Good evidence for the nonviolent response of Christian Roman society to overwhelming catastrophe and ever-present violence.

306   Neill. *History.* See **41**.

Excellent background to the activities of Christian missionaries among the barbarians, including Augustine of Canterbury and Pope Gregory the Great, Columba, Wilfrid, Columban, and Boniface of Crediton.

307   Opelt, Ilona. "Briefe des Salvian von Marseille: Zwischen Christen und Barbaren," *Romanobarbarica* 4 (1979): 161-82.

There is little trace of the barbarian invasions in Salvian's letters, which fully reflect the nonviolent spirituality of Lérins. Themes of reconciliation of Roman and barbarian found in Livy, of Christian humility, mutual love and compassion (*amor, caritas, affectus*) go hand in hand with a sense of community with the whole human race.

308   Talbot, C.H., ed. *The Anglo-Saxon Missionaries in Germany.* New York: Sheed & Ward, 1981.

A good account of the missions, the personalities, and the issues involved.

309   Thompson, E.A. "Christianity and the Northern Barbarians." See **187**, 56-78.

No evidence exists that the Roman missionaries under the empire played any significant role in converting the barbarians outside its borders before 476. Most converts during this period were barbarians serving in the Roman army, Christian captives who converted their captors, and missionaries on trade routes. All three methods were haphazard and unorganized. Nevertheless, Thompson does provide some excellent material on early Christian peacemakers and the barbarians, including Niceta of Remesiana, Queen Fritigil of the Macromanni, Victricius of Rouen, and Amantius of Aquileia.

310   Vogt, Hermann Josef. "The Missionary Work of the Latin Church." See **288**, 517-601.

Ranges from St. Patrick and Irish monasticism to Columban and the conversion of the Franks and Burgundians up to the reign of Clovis. Then deals with church councils, Columban, northern and eastern Gaul, Switzerland and extends into the late seventh century.

311   Waddell, Helen. *The Wandering Scholars*. Garden City, NY: Doubleday, 1961.

Discusses the more literary aspects of such peacemakers as Sulpicius Severus and Paulinus of Nola.

Educating the Barbarians for Peace: Penitentials and Canon Law

312   Bieler, Ludwig. *The Irish Penitentials*, in *Scriptores Latini Hiberniae* 5. Dublin: Dublin Institute for Advanced Studies, 1963.

Penalties for homicide and for killing in war or tribal strife exist as early as the *Welsh Canons* of the sixth century. The *Old Irish Penitential*, for example, seems to have equated violence done in war with that in a brawl or in an ambush, and imposes a penance of as high as a year and a half.

313 ——."Penitentials," *NCE* 11: 86-87.

A brief introduction.

314 Frantzen, Allen J. *The Literature of Penance in Anglo-Saxon England.* New Brunswick, NJ: Rutgers University Press, 1983.

Fine overview of the subject, with chapters on Irish sources, Frankish developments, penance and prayer, preaching penance through homilies, handbooks, and prayers, penance as a theme in Old English poetry. Good general background with some references to violence and warfare. Excellent bibliography.

315 ——."The Penitentials Attributed to Bede," *Speculum* 58, 3 (1983): 573-97.

Useful as a review of current research and historiography.

316 ——."The Significance of the Frankish Penitentials," *Journal of Ecclesiastical History* 30 (1979): 409-21.

Their sources, spread and influence on life and legislation.

317   —.—."The Tradition of Penitentials in Anglo-Saxon England," *Anglo-Saxon England* 11 (1982): 23-56.

A good summary of recent research.

318   Hallam, Elizabeth M. "Monasteries as War Memorials: Battle Abbey and La Victoire." See **53**, 47-57.

While no contemporary documents for the foundation of either house exist that can give us explicit information on the motives of their founding, there are later "copies" of both charters, one dating from the nineteenth century. Despite this lack of first-hand material, Hallam rejects outright the penitential motive of William the Conqueror's founding of Battle Abbey to atone for the deaths of Hastings. Even the explicit wording of the existing charter, "let it be an atonement," is dismissed. What we have in both cases is pure military celebration and the visible manifestation of strong rulers' ability to stamp their bellicose policies on the institution of the church.
Hallam may be reading too much of Thatcher's Britain into the Middle Ages.

319   Hanson, R.P.C. *The Life and Writings of the Historical Saint Patrick.* New York: Seabury, 1983.

Not seen.

320   Le Bras, Gabriel. "Pénitentiels," *DTC* 12 (1933): 1160-79.

Defines the literary form and discusses origins and historiography. Then briefly surveys their development up to the mid-seventh century, their apogee between 650 and 800, the Carolingian reform, Pseudo-Isidore, and the penitentials' incorporation into Gratian's *Decretum* and thus into the general canon law of the church.

321   McNeill, John T., and Helen M. Gamer. *Medieval Handbooks of Penance.* New York: Columbia University Press, 1938.

An excellent and far-reaching collection of penitential literature, well edited and presented with useful introductory materials. Offers numerous sources for the history of nonviolence as found in penitential regulations against bloodshed in personal vendettas, feuds, and warfare, with specific penances, often quite severe, attached to each form of violence. These reflect both the violence of the age and very real attempts to curb it.

Useful sources include the Canons attributed to St. Patrick, the Penitentials of Finnian, Cummean, the Irish Canons, the Law of Adamnan, the Old Irish Penitential, the Welsh Canons, the Penitential of Theodore, that attributed to Bede, of Columban, the Burgundian, Paris and Solos Penitentials, and the Laws of Edmund. They range from Ireland to the Continent and from the sixth to the tenth century. The penitentials edited here represent the continuing tradition of Christian peacemaking, even in the darkest of the Dark Ages, that sought to bring peace and to outlaw war.

322   Oakley, T.P. "Cultural Affiliations of Early Ireland in the Penitentials," *Speculum* 8 (1933): 489-500.

A survey of the known Irish penitentials as a source for social mores in lay society as a whole. Such evidence provides useful arguments against those who contend that medieval peace represented a turning away from social issues of peace and justice.

323   Vogel, Cyrille. *Le pécheur et la pénitence au Moyen Age.*
        Paris: Éditions du Cerf, 1969.

        Good collection of texts in Latin, with comprehensive
        introduction. Useful selections include the Penitential
        attributed to Bede, which imposes penance for killing in
        war, and the Penitential of Finnian.

324   Watkins, Oscar Daniel. *A History of Penance.* 2 vols.
        London: Longmans, 1920.

        Volume 1 focuses on the development of the sacra-
        ment, volume 2 on the penitential literature. Selections
        highlight the penances imposed on both clergy and laity
        for violence, murder, and war.

Early Medieval Europe: The Continuing Tradition of Peace

325   Bloch, Marc. *Feudal Society.* L.A. Manyon, transl. 2
        vols. Chicago: University of Chicago Press, 1965.

        Chapters 21-23 in volume 2 remain the best intro-
        duction to the warrior life and mores of the Middle Ages.

326   Bonnaud-Delamare, Roger. *L'idée de paix à l'époque
        carolingienne.* Paris: Domat-Montchrétien, 1939.

        Christian notions of peace were sorely strained under
        the impact of the Germanic invasions. The *pax ecclesiae,*
        already a juridical and political concept under the Imperial
        Church, took on the notions of the *pax* of the German
        warlord — his personal protection — becoming translated as
        the immunities enjoyed by, or extended by, the church to
        its dependents. Germanic law codes contained few refer-
        ences to peace. The *Lex Alamannorum* and the *Lex*

Visigothorum use it in the sense of special protections mentioned above.

327 Brock. *Roots.* See **8.**

Quite simply, "the barbarians militarized Christianity," and Christian peacemaking was submerged for a millennium until the advent of the Protestant pacifist sects of the Reformation. The clergy existed as an elite group of "vocational noncombattancy." No mention is made of the impact of Christianity upon the barbarians, or of the work of scores of Christian peacemakers: monks, martyrs, and missionaries. On the whole, for the medieval Church "the radical antimilitarism of the early Church found no place in its teachings." What criteria Brock uses to distinguish the clerical pacifists of the early church, our chief documentary source for early Christian pacifism, from the same clerical pacifists of the early Middle Ages are unspoken.

328 *La conversione al cristianesimo nell' Europa dell' alto medioevo.* Vol. 14 in *Settimane di studio.* Spoleto: Centro italiano di studi sull'alto medioevo, 1967.

A good collection on recent research on all aspects of the conversion process.

329 Dalbey, Marcia A. "The Good Shepherd and the Soldier of God: Old English Homilies on St. Martin of Tours," *Neuphilologische Mitteilungen* 85, 4 (1984): 422-34.

This traces the influence of Sulpicius Severus' *Life of Martin of Tours* in England during the period of the Viking invasions. Both in the Old English homilies of c. 960, written during a lull in the attacks and in Aelfric's life c. 990, written in the context of real war and invasion, St.

Martin of Tours remains a nonviolent soldier of Christ who overthrows the devil and establishes Christianity through spiritual weapons. He is the shepherd, educating and converting. While Aelfric admits the need to defend the nation, the tradition of nonviolence exemplified by St. Martin remained strong even in this darkest of the dark ages.

330   Danielou, J., S.J., and Henri-I. Marrou. *The First Six Hundred Years*. Vincent Cronin, transl. New York: McGraw-Hill, 1964.

An excellent reference history.

331   Du Cange. "Pax." See **19**, 3-43.

The early Middle Ages brought new meanings to the word *pax*, largely borrowed from the world of the barbarians. These include the concept of the *pax regis* as the special protection granted the king to his dependents, and the *pax firma*, security or immunity from harm. The *pax ecclesiae* between the Christian Empire and the Imperial Church brought the *pax Sancti Petri*, a municipal peace enforced by imperial police, the *pax domini*, a liturgical instrument used by the bishop to show himself the vicar of Christ, and the liturgical forms, *pax vobis*, a salutation, and the *pax dare*, the kiss of peace.

332   Erdmann. *Idea of Crusade*. See **21**, 3-80.

The absorption of the Germanic barbarians into Christianity took centuries, but the work was undertaken constantly and consistently. The barbarian moral exaltation of war, heroism, famous deeds, loyalty to leader and contempt for civilized life had first to be overcome. Rather than accommodating to this warrior ethic, however, the church took an even more rigorous view of war than before, forbidding the clergy from participating in bloodshed and using the penitential system to educate the barbarians to peace. Martin of Tours and Boniface of Crediton are examples of medieval peacemakers. Erdmann's evidence could lead one to conclude that the numerous stories of miraculous defenses without recourse to arms by such saints as Aimoin, Benôit, Fidis, Andreas of Fleury, and Bernard of Angers are simply the medieval interpretation of the effects of nonviolence.

333   Goffart, Walter. *Barbarians and Romans A.D. 418-584.* Princeton: Princeton University Press, 1980.

The barbarians who overwhelmed the Roman world were small in number, and their assimilation was essentially peaceful.

334   Haines, Keith. "Attitudes and Impediments to Pacifism in Medieval Europe," *Journal of Medieval History* 7 (1981): 369-88.

While medieval pacifism must be understood in the context of the brutality and warfare of the period, it existed quite over and above any medieval longings for peace in a general way. Nevertheless, the just-war and Augustinian traditions dominated most of medieval thought on war and peace despite an ambivalence and some confusion between concepts of earthly and spiritual peace. The penitentials imposed some curbs on the violence of the age.

335   Hornus. *It is Not Lawful.* See **201**, 3-69.

The early Middle Ages saw two major trends in Christian peacemaking. The newly Christianized *Pax Romana* celebrating the alliance of the empire and the

church on behalf of a Christian world order — represented
by such writers as Lactantius and Eusebius — and the
continuing tradition of prophetic protest, now allied with
monastic revolt, typified by Martin of Tours. His life, and
those of his associates in southern Gaul in the fourth
century, was not some monastic hagiographic legend, but
a truly antimilitarist movement of protest. By the fifth
century these two strains had produced real conflicts of
conscience within the Christian community that emerged in
regulations for clerical nonviolence and penitential penalties for murder and participation in war by the laity.
Nevertheless, Constantine's conversion does represent a
true turning point in the history of Christian nonviolence.

336   Isidore of Seville.

His *Differentiarum* 10.243 (PL 83: 35), *Epistemo-
logiarum*   10.1.11, *Sententiarum* 3.51.6 (PL 83), and
Synonymorum 2.38 (PL 83: 854) provide rich material for
the student of early medieval concepts of peace, combining
barbarian notions of peace as protection and privilege,
Roman notions of treaty alliance, and Christian ideas of
love and tranquility.

337   Le Bras, Gabriel. "The Sociology of the Church in the
        Early Middle Ages," *Early Medieval Society*. Sylvia
        Thrupp, ed. New York: Appleton-Century-Crofts,
        1967, 47-57.

The work of the church in the early Middle Ages was
to bring about a Christian society. "The invasions, far
from interrupting the preaching of the Gospels, made it
even more necessary."

338   McNeill, John T. "Asceticism versus Militarism in the
        Middle Ages," *Church History* 5 (1936): 3-28.

        A basic work on the history of peacemaking in the
        Middle Ages. Focuses on the development of monas-
        ticism as the new *militia Christi* waging a spiritual warfare
        against Satan. This was essentially a pacifist notion, and
        the monastic leader was par excellence the peacemaker.
        These ascetics, typified by Martin of Tours and his
        conversion from soldier to monk, represented a "flat
        repudiation of militarism."

339   Paradisi, Bruno. "L'organisation de la paix aux ive et v^e
        siècles." See 47, 321-95.

        Early medieval ideas of peace were borrowed from the
        late Roman Empire. Peace was a juridical concept, the
        societas hominum, the transcendent unity existing within
        the Christian Empire. To the meanings of peace in the
        words *pax* and *eirene* were added those of *concordia* and
        homonoia, the world order and tranquility of the Roman
        Empire. Nevertheless, Christian thinkers retained, and
        even strengthened, biblical meanings of peace. Augustine,
        for example, criticized the *Pax Romana* as a negative
        peace, wrought by war and discord. Justice, instead, is
        the true basis of peace, and this is based on the love within
        the Mystical Body. With the coming of the barbarians,
        peace took on even newer meanings, as *foedus*, a treaty
        condition of peace gained with Rome, the result of a pact.
        This meaning was handed on to the Middle Ages through
        Isidore of Seville. At the same time personal peacemaking
        tended to become internalized, a transcendental condition.

340   Renna, Thomas. "The Idea of Peace in the West, 500-
        1150," *Journal of Medieval History* 6, 2 (1980): 143-
        67.

    The peace tradition in the early Middle Ages has thus
far been neglected, and no synthesis has yet been attempted. Constantine probably did not understand the Christian
idea of peace and gave the Middle Ages, instead, a notion
of peace as unified control. During the Merovingian
period this became an extraordinary privilege, a protection,
granted to individuals or churches. *Pax Christi* was taken
as a personal, not a societal condition, an otherworldly
extension of monastic notions of *hesychia* and *tranquillitas*,
earthly detachment and the approach to heavenly peace.
Augustine is typical of this development in his contrast
between *pax Christi* and false, external peace.
    Yet there were exceptions. One strain in Christian
thought held that peace was not simply an inner
disposition but a social goal. Gregory the Great believed
that conversion of the barbarians could be achieved
through the example of charismatic peacemakers. By the
sixth century churchpeople were attempting to bring peace
by curtailing feuds, and by the eighth century imperial
notions of peace had fused with ecclesiastical ideas of
internal peace. Thus external order was seen as the
precondition of internal peace. While an indispensablee
overview, this article concentrates on official notions of
peace, as a concept forced from the top down.

341   Rusch, William G. *The Later Latin Fathers*. London:
        Duckworth, 1977.

    Brief introductions to the life and writings of the
Christian thinkers of the late empire and early Middle
Ages, including Damasus I, Hilary of Poitiers, Ambrose
of Milan, Paulinus of Nola, Augustine, Vincent of Lérins,

Hilary of Arles, Gregory the Great, Gregory of Tours, and
Victor of Vita.

342   Severus, Sulpicius et al. *The Western Fathers*. F.R.
       Hoare, ed. and transl. New York: Harper & Row,
       1965.

Excellent source materials for the lives of some of the
early Middle Ages' most energetic and attractive peacemakers, including Ambrose and his confrontation with the
emperor Theodosius, Augustine and his *Letter to
Honoratus* (recommending martyrdom or flight rather than
violence against the invading barbarians), Sulpicius
Severus' life of Martin of Tours, Honoratus of Arles'
biography of Hilary of Arles, and the fascinating life of
Germanus of Auxerre by Constantius of Lyons. Hoare's
introductions also remind us that the spirit of nonviolence
that breathes through many of these works reflects not
only the peacemaking of the heros they praise but also the
living tradition of nonviolence of the bishops who commissioned the works and the writers who composed them.
The works themselves are evidence of a Catholic pacifism
still flourishing in the late fifth century.

343   Thompson, E.A. *Saint Germanus of Auxerre and the End
       of Roman Britain*. Woodbridge, Sussex: Boydell
       Press, 1984.

This is an excellent study in source analysis. While
Thompson's concern is British history, its sources and
dating, by and large Constantius' picture of Germanus is
historically accurate. The British under Germanus' guid-
ance did win their Alleluia victory without a blow being
struck or a prisoner being taken; Germanus did stop an
army single-handedly with his stern rebuke to the barbarian King Goar; he did defy the vengeance of the Roman

general Aetius; and did travel to Ravenna to work justice for the Armoricans.

344   Zampaglione. *Idea of Peace.* See **58**.

An excellent survey of the theory of Christian peace-making in the late empire and early Middle Ages. Topics discussed include the Council of Arles in 314, which Zampaglione asserts abandoned pacifism in favor of Christian military service, and the reassertion of this service in the council of Nicea in 325. On the other hand, the Greek Fathers continued to condemn war. These include Gregory Nazianzen, Gregory of Nyassa, and the mystical peace of Dionysius the Areopagite, who saw earthly and community peace as a reflection of divine peace. In the West, the stronger the relation to secular power, the weaker the Christian message of peace tended to be. Nevertheless, Zampaglione cites many early medieval peacemakers, including Hilary of Poitiers, Marius Victorinus, Prudentius, and Ambrose of Milan. His treatment of Augustine is fundamental to any historical approach to Catholic peacemaking.

*   *
*

CHAPTER 5: *From Carolingian Peace To People's Peace, 800-1100*

General Introduction

345   Boussard, Jacques. *The Civilization of Charlemagne.* New York: McGraw-Hill, 1968.

An attractive and readable introduction to the Carolingian period, with emphasis on the institutions and cultural life of the Carolingian Empire. Useful background reading, with helpful bibliography.

346   Brooke, Christopher. *Europe in the Central Middle Ages, 962-1154.* New York: Holt, Rinehart and Winston, 1964.

Useful and detailed background reading for the events, personalities, and institutions of the post-Carolingian period, in which the Peace and Truce of God flourished. Good bibliography.

347   Fichtenau, Heinrich. *The Carolingian Empire.* Peter Munz, transl. New York: Harper & Row, 1964.

This standard history of Carolingian institutions and ideas provides valuable background to their notions of peace as order and balance, the secular arm's duty to preserve and extend Christianity by force of arms, and of Carolingian social and political structures, including the role of the popular assembly and the clergy. Carolingian spirituality, including that of Alcuin and his circle,

Fichtenau insists, was external and superficial, removed from any notion of Christian ethics.

348   Ganshof, F.L. *Feudalism.* Philip Grierson, transl. New York: Longmans, 1952.

The best introduction to the origins, growth, and institutions of feudalism as a social and political phenomenon that set the scene for Christian peacemaking throughout the Middle Ages.

349   Loud, G.A. "The Church, Warfare and Military Obligation in Norman Italy." See **53**, 31-45.

The attempt to reconcile the Christian message with war was "one of the most important intellectual problems of the Middle Ages," Loud asserts. The "presense of, and the necessity for, war" is always a problem for the institutional church. In Norman Italy the church's institutional power meant wealth and land, and therefore military service on that land, both for self-defense and to fulfill feudal obligations.

350   Nelson, Janet L. "The Church's Military Service in the Ninth Century: A Contemporary Comparative View." See **53**, 15-30.

Examines the problem of provisioning the English and Frankish warrior class and the question of military service rendered by the church for its large land holdings. The church thus performed an "institutionalized military service."

351   Ullmann, Walter. *The Carolingian Renaissance and the Idea of Kingship.* New York: Barnes and Noble, 1969.

Good background reading for the intellectual universe of the Carolingians. While the period was decidedly one that prized the warrior, the cultural tradition of the empire was that of Christian Rome that took the Bible as its source of social as well as religious life. Thus the purpose of the empire for Charlemagne and his successors was to transform the world into a Christian republic. This, at least in theory, gave room to calls for Christian virtues as modes of social life. This effort is reflected in the Carolingian Capitularies, its court literature, and its church legislation.

Carolingian Peace

352   Attwater. *Saints.* See **1**.

Good biographies, with some bio-bibliographical references, for such peacemakers as Adalbert of Prague, Aurelius and Natalia, Boniface of Querfurt, Columba of Cordoba, Eskil, Eulogius of Cordoba, Flora and Mary of Cordoba, Pope Nicholas I, Odilo of Cluny, and Romuald.

353   Bonnaud-Delamare. *L'idée de paix.* See **326**.

The best and most comprehensive introduction to peacemaking during the early Middle Ages. Provides both overall interpretation and careful readings of individual thinkers and texts. Carolingian peace was a combination of Germanic *pax*, royal power to protect and maintain order, and Christian *pax*, peace of the heart. Earthly peace and order reflect the heavenly. Traces the development of these theories from the royal apologists in Pepin's and Charlemagne's courts through Alcuin and the Carolingian capitularies and councils, to monastic thinkers like Smaragdus, Druthmar of Corbie, and Rabanus Maurus, and to the capitularies of Louis the Pious. Also analyzes the notions of peace found in the *False Capitularies* and *False Decretals* produced during the decline of the Carolingians. Finally, it shows how the Carolingian councils passed on all these notions of peace to the Peace and Truce of God.

354   Cowdrey, H.E.J. "Bishop Ermenfrid of Sion and the Penitential Ordinance Following the Battle of Hastings," *Journal of Ecclesiastical History* 20 (1969): 225-42.

The very specific penances imposed by the Norman Council of Westminster upon the victors of the Battle of Hastings for their participation in war had a long tradition in the church legislation found in the penitential literature. This goes back to the Carolingian revival of earlier penitential literature and finds expression in Burchard of Worms and Fulbert of Chartres, among others. See **312** to **324**.

355   Delaney. *Dictionary.* See **15**.

Brief biographies of many of the most important Catholic peacemakers of the period, including Angilbert, Eulogius of Cordoba, Frederick of Utrecht, Guibert, Pope Nicholas I, Odilo of Cluny, Odo of Beauvais, Romuald, Stanislaus of Poland, and Theobald of Champagne.

356   Delaruelle, Étienne. *L'idée de croisade au Moyen Age.* Turin: Bottega d'Erasmo, 1980, 1-23.

A complete survey from Charlemagne through Urban II to St. Louis. These pages provide some background to Carolingian notions of peace.

357   Du Cange. "Pax." See **19**.

Pax took on several new meanings and deepened others during the Carolingian period. These range from legal pardon, religious absolution, and the forgiveness of sins to sworn oaths and a call for silence ("Peace!"). It also retained the Germanic notions of special protection or law: the *pax regis* (the king's peace), the special protection granted by the king to his retainers, his court, his high roads, and his law and order, the peace of a village and even the village district itself. Stemming from these notions of special protections came the linguistic development inherent in the Peace of God: the special protection afforded various groups, and the *pax totius hebdomadae* (the peace of the entire week), which eventually emerged into the Truce of God. In all these usages medieval *pax* seems to have taken on the nature of a commodity to be granted, shared, or won.

358   Duval, Frederic Victor. *De la paix de Dieu a la paix de fer*.
       Paris: Paillard, 1923.

Traces the development of the Peace of God and its popular assemblies to its cooptation into the Truce of God controlled by the princes and used as an instrument of law and order, as often as not insured through compulsion and violence. Useful, though at times overly apologetic for this course of events.

359   Erdmann. *Idea of Crusade*. See **21**.

Despite his main topic, the origins of the concept of the crusade, Erdmann is indispensable for the history of medieval peace movements and ideas. Reviews the continuing tradition of Christian nonviolence and condemnation of warfare found in the penitential literature from

Rabanus Maurus to Fulbert of Chartres and Burchard of Worms. Also recounts the condemnations of military life found in Gerhoh of Reichersberg, Rather of Liège, Hincmar of Reims, Atto of Vercelli, and Odo of Cluny. Erdmann reviews the development of Carolingian ideas of peace as order and military stability and traces the origins of the Peace of God. This, he states, shows a new shift of emphasis to the peasant and the ecclesiatic and away from the warrior and represents the first mass religious movement of the Middle Ages.

360   Fournier, Paul E.L., and Gabriel Le Bras. *Histoire des collections canoniques en Occident depuis les Fausses Décretales jus qu'au Décret de Gratien*. 2 vols. Paris: Sirey, 1931.

On the legal basis of Carolingian peace. Surveys the extent of canon law during the late Carolingian period, including some collections that have direct bearing on Carolingian and later concepts of peace and peacemaking. These include the *False Capitularies, False Decretals*, and the tradition of the penitentials.

361   Fuhrmann, H. "False Decretals (Pseudo-Isidorian Forgeries)," *NCE* 5: 820-24.

Detailed analysis of the sources and composition of this legal collection, including much of the penitential literature, and of its later influence. Useful background to the history of peace legislation during the period.

362   Ganshof, F.L. "La paix au très haute Moyen Age." See **46**, 207-35.

Examines the attempts at peace as political stability achieved through treaty agreements between the various barbarian successor states. Also follows later Carolingian measures to maintain some semblance of this order. Into the mid-ninth century peace thus meant maintaining both the order of the empire and protection over the church.

363   Prinz, Friedrich. *Klerus und Krieg im Früheren Mittelalter*. Stuttgart: Hiersmann, 1971.

Useful background material for the continuing tradition of clerical nonviolence into the Merovingian and Carolingian periods, but relies on Erdmann (**21**) to a great extent.

364   Renna. "Idea of Peace." See **340**.

Official Carolingian and post-Carolingian ideas of peace seem to have been primarily those of law and order, the internal order of empire and its defense against external enemies. At the same time, Carolingian monastic thought held that only the ascetic can achieve true spiritual peace. Yet this monastic virtue put pressure on the monk to become the peacemaker, and the Cluniacs were among the first to take up this call. The Peace of God emerged from these traditions as a means to bring about Christ's peace on earth by using his spiritual weapons. No pacifism in the twentieth-century sense existed.

365   Rosenthal, J.T. "The Public Assembly in the Time of Louis the Pious," *Traditio* 20 (1964): 25-40.

Traces the origins of the popular assembly to its Germanic tribal roots, notes that the assemblies were non-military in nature, and then demonstrates that they were held at a rate of two to three a year between 814 and 840. These assemblies discussed all sorts of issues, including those of war and peace. While the "people" were not given any significant role at these assemblies, they certainly were in attendance and were sometimes appealed to for at least a formal acclamation. In theory, and sometimes in practice, then, the Carolingians preserved the voice of the people that was later to come to the fore in the the peace demonstrations of the Peace of God.

366   Russell. *Just War*. See **50**, 4-30.

During the collapse of the Carolingian Empire individual writers, such as Agobard of Lyons and Rabanus Maurus, and the penitential literature attempted to stem the tide of war by stressing the nonviolence of the Christian message or by imposing sanctions. The Peace and the Truce of God, while not necessarily pacifist, also sought to bring peace by limiting war.

367   Ullmann, Walter. "Public Welfare and Social Legislation in Early Medieval Councils," *Studies in Church History* 7 (Cambridge, 1971): 1-39.

During the Carolingian period the Frankish bishops met regularly to legislate on a wide variety of religious and social issues, from weights and measures to due process in property transfers, to ameliorating the condition of slaves and the plight of the poor, of the workers, unwed mothers, Jews, the sick, the imprisoned. The central concern of all their legislation was to translate the New Testament virtue of charity into the concrete world. The Frankish councils thus naturally legislated against capital punishment and attempted to eliminate violence or to protect society's weakest members from it. Ullmann unabashedly seeks to draw modern attention to earlier parallels in an age thought barbarian and indifferent to suffering.

Carolingian Monasticism, Missions and Antimilitarism

368   Bishop, Jane Carol. "Pope Nicholas I and the First Age of Papal Independence." Ph.D. dissertation. New York: Columbia University, 1980.

Useful for the life and reign of this remarkable pope, with a comprehensive bibliography.

369   Latourette, Kenneth S. *History of the Expansion of Christianity.* 7 vols. New York: Harper & Row, 1937-1945. Vol. 2, *The Thousand Years of Uncertainty, A.D. 500-A.D. 1500.* Reprinted Grand Rapids, MI: Zondervan, 1976.

Still the best historical synthesis of missionary history. Comprehensive, well written, and given to useful detail on the lives of many of the period's foremost peacemakers.

370   McNeill. "Asceticism." See **338**.

Medieval monasticism was a direct response to the militarism and violence of the feudal class and an attempt to tame its barbarism. Uses several examples of knights who convert to the monastic life and become leading peacemakers, especially among the Cluniacs. "All in all, before the rise of the university, the monasteries were the principal cultural agency leading Europe toward a pacific and progressive civilization."

371   Sullivan, Richard. "The Carolingian Missionary and the Pagan," *Speculum* 28 (1953): 705-40.

Outlines the methods used to contact, convince, and teach the barbarian. For the Carolingians the use of force certainly played a part in conversion. Important reminder that not all Christian missionary work was exemplary of nonviolence and that violent conversion was not without result.

372   ——,"Carolingian Missionary Theories," *Catholic Historical Review* 42 (1956-57): 273-95.

Forced conversion was the Carolingian norm, although much theoretical ink was spilt on nonviolent alternatives. Nevertheless, a tradition of peaceful conversion in action certainly existed. Nicholas I and Boniface of Crediton offer examples of the methods used.

373   ——."Early Medieval Missionary Activity: A Comparative Study of Eastern and Western Methods," *Church History* 23 (1954): 17-35.

Despite the violent methods normal for Carolingian missions, peaceful means were often attempted. Alcuin's criticisms of Charlemagne's forced conversion of the Saxons and Willehad's and Ludger's activities are examples.

374   ——."Khan Boris and the Conversion of Bulgaria: A Case Study of the Impact of Christianity on a Barbarian Society," *Studies in Medieval and Renaissance History* 3 (1966): 53-139.

Pope Nicholas I's response to Khan Boris' request for Christian instruction. Included in Boris' questions and the pope's reply is a lengthy discussion on Christian preparation for war in which Nicholas advises Boris to embrace actions and attitudes that directly contradict all the norms of a warrior society and reveal the existence of a thriving tradition of Christian nonviolence.

375 ——."The Papacy and Missionary Activity in the Early
Middle Ages," *Mediaeval Studies* 17 (1955): 46-106.

An excellent review of the role the papacy played in
formulating and coordinating the Christian response to the
barbarians.

The Martyrs of Cordoba

376 Colbert, Edward P. *The Martyrs of Cordoba (850-859). A
Study of the Sources.* Washington, DC: Catholic
University, 1962.

The best general introduction to the sources,
historiography, and problems. Introduces the literature,
doctrine and theological controversies of the Cordoban
church and gives special attention to Eulogius and
Alvarus, the leading figures of this decade of Christian
nonviolent resistance to Islam.

377 Cutler, Allan. "The Ninth-Century Spanish Martyrs'
Movement and the Origins of Western Christian
Missions to the Muslims," *Muslim World* 55 (1965):
321-39.

The Cordoba martyr movement was the first Christian
mass movement and had profound importance for the
history of later Christian missions. Recounts the main
personalities and events and stresses the apocalyptic
motivations of many in the movement. Cutler, however,
sees its apocalyptic drift as the first step in a violent
revolution and links it directly to the Crusades movement.
He does this in the face of all the evidence explicitly
praising the nonviolence of the martyrs, and lacking

evidence supporting his notion of such a cynical maneuver on the part of the Christian leadership.

378   O'Callaghan, Joseph F. *A History of Medieval Spain*. Ithaca: Cornell University Press, 1975.

Good introduction to the historical background. Pages 109-12 review the martyr movement, which O'Callaghan calls a "resistance" movement, detailing the causes, the main personalities, and the events.

379   Waltz, James. "The Significance of the Voluntary Martyr Movement of Ninth-Century Cordoba," *Muslim World* 60 (1970): 143-59, 226-36.

Excellent analysis of the martyr movement that links its religious motivation and response to very concrete political and social issues, focusing on the widespread conversion to Islam brought about by taxes on Christians, the appeal of Sufic asceticism, and the high social status often accorded Christian converts. Nevertheless, Waltz stresses that the Christian response was not simply a negative reaction but a positive cultural and religious revival that soon matched Islam's appeal and spurred the martyrdoms as an active demonstration of a reborn Christianity. Waltz traces in detail the progress of the movement, yet concludes, rather in the face of the evidence, that an appeal to force was an essential ingredient of the martyrs' witness.

The Peace and Truce of God

380   Bisson, Thomas N. "The Organized Peace in Southern France and Catalonia c.1140-c.1233," *American Historical Review* 82: 2 (1977): 290-311.

Treats the institutional, centralized peace of the feudal
lord, the instrument of authority, not the "sanctified" or
popular peace movement. Valuable analysis of how the
Peace of God, originally intended to protect the poor and
weak from the violence of the feudal warrior, became an
instrument of power in the hands of feudal government.
Briefly traces the origins of the Peace of God in its
religious and legal traditions in the influences of
monasticism, in the penitentials, and in popular spirituality. By the time of the Council of Clermont in 1095 this
peace movement had been institutionalized and made an
instrument of royal and papal power. By the late twelfth
century in Catalonia *pax* had lost its otherworldly
meanings and had come to mean simply the lord's militia
and his rule of law. By the thirteenth century tax levies to
maintain peace forces were actually being converted into
war taxes.

381   Bloch. *Feudal Society*. See **325**.

While his treatment takes up only a few pages (2: 412-
19), Bloch was one of the first to discuss the Peace and
Truce of God in any comprehensive manner, and his vast
prestige as a medievalist and the value of this book has
impressed his views on all subsequent students of the
movements. Bloch traces the origins of the Peace to
Carolingian notions of the peacemaker as one who
imposes order. Peace was imposed from above, and the
Peace movement had its direct origins in councils of
bishops legislating for flocks. As a spiritual movement
both the Peace and the Truce were severely limited and
needed the sanctions of law and civil authority. Nevertheless, at its height the Peace movement was truly revolutionary, not in its occasional violence but in its insistence
on mutual oaths of peace sworn between equals. It thus
posed a threat to the hierarchical order of society and

provided a basis for the later urban communal movements.

382   Bonnaud-Delamare, Roger. "Fondement des institutions
       de paix au xi⁰ siècle," *Mélanges d'histoire du Moyen
       Age dédies à la mémoire de Louis Halphen*. Paris:
       Press Universitaire, 1951, 19-26.

       A brief introduction.

383   ——."Les institutions de paix en Aquitaine au xiᵉ siècle."
       See **47**, 415-87.

       The Peace of God in Aquitaine was essentially the
       ducal peace, forced from the top down. The people did
       not participate in its creation. Nevertheless, it depended
       upon the institutions of popular spirituality to bind its
       adherents: the relics of the saints, anathemas and
       interdictions on those who defied its bans. Sermons by
       bishops spoke of both peace and justice and emphasized
       the role of the Peace in protecting the powerless. Yet their
       definitions were along older Carolingian lines of peace as
       order and of justice as law. Also traces the progress of the
       movement through its individual councils.

384   ——."La paix d'Amiens et de Corbie au xiᵉ siècle," *Revue
       du Nord* 38 (150) (1956): 167-78.

       Based on the account of Gerard, abbot of Sauve-
       Majeure in the diocese of Bordeaux from 1080 to 1095.
       His *Life of Adalhard* provides evidence for the popular
       assemblies that gave form to the Peace of God.

385   Bouard, M. "Sur les origines de la trêve de Dieu en
       Normandie," *Annales de Normandie* 9 (1959): 168-
       89.

First traces the origins and development of the Truce in Northern France and Flanders and its royal and papal support, then focuses on its career in Normandy, where Richard de Saint Vanne played a key role. In Normandy the Truce proved an instrument of ducal centralization. The elimination of private wars and the penances, including exiles, imposed on violators all had ecclesiastical backing, strengthened by the force of councils. Bouard then details the elements of the Truce and analyzes its vocabulary in its Gothic, Frankish, and Languedocian roots, showing how in Normandy the vocabulary of the Truce was used interchangeably with that of the Peace. By the late eleventh century both had come to be the exclusive realm of the prince.

386   Callahan, Daniel F. "Adhemar de Chabannes et la paix de Dieu," *Annales du Midi* 89, 1, 131 (1977): 21-43.

Uses the *Chronicle* of Adhemar de Chabannes and his *Vita* of St. Martial as sources for the birth and spread of the popular peace movement, which Callahan terms one of the most important phenomena of the eleventh century. Adhemar describes the Peace assemblies in great detail: the participants, oaths, the condemnations of the warrior class, sanctions against violators, and the sermons of bishops who promoted the Peace of God.

387   Cowdrey, H.E.J. "The Peace and Truce of God," *Past and Present* 46 (1970): 42-67.

Valuable synthesis traces the origins and development of both the Peace and Truce of God, discussing the major sources, and detailing the elements of the assemblies, the special protections against feudal violence afforded to classes of people and to times of the year, the oaths, and sanctions imposed on violators. Cowdrey stresses that the Peace movements were more than a mere protection of property or of law and order. They were true religious movements at heart, intent upon renewing the Gospel peace of Christ and of the Apostolic age among all classes of society. Finally, however, the movement was coopted by secular authorities and by a crusading papacy into exactly its antithesis: a call to arms.

388   Delaruelle, Étienne. "Paix de Dieu et croisade dans la chrétienté du xiie siècle," in *Paix de Dieu et guerre sainte en Languedoc au xiiie siècle*. Cahiers de Fanjeaux 4. Toulouse: Privat, 1969, 51-71. Reprinted in **356**, 233-53.

Highlights the various aspects of the Peace: socio-political, ecclesiastical, popular, and religious and mystical, but accepts the coopted language of the Peace and Truce of God used by the Crusades as if the three were really all part of the same movement. Implies that conquest and forced conversion were also the same as nonviolent missionary work.

389   Duby, Georges. "Laity and the Peace of God," in *The Chivalrous Society. Essays by Georges Duby*. Cynthia Postan, transl. London: Edward Arnold; and Berkeley: University of California Press, 1977, 123-33.

While the original inspiration for the Peace came from the bishops and abbots, they soon gained the adherence of the feudal aristocracy and, then, of the lower laity. While at first the Peace movement made no attempt to restructure society, its continuing attacks on the violence of the nobility soon emerged into an idealization of pacifism as a form of Christian purity, akin to poverty and chastity. The poor and the unarmed became an ideal figure, linked to the purity of the penitential system, as a renunciator of the old world of sin, violence, and exploitation.

390 ——.*The Three Orders: Feudal Society Imagined.* Chicago: University of Chicago Press, 1980.

Sections on Gerard of Cambrai (pp. 21-43), Adalbero of Laon (13-19), and the Peace of God (134-39) are of fundamental importance for understanding the Peace movement. Both bishops represent the old Carolingian aristocracy and reflect their disdain for the Peace of God. They see this as a movement of peasants and other inferiors intent upon turning the God-given order of things on its head by assembling together and swearing mutual oaths of love and peace, daring to judge the violence of their superiors. Peace, they contend, is hierarchical order and authority imposed from above. In reaction they crystallize the theory of the three orders of society: those who pray, those who fight, and those who work. Duby's brilliant analysis highlights how the Peace movement transformed passive victims into truly active agents of peace and made poverty a virtue to be pursued as a criticism of feudal wealth, violence, and exploitation.

391 Gernhuber, Joachim. "Staat und Landfrieden im deutschen Reich des Mittelalters." See **48**, 27-78.

The application of the Truce of God as the Imperial Peace spread and enforced by the emperor, parallel by numerous local peaces enforced by the princes of the empire.

392   Glaber, Ralph. *Five Books of Histories.* See **3**, 221-22.

Book IV, 5 gives an account of the Peace movement, detailing its most important features.

393   Gleiman, L. "Some Remarks on the Origins of the Treuga Dei," *Études d'histoire litteraire et doctrinaire.* Montréal: Université de Montréal. Institut d'Études Médiévales. Publications. 17 (1962): 117-37.

Sets the Peace and Truce of God within their context of constant feudal warfare, reviews the historiography of the movements and the problems of interpretation. Gleiman stresses that the Peace of God is well documented in the writings of the period: the movement is rooted in monastic discipline and sought the imitation of Christ and the restoration of peace and justice. In fact, there seems some evidence of total pacifism, but this Gleiman attributes to some heretical, perhaps Manichean, bent.

394   Haines. "Attitudes and Impediments." See **334**.

While the Peace and Truce of God were never very successful, peace remained an ideal. It was the highest goal for a ruler and the goal of the urban communal movements, which called themselves "peace." A medieval pacifism did exist, but this was restricted to individuals and was commonly lost amid the constant suspicions and conflicts of the period.

395   Heyn, Udo. "Arms Limitation and the Search for Peace in Medieval Europe." *War and Society* 2 (Sept. 1984): 1-18.

A review of medieval attempts to limit the effects of war that focuses on the Peace, Truce, and "Imperial" peace. While his notes and bibliography are excellent — this is a superior introduction to the materials in the area — this is really history of the old school.

Heyn's assumptions are explicit: "to the extent that its causes are atavistic, war must be reckoned endemic to human nature....The only sensible, the only moral, course of action is to plan to conduct [wars] with as much moderation as is humanly possible." Peace is the equivalent of "society's stability" insured by a "superior authority" that will insure ordered change through legal systems, "directed towards the end of psychic and physical survival — whose historical instrumentality has become, and is likely to remain indefinitely, the sovereign state."

Heyn's methods are thus sociological and legal, and it comes as no surprise that in his analysis of medieval peace movements there is not a single reference to the Gospels, the imitation of Christ, the poverty movements, the cult of saints, the Third Orders, missionary work, or anything touching on popular imagination or aspirations, except to say that authority flowed from the top down and the burden of peace, as of war, rested on the peasants.

396   Hoffmann, Harmut. *Gottesfriede und Treuga Dei*. MGH, *Scriptores* 20. Stuttgart: Hiersmann, 1964.

Among the most useful general introductions, this book sets the movements into their historical context, then traces each region by region and chronologically. It also gives attention to major treatises, papal letters, and canon law. Appendixes print important sources. Excellent bibliography.

397   Joris, André. "Observations sur la proclamation de la trêve
         de Dieu à Liège à la fin du xie siècle." See **47**, 503-45.

         The Truce first reached the Holy Roman Empire in
         1082 at Liège. Joris details the assemblage here, the
         special prohibitions against violence in certain seasons, on
         certain feast days and days of the week, the sanctions
         imposed against violators, then goes on to discuss the
         problems posed by the sources.

398   Kennelly, Karen. "Catalan Peace and Truce Assemblies,"
         Studies in Medieval Culture 5 (1975): 41-51.

         Traces the progress of the Peace and Truce through
         the eleventh century in church councils attended by clergy,
         nobility, and laity and notes that toward the end of the
         century the movements were even used to prepare public
         opinion for crusades. In general their main functions in
         the twelfth century seem to have been to protect property
         and to establish royal authority. By the fourteenth century
         the Peace was simply identified with the royal protection
         over the realm.

399   ——."Medieval Towns and the Peace of God," *Medievalia
         et Humanistica* 15 (1963): 35-53.

         Attempts to examine some practical effects of the
         Peace movement, here reviewing the historiography as far
         back as Pirenne and questioning whether the commercial
         movement of the Middle Ages, the "peace" of the towns,
         was a result of the Peace of God. While she answers in
         the negative, Kennelly does conclude that the Peace of
         God did lend some of its vocabulary and its methods to the
         urban communal movement of sworn associations and
         strengthened the idea that peace was the outcome of people

coming together to attain it. In this she agrees with Bloch (**381**) in seeing the Peace as a revolutionary movement. Good bibliography.

400 ——."The Peace and the Truce of God: Fact or Fiction?" Ph.D. dissertation. Berkeley: University of California, 1962.

Not seen.

401 MacKinney, Loren C. "The People and Public Opinion in the Eleventh-Century Peace Movement," *Speculum* 5 (1930): 181-206.

The Peace of God grew out of the church's desire to aid the defenseless and from a popular desire for peace. It ended by being coopted by the princes, who used it as an instrument for their own power. Details the progress of the Peace movement: the church councils, the elements of the assemblies, the aspects of the Peace, the sanctions, and the effects of the Peace. Then treats the Truce of God as an extension of the Peace, follows its spread and the opposition that it met from the entrenched hierarchy. The Council of Clermont was both the climax of the Peace and the Truce, which succeeded in creating internal peace, and paradoxically, their transformation into a mechanism for foreign war, which they were unable to prevent.

402 Mayer, Hans Eberhard. *The Crusades*. John Gillingham, transl. New York: Oxford University Press, 1972.

The Peace of God grew out of the church's desire to preserve its own privileges and properties. Despite the church's own self-interest, however, benefits did accrue. Armed enforcement was essential to the movement.

Mayer is, of course, writing a history of the Crusades, but his unspoken cynicism about any form of antimilitarism during the period should be treated warily.

403   Runciman, Steven. *A History of the Crusades.* 3 vols. New York: Harper & Row, 1964-1967; reissued, New York: Penguin Books: 1972. 1: 84-87.

While Runciman's topic is the crusades, this admirably comprehensive and fair-handed account provides valuable judgments and a useful summary on the development and spread of the Peace and Truce of God.

404   Strubbe, E.I. "La paix de Dieu dans le Nord de la France." See **47**, 489-501.

Traces the spread of the Peace of God throughout southern France, then into northern France via Burgundy. Emphasizes that in the north the Peace and the Truce were essentially the creatures of the prince, and that in its earlier form the Peace's spiritual sanctions were drawbacks in a society where physical force ruled.

405   Töpfer, Bernhard. *Volk und Kirche zur Zeit der beginnenden Gottesfriedensbewegung im Frankreich.* Berlin: Rutten & Loening, 1957.

This is a work of synthesis that reviews the origin and development of the Peace of God in great detail and with a careful eye to chronology. Töpfer remains true to his Marxist historical tradition in stressing the popular nature of the Peace of God, calling it a true people's movement, yet here he also depends on the populism of American historians of the 1930s, like MacKinney. See **401**.

406 Wohlhaupter, Eugen. *Studien zur Rechtsgeschichte der Gottes- und Landfrieden im Spanien.* Heidelberg: Winter, 1933.

Concentrates on the legal aspects of the peace movement in Spain from the eleventh to the fourteenth century.

* *
*

CHAPTER 6: *The Era of the Crusades.*
Peacemaking in Europe 1100 to 1400

General Introduction

407   Brooke. *Europe.* 237-93. See **346**.

Good background to the events, personalities, and issues of the period, including the Investiture Conflict.

408   Heer, Friedrich. *The Intellectual History of Europe.* Jonathan Steinberg, transl. 2 vols. Garden City, NY: Doubleday, 1968. 1: 94-196.

Excellent introduction to the intellectual and cultural issues of the period.

409   Larner, John. *Italy in the Age of Dante and Petrarch 1216-1380.* New York: Longmans, 1984.

Most of the peace movements of this period studied by historians took place in Italy. This provides an excellent introduction to the period's culture, politics, society, and economy, with careful attention paid to popular spirituality. Pages 243-52 provide some background and good bibliography on the Italian peace movements of the era.

Background for the Crusades

410   Alphandéry, Paul. *La chrétienté et l'idée de croisade.* Paris: Albin Michel, 1954.

Excellent introduction to the historiography of the

Crusades in the nineteenth century, when the movement first came to the center of historians' interests. While the book in no way takes a Marxist point of view, it does tie the interest in the historical movement to European colonialism and imperialism in the nineteenth century. The Suez Canal Project, for example, set off a new wave of French interest in the Middle East and in France's historical role there. European interest in the decaying Ottoman Empire and the entire "Eastern Question" also roused interest in the region. Soon "crusade" had come into common parlance for any campaign involving large social forces or ideals. "Crusade in Europe," "Crusade of Charity," "Crusade Against Slavery," all lent moral grandeur to the causes, and at the same time helped ennoble the original Crusade movement.

411   Atiya, Aziz S. *The Crusade. Historiography and Bibliography.* Bloomington, IN: Indiana University Press, 1962.

Pages 17-28 briefly review the historiography of the sources from the Middle Ages to the twentieth century. The seventeenth and eighteenth centuries condemned the Crusades, and the nineteenth century saw new editions of sources prepared by the Maurists and others. As yet, Atiya notes, Crusade historiography is still in need of a comprehensive monograph.

412   Brundage, James A. *The Crusades: Motives and Achievements.* Boston: D.C. Heath, 1964.

The review of earlier historiography reveals that before the nineteenth century the Crusades were generally interpreted unfavorably, either as manifestations of medieval religious fanaticism (Gibbon) or Catholic corruption (Fuller). Only with nineteenth century historians, such as Brehier, are the Crusades seen in any altruistic light. This shift was probably tied to French geographical and economic expansion and their "protectorate" in Syria.

413 ——.*Medieval Canon Law and the Crusader.* Madison, WI: University of Wisconsin Press, 1969.

Pages 3-29 provide valuable background to the very strong penitential pilgrimage tradition that predated the Crusades, and to a large extent characterized the movement for the unarmed poor, who formed the vast majority of crusaders.

414 Mayer. *Crusades.* See **402**.

A good one-volume introduction.

415 Riley-Smith, Louise. *The Crusades: Idea and Reality, 1095-1274.* London: Edward Arnold, 1981.

A collection of primary sources in translation, focusing on the premise that the Crusades were "holy wars authorized by the pope." The work is an explicit attempt to present texts that extol "sacred violence." It was undertaken, its author notes, because "too many militant theologians, mistakenly convinced of the novelty of the premises they use, do not realize that Christians have been committed to an ideology of violence before, with very unfortunate consequences."

416 Runciman. *Crusades.* See **403**.

Still the best history in English. Runciman was a Byzantinist at heart, and his sympathies lay in the East, not

with the barbaric Westerners who descended on the Levant
and the Byzantine Empire. His account, always stirring, is
thus tempered by a good deal of skepticism concerning the
virtue and altruism of the Western crusaders.

417   Setton, Kenneth Meyer. *History of the Crusades.* 6 vols.
         Madison, WI: University of Wisconsin Press, 1955-
         1983.

         The most comprehensive account available in English.
         A collection of essays by distinguished scholars, divided
         into volumes by general topic area. While this lacks the
         cohesiveness and drama of Runciman's masterful nar-
         rative, it is an invaluable reference resource.

Chivalry and Just War: Civilizing the Soldier?

418   Althoff, Gerd. "Nunc fiant Christi milites, qui dudum
         extiterunt raptores. Zur Entstehung von Rittertum und
         Ritterethos," *Saeculum* 32 (4, 1981): 317-33.

         On the shift from the Peace and Truce to the Crusades
         and the development of chivalry as a conscious attempt by
         the church to tame the violence of the feudal nobility.

419   Bloch. *Feudal Society* 2: 312-19. See **325**, 5-35.

         Still an excellent introduction to chivalry as the ethos
         of the feudal class as it was formed by the church in an
         effort to Christianize the warrior.

420   Bonnaud-Delamare, Roger. "La paix en Flandres pendant
         la première croisade," *Revue du Nord* 39 no. 154
         (1957): 147-52.

         Focuses on the peace synod called sometime between

1083 and 1092 by the Archbishop of Reims, Raynaud du Bellai. Demonstrates the confluence of the Peace and Truce with the Crusade movement.

421   Delaruelle. "Paix de Dieu," 51-71. See **388**.

The development from the Truce of God, which provided an external control on feudal violence, to the new notion of chivalry, which internalized these controls into a new ethos of the Christian warrior, was a gradual process that led eventually to the Crusades. The Crusades, in fact, coopted many of the elements of the old Peace assemblies: the oath, a sacred literature expressing its meaning, the espousal of peace as the final aim, a militia or knighthood sworn to this peace, the depiction of the enemy as the foe of Christian peace, and the very emblem of the Peace and Truce: the Cross. The same papal bulls, mobilization of popular forces, and the end of internecine strife accompanied both movements. St. Bernard was a leader in this transformation. Delaruelle concludes that because the Crusades coopted the language of pilgrimage, peace and conversion, they were actually part of the same movements.

422   Duval. *Paix*. See **358**.

The evangelical reform, which included that of the new poverty movements, made a return to the roots of Christian tradition its ideal. The Gospel ideal was therefore as incompatible with war and violence and it was consistent with poverty and penitence. Such a linkage was central to the spirituality of Peter Damian, St. Francis, and the Franciscan Third Order. Duval's treatment is balanced, however, and the new age of reform also applied to the feudal class. Church leaders actively tried to civilize the knight through the ethos of chivalry. The

Crusades themselves witnessed the new military monastic orders, and the application of just-war theory.

423   Erdmann. *Idea of Crusade.* See **21**.

The Investiture Conflict between the popes and German emperors gave birth to a whole pamphlet literature by intellectuals and propagandists on both sides. Among the more interesting discussions was the imperialist condemnation of the pope for waging war and "killing Christians for Christ." Christ himself marked his *milites* with the seal of peace and love, not the banner of war. God himself desires peace. The pope brings only war. While much of this literature was obviously partisan, its popular appeal helped instill the notion that real political peace was a goal of the Christian church. The propaganda campaign also showed up the contradictions in just- and holy-war theories.

424   Grabois, Aryeh. "De la trêve de Dieu à la paix du roi. Études sur la transformation du mouvement de la paix au xiie siècle," *Mélanges offerts à René Crozet.* Poitiers: Société d'Études Médiévales, 1966. 1: 585-96.

Not seen.

425   Herlihy, David. *The History of Feudalism.* New York: Harper & Row, 1970, 281-344.

Part Four, "Chivalry," presents an excellent series of documents tracing the rise of this ideal from the Peace and Truce of God, through the writings of Bernard of Clairvaux, the Legend of St. George, to Raymond Lull's *Book on the Order of Chivalry.*

426   Holdsworth, Christopher J. "Ideas and Reality: Some
       Attempts to Control and Diffuse War in the Twelfth
       Century." See **53**, 59-78.

Holdsworth notes "how relatively unexamined the
actual working out of Christian ideas about war within the
medieval period is" and cites Russell (**50**) as the chief
resource on the period. Focuses on the historical work of
Odericus Vitalis as a good indicator of attitudes. While
Odericus is favorable to peacemaking, he describes battles
with more relish than peace negotiations. While clear on
clerical nonviolence, he treats sex and concubinage as
more serious a violation than killing. To emphasis this
point Holdsworth cites the Penitential of Theodore (see
312 to **324**) and notes that it imposes the same penance for
killing in war as for masturbation.
     On the whole, while Odericus does not condemn
pacifism, Holdsworth asserts that "indeed it is hard to find
such [pacifism] within orthodox circles in the twelfth
century, though some of the groups who came to be
regarded as heretical did believe that the command to turn
the other cheek had application to behaviour in society."
These long-unexamined assumptions, combined with a
somewhat misguided attempt at humor, cause this article to
fail the purpose of its opening remarks and make it less
valuable that it might have been.

427   Leclercq, Jean, O.S.B. "Saint Bernard's Attitude Towards
       War," *Studies in Cistercian History* 2 (1975): 1-39.

Bernard still bears a reputation as a man of war for his
vigorous support of two crusades. Yet this reputation
obscures his true nature as a man of peace. He always
stressed the just-war theory and preferred the *militia Christi*
to the *militia mundi*, calling his followers *bellatores*

pacifici, "peaceful warriors." He opposed war against other Christians, heretics, and Jews. Despite this, his attitude toward the barbarian Wends (against whom the Teutonic Knights waged a war of genocide) was "ambiguous." Leclercq's article reads like a rehabilitation of the saint suited to modern sensibilities.

428   Lorson, Pierre, S.J. "Saint Bernard devant la guerre et la paix," *Nouvelle Revue Théologique* 75 (1953): 785-803.

Bernard's ideas of peace remained hierarchical: peace was order imposed from above, or the right ordering of the bodily parts coordinated by the head, the harmony of all things in their proper place. Yet peace could also be monastic order and calm, the feudal peace arranged by arbitration and treaty, and international peace achieved by the same means.

429   MacKinney. "Public Opinion." See **401**.

The Crusades coopted for war the energies and popular support awoken by the Peace and Truce of God.

430   Painter, Sidney. *French Chivalry*. Ithaca: Cornell University Press, 1965.

This is an excellent introduction to the topic, with chapters on the French nobility, feudal chivalry, religious chivalry, courtly love, and the growing criticism by churchmen and poets of the feudal ethos of violence, even as expressed by chivalry.

431   Pissard, Hippolypte. *La guerre sainte en pays chrétien.* Paris: Picard, 1912; reprinted New York: AMS, 1980.

Pages 13-14 discuss Peter Damian's absolute nonviolence, based explicitly on the Sermon on the Mount.

432   Renna. "Idea." See **340**, 5-18.

Bernard of Clairvaux stressed that the Christian must have peace, hold peace, and make peace, thus combining the mystical and purgative elements of monastic peace with the activism of the Christian peacemaking tradition. The monk, in Bernard's eyes, was the chief agent of this synthesis.

433   ⸺."St. Bernard's Idea of Peace in Its Historical Perspective, 750-1150," *Res Publica Litteraria*.

Not seen.

Peacemaking and the New Poverty Movements

434   Attwater. *Saints*. See **1**.

Good biographies, with some bibliography, for such peacemakers as Adalbert of Prague, Boniface (Bruno) of Querfurt, Bridget (Birgitta) of Sweden, Hugh, Odilo, and Odo of Cluny, Peter Damian, Romuald, and Stanislaus of Cracow.

435   *Bibliotheca Sanctorum*. See **4**.

Good biographies, with excellent bibliography and complete artistic iconography, for such peacemakers as Adalbert of Prague, Boniface (Bruno) of Querfurt, Guibert, Hugh of Cluny, Odilo of Cluny, Odo of Beauvais, Odo of Cluny, Peter Damian, Romuald,

Stanislaus of Cracow, and Theobald of Provins, many of whom were soldiers who renounced the sword for the monastic life of peacemaking.

436   Butler. *Lives.* See **9**.

The most complete collection of biographies available in English for such peacemakers as Adalbert of Prague, Boniface (Bruno) of Querfurt, Gerard of Brogne, Guibert, Hugh of Cluny, Odilo of Cluny, Odo of Cluny, Peter Damian, Romuald, Stanislaus of Cracow, and Theobald of Provins.

437   Chenu, M.-D., O.P. "The Evangelical Awakening." See **439**, 239-69.

Good introduction to the spirit of reform that marked the high Middle Ages: the ideal of the Gospel life of Christ and the early church, and the life of imitation that that entails in the present. This includes, of course, the strict adherence to the beatitudes, including poverty and peacemaking.

438   ——."Monks, Canons, and Laymen in Search of the Apostolic Life." See **439**, 202-38.

Analyzes by group the forms of imitation of the life of the Gospels and the early church. Particularly interesting are his comments on lay spirituality and adherence to the beatitudes.

439   ——.*Nature, Man, and Society in the Twelfth Century.* Jerome Taylor and Lester K. Little, eds. and transls. Chicago: University of Chicago Press, 1979.

Collected essays, fundamental to understanding the poverty movements. Includes **437** and **438**.

440   Clasen, Sophronius, O.F.M. "Poverty Movement," *NCE* 11: 652-53.

Traces the origins of the poverty movement to northern France in the eleventh century, but ties the new poverty movements to feudal violence in a simplistic way: as the result of the Crusades. This movement, Clasen claims, brought Eastern monasticism and the imitation of Christ and the early church back to the West, thus spurring the new ideal of poverty.

441   Delaney. *Dictionary.* See **15**.

Includes brief biographies of the period's peace-makers, including Adalbert of Prague, Bridget of Sweden, Boniface (Bruno) of Querfurt, Guibert, Hugh of Cluny, Odilo of Cluny, Odo of Beauvais, Odo of Cluny, Peter Damian, Romuald, Stanislaus of Cracow, and Theobald of Provins.

442   Flood, David, O.F.M., ed. *Poverty in the Middle Ages.* Werl, Westfalia: D. Coelde, 1975.

A collection of essays by distinguished scholars on many aspects of medieval poverty. Includes **446**.

443   *La guerre et la paix, frontiers et violence au Moyen Age. Actes du 101ᵉ Congrès National des Sociétés Savantes, Lille, 1976. Section de Philologie et d'Histoire.* Paris, 1978.

Not seen.

444   Haines. "Attitudes and Impediments." See **333**, 5-48.

Many of the most important of the popular religious
movements of the high Middle Ages were, in fact,
thoroughly pacifist and orthodox, even in their combination of poverty and millennial ideals. These movements included the Penitenti, Humiliati, Flagellants, the
Great Alleluia of 1233, the Beguines and Beghards, and
the lay Third Orders of the cities. St. Francis and his
order were yet another example of this widespread
phenomenon. Yet this pacifism was not without risk. The
obligation of most communal citizens to bear arms gave
rise to great resentment against those who refused to do so
on any grounds. The common refusal of such pacifists to
swear oaths, in imitation of the early church, went against
the core of feudal bonds and made them uncomfortably
akin to many heretical groups.

445   Labande-Mailfert, Yves. "Pauvreté et paix dans l'icono-
        graphie romane, xie-xiie siècles." See **447**.

In iconographic programs, such as that of the church
of Notre Dame in Clermont, *ira* (violence) is linked with
avaritia (greed) in opposition to *caritas* (Christian love) and
misericordia (mercy).

446   Little, Lester K. "Evangelical Poverty, the New Money
        Economy, and Violence." See **442**, 11-26.

The links between the evangelical ideal, economic and
social realities, and the link between poverty and peacemaking.

447   Mollat, Michel, ed. *Études sur l'histoire de la pauvreté.*
       Moyen Age —xvie siècle. 2 vols. Paris: La Sorbonne,
       1974.

       An excellent collection examining poverty as a real
       physical state, a religious ideal, and an intellectual and
       artistic theme.

448   ——."Les pauvres et la société médiévale," *Rapports du
       xiiie Congrès International des sciences historiques* 1.
       Moscow, 1973, 162-80.

       The poor in life and in religious ideal.

449   *La pace nel pensiero, nella politica, negli ideali del
       trecento. Convegni del Centro di Studi sulla
       Spiritualità medievale* 15. Todi, 1975.

       As the title indicates, it covers the entire range of peace
       topics from intellectual tradition to political institutions,
       popular spirituality, and the lives and thought of
       individuals. Includes **498, 499, 502, 503, 505-507,** and
       586.

Popular Peace Groups: Humiliati and Poor Catholics

450   Bolton, Brenda M. "Innocent III's Treatment of the
       Humiliati," *Studies in Church History* 8 (Cambridge,
       1972), 73-82.

       The pope's changing attitudes to the group's
       orthodoxy. A good introduction to the topic.

451   Da Milano, Ilarino, O.F.M., Cap. "Umiliati," *Enciclopedia Cattolica* 12: 754-56.

Good background for the origins and rapid spread of the movement, with some interesting estimates of the numbers involved.

452   Grundmann, Herbert. *Religiöse Bewegungen im Mittelalter.* Darmstadt: Wissenschafliche Buchgesellschaft, 1961. Transl. with new intro. as *Movimenti religiosi nel Medioevo.* Bologna: Mulino, 1974.

A fundamental work for the study of medieval popular spirituality, provides excellent background for the Humiliati, Poor Catholics, and the rapid spread of these and other poverty movements.

453   Laughlin, M.F. "Humiliati," *NCE* 7: 234.

Outlines the origins, development, and central tenets of the group, including their refusal to bear arms. Makes some attempt to fix the social origins of the members to manual laborers and wool-industry workers.

St. Francis and the Franciscans

454   Cousins, Ewert, ed. and transl. *Bonaventure.* New York: Paulist Press, 1978.

In such works as the *Tree of Life* and the *Soul's Journey to God* Bonaventure makes clear his idea of peace as a union with God, a quiet silence, and a universal peace of calm. Francis prepared our way to God with a path of light and peace. This edition presents English translations, with notes and bibliography. A good introduction.

455 Daniel, E. Randolf. *The Franciscan Concept of Mission in the High Middle Ages.* Lexington, KY: University Press of Kentucky, 1975.

"St. Francis was not a pacifist, but he lived as if he were." Daniel's comment begs the point, for he stresses that for Francis and the Franciscans example of life was always placed above the word. His example of peace, of reconciliation, and the forgiveness of sins set the tone for the mendicant movement more than any rules or writings.

456 Dubois, Leo L. *St. Francis of Assisi, Social Reformer.* New York: Benziger Brothers, 1906.

Pages 59-61 discuss the pacifism of the Third Orders, their rapid spread, and their great impact on medieval society.

457 Fortini, Arnaldo. *Francis of Assisi.* New York: Crossroads Press, 1981.

The peacemaking of St. Francis and of the Tertiaries that he founded were clear examples of pacifism in the Middle Ages.

458 Francis of Assisi. *Francis and Clare. The Complete Works.* Regis J. Armstrong, O.F.M., Cap. and Ignatius Brady, O.F.M., transls. and eds. New York: Paulist Press, 1982.

An excellent English edition, in the Classics of Western Spirituality series.

459   ——.*Opuscula Sancti Patris Francisci Assisiensis.* Cajetan
          Esser, O.F.M., ed. Grottaferrata (Rome): Collegio
          San Bonaventura, 1978.

          The basic, Latin edition of Francis' works, with
          scholarly annotations concerning authenticity and manu-
          script tradition. An analytic index of important words and
          ideas makes this a useful reference tool.

460   ——.*Writings and Early Biographies. English Omnibus of
          the Sources for the Life of St. Francis.* Marion A.
          Habig, O.F.M., ed. Chicago: Franciscan Herald
          Press, 1973.

          The most comprehensive collection of Franciscan
          sources in English. A true omnibus of previous editions
          and translations drawn from several sources, including all
          of Francis' own works, all his contemporary major bio-
          graphies, and the works of the Spiritual tradition,
          including the *Fioretti* (Little Flowers) and the *Speculum
          perfectionis* (Mirror of Perfection), with invaluable indices,
          concordances, and bibliography.
          The interpretation of these Franciscan sources has
          been compared to that of the Gospels: problems of
          author's intent, literary form, historical context and
          authenticity, manuscript tradition, etc. must all be ad-
          dressed. Francis' thoughts on peace are, accordingly, not
          gathered into single texts or easily quoted: problems of text
          and context dictate that one study and evaluate his life as
          well as his words, and pay close attention to the intent of
          his biographers and those who edited and preserved his
          own works. Nevertheless, a clear pattern of Francis as a
          peacemaker emerges easily from these scattered writings.
          Indices and concordances help assemble key materials.

461   Habig, Marion A., O.F.M. *Francis of Assisi: Writer.*
       Chicago: Franciscan Herald Press, 1983.

       The subtitle reads "Supplement to the Omnibus of
       Sources on St. Francis." This includes discussion of
       Francis' own works, new translations of individual letters,
       and a bibliographical notation on the "Ten Best Books" on
       Francis of Assisi.

462   McNeill. "Asceticism." See **338**, 5-24.

       Francis of Assisi's conversion was one that explicitly
       linked peace and poverty as a witness against the alliance
       of feudal violence and new urban wealth. His order held
       its ministry of peace and peacemaking central. Such Fran-
       ciscan heroes as Anthony of Padua made the call to
       repentance, forgiveness, and peace essential. The Fran-
       ciscan Tertiaries often found themselves at odds with the
       civil authorities for their refusal to bear arms "against
       anyone."

463   Moorman, John. *A History of the Franciscan Order from
       its Origins to the Year 1517.* Oxford: Clarendon Press,
       1968.

       This is the standard and best history of the order in
       English, with an excellent bibliography.

464   O'Mahony, Donal, O.F.M., Cap. "St. Francis, Peace
       Spirituality and Life Style." See **44**, 129-44.

       A sensitive and highly insightful look into what made
       Francis a paramount Christian peacemaker: his imitation of
       Christ, his embrace of poverty as an alternative to the
       violence and exploitation of feudal society and as a sign
       that the truth of the Gospel is to be found in simplicity, and

his understanding and celebration of the wholeness of God's creation, which is, after all, the fullest meaning of "peace."

465   Peregrinus, Brother, O.F.M. "Evangelical Pacifism in the Age of St. Francis." *Blessed Are the Peacemakers.* Montreal: Canadian Catholic Pacifists' Association, 1944, 58-104.

Pages 78-90 concentrate on the pacifism and peacemaking of the Third Orders.

Peacemaking and the Third Orders

466   Duval. *Paix.* See **358**.

Duval discusses the Faenza affair of 1226/7, when the Franciscan Tertiaries appealed to Pope Gregory IX to intervene on their behalf against civil authorities who were attempting to draft them into the militia in violation of their rule of nonviolence. His account is balanced, however. Tertiaries did participate in armed struggle against the pope's enemies, as against Emperor Frederick II.

467   *I Frati Penitenti di San Francesco nella società del due e trecento.* Rome: Atti del secondo convegno di studi francescani, 1977.

Not seen.

468   Hallack, Cecily, and P.F. Anson. *These Made Peace.* Paterson, NJ: St. Anthony Guild, 1957.

A good, popular introduction to the work of the Franciscan Third Order in making peace. Surveys the period from 1174 to the nineteenth century, with short biographies of leading tertiaries, including Angela of Foligno, Elizabeth of Portugal, Bridget of Sweden, Elizabeth of Hungary, Delphine de Sabran, Raymond Lull, and others.

469 Hartdegen, S. "Third Orders," *NCE* 14: 93-96.

A basic introduction, with brief bibliography.

470 Hefèle, H. "Die Bettelorder und das religiöse Volkslebenorder im Mittelitaliens im xiii Jahrhundert," *Beiträge zur Kulturgeschichte des Mittelalters und der Renaissance* 9 (1910): 25-26.

Useful background to opposition to the Crusades in Italy, with some material on the Great Alleluia of 1233. Traces this opposition back to the poverty movements of the Humiliati, Franciscans, Dominicans, and others. Emphasizes the movement's rapid decline after the Verona demonstration.

471 Meersseman, Giles G., O.P. *Dossier sur l'ordre de la Pénitence au xiii⁰ siècle*. Fribourg: Éditions Universitaires, 1961.

This is the most comprehensive account of the Third Orders available, made even more valuable by Meersseman's thorough familiarity with the sources, and his editions of most of the orders' rules, privileges, commentaries, decrees of chapters general, papal bulls, and other relevant documents. These are arranged in chronological order, and numbered consecutively for easy reference. The collection provides many examples of the Third Orders' pacifism and their repeated efforts to retain their status as conscientious objectors in the face of government efforts to enlist them in military service.

Documents are not confined to this, however. They stress
the activist role of the Tertiaries in making peace among
their fellow citizens. Includes documents for the
Dominicans and Franciscans, the Humiliati, Poor
Catholics, Poor Lombards and their Penitents.

472   ——.*Ordo Fraternitatis. Confraternitate e pietà dei laici nel
             medioevo.* Rome: Italia Sacra, 1977.

A complete survey of lay fraternities from the
Carolingian period into the fourteenth century, along with
relevant documents. Meersseman traces the origins of the
confraternities back to the early church.

473   Moorman. *History.* See **463**.

Pages 40-45 treat the origins of the Franciscan Third
Order, 216-25 its rule and controversies surrounding its
provisions, 418-28 the fourteenth century, and 560-68 its
development into the sixteenth century. A refusal to bear
arms was central to the movement from its start, and this
exemption was reinforced by papal bulls and episcopal
protections against the civil authorities. Well into the
fourteenth century this strict adherence to nonviolence
remained a hallmark of the Franciscan Tertiaries.
Moorman agrees with those historians who stress and
large numbers of Third Order members and houses. He
emphasizes their respected place in medieval society, and
their appeal, even among the nobility, as a refuge from
violence and war.

474   "The Rule of the Third Order." See **3**, 350-56.

This reprints the Venice Rule of 1221 for the
Franciscan Tertiaries. Poverty and simplicity are clearly

joined to peacemaking here, while reconciliation with neighbors, the restoration of stolen goods, avoidance of formal oaths — and hence of feudal or even communal military loyalties — are all demanded of members. Most important, the Tertiaries "are not to take up lethal weapons, or bear them about, against anybody." The pacifism of the rule is obvious, as is the possibility for trouble with secular government. Provision is therefore made for the intervention of the bishops on behalf of the nonviolent when the state took repressive action.

475   Tugwell, Simon, O.P. *Early Dominicans. Selected Writings.* New York: Paulist Press, 1982.

Pages 29-31 provide introduction to the Dominican Third Order, the Order of Penance, while pages 432-51 present English editions of several rules. "To foster mutual charity and love and harmony, to strengthen the bond of peace and to encourage everything that is good" are among the central aims of the confraternity.

The Great Alleluia of 1233

476   Coulton, G.G. "The Great Alleluia," in *From St. Francis to Dante. Translations from the Chronicle of the Franciscan Salimbene (1221-88).* Philadelphia: University of Pennsylvania Press, 1972, 21-37.

Salimbene's *Chronicle,* excerpted here in large part, with transitional commentary by Coulton, is probably the most important source for this movement. It sprang up almost spontaneously as a response to growing factional and regional strife and grew directly from Francis' appeals to peace and reconciliation. According to Salimbene, the Alleluia was a period of great processions, devotions, and

peace demonstrations held in all the cities of Italy, bringing
together all ages, sexes, and classes in rejoicing, reconciliation, "joy and exaltation." The movement was spread
by a layman, Benedict of Parma, a wandering preacher
who lived in poverty and urged repentance and
forgiveness as the foundations of peace.

477   Da Schio, O. *Giovanni da Vicenza e l'Alleluja del 1233.*
        Vicenza, 1901.

        Not seen.

478   Fumigalli, Vito. "In margine all' 'alleluia' del 1233,"
        BISIMEAM 80 (1968): 257-72.

        The term "alleluia" signifies peace, salvation, and
        mercy. This movement brought together the young, old,
        the high and low, city and country folk, men and women.
        Essentially it was a religiously motivated peace movement
        in which the influence of the Mendicants and their Third
        Orders was clear.

479   Salimbene de Adam. *Cronica.* O. Holder-Egger, ed.
        MGH, Scriptores 32. Hanover, 1905-13.

        An important Latin source for much of the popular
        spirituality of the time by an author who witnessed or
        knew those who witnessed the events he describes.

480   ——.Giuseppe Scala, ed. 2 vols. Bari: G. Laterza, 1966.

        A good, handy edition of this basic source for
        thirteenth-century spirituality in Italy. Pages 99-123 give a

detailed account of the peace movement called the Great Alleluia.

481 Sutter, Carl. *Johann von Vicenza und die italienische Friedensbewegung im Jahre 1233.* Freiburg-im-Breisgau: J.C.B. Mohr, 1892.

Not seen.

482 Symonds, J.A. "Religious Revivals in Medieval Italy," *Cornhill* 31 (181) (January 1875): 54-64.

Symonds looked back upon medieval Italy from a Victorian Protestant's point of view. Written in an age when popular spirituality — indeed all things "popular" — were suspect, his story is really one of medieval religious excesses. Viewing what he considered the sad spectacle of the Italian peace and penitential movements, Symonds concludes that "that Renaissance of Christianity, which we call the Reformation, could not have proceeded from a Latin people." Nevertheless, his Victorian fascination with religious passion did help him provide one of the earliest accounts of the Great Alleluia of 1233, its origins, rapid spread and culmination at the Plain of Paquara outside Verona in August 1233, where 400,000 assembled to hear John of Vicenza preach peace and reconciliation. Also provides useful information on John himself.

The Flagellants

483 Delaruelle, Étienne. "Les grandes processions de pénitents." See **488**.

A good introduction to the events and sources.

484   Frugoni, Arsenio. "Sui flagellanti del 1260," *BISIMEAM* 75 (1963): 211-37.

Both the Franciscan call to reconciliation and peacemaking and Joachite expectations of the Apocalypse fueled the movement. It sprang up in the wake of the bloody battle of Montaperti in September 1260 and saw thousands of penitents descending on Rome, naked, begging God for mercy and peace. The most startling aspect of the movement was the flaggelations inflicted by the marchers on themselves to demonstrate their willingness to suffer martyrdom for peace and to ask for mercy for their neighbors and enemies.

485   Leff, Gordon. *Heresy in the Later Middle Ages.* 2 vols. New York: Barnes & Noble, 1967, 2: 485-93.

While this is essentially a survey of *heretical* movements, these pages provide useful background and bibliography to the orthodox Flagellant movement.

486   Meersseman, Giles G. "Disciplinati e penitenti nel duecento." See **488**.

The Flagellant movement in the thirteenth century with careful attention to source materials.

487   Morghen, Rafaelo. "Ranieri Fasani e il movimento de Disciplinati." See **488**.

Not seen.

488   *Il movimento dei Disciplinati nel settimo centenario dal suo inizio.* Lodovico Scaramucci, ed. 3 vols. Perugia Deputazione di storia patria per l'Umbria, 1962.

For the Flagellants. Includes **483, 486, 487, 489**.

489   Tammi, G. "Lo statuto dei Disciplinati di S. Maria Maddelena di Bergamo." See **488**.

A local rule for a group of Flagellants.

Venturino da Bergamo

490   Altaner, A. "Venturino von Bergamo, O.Pr. (1304-1346). Eine Biographie. Zugleich ein Beitrag zur Geschichte des Domenikanerordens im 14. Jahrhunderts." Ph.D. thesis. Breslau: University of Breslau, 1911.

Not seen.

491   Clementi, Giuseppe. *Il Beato Venturino da Bergamo dell'Ordine di Predicatori (1304-1346). Storia e Documenti*. Rome: Libreria Salesiana, 1904.

Traces his life and preaching.

492   ——.*Un Savonarola del secolo xiv. Il Beato Venturino da Bergamo*. Rome: Libreria Salesiana, 1899.

An earlier version of **491**.

493   Gennaro, Clara. "Venturino da Bergamo e la peregrinatio romana del 1335," *Studi sul medioevo cristiano offerti a Raffaelo Morghen*. Rome: Istituto Storico Italiano per il Medioevo, 1974. 1: 375-406.

This was a great peace crusade, a flagellant pilgrimage that descended on Rome largely as a result of Venturino's preaching of peace and reconciliation. Estimates of the

movement's strength range from an anonymous
Florentine's three million to Villani's 10,000. Perhaps
three thousand reached Rome. The processions and demonstrations stretched through Milan, Florence, Ferrara,
Orvieto, Lodi, Cremona, Mantova, Siena, Viterbo and
Rome and brought together all classes and social groups.
Far from the grim scenes of the film-makers' flagellants,
the processions were occasions for peace festivals in the
towns they passed. The "pilgrimage" image, usurped by
the Crusades, was consciously used to emphasize the
physical bravery, but nonviolence, of the participants.

494   Grion, Alvaro, ed. "*Legenda Beati Fratris Venturini
            O.P.,*" *Bergomum* 30,4 (1956): 11-110.

A good edition of an excellent source for popular
peacemaking during the Middle Ages. Grion's introduction (pp. 11-37) reviews Venturino's life, his
preaching, and his peace crusade, his journey to Avignon
and examination by the pope, his preaching of a general
crusade against the Turks, his journey east with the
crusaders, and his death at Smyrna in 1346. He also
examines the historiography, the manuscripts of the
Legenda, and the work's value as a source.

Pages 38-110 present the text. Venturino is a complex
personality to study. He preached a true nonviolent
crusade of peacemaking throughout Italy in his great pilgrimage to Rome, making the pilgrims' cry of "mercy,
peace, penance" known throughout Italy. Once in Rome
however, as his orthodoxy and his right to lead such a
mass movement was questioned by religious authorities
he suddenly began preaching a *passagium generale,* that is
a crusade against the Turks. During his inquisition i
Avignon he swore to the pope that he never made a pac
with anyone to make a crusade, except one "for concord
and peace, and the unity of citizens." Was this crusade hi

intent all along? Was it an expedient to win the pope over to his side and escape the inquisition? This is hard to say.

The Bianchi of 1399

495   Frugoni, Arsenio. "La devozione dei Bianchi del 1399," in *L'attesa dell'età nuova nella spiritualità della fine del medioevo.* Todi: Centro di Studi sulla Spiritualità Medievali, 1962, 232-48.

A review of the movement with special emphasis on their millennial expectations that their peace movement was a prelude to the new age about to dawn with the turning of a new century.

496   Tognetti, G. "Sul moto dei Bianchi del 1399," *BISIMEAM* 78 (1967): 205-343.

A careful piece of history writing, reconstructing events from regional sources, many still in manuscript, separating out legend from actual events. Tognetti hypothesizes that the spirituality of Vincent Ferrer may well have been a source that percolated through the culture of Provence and emerged into the peace movement of the Genoese Riviera.

The Bianchi moved from town to town in nine-day processions, with chants of "mercy" and "peace," abstaining from meat, going barefoot, and wearing simple white dress, all penitential elements designed to signify their inner conversion as a prerequisite to converting their neighbors to peace. The movement affected most of northern and central Italy as it converged on Rome.

Similar peace movements included that of Venturino da Bergamo in 1335, the Pistoia movement of 1402, that of Cuneo in 1464, and that of Perugia in 1476 and 1486, all with remarkably similar language to that of the Bianchi.

497   Webb, Diana M. "Penitence and Peace-Making in City and
        Contado: The *Bianchi* of 1399," *Studies in Church
        History* 16 (1979): 243-56.

        This is the best, and still the only comprehensive
        English, account of this movement, so named after the
        white (*bianco*) dress of its members. Webb first traces the
        origins and follows the course of this wave of penitential
        pilgrimages that swept over Northern Italy, beginning in
        the Piedmont and converging south on Rome, spreading
        from the countryside to the cities, bringing reconciliation in
        the wake of processions, peace demonstrations, and
        festivals. The Bianchi's numbers were large, often in the
        thousands. The movement brought together peasants and
        cityfolk, the rich and poor. Webb stresses that "every-
        where the Bianchi went, peacemaking was their major
        function."

Other Movements and Aspects

498   Carli, Enzo. "La pace nella pittura senese." See **449**, 225-
        42.

        Focuses on Sienese painting, especially the great
        public works, "Maestà by Duccio di Buoninsegna and
        "Good and Bad Government" by Ambrogio Lorenzetti.
        Most especially in Lorenzetti's work, peace is inseparable
        from reconciliation among citizens and is, above all, the
        work of justice.

499   De Matteis, Maria Consiglia. "La pacificazione cittadina a
        Firenze nelle componenti culturali di Remigio de'
        Girolami." See **449**, 199-224.

        Focuses on Remigio's *De bono pacis*, the product of

the grave political crisis of 1302-4. While Dante sought peace through a universal monarch who would impose order upon Italy's unruly cities, this work is a plea for internal reconciliation and harmony in order to secure the survival of the Florentine republic against external enemies. Its basic outlook is Aristotelian and Thomistic: the good of the whole community is greater than that of any individual or faction.

Yet for Remigio this peace is not simply an imposed order, but the product of forgiveness of injuries and damages between citizens. Like the public state itself, it is based on Christian charity, which is the highest civic virtue. Far from hindering the happiness and virtue of the individual, the state and its peace is actually the chief means toward this human perfection. Peace is both temporal and spiritual, but unlike Thomas Aquinas, Remigio does not argue that external peace is inferior to the internal.

Also briefly traces Remigio's intellectual sources, and the evolving meaning of peace in the Western tradition.

500   Frugoni, Arsenio. "Il giubileo di Bonifacio VIII," *BISIMEAM* 62 (1950): 1-121.

Traces the history and the concept of the jubilee and the apocalyptic implications of great turnings of the century and shows the influence of Franciscan, Joachite, and Roman traditions in the feast. Then follows the history of the great pilgrimage of 1300 that brought together all classes, ages, and sexes in a spirit of penitence, reconciliation, and peacemaking in imitation of the Christians of the early church.

501   Gennaro, Clara. "Giovanni Colombini e la sua 'brigata'," *BISIMEAM* 81 (1969): 237-71.

This was a penitential movement dominated by the

"Gesuati." Poverty and reconciliation were their central motivations. The movement was centered on Siena but spread rapidly through Tuscany and Umbria in the 1360s. Members included both clergy and laity, and their influence on Siena had become so strong by the late 1360s that the authorities expelled them from the city, citing the influence of their ideas for the city's new divisions and "depopulation." An interesting example of how a peace movement can bring on repression and discord through its very attempts at reconciliation.

502   ——."Movimenti religiosi e pace nel xiv secolo." See 449, 91-112.

An excellent introduction to the Italian peace movements of the fourteenth century and a basic work in medieval peace studies. Surveys the Flagellanti in Lombardy, the Genoese coast and Tuscany in 1311, Venturino da Bergamo in 1335, Giovanni Colombini at Siena from 1350 to 1360, the Disciplinati at Florence in 1377, and the Bianchi throughout northern Italy in 1399. Peace — personal, familial, socio-political and religious — was at the center of all these movements. Their roots lay in the Bible and its Apocalypse, in penitential, monastic, and Franciscan traditions. Pilgrimages involving highly visible peace demonstrations, penitence, and the refusal to bear arms were all essential parts. In such movements as Venturino da Bergamo's the element of the nonviolent crusade was clearly emphasized.

The movements met with considerable hostility, especially in the cities, where such true pacifists as Giovanni Colombini and his followers were exiled under the accusation of dividing the citizenry. During the War of the Eight Saints in Florence (1375-78), the Disciplinati were suspected of treason by the government because of their pacifism and were eventually expelled from the city. Nevertheless, it was in the cities that the peace movements met their greatest success at bringing about reconciliation. Thus the ideal of the mendicant orders, that society's outcasts, the marginal *poveri*, become a religious and social ideal was fulfilled here.

503 Manselli, Raoul. "Equilibrio politico e ideali di pace al tempo di Giovanni di Boemia." See **449**, 155-74.

All the intellectual discussions of peace and the religious movements of repentance and reconciliation of the century derive from the tormented reality of Italian politics during the period. This article briefly outlines the political maneuvering around John of Luxembourg, king of Bohemia's role in Italy's troubles and the ultimate political settlement that attended it. Good background.

504 Miccoli, Giovanni. "Giovanni Colombini," *Storia d'Italia*. II, 1. Turin: Einaudi, 1974, 914-24.

A review of the movement set in the context of many of the spiritual and peace movements of the late fourteenth century. Other topics include Catherine of Siena, Giovanni delle Celle, and Bridget of Sweden.

Miccoli's account of Colombini is based largely on Gennaro (**501**), but he emphasizes that the heart of the movement was a mystical transformation, not simply the imitation of Christ's life of poverty found in many late medieval reformers. The greatest effect of the movement was among the poor and the marginal in Italian society.

505 Miglio, Massimo. "Gli ideali di pace e di giustizia in Roma a metà del Trecento." See **449**, 175-97.

Focuses on the ideas and actions of Cola di Rienzo,

who led a revolution restoring the Roman republic in 1347. While Rienzo is not a peacemaker in the sense we use the word here, Miglio's purpose is to demonstrate Roman concepts of peace by using the sources available for Cola's revolution. These include notarial documents, the anonymous *Life*, Cola's letters, and the letters of his friend and propagandist, Petrarch.

The sources make clear for us the intimate connection in late medieval thought between peace and justice, and the connection made in urban societies between these and political liberty. The sources also emphasize, however, that the justice Cola speaks of and provides is for the merchant classes of the city that will restore order and prosperity.

506   Petrocchi, Giorgio. "La pace in S. Caterina da Siena."
          See **449**, 9-26.

Catherine repudiated violence and factional strife within and among the Italian city-states. She was a true pacifist, who saw sin as the root of all conflict. Her concept of peace was both mystical and very practical. Peace is not simply *quies*, but is an activist seeking after reconciliation and reform.

Petrocchi analyzes her imagery, which is truly mystical, apocalyptic and Christocentric. Her notion of peace is linked inextricably to the welfare of the poor, the chief victims of violence. Her aims were three-fold: Christian unity, brought about in part through a crusade against the Turks; the unity of the church; and the return of the pope to Rome through nonviolent means. For her attempts to reconcile the pope to the Italian communes an assassination attempt was made on her, which she accepted as the price the peacemaker must be willing to pay.

507   Prandi, Adriano. "La pace nei temi iconographici del
       Trecento." See **449**, 243-59.

       Traces the concept both in its etymology and in its
artistic iconography in Greek, Roman and Hebrew senses.
While "Peace" was always a clear symbolic figure for the
Romans, in the Middle Ages peace is portrayed only once,
in Siena, as a figure (see **498**). In Trecento art it is relayed
through the kiss of peace, through the embrace of
forgiveness and reconciliation, through the dance, and
through the delightful summer garden, among other
images.

                        *   *
                          *

CHAPTER 7: *Alternatives to the Crusades. Peacemaking in the Non-Christian World 1100-1400*

Conversion as an Alternative to the Crusades

508   Berry, Virginia. "Peter the Venerable and the Crusades," in Giles Constable and James Kritzeck, eds. *Petrus Venerabilis 1156-1956*. Rome: Studia Anselmiana, 1956, 141-62.

Despite arguments that Peter opposed the Second and Third Crusades, this article presents evidence that this well-known peacemaker actually sympathized with these expeditions. See **516** for the opposing view.

509   Burns, R.I. "Christian-Islamic Confrontation in the West: The Thirteenth Century Dream of Conversion," *American Historical Review* 76 (1971): 1386-1434.

Christian attempts to win over Islam through nonviolent means went back to at least the eleventh century: translation projects and missions were all urged by such major figures as Peter the Venerable, abbot of Cluny, Jacques de Vitry, and Roger Bacon. By the thirteenth century these nonviolent methods had taken several distinct forms: secret persuasion via commerce; chaplains at Islamic courts; the direct approach of the Franciscans and other missionaries aimed at nonviolent confrontation.

Intellectual dialogue was carried on most importantly by the Dominicans, who opened language schools for missionaries and wrote intellectual treatises like Thomas Aquinas' *Summa Contra Gentiles* to confront the Moslems on the basis of doctrine and reason. Diplomatic work aimed at converting the Moslem leader; and finally, as a last resort, came the military solution. Burns' carefully balanced article should be read as a caveat to those who would make too simplistic and tight a chronological periodization between mission and warfare. See **515**.

510   Cutler, Allan. "Catholic Missions to the Moslems to the End of the First Crusade (1099)." Ph.D. dissertation. Los Angeles: University of Southern California, 1963.

Not seen.

511   ——."The First Crusade and the Idea of Conversion," *Muslim World* 58 (1968): 57-71, 155-64.

Cutler associates the Crusade with nonviolent conversion because both movements were concerned with winning over the Moslem. As examples of the "missionary" spirit of the First Crusade he cites Peter the Hermit, whose excesses at the head of a band of marauders can scarcely be called either nonviolent or aimed at conversion. Excerpted from **510**. See **522** for rebuttal.

512   Dunlop, D.M. "A Christian Mission to Muslim Spain in the Eleventh Century," *Al-Andalus* 17 (1952): 259-310.

Concerns a letter sent with a Christian mission by an anonymous "monk of France" to al-Mugtadir bin Hud, ruler of Saragossa (1049-81), urging him to convert to Christianity. The letter and its reply, written in the eleventh century, provide evidence for an alternative to the French "crusaders" then fighting in northern Spain.

513   Flahiff, George B. "Deus Non Vult: A Critic of the Third Crusade." *Mediaeval Studies* 9 (1947): 162-88.

On Ralph Niger's systematic criticism of the Third Crusade, written in 1189. The military pilgrimage to Jerusalem is of no avail unless it is joined by a spiritual pilgrimage to the mystical Jerusalem. While no "pacifist," Niger took a "non-interventionist" position condemning the war for several reasons. These include the need to address the "West's" own problems, largely heresy; the questionable value of intervention in the "East"; and the physical dangers of the journey. Niger also excludes several groups from participation: clergy (for their pacifism), penitents, women, the poor, the old, and the retired.

Flahiff's treatment is even-handed but is marked by Cold War assumptions.

514   ——."Ralph Niger: An Introduction to his Life and Works." *Mediaeval Studies* 2 (1940): 119-20.

Uses Niger's *De re militaris et triplici via peregrinationis Ierosolimitane* to illustrate his opposition to the crusades.

515   Kedar, Benjamin Z. *Crusade and Mission*. Princeton: Princeton University Press, 1984.

This is an important book both because of its sweep of the literature and the general balance of its conclusions. Kedar seeks to distinguish clearly the two movements of crusade and missionary activity and to then analyze the relationship between them, in the process exposing scholarly assumptions that, he contends, have conflated them. The book is divided into chapters dealing with the early centuries, the Christian reconquest of Spain, the problem of mission espousal and whether this was actually criticism of the crusades, the mendicant movement, and the contested thesis that crusading was actually seen as a means of advancing missionary work.

Kedar examines several movements that have been seen as precursors. The martyrs of Cordova, he asserts, were not seeking conversion but martyrdom; their non-violence was an act of defiance; and Albar's "sancta crudelitas" was actually a call for holy war. Conversion was avoided in Norman Sicily, since it would then be more difficult to exploit the conquered Moslems. Conversion was not a specific goal of Urban II at Clermont, nor does it appear as a motive in any extant papal letters for later crusades.

Kedar does find some evidence that espousal of missionary conversion was an implied criticism of the crusades but asks to what extent this was a direct outcome of moral criticism. He rejects such theories by Kritzeck (516) and Daniel (528), but corrects the overstated critique by Siberry (567) that Joachite influence was minimal. While Isaac de l'Étoile, Walter Map and Ralph Niger may have criticized the Crusades, Jacques de Vitry and Francis of Assisi praised the crusaders. The mendicants themselves may have preached the gospel to the Saracens, but they simultaneously preached the cross to Christians.

Kedar does demonstrate fairly convincingly that one should not see crusade and mission as part of the same movement. He overstates his position, however. Despite some evidence of "those Christians who objected in principle to all bloodshed," presumably clergy, there were also those "laymen in search of a high-minded reason for dodging a crusade." "While mendicants did provide martyrs, practical men could not regard this mendicant activity as a viable solution." Opponents of the crusades, including William of Tripoli, Roger Bacon ("too much a realist"), John Gower and others cited by Humbert of Romans were certainly not pacifists. Throop (**569, 570**) has mistakenly convinced all later historians that this was the case. Ramon Lull's stated desire for a life of missionary work was "of course, a literary device."

In the end Kedar exhibits the same value-laden history writing that he begins his book by criticizing. He reveals a modern preoccupation with current political trends and a cynicism toward evidence of peacemaking.

516	Kritzeck, James. *Peter the Venerable and Islam.* Princeton: Princeton Oriental Studies. Vol. 23, 1964.

An excellent analysis of the abbot of Cluny and his role in the major movements of the day, most especially his attempt to offer an alternative to the Crusades preached by his friend Bernard of Clairvaux. Kritzeck states at the outset that "Peter has been singled out, more than once, as the most peaceful man of his age." He gained a solid reputation in Europe for his political arbitrations and conciliations, as well as for his staunch opposition to Islam and insistence that the Holy Places be in Christian hands. His calls for the study of Islam and a campaign to convert it therefore show an activist approach to peacemaking and a truly nonviolent alternative to the Crusades in an age that knew little of modern toleration. Kritzeck prints the text of his *Liber contra sectam sive haeresim Saracenorum* pages 220-91.

517	Latourette. *Expansion.* See **369**, 2: 319-42.

Offers the best introductory survey of the missionary activity conducted as an alternative to the Crusades.

518   Marsh, Adam. *Epistolae.* J.S. Brewer, ed. *Monumenta
       Franciscana.* Roll Series, vol. 4. London: Longmans,
       1858, 413-37.

       Letter 246 of 1250 extolls martyrdom in the pursuit of
       peaceful conversion of the non-Christian.

519   Muldoon, James M. *Popes, Lawyers, and Infidels: The
       Church and the Non-Christian World 1250-1550.*
       Philadelphia: University of Pennsylvania Press, 1979.

       This recounts the history of Christian missions from
       the papal point of view. We see the papacy as actively
       involved with attempts at nonviolent conversion, using its
       diplomatic channels to assure the access and safety of
       missionaries in North Africa and in Asia as far as Tartary
       and China. An apocalyptic sense of the nearness of the
       last days and the necessity to convert the non-Christian
       world before the end certainly played a part in motivating
       the popes. Papally sponsored canon law also saw the
       possibility of coexisting peacefully with the Moslem
       world. By the late fourteenth century the main interest of
       the papacy in the Holy Land lay more in protecting
       pilgrims bound there than in stirring up yet another
       unsuccessful crusade.

520   Richard, Jean. *La papauté et les missions d'Orient au
       Moyen Age (xiiiᵉ-xvᵉ siècles).* Rome: École Française
       de Rome, 1977.

       An excellent survey of the topic. Traces papal support
       for, and formulation of, missions to the non-Christian
       world, ranging from the Levant to China. Papal motives
       were diverse, ranging from the political to the spiritual, but
       such missions as that of the Franciscans to the Levant did

offer an alternative to the violence of the crusades.

521 Southern, Richard W. *Western Views of Islam in the Middle Ages.* Cambridge, MA: Harvard University Press, 1962.

Reviews the wide range of Christian attitudes. Useful sections on Peter the Venerable, Joachim of Fiore, Roger Bacon, and William of Tripoli, all of whom recommended nonviolent conversion as an alternative to the Crusades.

522 Waltz, James. "Historical Perspectives on 'Early Missions to the Muslims': A Response to Allan Cutler," *Muslim World* 61 (1971): 170-86.

Takes up Cutler's (**510, 511**) association of crusader with missionary. A good rebuttal.

The Missionary Orders

523 Alphandéry. See **410**. II: *Recommencements nécessaires (xiie-xiiie siècles).* Alphonse Dupront, ed. Paris: Albin Michel, 1959, 210-237.

The Franciscan missions were very consciously seen as an alternative to the Crusades.

524 Bacon, Roger. *Opus Majus ad Clementem quartem.* J.H. Bridges, ed. Oxford: Oxford University Press, 1900, 3: 120-22.

Bacon's *Opus Majus* covers the intellectual universe of the medieval world. The book, "The Study of Tongues," chapters 13-14, presents an eloquent plea for the use of words above weapons in the conversion of the non-Christian. Toleration and missionary work for Jews,

Saracens, and pagans to the North and East are preferable to their destruction. In the case of the Crusades war brings only hatred and sends the unbeliever to Hell. True Christianity, on the other hand, was spread by simplicity of preaching and purity of life. History recounts many tyrants and evil men who have been overcome by nonviolence. The Teutonic Knights have actually maintained their Slavic victims in paganism because of their brutality. Bacon does not hesitate to expose the myth of the Crusades: the Teutonic Knights do not really want peace but to subject a people to slavery.

525   ——,*Opus Majus*. Robert B. Burke, transl. New York: Russell & Russell, 1962, 110-15.

Another, equally useful, edition.

526   Bonaventure. *Legenda maior* 9.5-9. See **454**, 266-71.

These chapters reveal Francis' desire to imitate Christ, even to his suffering and death. His desire for martyrdom lead him to the East to convert the Moslems or to be killed in the effort. A cogent rebuttal to those who would argue that the crusader, who sought to kill the non-Christian or to take his land, and the missionary, who saw his role as converting the non-Christian or being killed in imitation of Christ, were actually part of the same broad movement.

527   Christiansen, Eric. *The Northern Crusades*. Minneapolis: University of Minnesota Press, 1980.

Pages 145-46 summarize Roger Bacon's criticisms of the Crusades against the Slavs.

528   Daniel. *Concept.* See **455.**

The Franciscan concept of mission was based primarily on St. Francis' desire to imitate Christ through suffering and martyrdom. Their efforts were paralleled to an extent by those of the Dominicans, who established missionary colleges, wrote treatises encouraging toleration for the Moslems, and urged peaceful conversion rather than bloodshed. Yet the Franciscan tradition seemed to have been more radical in its approach. Francis set the tone and method in his own missions to the Moslems. Even during Francis' lifetime, the Franciscans were suffering martyrdom, choosing public confrontations on Islam's own field to proclaim Christ. Their peacemaking was thus an activist one. Roger Bacon, Raymond Lull, Peter John Olivi, and the radical Franciscan Spirituals all condemned the Crusades and urged nonviolent conversion. Well into the fourteenth and fifteenth centuries Franciscan missionaries were extending themselves out into Asia and the Near East, preaching conversion, willing to face martyrdom in imitation of Christ.

529   Duval. *Paix.* See **358.**

Briefly surveys the efforts of the Franciscans and Dominicans at nonviolent conversion and their criticisms of the Crusades.

530   Francis of Assisi. *Opuscula.* See **459.**

Esser's edition provides the best Latin text of Francis' works. An analytical index of important words and ideas makes this a useful reference tool. See **531.**

531   ——.*Omnibus.* See **460.**

Francis' *Rules* and Celano's *Life* provide ample
evidence of his willingness to lay down his life in imitation
of Christ in order to attempt the peaceful conversion of the
non-Christian. Nowhere does he show the slightest support of the Crusades. In fact, Celano recounts the story of
his condemnation of the Fifth Crusade against Damietta
while in the Crusaders' camp there. Like Christ, Francis
sent off his followers two by two to preach the Gospels,
"gathering the dispersed of Israel."

532   Moorman. *History.* See **463,** 226-39, 429-38.

Excellent background to the history, personalities, and
motivations of the Franciscan missions to the end of the
Middle Ages. Still the best available in English.

533   William of Tripoli. *De statu saracenorum.* H. Prutz, ed.
              Kulturgeschichte der Kreuzzuge. Berlin: Beilagen,
              1883, 573-98.

Recommendations for the nonviolent conversion of
the Saracens by one who lived on the spot and knew them
and the results of crusading warfare well.

Ramon Lull

534   Altaner, Berthold. "Raymundus Lullus und der Sprächen-
              kanon des Konzils von Vienne," *Historisches
              Jahrbuch* 52 (1933): 190-219.

Analyzes Lull's successful role in lobbying at the
general council of Vienne (1311-12) for the inclusion of
the decrees mandating the teaching of oriental languages at

major European universities to prepare missionaries for their work of nonviolent conversion of the non-Christian.

535   Atiya, Aziz S. *The Crusade in the Later Middle Ages*. 2nd ed. London: Butler and Tanner, 1938; reprint, New York: Kraus Reprints, 1965.

Pages 74-94 provide good biography and analysis of Lull's place in the history of the Crusades and in nonviolent conversion. Surveys some of his works, his travels around the Mediterranean, and his ideas on conversion and the study of languages for missionary work.

536   Brummer, Rudolf. *Bibliographia Lulliana. Ramon Llull Schriften 1870-1973*. Hildesheim: Gerstenberg, 1976.

A useful collection, 1331 items, unannotated, with an index of authors. Pages 61-64 list works on his missionary work and crusade ideas (nos. 873-923). English translations of his works are listed on page 17 (nos. 139-144).

537   Daiber, H. "Der Missionar Raimundus Lullus und seine Kritik am Islam," *Estudios Lullianos* 25, 1 (1981-1983): 47-57.

Not seen.

538   De Urmeneta, Fermin. "El pacifismo luliano," *Estudios Lullianos* 2 (1958): 197-208.

Modern reflections on the spirit of Lull's nonviolence. Less useful for a historical understanding.

539   Gibert, Rafael. "Lulio y Vives sobre la paz." See **48**, 125-
           70.

           The first part of this article examines Lull's writings
           and sees him as an early internationalist. Analyzes his
           approach to the winning of the Holy Land as a dual path:
           one of sensual war and one of intellectual war, for both of
           which one interested in peace must prepare. Peace is the
           result of an international order, brought about by an
           overriding international authority and by its agents, a
           knighthood devoted to Christian peace. Gibert emphasizes
           Lull's military schemes, his sensual war, more than his
           intellectual war, his plans for nonviolent conversion.

540   Hallack and Anson. *These Made Peace.* See **468**.

           Pages 65-73 offer a good, brief biography, placing
           Lull in the context of other medieval peacemakers.

541   Lull, Ramon. *Blanquerna: A Thirteenth-Century
           Romance.* E. Allison Peers, ed. London: Jarrold's,
           1926.

           The novel is Lull's treatise on Christian chivalry and
           his recommendations for its implementation. Chapters 80,
           "Gloria in excelsis Deo," and 81, "Et in terra pax
           hominibus bonae voluntatis," deal explicitly with Lull's
           plans for the papacy as a European peacemaker, which
           would then coordinate missionary efforts to convert, rather
           than conquer, the non-Christian world. This edition could
           use an update.

542   ——.*Selected Works of Ramon Llull (1232-1316).* Anthony
           Bonner, ed. and transl. 2 vols. Princeton: Princeton
           University Press, 1985.

A good, very well illustrated and edited collection. Good indexes. Not very useful for Lull as a peacemaker, however.

543   Peers, E. Allison. *Ramon Lull*. London: S.P.C.K., 1929.

A good biography with analysis of his works and missionary ideas. Still the best available in English.

544   Petry, Ray C. *Late Medieval Mysticism*. Philadelphia: Westminster Press, 1957, 142-69.

Reprints sections from Peers' edition of the *Blanquerna*.

The Apocalyptic Tradition

545   Bloomfield, Morton W. *Piers Plowman as a Fourteenth-Century Apocalypse*. New Brunswick, NJ: Rutgers University Press, 1962.

The apocalyptic tradition of *Piers Plowman* stretches back to the early Christian literature of consolation in tribulation, a promise of coming perfection, and the end of suffering. It offers a vision of unarmed struggle and nonviolent victory brought about through virtue and faith.

546   Costa, Dennis. *Irenic Apocalypse: Some Uses of Apocalyptic in Dante, Petrarch and Rabelais*. Vol. 21 of Stanford French and Italian Studies. Saratoga, CA: Anma Libri, 1981.

This is a dense, very difficult, but ultimately rewarding study of the apocalyptic subtext of several important works. Of interest here are Costa's comments on the uses of apocalyptic imagery and structures in *Piers Plowman*, Petrarch, and Dante's *Divine Comedy*. Apocalyptic is essentially a nonviolent process of transformation, of revelation, and of renewal that emphasizes the *patientia*, or nonviolent suffering of the apocalyptic characters. It is an anticipation of Paradise on earth that is made present in the very process of tribulation.

The medieval exegetical tradition, as exemplified by Rupert of Deutz, understood the nonviolence of the apocalyptic text; and Dante clearly understood that the text implied the passage to Paradise of an elect threatened by the violence of the age. Petrarch's *De vita solitaria* expressed this apocalyptic experience for the layperson, using the tradition of monasticism as a bloodless martyrdom.

547   Daniel, E. Randolf. "Apocalyptic Conversion: The Joachite Alternative to the Crusades," *Traditio* 25 (1969): 127-54.

This is a groundbreaking article, one of the first to make the connection between the Apocalypse and nonviolence in medieval society. The impact of this work is even more striking in that it discusses a group long considered one of the most dangerously "revolutionary" in the medieval church: the Franciscan and other Joachites. The anti-Crusade tradition was strong among these Joachites and can be traced back to the influence of the Calabrian abbot, Joachim of Fiore.

Joachim wrote of the events of his own lifetime in apocalyptic terms, and he saw the Moslem occupation of the Holy Land as one of the signs of the end time. Saladin was thus God's instrument to war against the Lamb sent to kill both the impious and the innocent in the process. Yet

Joachim himself experienced a conversion from whole-hearted support of the Crusade effort to opposition, realizing that the suffering of the innocent in the Apocalypse was that of nonviolent martyrs, not of earthly warriors. Christianity would triumph, he concluded, not by military victory but by preaching the word, by the faith and patience of those holy people who would introduce the Third Status of world history. Military struggle would only interfere with God's historic plan. In the end the "spiritual men" of the last days would convert the Saracens, the schismatic Greeks, and the Jews without violence, and all humanity would be united in peace, freedom, and contemplation.

With the development of the Spiritual faction within the Franciscan Order, this role was naturally associated with these contemplatives devoted to a life of poverty. Their literature, in works like *Super Hieremiam*, criticized papal efforts to launch further crusades. Any attempt to conquer the earthly Jerusalem ignored the historical role of the Heavenly Jerusalem, the apocalyptic Vision of Peace. Salimbene da Adam (**476, 479, 480**) recounts the widespread anti-crusade feeling among these and in the Dominican order. Such Spirituals as Angelo Clareno, Peter John Olivi, and Ubertino da Casale, when they did speak of the Crusades, expressed only opposition. The article concludes with a selection of texts from Joachim and the Joachite tradition expressing this opposition.

548 ——.*Concept.* See **528**, 76-100.

Incorporates much of the materials of **547** into a larger analysis of Franciscan opposition to the Crusades and alternative means of peacemaking.

549   ——."The Medieval Crusade and Vietnam: A Debate About War," *Lexington Theological Quarterly* 6 (1971): 93-101.

Not seen.

550   Douie, Decima L. *The Nature and the Effect of the Heresy of the Fraticelli.* Manchester: University of Manchester Press, 1932; reprint, New York: AMS, 1978.

Provides the best introduction to the lives, works, and ideas of the leading Spirituals discussed by Daniel in **547** and **548**, including Peter John Olivi, Ubertino da Casale, and Angelo Clareno.

551   Duby. *Three Orders*. See **390**.

The image of Jerusalem as the Vision of Peace, the Heavenly City, became associated in the eyes of many of the poor pilgrims who made up the mass of crusaders with the real physical city. Duby pinpoints the apocalyptic role that the city and the pilgrimage to it thus played.

552   Mayer. *Crusades*. See **402**, 9-40.

Both the millennial expectations of reaching the Heavenly Jerusalem and the long tradition of penitential pilgrimage combined in the popular imagination to launch thousands of the poor and unarmed toward the earthly Jerusalem both before and during the Crusade era. In fact, in launching the Crusades Pope Urban II tapped both eschatological and penitential currents. He also used the imagery of the Peace of God to stir Europeans to make the journey. While the military class may have been partially motivated by greed for conquest, the mass of Christians went to the Holy Land for three reasons: pilgrimage, penitence, and eschatology.

553   Porges, W. "The Clergy, the Poor, and the Non-Combatants on the First Crusade," *Speculum* 21 (1946): 1-23.

Urban II knew that an appeal to a purely military expedition would not rouse Europe to the Crusade, but that an appeal to pilgrimage would. He had a long tradition of unarmed pilgrimage to draw on, one that saw as many as 12,000 unarmed Christians make their way toward Jerusalem in a single expedition. When the pope realized the groundswell of support among the *unarmed*, he tried to eliminate or arm them, but all to no avail. The ranks of the Crusaders were swelled with the sick, the old, the unarmed, prostitutes, penitents, and pilgrims of all types seeking the New Jerusalem. Only one-sixth of the expedition were fully armed by the time it reached Nicea in Asia Minor, thereupon the proportion of the unarmed became even greater. Porges then goes on to analyze the various groups that made up the crusade: clergy, poor, women, children, etc.

554   Reeves, Marjorie. *The Influence of Prophesy in the Later Middle Ages.* Oxford: Clarendon Press, 1969.

The best introduction to the medieval Joachite tradition of apocalyptic prophesy and expectation.

555   ——*Joachim of Fiore and the Prophetic Future.* London: S.P.C.K., 1976.

A shorter version of **554**, with some new research.

556	Runciman. *Crusades.* See **403**, 1: 38-50.

Provides useful background to the long tradition of penitential pilgrimage to the Holy Land dating back at least to St. Helena in the fourth century. By the eleventh century unarmed pilgrims numbered in the thousands.

557	Vogel, C. "Les pèlerinages pénitentiels," *Revue des Sciences Réligieuses* 38 (1964): 113-45.

Not seen.

Voices of Protest

558	Adams, Robert P. "Pre-Renaissance Courtly Propaganda for Peace in English Literature," *Papers of the Michigan Academy* 32 (1946-48): 431-46.

English writers in the courtly tradition, from Hoccleve to Caxton, paid lip service to the idea of the just war, yet their works reveal some very urgent pleas for peace and condemnations of the disastrous effects of war upon a people. Such criticism came from a variety of sources: the standard medieval arguments against the spilling of Christian blood, the fact that war was both unprofitable and unreasonable, and a new bourgeois aversion to the disruption of commerce that war entailed. Some criticism also derived from the genre of advice to princes, reminding the prince that peace was one of his chief functions. Useful reminder that while such sentiments may well have been commonplace, the age saw no blanket glorification of war, even in the literature aimed at the warrior class.

559	Delaruelle, Étienne. "La critique de la guerre sainte dans la littérature méridionale." See **356**, 128-39.

This criticism stemmed from several sources. These include the Cluniac order and its emphasis on preaching and conversion, and the poets of Languedoc in their criticisms of the Albigensian Crusade.

560   Gower, John. *Confessio Amantis*. Terence Tiller, transl. and ed. Baltimore: Penguin Books, 1963.

Book III, lines 2226-2626, presents a detailed discussion of the merits of the just-war theory. Gower concludes that wars are really fought out of greed and bring destruction on nature, human virtue, God's law, and Christ's commandments. He then turns to the Crusades and determines that Christ preached peace and sent his disciples to do the same, not by killing but by the example of peace. He concludes by stating that all slaying is evil, no matter what the excuse. Tiller provides a good introduction to Gower's life and historical setting.

561   Langland, William. *Piers the Plowman*. J.F. Goodridge, transl. and ed. Baltimore: Penguin Books, 1968.

Books III, IV, and XV offer some glimpses into the popular expectations of apocalyptic conversion of the Saracens without the need for the Crusades. A good modern English edition.

562   Morris, Colin. "Propaganda for War. The Dissemination of the Crusading Ideal in the Twelfth Century." See **53**, 79-101.

A good reminder that the same forms of communication — troubadours poetry, pulpits, the influence of princely courts, the use of religious symbols like the cross

— were used to promote, as well as to criticize, the Crusades.

563   Owst, G.R. *Literature and Pulpit in Medieval England.* 2nd, rev. ed. New York: Barnes & Noble, 1961.

This study, still of use to students of literature and popular religion, analyzes sermons for insights into popular attitudes and literary genres that found their way into popular literature. Devotes some attention to sermons on war, the just war, and the knight. On the whole, as one might expect, unjust wars are condemned. Yet, at the same time, even just wars come in for some criticism, since it is usually the poor called upon to defend a land who are made to suffer for the conflicts of the nobility. The knights themselves are a lawless class who plunder the poor in peacetime and who flee battle in war, who despoil the church and crucify Christ. They are a burden on the people in both war and peace. Though many of these are stock topoi of the genre, the fact that such criticism was made before the most popular audience, sermon hearers, meant that a definite strain of antimilitar- ism did exist in late medieval England, one that finds its way into the more sophisticated pages of Langland and Gower.

564   Prawer, Joshua. *Histoire du Royaume latin de Jérusalem.* G. Nahon, transl. 2 vols. Paris: Editions du Centre National de la Recherche Scientifique, 1969-70.

Volume 2: 375-95 discusses medieval criticisms of the Crusades, relying heavily on Throop (**569, 570**).

565   Purcell, Maureen. *Papal Crusading Policy 1244-1291.* Leiden: E.J. Brill, 1975.

While Purcell's aim is to outline papal attempts to promote crusades with spiritual and material incentives, her introductory comment that the crusade was a form of imperialism whose demise escaped its proponents in large part because of the papacy's own role in diverting them to its own political ends is worth noting.

566   Runciman, Steven. "The Decline of the Crusading Idea," *Relazioni del x° Congresso Internazionale di Scienze Storiche* 3. Florence: International Congress of Historical Sciences, 1955, 637-52.

The major obstacle to further crusades at the end of the Middle Ages was the widespread skepticism about their Christian value. By the time of the Fifth Crusade peaceful conversion had become a major alternative the the Crusade movement. These strains of skepticism are reflected in as divergent sources as Humbert of Romans' *Opus tripartitum* and in Langland's *Piers Plowman*.

567   Siberry, Elizabeth. *Criticism of Crusading 1095-1274*. New York: Oxford University Press, 1985.

Like Kedar's work (**515**), this book's explicit purpose is to "refute" both the notion that there was a religious opposition to the crusades that offered conversion as an alternative to violence and that the crusades themselves were actually fought to further missionary conversion. Using much of the same evidence, uncovering more, and ignoring some more, Siberry rejects out of hand, and one by one, the theses of Kritzeck (**516**), Throop (**569, 570**), Daniel (**528, 547**), Prawer (**564**) and Richard (**520**), among others cited.
    While the criticisms collected by Humbert of Romans were certainly strong and reflected real opposition, they

were overwhelmingly intended to reform the crusade mechanism and aimed against specific abuses, not against the movement as a whole. Despite the fact that the thirteenth century saw the end of the crusades, Siberry asserts that these "still enjoyed considerable support from the faithful. There is no evidence to justify the claim that the thirteenth century saw a significant decline in popular enthusiasm." To explain away the discrepancy between the reality and her assertions, Siberry resorts to what could be called the post-Vietnam, Westmoreland syndrome: "A number of recent studies have shown that in the fourteenth century princes and nobles remained eager to avenge the Muslim victories, but their efforts were frustrated by dissension and internal problems in the West." In short, while popular support remained strong, and the military was eager to fight it out, "dissension" at home frustrated adventures abroad.

Good bibliography and excellent notes.

568   ——."Missionaries and Crusaders, 1095-1274: Opponents or Allies?" See **53**, 103-110.

A prelude to **567**. Siberry's use of Humbert of Romans' *Opus tripartitum* (see **569**) to show strong support for the crusade movement is akin to using General Westmoreland's suit against CBS to show continuing support for the war in Vietnam.

569   Throop, Palmer A. *Criticism of the Crusades: A Study of Public Opinion and Crusade Propaganda.* Amsterdam: Swets & Zeitlinger, 1940; reprinted Philadelphia: Porcupine Press, 1975; New York: Gordon Press, 1983.

This is one of the most important books for the history
of Christian peacemaking and for the peace tradition in the
Middle Ages. It directly tackles the topic of opposition to
the Crusades. This sprang up from the twelfth century,
almost from the start of the expeditions. Even the heroic
chansons de geste contained some sentiment for the
conversion of Moslems, rather than for their destruction.
The troubadour *sirventes* expressed the widespread horror
at the Christian crusade against the Albigensian heretics of
southern France. Roger Bacon expressed similar mis-
givings at the Teutonic Knights' efforts in the Baltic.
William of Tripoli, writing in the Holy Land, called for the
peaceful conversion of the Moslem. Throop examines this
form of missionary pacifism at some length, tracing the
Franciscan and Dominican traditions.

By the late thirteenth century this sentiment had grown
so widespread that Pope Gregory IX found himself unable
to stir further crusade fever. He therefore commissioned
the Dominican Minister General, Humbert of Romans, to
launch an investigation and to report his findings. The
result was Humbert's *Opus tripartitum*. According to
Humbert, among the opponents to the Crusades pacifists
were the most important element, and the most dangerous,
since their opposition was based solely on the teachings of
the Gospels. Then there were the missionary pacifists,
and the selective pacifists, who saw just-war criteria as
inapplicable to the Crusades, then the Joachites who
expected a nonviolent conversion foreshadowed by the
Apocalypse, then the troubadours, and wives separated
from their husbands, and so on through all the classes and
most of the occupations of medieval society.

570 ——."Criticism of Papal Crusade Policy in Old French and Provençal," *Speculum* 13 (1938): 379-412.

This criticism came from all walks of life. The greater part of the critics were laypeople of all social classes and occupations from tailor to courtly poet. Much of this article is incorporated into **569**.

571 Wentzlaff-Eggebert, Friedrich-W. *Kreuzzugsdichtung des Mittelalters*. Berlin: De Gruyter, 1960.

Surveys the large medieval literature in favor of the Crusades, including the writings of Bernard of Clairvaux. A good reminder that issues and positions were as complex in the Middle Ages are they are today.

572 Wood, Mary M. *The Spirit of Protest in Old French Literature*. New York: Columbia University Press, 1917, reprint, New York: AMS, 1983.

Examines the literature of the southern French troubadours who criticized the Crusades as un-Christian and the churchmen who called for them as corrupt. Criticism was leveled not only against the church, but also the nobility, who in both war and peace used their power to exploit the poor. The poets thus make clear the connection between peacemaking and social justice Examines such poets as Étienne de Fougères, Guillaume le Clerc, and Guilhem de Tudela.

* *
*

CHAPTER 8: *The Papacy As Peacemaker 1100-1500. Arbitration, Canon Law, and the Rights of Conscience*

Papal Diplomacy and Arbitration

573   *Archivum Historiae Pontificae.*

There is no general history of papal diplomacy in English. For specific studies see the yearly bibliographies in this journal devoted to the papacy and all aspects of its life.

574   Bainton. *Attitudes.* See **2**.

Pages 116-17 discuss medieval Catholic attempts to settle war by arbitration. While the discussion is largely based on Novacovitch (**599**), Bainton interprets his source to conclude that the medieval church's record on arbitration was poor. He does not cite Novacovitch's ample documentation for this, and omits all papal arbitrations before the Hundred Years War, and most during it.

575   Barraclough, Geoffrey. *The Medieval Papacy.* New York: W.W. Norton, 1979.

An excellent, popular introduction to general papal history. Includes discussion of the diplomatic activity of Gregory I and Benedict XII.

576   Barry, Colman J., O.S.B. *Readings in Church History.*
        Vol. 1, *From Pentecost to the Protestant Revolt.*
        Westminster, MD: Newman Press, 1966.

        Pages 621-25 present the text of the papal bull *Inter
        caetera* and of the Treaty of Tordesillas, which settled the
        dispute between Spain and Portugal over the extent of their
        colonial empires and helped set a precedent for arbitration
        in the early modern period.

577   Beales, Arthur C.F. *The Catholic Church and International
        Order.* Harmondsworth: Penguin Books, 1941.

        Where Bainton (**574**), from a Protestant point of view,
        attempts to downplay the peacemaking role of the medieval
        church hierarchy, Beales uses the same raw material, the
        evidence provided by Novacovitch (**599**), to paint a far
        more positive picture. Beales' main concern is with the
        twentieth century, but he does include material from the
        Middle Ages. Pages 28 to 35 deal with papal arbitrations
        and he sees the number of these in the period from 1150 to
        1450 as "enormous," with 100 cases in Italy alone.

578   Blet, P. "La répresentation pontificale de Gregoire I à
        Gregoire XIII," *Divinitas* 19 (1975): 335-52.

        Not seen.

579   Chaplais, P. "Le règlement des conflits internationaux
        franco-anglais au xive siècle." *Le Moyen Age* 57
        (1951): 269-302.

        Not seen.

580   Duval. *Paix.* See **358**, 64-98 *et passim.*

Contains excellent material on papal peacemaking through moral persuasion, the development of concepts of international law, the Peace and Truce of God, Third Orders, the just-war theory, and arbitration and other diplomatic work. Duval's scope is the entire Middle Ages and Renaissance. His discussion of papal diplomacy begins in detail with Nicholas I, but it concentrates on the period from the thirteenth through the fifteenth centuries. His approach is chronological, detailing the arbitrations, treaties, bulls, diplomatic and personal correspondence, interdicts and excommunications and other means used by individual popes to curb war. At least two dozen popes are discussed, concluding with Alexander VI (1492-1503). At times Duval tends to grasp at straws, equating genuine, and disinterested, papal attempts to settle international disputes with their political alliances with the Italian city-states and European monarchies. Duval is also led to explain papal plans in preparing crusades against the Turks as acts of peacemaking.

581   Fernessole, Pierre. *La papauté et la paix du monde de Gregoire XVI à Pie XI*. Paris, Beauchesne, 1948.

This is a survey from the late Middle Ages to the nineteenth century. Fernessole notes that Catholic peace is only indirectly the product of justice. Ultimately it is the work of charity. Pages 7-50 review the diplomatic activities of the medieval papacy.

582   Fliche, A. "Le rôle international de la papauté au Moyen Age," *Bulletin du comité internationale des sciences historiques* 1 (1928): 584-97.

Not seen.

583   Fowler, Linda. "Forms of Arbitration." See **615**, 133-47.

On the mechanisms and nature of arbitration in medieval society, with some attention to papal efforts.

584   Ganshof, F.L. *The Middle Ages.* Remy I. Hall, transl. New York: Harper & Row, 1970. From his *Histoire des relations internationales* I: *Le Moyen Age.* Paris: Hachette, 1953.

Though similar to Duval's (**580**), Ganshof's emphasis is the general history of diplomacy, not that of Christian peacemaking per se. In many ways this makes Ganshof's work less apologetic and more selective, but his treatment less unified. There is still a large storehouse of information on papal peacemaking here, but one must assemble it from the comprehensive, and chronological, treatment of the material. Papal diplomatic work begins in earnest with Gregory I (590-604) in his attempts to bring peace among contending barbarian peoples and to keep them from devouring the papal protectorate around Rome. With the creation of the Papal State by the Carolingians, the papacy bolstered its moral calls for peace with a physical base and the beginnings of a diplomatic apparatus. From the eighth century popes are actively negotiating treaties of peace and alliance, a role eclipsed in the ninth and tenth centuries by internal Roman disputes, but fully resumed during the Investiture Conflict.

In the high Middle Ages the pope became the arbiter par excellence, using a variety of means already in place for its own administrative needs to international disputes. These included papal legates, bulls and other diplomatic letters, legal appeal to Rome's powers of arbitration and final decision, the summoning of councils, the codification and dissemination of canon law as an international standard, and the foundation of the new monastic and mendicant orders, which often acted as an international corps of papal agents. From the time of Innocent II, the papacy's role as the supreme judge with unmatched spiritual, and considerable temporal, powers made it the arbiter of choice or of necessity among European rulers. With the removal of the papacy to Avignon, however, and the diminution of papal prestige in the fourteenth century came a new emphasis on real diplomacy, with the papacy acting very often as a disinterested third party, a truly honest broker. Ganshof details the institutions and methods of papal diplomacy during the late Middle Ages, it legates and nuncios, its peace conferences and diplomatic missions, and its role in developing such modern practices as diplomatic immunity and permanent missions. By the fifteenth century, however, the rise of the nation-states pushed the papacy from the center of active arbitration. Rulers now insisted that the popes carry on diplomacy only as private persons with no overriding authority to compel. By 1450 the papacy's modern role in international affairs was largely set.

585   Gaudemet, Jean. "Le rôle de la papauté dans le réglement des conflits entre états aux xiiie et xive siècles." See **48**, 79-106; reprinted in his *La société ecclésiastique dans l'occident médiéval*. London: Variorum Reprints, 1980, 79-106.

This is an important article, dense with useful information. Surveys the period from the Investiture Conflict, but concentrates on the important era of the Hundred Years War between England and France (1337-1453). Papal diplomacy had three purposes: the humanitarian, to allay and avoid the horrors of war; the evangelical, to spread the peace of the Gospels; and the practical, to forge a Christian unity to reduce the threat of external aggression or to preach and launch crusades. On the whole, papal diplomacy changed in effectiveness and forms from the eleventh to the fifteenth centuries. These forms ranged from outright intervention, to exercise of the pope's good offices, mediation, arbitration, and judgments, all ultimately sanctioned by the papal powers of interdict and excommunication. In the earlier period, that of the monarchical papacy of Innocent II and his successors, the papacy was able to intervene forcefully into the affairs of princes, claiming its place as the supreme judge of all Christendom, imposing settlements or arbitrations in conflicts, often through papal legates acting with full papal powers.

The reign of Boniface VIII and of the succeeding Avignon Papacy (1305-1378) marked a drastic shift. The rising power of the new nation-states and the decline of papal prestige through its overuse of spiritual sanctions for secular ends brought princes to regard the papacy with suspicion and to insist that it carry on diplomacy as a private person with no powers of compulsion. Yet during the Avignon period papal diplomacy reached new levels of sophistication precisely because of these new restrictions. Diplomacy was now carried out through a wide variety of personnel: curial officials, chaplains, apostolic notaries, penitenciaries, and, sometimes, high ranking clergy. Gives dozens of examples of papal efforts at peacemaking, treaties, arbitrations, and diplomatic missions and negotiations, arranged by papal reign. Offers a good review of scholarship up to 1961.

586 Giocchi, Orio. "L'opera di pace del pontificato romano nel Trecento." See **449**, 69-89.

Surveys the theory underlying the papacy's activities as arbiter in the fourteenth century. This theory was quite different from that of Pius XII, Benedict XV, Paul VI, and other modern popes, since medieval popes based their notions of peacemaking on the Gelasian theory of the two swords, which stated that the spiritual sphere, or sword, was superior to the temporal, and that the papacy had a jurisdictional authority over all secular states as members of Christendom. Thus papal efforts at peacemaking were actually those of a supreme judge who could impose settlements.

This is the theory presented in works by Egidio Romano, Giacomo di Viterbo, Agostino Trionfo, and Alvaro Pelajo on behalf of papal claims. Marsiglio of Padua, on the other hand, followed the Aristotelian notion of the natural autonomy of human society and declared that the secular authority was supreme in it.

Giocchi concludes by contrasting the high-flown claims of fourteenth-century papal theory with its rather unsuccessful attempts at imposing peace settlements.

587   Gruber, John. "Peace Negotiations of the Avignonese Popes," *Catholic Historical Review* 19 (1933-34): 190-99.

On the whole the partiality and ineffectiveness of the Avignon popes in bringing peace to Christendom have been exaggerated. Analyzes the diplomatic activity of each of the Avignon popes: Clement V, Benedict XII, Clement VI, Innocent VI, Urban V, and Gregory XI, who all tried to bring an end to the Hundred Years War. Papal efforts had three purposes: to alleviate the suffering of Europe's peasants, who were the chief victims of the war, to protect the property of the church and the unarmed, and to organize Christian resistance to the Turks. Gruber concludes that all through the Avignon papacy, "the Crusades were still at the heart of papal politics."

588   Hallenbeck, Jan T. "Instances of Peace in Eighth-Century Lombard-Papal Relations." See **574**, 18 (1980): 41-56.

A general survey of these relations. Concludes that, even in this dark age, the relations between papacy and barbarians were "at once more pacific and less hostile than is commonly supposed."

589   Hill, David J. *A History of Diplomacy in the International Development of Europe.* 3 vols. New York: Longmans, 1905-1914.

Volume one treats the period from the fall of Rome to Boniface VIII, volume two the fourteenth century to 1648, volume three to the modern period. Hill believes that the papacy acted largely out of self-interest and through cynical pronouncements of Christian goals. During the Hundred Years War it secretly served the interests of the French against the English, or generally of any "papist" party. Even such a pacifist pope as Benedict XII acted out of cynical motives of papal supremacy when he avoided all alliances with secular princes. His work for peace was actually an attempt to paralyze the initiatives of princes in the name of papal interests. John XXII's calls for a crusade to bring peace among warring princes was no more than a cynical ploy. Out of date, decidedly slanted toward the nation-state, especially the Anglo-Saxon variety, generally anti-papal, and subtly anti-Catholic.

590   Jenkins, Helen. "Papal Efforts for Peace Under Benedict XII, 1334-1342." Ph.D. dissertation. Philadelphia: University of Pennsylvania, 1933.

This is a detailed analytic study of an individual's work for peace. Introduces the personality of this pope, the former inquisitor and staunch opponent of heresy, Jacques Fournier. This rigid, honest monk had been an abbot and bishop, an authoritarian man devoted to justice, not especially suited to diplomacy and its compromises. While Benedict was no absolute pacifist — he favored war against heretics and infidels when necessary — peace among Christians was an absolute moral imperative, both for its own sake and as an example to non-Christians.

Jenkins emphasizes that Benedict retained his authoritarian rigidity even when dealing with princes. He disdained secular mediation and insisted on papal arbitration. Nevertheless, his reign was devoted to preventing, and then to ending, the Hundred Years War. His methods ranged from the promise of a crusade to unite the West, threats of excommunication and interdict, and the granting of dispensations. But the most frequent tool was his use of papal legates and nuncios, letters, and the influence of local clergy.

Benedict's policies were seldom successful. The reasons ranged from the belligerence and suspicions of the warring parties and his insistence that war could be used against heretics and infidels, which was exploited by secular princes to undermine his entire anti-war message. Benedict was also naive as to what made for lasting peace. Nevertheless, this study details the pope's continuing efforts to bring about a settlement of the war between England and France and his many arbitrations elsewhere in Western Europe.

591   Kyer, Clifford Ian. "*Legatus* and *nuntius* As Used to Denote Papal Envoys: 1245-1378," *Mediaeval Studies* 40 (1978): 473-77.

The shift from the papacy's use of legates with full powers to bind and loose to nuncios with limited missions and authority was a result of the new powers of the princes and their emerging nation-states. The papacy could also control nuncios far more effectively, and could use them to collect revenues. A useful, if limited, study. Kyer also lists all papal legates dispatched between 1243 and 1378 on peace and other diplomatic missions.

592   ——."The Papal Legate and the 'Solemn' Papal Nuncio, 1243-1378: The Changing Pattern of Papal Representation." Ph.D. dissertation. Toronto: University of Toronto, 1979.

A more comprehensive and detailed treatment of the materials outlined in **591**.

593   Lange, Martin. "Benoît XII, Pape Conciliateur." Ph.D. thesis. Paris: La Sorbonne, 1955.

Not seen.

594   Mattingly, Garrett. *Renaissance Diplomacy*. Baltimore: Penguin Books, 1964.

This is the classic work in English on the origins of modern diplomacy and its institutions. Discusses papal diplomacy only in the larger context of European trends. Pages 30-38 discuss papal practices in some detail. Useful account of the activities of Nicholas V (1447-55) and his work in making Rome the center of European diplomacy in the late fifteenth century.

595   McHardy, A.K. "The English Clergy and the Hundred Years War." See **53**, 171-78.

Focuses on the "immense" clerical contribution to the

English war effort. While there was some criticism of the war — Thomas Hoccleve and William Langland, for example, "show signs of pure pacifism" — "their anti-establishment and hence anti-war, attitude could be attributed to disappointed ambition," as both were disappointed office seekers. There were also some heretical Lollards who were against the war.

McHardy adopts outmoded historical assumptions about the un-"orthodoxy" of peacemaking in the Middle Ages and appears to reveal more about late twentieth-century British attitudes to war and peace than about fourteenth-century ones. His assertion that opposition from war stems from anti-establishment views and not, perhaps, vice-versa reveals dangerously unexamined assumptions about the past and the present, about what the "establishment" represents and what the nature of dissent is. One might as well ask whether disappointed office seeking is the result of pacifism and not vice-versa, as he asserts.

596   Mollat, Guillaume. "La diplomatie pontificale au xive siècle," *Mélanges...Louis Halphen*. Paris: Press Universitaire, 1951, 507-12.

A brief, and general, account of the methods of papal diplomacy during the period. A good supplement to the scattered material on personalities, institutions, and events found in **597**.

597   ——.*The Popes at Avignon*. New York: Thomas Nelson, 1963.

Mollat's primary purpose here is an account of the papacy's development during the Avignon period. Papal diplomacy is treated at various points in his discussions of individual reigns, institutions, finances, and politics. In general the Avignon popes had a three-fold foreign policy: to bring peace back to Europe, to recapture the Holy Land, and to bring the papal states back under papal control. At times these interests coincided, at times papal interests in each sphere conflicted with those in others. Good background for individual popes.

598   Muldoon. *Popes.* See **519**.

Briefly discusses the significance and consequences of the papal bulls *Inter caetera* and *Eximinae devotionis*, which settled conflicting claims between Spain and Portugal over New World settlements and conquests. While these bulls laid the foundations for later just-war claims to colonial conquests, they rested on the precedents of *Romanus Pontifex*, which actually ended the threat of war between the two nations over the Canary Islands. Papal arbitration was thus used as both a plowshare and a sword.

599   Novacovitch, Mileta. *Les compromis et les arbitrages internationaux du xiie au xve siècle.* Paris: A. Pedone, 1905.

Treats all arbitrations during the period, both secular and religious. Part I details the essential traits of medieval arbitration, individual cases, and the legal issues involved. Part II provides a chronological list of arbitrations. This gives few details of the cases themselves, but it does name the parties involved and the arbiters. Most arbiters listed are lay, but there are dozens of instances of clerical and papal arbitrations.

600   Perroy, Edouard. *The Hundred Years War.* New York: Capricorn, 1965.

Perroy wrote this classic history of the English invasion and occupation of his country while memories of the Nazi occupation were still fresh in French minds. His work is thus unabashedly pro-French, but also decidedly anti-negotiation, concession, what anyone brought up in the era of World War II would call "appeasement." For such history, then, any papal attempts to find a negotiated settlement to the Hundred Years War could only be seen as playing into the hands of the English, either out of clerical naiveté of the ways of the world, or through some form of active malice. Thus Benedict XII fares as poorly in Perroy's French version of his peacemaking as he does in Hill's Anglo-Saxon version. See **589**. Nevertheless, this work provides very useful background and detailed accounts of the peace negotiations that halted or finally ended the various phases of this war.

601   Schmutz, Richard. "Medieval Papal Representatives: Legates, Nuncios, and Judges," *Studia Gratiana* 15 (1972): 443-63.

Not seen.

602   Seward, Desmond. *The Hundred Years War: The English in France 1337-1453.* New York: Athenaeum, 1982.

A general narrative of events and personalities, with adequate bibliography and index. One must beware of Seward's viewpoint, however. He sees the systematic plunder of the French countryside and the massacre of its countryfolk as a business venture for the English nobility. He states that "it is arguable that the Hundred Years War was medieval England's greatest achievement."

603   Swanson, R.N. "The Way of Action: Pierre D'Ailly and

the Military Solution to the Great Schism." See **53**, 191-200.

Focuses on D'Ailly's thoughts on the ending of the schism between rival papal lines and his consideration of the use of force to bring one side or the other to terms. After giving all the pros and cons in good scholastic fashion, D'Ailly rejects the military option as both too risky logistically and as morally unacceptable.

604   Thomson, John A.F. *Popes and Princes 1417-1517*. London: Allen & Unwin, 1980.

Pages 98 to 103 briefly trace the evolution of papal diplomatic methods and institutions during the period, including the *secretarius domesticus,* the papal diplomatic secretariat, the development of the papal Curia as a center of international diplomacy, and the papacy's gradual shift from the use of ad hoc legates to more permanent nuncios and permanently based missions.

605   Ullmann, Walter. *The Growth of Papal Government in the Middle Ages*. 3rd ed. London: Methuen, 1970.

Pages 204-11 discuss the diplomatic activities of Nicholas I and Adrian II and their role in making the papacy a peacemaker for Europe.

606   ——."The Medieval Papal Court as an International Tribunal," *Virginia Journal for International Law* 11 (1971): 356-71.

Since the papal court possessed compulsory jurisdiction, at least during the high Middle Ages, it had the authority to lay down, interpret, and develop international standards that had a reasonable likelihood of enforcement. It could, and did, use both spiritual and secular power to impose treaties, end hostilities, eliminate barriers to trade and free travel, and depose unjust rulers.

607   Wood, Diana. *"Omnino Partialitate Cessante:* Clement VI and the Hundred Years War." See **53**, 179-89.

Here is the British equivalent of Perroy's thesis (**600**): the papacy, in this case Clement VI, lost all credibility as a peacemaker both because of the pope's desire to avoid war at all costs (appeasement) and because of his total partiality to France (betrayal). National divisions made all the papacy's international efforts hopelessly futile.

608   Wynen, A. *Die päpstliche Diplomatie.* Freiburg-im-Breisgau, 1922.

Not seen.

The Just War and the Rights of Conscience

609   See **266** to **284**.

610.   Hehir. "Just-War Ethic." See **29**, 4-24.

Thomas Aquinas systematized the thought of St. Augustine on the just war. His theory was an attempt to limit the scope of violence and to submit the warrior to the ethic of charity and the ideal of the common good. Just cause, legitimate authority, and right intention are the three foundations of Aquinas' theory.

611   Hubrecht, George. "La juste guerre dans la doctrine
        chrétienne, des origines au milieu du xvie siècle." See
        48, 107-25.

        Traces the theory from the New Testament to the
        period just before Vitoria and Grotius in the sixteenth
        century. Patristic thought, including Augustine, Isidore of
        Seville, Anselm of Lucca, Gratian, and Thomas Aquinas
        are among the chief formulators of the evolving theory.
        Luther and Erasmus are also examined. Relies heavily on
        Lebreton and Zeiller (**169**) for earlier sections.

612   Johnson, James T. "Historical Tradition and Moral
        Judgment: The Case of the Just War Tradition,"
        Journal of Religion 64 (July 1984): 299-317.

        Examines the role of the moralist in society, more
        specifically that of moral reflection in the just-war tradi-
        tion. To discuss war we must admit not only the strong
        tradition of pacifism, but also the role of the just-war
        tradition in limiting war.
        This article is a startling reversal of roles, reflecting
        the new strength of "pacifism" and the growing disrepute
        of the just-war among both activists and, apparently,
        scholars.

613   ——*Ideology, Reason, and the Limitation of War: Religious
        and Secular Concepts 1200-1740*. Princeton: Princeton
        University Press, 1975.

        While Russell (**617**) is cited by most medievalists as
        the best available reference on the just-war theory,
        Johnson proves far more useful and comprehensive. He
        covers not only the canon-law sources found in Russell,
        but also scholastic theory, the literature of chivalry, and the

tradition of *ius gentium* inherited from the Romans. Each, according to Johnson, appealed to a different class in medieval society. The first two to the clergy, the last two to the laity. In itself, Johnson stresses, the just-war theory is in no way Christian in the sense of biblical, theological, or canonical. It is the product of forces from both within and without the church, both secular and religious. Neither is it particularly Christian in its expression or application. Nor, Johnson asserts, can the full-blown just-war theory be read back into the Middle Ages, as Vanderpol (**618**) would assert.

Johnson clearly distinguishes the *ius ad bellum*, the just-war criteria for entering a war, to the *ius in bello*, the laws governing the conduct of a war. Both these concepts, he indicates, are really only fully developed in the modern era. Excellent summary of all four strains of the just-war tradition, with useful analysis of other major historians of the theory. In one respect, however, Johnson might be faulted for too literal acceptance of the chivalric literature concerning the proper conduct and rules of war, in part derived from his reliance on Keen (**614**).

614   Keen, M.H. *The Laws of War in the Late Middle Ages*. London: Routledge and Kegan Paul, 1965.

Uses contemporary literary sources to examine the nobility's attitude toward war and its proper conduct. Concludes that medieval warfare was, in fact, waged according to the chivalric standards that the romances and epics extol. Keen's chief sources, however, are aristocratic accounts like Froissart's *Chronicles*, a deliberate attempt to put the early events and personalities of the Hundred Years War into as heroic a framework as possible, concentrating on the deeds of the "noble," and ignoring the lives and sufferings of the poor. To realize the unreliability of Keen's interpretation, one need only

compare Froissart's stories of noble knights to the dry
accounts of slaughter and destruction found in other
chronicles or in such documents as papal letters and in
contemporary satiric or moral literature. See **558** to **571**.

615.   Kuttner, Stephan, ed. *Proceedings of the Fourth
International Congress of Medieval Canon Law.*
Vatican City: Bibliotheca Apostolica Vaticana, 1976.

Includes **583** and **616**.

616   Russell, Frederick H. "Innocent IV's Proposal to Limit
Warfare." See **615**, 383-99.

Innocent was the foremost canonist of his day, a
shrewd and subtle legal reasoner. His analysis of the just
war focuses here on the the issue of the lord's right, and
prudent decision, to wage war. Drawing on the previous
tradition of legal interpretation in Gratian, the Decretists,
and the Decretalists, Innocent focused his discussion of
obedience to a lord's commands by applying the Roman
law criteria of mandate to feudal relationships. For
Innocent concern over a vassal's property rights stemming
from either just or unjust war provided the check of
prudence over a vassal's — and thus a lord's — willingness
to begin a war. Self-interest seems Innocent's criterion.
Russell concludes that Innocent "discarded as unrealistic
an attempt to halt all recourse to wars and violence
between feudal lords" and that his theory had little practical
effect.

617   ——*Just War.* See **50**, 4-30.

The examination of a particular theory, intellectual

tradition, social or political institution through the provisions of canon law has been a highly popular and often
successful means of research since the 1960s. Church
law applied both to clerics and laypeople, and thus
collections of canon law have much to say about
contemporary attitudes and intellectual positions.
Russell's approach to the just-war theory was one of the
first and most influential of this school, and his findings
were taken by many to speak fully not only for the just-
war tradition but for the medieval church's entire attitude
toward war and peace. His range is both far more
restricted and more flexible than that, however; and this
book provides much useful discussion and material on
both the legal traditions and the real political and moral
dilemmas that gave rise to the church canons.

Russell's account shows the gradual evolution of just-
war criteria as applied in the writings of Gratian, the
Decretists, and the Decretalists, commentators on the
various collections of canon law. Their attitudes ranged
from Gratian's unequivocal call on subjects and vassals to
obey their lords, even in unjust wars; to his successors',
the Decretists', insistence that just wars need just authority
to declare them and that the prince's orders cannot be
obeyed if they contradict divine law; to the Decretalists'
insistence on the Golden Rule, forbidding war among
Christians. Russell traces the evolution of this and other
elements of the just-war theory, including the problem of
what constitutes just authority, how is the individual's
conscience informed, how is consensus concerning the
justness of a war derived. While most of his scholarship is
devoted to canon law, Russell does include some material
from the theological discussion of the thirteenth century,
which was generally more pacifist than the legal one.

618   Vanderpol, Alfred. *La doctrine scholastique du droit de guerre*. Paris: A. Pedone, 1919.

Still the best account on the development of the just war theory among Aquinas and his fellow scholastics.

Liberty, Conscience and Dissent

619   Baylor, Michael George. *Conscience in Late Scholasticism and the Young Luther*. Ann Arbor, MI: University Microfilms, 1971.

A scholarly treatment of the subject, at times difficult and dense, but even for the general reader it offers an excellent account of the development of the medieval, and Catholic, theory of conscience. Baylor's approach is both historical and topical. Concepts are introduced briefly, but fully explored within their historical development. Explores the Pauline notion of *syneidesis* and its later, broader, Vulgate translation as *conscientia* and the transmission of the idea of fear and shame from Jerome to Peter Lombard. Traces the notion of *synteresis*, as an innate sense of moral order among the scholastics from Peter Lombard to Abelard, Aquinas, and Bonaventure, and then proceeds on to Ockham and the late Scholastics, such as Gabriel Biel. Important background to what medieval political and religious thinkers meant when they discussed such notions as individual conscience, its education, its conformity to — and conflict with — human reason and law, moral commands, and divine revelation.

620   Bainton. *Attitudes*. See **2**.

Briefly discusses, on page 107, the developing theory of conscience from Abelard to Bonaventure. This finds its roots in Paul's Epistle to the Romans. Contrasts Abelard's notion that the individual conscience can be objectively wrong, but still subjectively right, with Bonaventure's notion that *synteresis,* our inner moral capacity, will — or should — always bring individual conscience into line with the revealed teachings of the church. While Bainton's discussion is brief, his influence has been great. His assertion that Bonaventure represents all of medieval Catholic doctrine on this matter is far too simplistic.

621   Callahan, E.R., C. Williams, and W. Dupré. "Conscience," *NCE* 4: 198-202.

A good introduction to Catholic teaching.

622   Chenu, M.-D. *L'eveil de la conscience dans la civilisation médiévale.* Montréal: Institute of Medieval Studies, 1969.

An impressionistic tracing of the development of the concept.

623   Congar, Yves M.-J. "Incidence ecclésiologique d'un thème de dévotion mariale," *Mélanges de Science Religieuse* 7 (1950): 277-92.

On obedience and authority within the church. Examines the theme, popular among Franciscan Spiritual dissidents, that at the time of the crucifixion, when all the Apostles and disciples had abandoned Christ, the church remained faithful in one person alone, the Virgin Mary at the foot of the cross. A vivid example of how Catholic tradition formulated the rights of individual conscience set against the power and authority of institutions and majorities.

624   ——."Les positions ecclésiologiques de Pierre Jean Olivi," in *Franciscains d'Oc. Les Spirituels ca. 1280-1324.* Cahiers de Fanjeaux 10. Toulouse: Privat, 1975, 155-65.

Explores the Franciscan's ideas of church government, authority, and the rights of individual dissent. While Olivi's notions of authority followed the traditional hierarchical model established by Dionysius the Areopagite, and while he considered the papacy as the natural head of the body of Christ on earth, despite the lives of individual popes who occupy the office; he stressed that the church is made up of all the faithful. The church bases the authenticity of its teachings on the Gospels; but the laws of Christ are also written in the hearts of the faithful by the Holy Spirit. When the pope or hierarchy fall into error, therefore, these truly faithful can constitute the true church. Should the truly faithful ever come into conflict with authority, and that authority should be in error, then they must follow their duty to disobey, relying on the light of their own consciences informed by revelation. Important analysis of an early exposition of the rights of conscientious objection.

625   Douie. *Fraticelli.* See **550**.

Still the best English introduction to the issues and personalities in the struggle between the Spiritual Franciscans and the papacy, including discussions of Peter John Olivi and Angelo Clareno, and the conflict between the Franciscans and the papacy.

626   Paul, Jacques. "Les Spirituels, l'église et la papauté," in *Chi erano gli Spirituali, Atti del III Convegno*

Internazionale. Assisi: Società Internazionale di Studi Francescani, 1976, 221-62.

The essential dilemma of the Franciscan Spiritual position — that the pope had no right to make any regulations altering the Franciscan Rule against the explicit wishes of St. Francis — forced them to develop an ecclesiology of dissent and the rights of individual conscience against the dictates of supposedly unjust authority. Such Spiritual thinkers as Peter John Olivi developed a theory to explain the suffering and deaths of the Spirituals at the hands of the hierarchy: like Christ condemned by the leaders of the synagogue, the Spirituals are the vanguard of a new age of the church. They retain the truth of Christian revelation, while any pope who alters the Rule of St. Francis is no longer the true pope, but a heretic who loses his jurisdictional powers. Thus, even while the papacy may be infallible, the individual person of the pope may err. Individual Christians must, therefore, follow the dictates of their own conscience, informed by the Holy Spirit, even if this brings them into conflict with authority.

627 Potts, Timothy C. *Conscience in Medieval Philosophy.* New York: Cambridge University Press, 1980.

Traces the development of such notions as *synderesis* (innate moral criteria), *scientia* (knowledge of temporal and changeable things), *sapientia* (the intellectual perception of divine truths), and *conscientia* (the human faculty that applies knowledge and innate criteria to individual cases). Analyzes the thought of Augustine, Peter Lombard, Aquinas, and Peter the Chancellor. Good background for a understanding of medieval perceptions of the rights and duties of the individual conscience.

628   Tierney, Brian. *Foundations of the Conciliar Theory*. New
        York: Cambridge University Press, 1968.

        One strain of influence on the Conciliarists' theory
        was the Franciscan Spirituals' assertion that the church's
        authority was diffused throughout the Mystical Body in
        both head and members, and that the individual had the
        right to dissent from papal authority if that authority were
        compromised. One method of expressing this was the
        story, popular among the Spirituals, that at the time of the
        crucifixion, when all the apostles and disciples had
        abandoned Christ, the true church lived on in one person
        alone, the Virgin Mary at the foot of the cross. Valuable
        study of how a theory of individual conscience can affect
        political structures. See **623**.

629   ———.*Ockham, the Conciliar Theory, and the Canonists*.
        Philadelphia: Fortress Press, 1971.

        Examines Ockham's analysis of the problem of
        individual conscience and its rights vis-à-vis the authority
        of institutions. Tierney traces Ockham's argument to its
        logical conclusions: that the individual following the
        dictates of conscience has the right and duty to disobey the
        church if it has strayed from the faith. While the pope may
        be infallible, it was up to the individual Christian to decide
        what pronouncements were in fact infallible and which
        deserving of obedience. Tierney pinpoints the danger in
        such a radical view of conscience: in the end it could be
        "utterly destructive" of consensus, tradition, and unity.
        This provides useful evidence that the medieval debate
        over conscience and duty was lively and open.

630   ———.*Origins of Papal Infallibility 1150-1350*. Leiden: Brill,

1972.

Tierney considers the debate over the Franciscan Rule as one of the primary sources for this theory, and focuses on the writings of Peter John Olivi. While Olivi stressed the infallibility of the papal institution, for precisely this reason he put special emphasis on the suitability of the individual occupying the office. For although the papacy was always worthy of obedience to its *magisterium,* its teaching authority, should the commands of an individual pope be contrary to the law of Christ, they must be disobeyed. This, he held, was the case in the pope's attempts to alter the Franciscan Rule. Those true adherents of the Rule, who defied the power of a heretical pope, were themselves the true church who maintained the light of revelation. It is thus up to the individual Christian to uncover the "keys of knowledge" hidden in Scripture and to judge papal decrees according to these.

631   Truhlar, K.V. "Obedience," *NCE* 10: 602-6.

Generally strongly authoritarian in tone, in keeping with the encyclopedia's Constantinian viewpoint. In his selection of biblical texts on obedience, Truhlar omits Peter's injunction in Acts 5:30 to obey God above man. Nevertheless, he does caution that obedience to human laws must be moderated by the degree to which human laws are informed by divine law.

632   Von Auw, Lydia. "La vraie église d'après les lettres d'Angelo Clareno," in *L'attesa dell'età nuova nella spiritualità della fine del medioevo.* Todi: Centro di studi sulla spiritualità medievale, 1962, 433-42.

Clareno was one of the leading Franciscan Spirituals, and his letters offer a rich source for their ecclesiology. In general, while Clareno stressed the duty of obedience to authority, and even the faithful's suffering under unjust authority, he argued that where the pope or hierarchy teaches anything that actively contradicts the laws of Christ as taught in the Gospels and revealed again in the Rule of St. Francis, the faithful must renounce their obedience, even if this means suffering and death in imitation of Christ and the Apostles. While not as radical as Olivi or Ockham, Clareno still clearly emphasizes the rights of individual conscience.

*   *
*

CHAPTER 9: *Humanist Peacemakers.*
The Sixteenth Century

Introduction

633 Gilmore, Myron. *The World of Humanism 1453-1517.*
New York: Harper & Row, 1952.

Despite its age, this is still an excellent introduction to
the age of the Humanists. The bibliography, though quite
out of date, is excellent for older scholarship.

634 Hale, J.R. *Renaissance Europe 1480-1520.* London:
Fontana, 1973.

A good introduction to the politics, culture and society
of the time. Hale draws a good balance between material
and cultural elements. Pages 87-100 deal with the
Humanists and briefly discuss their pacifism.

635 Harbison, E. Harris. *The Christian Scholar in the Age of
the Reformation.* New York: Charles Scribner's,
1956.

A general introduction to the Christian Humanists of
the Renaissance.

636 Hyma, Albert. *The Christian Renaissance.* Hamden, CT:
Archon Books, 1965.

Hyma has been often criticized for his insistence on a
"Christian Humanism," as if Renaissance Humanism grew
out of a secularist, antireligious spirit. Nevertheless, this

book well traces the spirit and accomplishments of Renaissance intellectuals, like Erasmus, for whom the revival of ancient learning and elegance went hand in hand with a revival of the most fundamental Christian values. Good background for understanding exactly what the Humanist peacemakers prized and why they often so bitterly criticized their contemporaries.

637   Kempis, Thomas à. *Of the Imitation of Christ.* Abbot
        Justin McCann, ed. New York: Mentor-Omega, 1962.

Thomas à Kempis is the best known product, after Erasmus, of the movement generally known as the Brethren of the Common Life. His spirituality was the epitome of the *Devotio Moderna,* a blend of simple ethical Christianity, the imitation of Christ, and a renewed emphasis on returning to the sources of Christian piety and learning. His work was, and remains, a best seller of enormous impact. This book has been translated into over fifty languages worldwide. It is important both for tracing the survival of monastic notions of inner peace into the end of the Middle Ages and for understanding some of the origins of the Humanist concepts of peace.

Thomas' work is divided into books dealing with the control of vices and the education of virtues. Peace is one of these virtues. It is the disposition of the inner person, a stillness and dispassion accompanied by an outer humility. Yet peace also implies an outer toleration and charity. True peace is not contentment, or remaining undisturbed, or mastery, but the life of imitating Christ. This is a handy edition.

638   *New Cambridge Modern History (NCMH).* Vol. I, *The
        Renaissance 1493-1520.* Denys Hay, ed. New York
        Cambridge University Press, 1975.

Newly revised, this is a standard reference work for Renaissance and early-modern European history. Essays on religious, political, social, economic, artistic, and intellectual life by renowned specialists in their fields. Well indexed. The volumes lack bibliographies.

639   ——.Vol. II, *The Reformation 1520-1559*. G.R. Elton, ed. New York: Cambridge University Press, 1975.

Continues the historical background into the Reformation era.

640   Ozment, Steven. *The Age of Reform 1250-1550*. New Haven: Yale University Press, 1980.

A excellent introduction to the political, spiritual and intellectual trends of the time. Topics include literacy and reading public, political institutions, especially the new monarchies, monastic piety, mysticism, the Franciscan reform, the *Devotio Moderna,* the Brethren of the Common Life, the Humanists, Erasmus and Luther. Ozment seeks to show that the period is not one of sudden break from medieval to Renaissance and Reformation, but really one of continuity of theme and accomplishment: the renewal of Christian life and learning.

641   Post, Regnerus R. *The Modern Devotion: Confrontation with Reformation and Humanism*. Leiden: Brill, 1968.

A review of the movement of simple, biblical spirituality and ethical life, including its manifestations in the Brethren of the Common Life, Thomas à Kempis, Erasmus and Luther's Reformation.

642   Rice, Eugene F., Jr. *The Foundations of Early Modern Europe, 1460-1559*. New York: W.W. Norton, 1970.

This is one of the best histories of the period. While it offers excellent analysis of the intellectual and reform trends of the day, it also places them fully within the material structures of the times.

Renaissance Thought on War

643   Bense, Walter F. "Paris Theologians on War and Peace, 1521-1529," *Church History* 41 (1972): 168-85.

Focuses on the controversy at the University of Paris over the crusade against the Turks and the impetus that it gave to Catholic theologians to derive the modern theory of the just war. The controversy came to a final head with Martin Luther's publication in 1529 of *On War Against the Turks*. Luther condemned the expeditions on several grounds: the papal Crusades were simply pretexts to raise money, no military effort could be fruitful without real penitence, and the Gospels condemned war. Luther's ideas and criticisms had long been in the air. As early as 1523 Josse Clichtove had embraced the just war in reaction to them, claiming that all wars against heretics and those attacking Christendom were just. Nevertheless, just wars must be entered and fought according to very strict criteria. In the meanwhile the church has not done enough for true peace, which includes inner serenity, social justice, and international cooperation. In the end however, war can be justified, since man has the moral duty of self-defense.

More vitriolic in his attacks was Noel Beda

Opposed to the Humanists and their new learning and
techniques, the Scholastic Beda attacked both Jacques
Lefevre's and Erasmus' biblical commentaries and urged
their public condemnation as "clandestine Lutherans."
Beda condemned the Humanists' emphasis on the New
Testament command of love of enemy and stressed the
importance of the Old Testament and the Church Fathers
instead. He argued that natural law and ancient custom
override Christ's words in the Gospels. Beda's most
effective attacks, however, were not intellectual but his
insinuations that the two Catholic reformers were "just like
Luther."

Robert Ceneau, on the other hand, stressed the virtue
and glory of the prince or princess who brings peace.
Peace among Christians should be the highest ideal. Like
Beda, however, he too argued that the Turks were not
heirs of Christ's peace, and therefore should be attacked.

Bense clearly demonstrates the mixture of academic
and nationalistic politics that went toward Paris' condemnation of Erasmus' *Complaint of Peace* as Lutheran heresy
and shows how the atmosphere of Counter Reformation
had already begun to link pacifism with subversion.
Henceforth Catholic orthodoxy would tend to equate nonviolence with the clergy, to stress the duty of war against
the enemies of that orthodoxy, and to be wary of the
enemy within who preached toleration.

544   Hale, J.R. "Armies, Navies, and the Art of War," *NCMH*
       2: 481-509.

A good review of the institutions, technologies, and
theories of war in the Renaissance and Reformation
periods.

645   ——."Sixteenth-Century Explanations of War and Vio-
        lence," *Past and Present* 51 (1971): 3-26.

The fifteenth and sixteenth centuries brought a new
emphasis on the warrior ethos and the "philosophy of
war." In place of a religious tradition toward war, "the
vein of masochism deeply implanted by the Christian
moral code," Hale sees a brave new world of "the learned
soldier, to whom the pen was almost as manageable as the
sword." This tough and trim new outlook coincided with
a vast new geographical learning that forced men to "think
from the world rather than from the Bible to seek guide-
lines."

According to Hale, moral considerations gradually
gave ground as an explanation for the causes of war. This
was due to the cynicism aroused by crusades, religious
wars, and papal political ambitions. During the sixteenth
century, the moral outlook was replaced by a psychological causality. The conflict between the virtues and
vices were now fought out within the individual, violence
itself being a form of psychological anger, or *ira*.

Hale also analyzes the "naturalist" tradition of war
criticism. Here the animal and plant kingdoms were
studied for analogies to human behavior. The author
makes it clear that these comparisons — of cooperation
nurturing, and toleration — are specifically analogical, and
that the study of nature in no way implied a theory of
biological determinism for Renaissance thinkers. Nature
on the contrary, is good in itself. Violence and evil stem
from some unnatural defects in it.

Hale is helpful in pinpointing literary themes. War as
a solution to domestic unrest becomes a common theme in

the sixteenth century, as does the literature of military service: morale, diet, pay, leave, etc. No other occupation, he asserts, is given such treatment.

646   ——,"War and Public Opinion in the Fifteenth and Sixteenth Centuries," *Past and Present* 22 (1962): 18-35.

"Public opinion about war did not become complex until the fifteenth century. During the Middle Ages there had been a preoccupation with the etiquette of personal combat . . . but war itself was taken for granted, and the arguments for and against it hardly discussed." Throughout the Middle Ages "there had indeed been a thin stream of pacifist argument passing from heresy to heresy." But only with the fifteenth century and the heretical Hussites, the Humanists, and the Protestant Anabaptists did any real pacifist movement emerge.

Hale also analyzes the culture of militarism. With the fifteenth century the military had finally come into its own. The Turkish threat spurred the creation of a new, slim and trim ethos for the fighting class, emphasizing the elimination of luxury and vice; a new warrior literature; and a new "aesthetic" of war, in fact a new "cult of war." An entirely new "polite conversation" developed on themes of war, a parlor game culture of strategies, justness, evils, and results. The printing press aided in the spread of this "new" militarist culture, and by the late sixteenth century governments were sponsoring history texts that were little more than propaganda pieces recounting history as a string of battles and victories. War propaganda poured forth from pulpits, theaters, and orations. Even the religious language of the Bible took on a new militarist tinge.

647   Solon, Paul D. "Popular Response to Standing Military
        Forces in Fifteenth-Century France," *Studies in the
        Renaissance* 19 (1972): 78-111.

        Not really the "popular" response, if by "popular" we
        mean the mass of people affected by war and peace, but
        that of the urban communes toward issues of taxation
        designed to pay for the new monarchies' wars. Solon also
        traces the new intellectual debate over the theory of a
        standing royal army.

The Humanists as Peacemakers

648   Adams, Robert P. *The Better Part of Valor: More,
        Erasmus, Colet, and Vives on Humanism, War and
        Peace 1496-1535*. Seattle: University of Washington
        Press, 1962.

        This is the most important work written to date on
        peacemaking during the Renaissance. Adams does an
        excellent job of setting the literary and scholarly careers of
        the Humanists into the historical context of war and peace.
        He focuses on the "London Reformers" (See **663**), who
        realized that no social reform or progress was possible
        without peace, and who therefore devoted much of their
        literary energies to it. These Humanists shared the
        Renaissance's great faith in human nature and therefore
        had a natural sympathy with the common folk of Europe
        and their plight at the hands of Europe's warlords.
        Drawing on medieval Christian ethics, a revived early
        Christian pacifism, and the neo-Stoic ideal of universal
        brotherhood, they questioned the basis of Europe's
        contemporary wars, generally concluding that if the just-
        war criteria of their religion and philosophy were
        scrupulously applied, a just war would be rare indeed.
            The Humanists' literary efforts were set in a very real,

and dangerous, context: the wars of Henry VIII, François I, Maximilian, and Charles V. To speak out against these absolutists was to risk one's career and, sometimes, one's freedom and life. Yet beginning with the Oxford lectures of John Colet in 1496 and continuing through the careers of Thomas More, Erasmus, and Juan Luis Vives, they bravely defended the cause of peace and of the common folk of Europe, condemning the savagery, mocking the social pretensions, and appealing to the Christian purpose of Europe's military nobility. It was Colet who first opened Erasmus' eyes to the need for this campaign, and Erasmus who made the first, and perhaps best, use of the new printing press to spread these ideas throughout the continent.

The tone, and fortunes, of their output varied with the outlook for war or peace in Europe, ranging from the bright optimism of Erasmus' *Praise of Folly* and Thomas More's *Utopia,* to the pessimism of Erasmus' *Julius Excluded* or of More's *Dialogue of Tribulation.* There was also the element of the educator in all the Humanists' works, aimed at the ruling classes in the hope that they might be converted to peace. Such works as Erasmus' *Education of the Christian Prince* and Vives' *Education of a Christian Woman* and *On Education* stress the destructive elements of a noble's education, the tales of violence and unrealistic deeds of bravery. They urged rather the true duty of the prince: the proper governing and protection of their peoples.

Adams stresses that the Humanists' words were not merely literary exercises. The Humanists had their enemies; they had often to face the accusation that they were soft on the Turks, opposing the crusade to defend Christendom. But all generally agreed that if a war against them could be waged according to all the criteria of the just war, it should then so be waged. They also observed, however, that if Christians truly lived as Christians and stopped killing one another, both their mutual strength and their example might even convert the Turk without bloodshed.

By the 1520s and the onset of both Reformation and a steady war policy, speaking out against war had become dangerous. Adams shows how the Humanists' letters reveal a new caution. More's letters become increasingly pessimistic of both chances for peace and the justice of Henry's rule as the Humanist is drawn further and further into the policy-making apparatus. Vives' letters urging Henry VIII to peace result in his being fired from his Oxford lectureship; his continued outspokenness on behalf of justice ended in his house arrest and final expulsion from England. Erasmus' continued message of peace ended in his vilification from both sides of the Reformation. More ended on the scaffold in defense of individual conscience and Christian unity.

649   ——."Pre-Renaissance." See **558**.

John Colet, Thomas More, and Erasmus, the "London Reformers," actually drew on a literary and social tradition of peacemaking in their works against war. Contemporary Christian reform movements, medieval and classical works on the blessings of peace, and the neo-Stoic ideal of universal peace were their chief sources. Their work stimulated both a courtly and a public acceptance of the idea. While their efforts had little immediate effect, their long-term impact was significant: their ideas set the pattern for all later forms of modern pacifism. Adams sees their pacifism as a dramatic break with medieval models, there having been, he asserts, little or no pacifism in the Middle Ages.

650   Bainton. *Attitudes.* See **2**.

Bainton has divided up Christian responses to war and peace into several, neat compartments. The early church was pacifist; the medieval, Catholic church clung to the Crusade and slowly evolved the just war. The Protestants, being the true inheritors of the early church, revived pacifism. Thus the Humanists, being by and large Catholics, adhered to the theory of the just war. Even such outright pacifists as Erasmus, Colet, Vives, Clichtove, and More used just-war criteria to condemn all real wars. While there is some truth to this, Bainton's oversimple scheme misses much.

651   Herding, Otto, and Robert Stüpperich, eds. *Die Humanisten in ihrer politischen und sozialen Umwelt.* Boppard-am-Rhein: Harald Boldt Verlag, 1976.

A collection of essays on the political and social context of the humanists. See **721** and **723**.

652   Hexter, Jack H. *The Vision of Politics on the Eve of the Reformation.* New York: Basic Books, 1973.

The Christian Humanists "were not philosophical observers analyzing the conditions of the world they lived in but committed men, wishing and hoping to change those conditions." Despite this, their relationship to Europe's ruling circle was ambivalent. The dilemma posed by Hythloday in Thomas More's *Utopia* typified their plight: should the independent intellectual and reformer ally himself to power in the hopes of bringing about change?

Their Humanism led them to assume that change was possible, and their role as educators encouraged their entry into the close circle of political advisors. On the other hand, their commitment to Gospel religion and its prophetic element led them to condemn much of contemporary life and politics. Their attacks on the ruling classes for their violence, their injustice, and their exploitation of the poor were not classical in inspiration, but biblical. Like unarmed prophets they sought not to bolster the status quo but to break it down and to change it with the fabric of Scripture.

But what place in the courts of princes was there for prophets? This is the situation that Hexter examines through the writings and careers of the Humanists, tracing their intellectual and religious backgrounds, outlining their major ideas for reform, and detailing their criticisms — including those of war and injustice — in contemporary Europe.

653   Hutton, James. *Themes of Peace in Renaissance Poetry.* Rita Guerlac, ed. Ithaca and London: Cornell University Press, 1984.

Surveys peace poetry in the Renaissance, which drew on a firm tradition of classical and Christian art. Only the "encomium," the pure peace poem, was new to the Renaissance.

Hutton divides his work into several thematic chapters. "Pax Aeterna" discusses the tradition in Greek and Roman poetry, including an excellent etymology of Greek and Latin terms for peace. This tradition extends through the Middle Ages and includes Dante, Petrarch, Jean Gerson, and the *Devotio Moderna,* as well as Erasmus and Clichtove in the Renaissance.

"Pax Poetica" examines the French literary tradition.

The form variously advocates peace, laments its absence, or awaits its near approach. While the Italian Humanists also used these topoi, the French really popularized them. "Pax Mundana: explores peace themes in sixteenth-century France, centering around the Italian wars, the Ladies' Peace, and other specific events and personalities. Later chapters deal with the theme of peace in the animal kingdom and with a renewed knowledge of Greek and Roman works and their use as models as late as Ronsard.

Well annotated, good indexes.

654   Lange, Christian Louis. *Histoire de la doctrine pacifique*. The Hague: Academy of International Law, 1927.

A survey that includes sections on several Renaissance peacemakers.

655   ——.*Histoire de l'internationalisme*. 3 vols. Kristiania (Oslo): H. Aschenhoug, 1919-1963.

Volume 1 presents discussions and selections from Erasmus, More, Vives, Josse van Clichtove, and Agrippa of Nettesheim. Lange's emphasis is on internationalism, not strictly nonviolence.

656   Patrides, C.A., and Joseph A. Wittreich, eds. *The Apocalypse in English Renaissance Thought and Literature*. Ithaca and London: Cornell University Press, 1985.

A collection of essays, with an excellent bibliography covering apocalyptic literature chronologically from the Bible to the twentieth century. Good index.

Essays by Bernard McGinn and Marjorie Reeves treat the medieval tradition; others focus on Elizabethan themes.

657   Woodward, William H. *Studies in Education During the Age of the Renaissance, 1400-1600.* New York: Columbia University Press, 1967.

An important introduction to the educational ideals and aims of the Humanists. Includes discussions of Agricola, Erasmus, Budé, and Vives.

John Colet

658   Colet, John. *John Colet's Commentary on First Corinthians.* Bernard O'Kelly and Catherine A.L. Jarrott, eds. and transls. Binghamton, NY: Medieval and Renaissance Texts and Studies, 1985.

Facing Latin and English texts of this landmark in biblical, and textual, criticism. Colet places Paul and his letter in their historical context. His commentary follows the epistle chapter and verse with careful analysis and very frank parallels to the pomp, vainglory, and corruption of his own time. The imitation of Christ and his folly, patience in tribulation and the life of love, service and wisdom are central themes that helped shaped the program of the English reformers.

Good introduction and notes.

659   Harbison. *Christian Scholar.* See **635**, 56-67.

Good introduction to Colet's life and ideas.

660   Jayne, Sears R. *John Colet and Marsiglio Ficino.* Oxford: Oxford University Press, 1963.

Traces the influence of the Italian Renaissance and its emphasis on human perfectibility, and ethical responsibility, on the English Humanist's ideas of reform.

661   Kaufman, Peter Iver. *Augustinian Piety and Catholic Reform: Augustine, Colet, and Erasmus.* Macon, GA: Mercer University Press, 1982.

The work of the Humanist reformers was based on fundamentally Christian sources, most especially in their emphasis on the ethical life of moral responsibility.

662   Schoeck, R.J. "Colet, John," *NCE* 3: 990-91.

A good, general introduction, with some bibliography.

Thomas More

663   Chambers, R.W. *Thomas More.* Ann Arbor, MI: University of Michigan Press, 1962.

Despite its Catholic and anti-Henrician biases, this remains the classic introduction to the man and martyr in his historical context. Chambers' interpretation has been the starting point for much of the historiography on More over the last generation. Chambers sees More as a liberal determined by the standards of his age: devoted to freedom of thought, if not of speech, of toleration of the bodies of heretics if not of their books, as long as they did not attempt to assert their beliefs as the one truth. As chancellor More attacked Wolsey as the prime mover of Henry's war policy. More died a true, and heroic, martyr to his ideals of a unified Christendom and of freedom of conscience.

664 Derrett, J. Duncan M. "St. Thomas More As a Martyr,"
 Downside Review 101 (July 1983): 187-93.

 A review of Jasper Ridley's *The Statesman and the
 Fanatic: Thomas Wolsey and Thomas More* (London:
 Constable, 1982). Derrett doubts Ridley's scholarship and
 criticizes his analysis of More from a twentieth-century
 point of view. More must be viewed in the context of his
 age. His convictions were genuinely religious, and he
 certainly did die the martyr's death for his witness.

665 Hexter, Jack H. *More's Utopia: The Biography of an
 Idea*. Princeton: Princeton University Press, 1952.

 Analyzes the hermeneutic process through which the
 author's idea is transformed into the reader's by the act of
 publication. This is a landmark study covering the ana-
 tomy of *Utopia* as a published work, various interpretations of its discourse, the "dialogue of counsel," More's
 inner debate on the role of the intellectual in service to the
 state. The study concludes with a very useful discussion
 of Cardinal Wolsey's disastrous policy of war, over-
 taxation, and social injustice and More's own catastrophe
 in playing a part in that policy through his service, just as
 Hythloday had warned.

666 Logan, George M. *The Meaning of More's Utopia*.
 Princeton: Princeton University Press, 1983.

 More's book has proven too sophisticated for its
 readers over the past five centuries. In the twentieth
 century much criticism has seen it as a "holiday piece," not
 to be taken seriously. Despite *Utopia's* obvious satire,
 however, it is essentially an accurate depiction of current
 European war and social policy.
 Utopia differs from Aristotle and Plato's vision of the

state, yet it does present a society unconstrained by "revealed Christian imperatives." While More does not approve of all the Utopians' actions, and clearly highlights their conflict with Erasmian ideals, he is creating a "best commonwealth" with all the wisdom available to the rational and secular. Thus Utopia's wars are not justified in any Christian sense, but on a natural-law basis. While *Utopia* does not offer an image of a reformed Europe, it does debunk the entire chivalric myth. In the end, however, More sets out to show the failings of both Christian Humanists and cynical "secularist" views. His work is a unique contribution to Western political thought.

Good notes, bibliography and index.

667   Marius, Richard. *Thomas More. A Biography*. New York: Alfred A. Knopf, 1985.

A modern portrait, fully in keeping with the 1980s in its demythologization of the saint and martyr and in its attempt to paint the complex, often contradictory, and sometimes dislikeable man. Nevertheless, Marius admits that he ended by liking the man and recognizing that he died a martyr to Christian unity. This biography treats More's life and career, both political and literary, and only tangentially discusses his pacifism. Nevertheless, it does make some very pointed remarks. More, for example, did fully support the good reputation of English arms abroad, if not all the war aims of Henry VIII. Even More's Utopians, while they loath war and butchery of any kind, still engage in both, if admittedly at second hand by hiring people to do it for them. Still, the Utopians fight only to avenge wrongs or depredations committed against them- selves or their neighbors, and they do not attempt wars of conquest. In short, though Marius does not analyze this, they follow the precepts of the just war.

More tried everything in his power as chancellor to

exterminate Protestant heretics, even taking glee when
some were burned at the stake.   Only Henry VIII's
backing away from a strict orthodox line in favor of
accommodation calmed More down.   In the end More
"seems much less the pacifist than modern scholars have
made him." Brief annotations, adequate bibliography.

668   More, Thomas. *A Dialogue Concerning Heresies*. Thomas
            M.C. Lawlor, Germain Marc'hadour, and Richard
            Marius, eds. See **673**, 6 (1981).

This is a work that must be considered in any
treatment of More's peacemaking, because here, as a
defender of Catholic orthodoxy, he urges the use of force
against Lutherans, equating them with Turks and thus the
object of the most heated war. Nevertheless, he does
warn that where no violence or compulsion is committed,
no one has the right to apply either.

669   ——.Excerpts in **672**, 196-216.

670   ——.*A Dialogue of Comfort Against Tribulation*. Louis L.
            Martz and Frank Manley, eds. See **673**, vol. 12.

This was written in 1534, when More was in the
Tower awaiting execution. The work is an extended
meditation on the Christian virtues of Faith, Hope, and
Charity in an attempt to alleviate his own fears and to
exhort others to nonviolent suffering under persecution. It
is a dialogue between an uncle and nephew in Hungary
just before the Turkish conquest in 1529. Their discussion
focuses on their fears of living under the tyranny of
infidels, and it concludes with their determination to
follow the example of Christ in defending their faith
without violence, even with their lives.

The point of the work was twofold. It was first a call on Catholics to resist evil, whether from Turk or Protestant, in a nonviolent, Christian way. Second, it was an indictment of the tyranny of Henry VIII and More's declaration of nonviolent resistance to it. Toward the end of the dialogue he declares that "the Turk is but a shadow" of the evil that all Christians must resist: the powers of violent tyranny. His ultimate refusal to violate his conscience in the end posed a far greater threat to Henry's tyranny than any violent opposition could ever hope to achieve.

671 ——,Leland Miles, ed. Bloomington, IN: Indiana University Press, 1965.

Another good edition.

672 ——.*The Essential Thomas More*. James J. Greene and John P. Dolan, eds. New York: Mentor-Omega, 1967.

A handy English, paperback edition of his works by two noted scholars. Their introduction provides a good brief biography and an appreciation of More's paradoxes and inconsistencies. They note that "men like More are a threat and a scandal to the single-mindedly earnest, to the 'true believers'." Includes **669** and **674**.

673 ——.*The Yale Edition of the Complete Works of Thomas More*. Various editors, 9 vols. to date, New Haven: Yale University Press, 1965-.

Excellent English editions, by scholars of note, of all of More's works. Among those published so far see **668**, **670** and **674**.

674   ——.*Utopia.* Edward Surtz, S.J. and Jack H. Hexter, eds. See **673**, vol. 4.

This book has stirred debate over its real meaning and intent since it was first published in 1516. More's vision took two parts. Book One criticizes contemporary European society through the observations of Hythloday, an explorer returned from the New World. Book Two details his observations on Utopia, the land he has visited. This framework allows More to make some damning criticisms of Christian Europe both directly and by way of contrast, and to suggest paths of reform.

Book One begins with a discussion of whether Hythloday should accept royal service as a state counselor. He refuses with an attack on Europe's princes for their preoccupation with war at the expense of wise administration. They are dominated by a lust for power that is fed on the false myths of chivalric romance and of ancient conquest. In reality war is the work of thieves, whose profession is indistinguishable from that of soldiers. Kings do not want peacemakers in their councils, in fact the entire structure of government is geared to a state of continuous war and war readiness. Such policies bring ruin to all civilized life as they impoverish people with heavy war taxes. Continuous war or war hysteria ultimately brings moral breakdown at home and a lust for violence until all creative, constructive, and peaceful pursuits are considered effeminate.

Book Two deals with Utopian customs and institutions. This is a description of a society guided solely by human reason, though open to divine grace. It is neither anti- or un-Christian but represents the ideal pre-Christian state capable of greater perfection. The Utopians are trained in the arts of peace. They reject even brutal sports, like the hunt, and even consider butchery a lowly trade. Nevertheless, being the product of natural reason alone, they are trained in defense and do conduct just wars, but only as a last resort. When exposed to the truths of Christianity, they embrace them eagerly.

More's treatment of domestic violence and the violence of injustice in Book One have become a classic in the Western tradition. Discussion focuses on the suggestion of a certain cleric that the chief way to reduce England's ever-increasing crime rate is greater punishment: the death penalty, even for theft. Hythloday gives More's answer: greater punishment is not deterrent; in fact, it even increases the boldness of criminals to commit murder rather than be caught for lesser crimes. The true solution to the crime rate is the alleviation of social injustice: poverty and exploitation, the greedy land grab of large landowners against small farmers who are pushed off the land and into the cities for lives of poverty and crime. Social justice, and less severe punishment, are his prescriptions.

Facing Latin and English texts, excellent introduction, commentary on each passage, excellent index and bibliography.

675 ——.See **672**, 23-96.

A good paperback edition.

676 Surtz, Edward, S.J. *The Praise of Wisdom: A Commentary on the Religious and Moral Problems and Background of St. Thomas More's Utopia.* Chicago: Loyola University Press, 1957.

An excellent commentary on the work's meaning and interpretation. Chapter 17, pp. 270-71 are especially useful for issues of war and peace.

Juan Luis Vives

677   Gibert. "Lulio y Vives." See **539**, 148-69.

Vives was a famous Humanist and internationalist. His literary works, letters to popes, kings and emperors, and his personal contacts all strove to carry on Erasmus' work. His themes were constant: the horrors of war, the insignificance of princes' motives for waging them, the suffering of the innocent, the need for educational reform and for Christian unity. Humanity is by nature peaceful, and this peace has been restored by Christ.

Vives also addressed the Turkish question and concluded that there were worse calamities than living under their yoke: the oppression of Christian princes who use fraud, conquest, and domination in place of Christian virtues of rule and justice. Christians should and can overcome the Turks, but they must do so with the spiritual and material goods of Christianity. These can be used after a general unification and reformation of Christendom. All Christians, of whatever station, must take on their duty to become peacemakers. This is especially true of Christian princes.

678   Tobriner, Marian Leona, S.N.J.M. *Vives' Introduction to Wisdom: A Renaissance Textbook.* New York: Columbia University Press, 1968.

This was Vives' most influential work, first published in 1540. Given the increasingly polarized state of Europe, its gentle tone is all the more surprising, but this goes far to explain its appeal. The book quickly became a standard textbook in the English school curriculum, and it appeared in 76 editions by the 1570s, including one in Mexico City. The work ranges over a broad field of topics: wisdom, beauty and strength, body and soul, learning, food, sleep, social life, love, religion, and Christ. It offers a compendium of Humanist teachings.

Humans are capable of the greatest love and peace, yet the violence of war reduces them to a level below that of beasts. The chapter "On Charity" presents Vives' prescriptions for peacemaking. Christ has given us his Golden Rule and ordered us to love our enemies and those who persecute us. Christ's own nonviolence is a compelling example for imitation. No true Christian can hate. Instead, true Christians "who study to bring peace among men, and to preserve tranquility safe and sound, shall be called the children of God."

Tobriner's introduction provides excellent background for the life and career of this disciple of Erasmus, including his difficulties with the English crown for his peacemaking activities.

679   Woodward. *Studies*. See **657**, 180-210.

Reviews his life, works, and educational and reform ideas, especially in his *De trahendis disciplinis* of 1531, a complete guide to educational training, staff, school site, curriculum, games, and exercise, all in an effort to produce the best Christians. Fully in the tradition of Erasmus.

Desiderius Erasmus

680   Bainton, Roland H. "Erasmus and the Persecuted." See **734**, 2: 197-202.

Not on Erasmus' views but on his active efforts to intercede for persecuted individuals. A good reminder that the Humanist writer lived as he wrote.

681   ——.*Erasmus of Christendom*. New York: Charles
        Scribner's, 1969.

An excellent review of Erasmus' life, friends, and
works set within their historical context. Bainton makes
good use of selections from the Humanist's works and
provides good analysis of most of these. He makes us
aware throughout that Erasmus was one of the first writers
to truly grasp the importance of the printing press. He also
allows us to appreciate Erasmus' life-long devotion to
Christian toleration, unity, and consensus. A late chapter
deals with his personality, personal appearance, and
habits; while the final one treats the growing suspicion and
irritability of his final years, his constant trouble from both
Protestant and Catholic sides, and emphasizes his claims
to belong to all Christendom. Handsomely illustrated
from contemporary sources, very well annotated, with
excellent bibliography.

682   ——."The Querela Pacis of Erasmus, Classical and Chris-
        tian Sources," *Archiv für Reformation Geschichte* 42
        (1951).

The sources for the *Complaint of Peace* lay in Stoic
philosophy and natural history.

683   Bietenholz, Peter G., and Thomas B. Deutscher, eds.
        *Contemporaries of Erasmus: A Biographical Register
        of the Renaissance and Reformation*. Vol. 1, A-E; vol.
        2, F-M. Buffalo: University of Toronto Press, 1985.

Well illustrated, brief biographies, arranged alphabetically, with good bibliographies. Volumes thus far
include such figures as Colet, Clichtove, and More.

684   Brachin, Pierre. "*Vox clamantis in deserto:* Réflexions sur
le pacifisme d'Erasme," *Colloquia Erasmiana
Turonensia.* 2 vols. Jean-Claude Margolin, ed.
Toronto: University of Toronto Press, 1972, 1: 247-
76.

Three themes dominated all of Erasmus' life and
work: the reform of literature, his "philosophy of Christ,"
and peace. On deeper examination these themes turn out
to be facets of the same reality: for Erasmus textual work
is born out of the need for internal renewal that will
overcome the evils of the church and of society.
Throughout his works he stressed that no matter how just
a war might seem, its crimes and calamities fell principally
on the innocent. His works on war and peace reached an
immense audience and were printed in dozens of editions.

Yet, for all of Erasmus' popularity, Brachin's assessment is negative: while the Humanist was deeply sincere in
his beliefs, his ideas affected only a very small circle of
intellectuals and had little impact on society. His analysis
also lacked any understanding of economic causality or of
the importance of the foreign policy of states. Instead, he
saw the chief cause of war in the failings and passions of
princes. His analysis of the conflicts of his day lacked any
understanding of the modern state or its institutions.
Instead, they sought causes in mental and moral frame-
works. In the end Erasmus was so unsuccessful because
his anthropology of violence was so naive and fantastic.

Brachin also analyzes Erasmus' ideas on the crusade
against the Turk. Generally he accepted the idea, if such a
war could be completely just in its motives and execution.
He rejected absolute pacifism, the type associated with
Luther (See **643**) and used nonviolence only as a tactic,
attempting to avoid the extremes of either side of the
Reformation debate. Brachin concludes that ultimately
Erasmus was stuck in the Middle Ages. The signs of his

times escaped him because he could not use modern psychology, sociology, or political economy. Today, on the other hand, we have institutes that can study war scientifically.

685   Broadhead, Meg. "War is Sweet to Those Who Have Not Tried It," *Catholic Worker* 45,1 (Jan., 1979), 8.

A modern appreciation of one of Erasmus' most popular adages against war. See **698**.

686   *Colloquium Erasmianum*. Mons: Centre Universitaire de l'État, 1968.

Includes George Chantraine, "*Mysterium* et *Sacramentum* dans le *'Dulce Bellum'*," on pages 33-45. For Erasmus the sacraments are the visible manifestations of Christ within the church, the *mysteria* of our relation with the sacred. These sacramental mysteries are at the root of Erasmus' view of Christ's peace as well, which is the visible manifestation of the mystery of his nature. Erasmus' spirituality, as well a his views of peace, were thus fully doctrinal and sacramental, not simply secular and ethical.

687   Chapiro, José. *Erasmus and Our Struggle for Peace*. Boston: Beacon Press, 1950.

A very personal and modern reappraisal, with a translation of the *Querela Pacis* as "Peace Protests." See **695**.

688   Cytowska, Maria. "Erasme et les Turcs," *Eos* 62 (1974): 311-21.

The Turkish question was the one major exception to

Erasmus' pacifism. Educated by the Brethren of the
Common Life, who produced a constant stream of anti-
Turkish propaganda in the fifteenth and sixteenth
centuries, and warned by the strong feelings of anti-
Lutheran hostility emerging in Europe, Erasmus thought it
best to accede to the call for a crusade lest he be accused of
heresy for his pacifism. Despite his approval of such a
war, however, Erasmus continued to stress that reason
would have greater effect than force of arms and that
Christians should destroy their own sins before setting off
to destroy those of the Turks.

His attitude to the Turks had three main elements: a
moral renaissance of Christians, an attempt to convert the
Turks by moral example, prayer and the proclamation of
Christian truths, and — only after all else fails — a crusade,
but this to be fought with the most just methods. Even if
such a war were waged, Christians killed were not to be
considered martyrs. These ideas are best expressed in
Erasmus' *Ultissima consultatio de bello Turcis inferendo*
(**715, 716**), which, according to Cytowska, is an intellectual justification of Hapsburg imperial policy.

689.   Erasmus, Desiderius. *The Adages of Erasmus*. Margaret
Mann Philips, transl. and ed. Cambridge: Cambridge
University Press, 1968.

An excellent translation and edition of these short
works on moral lessons and proverbs. See **698, 701, 712,**
and **717**.

690   ——.*Charon*. See **714**, 113-19.

Published in 1529, this is one of Erasmus' most
powerful, and popular, dialogues. Charon, the ferryman
of Hell, encounters Alastor, an avenging spirit. Charon is

busy preparing a large new ship for the sudden influx of souls damned to hell as a result of three Christian rulers — Henry VIII, François I, and Charles V — now busy preparing for a world conflagration and mass extermination. The war of words between Lutherans and Catholics will soon come to blows, and Charon will be fully employed. Up above the friars preach the false doctrine of the just war: to the French they say God is on their side, to the English and Germans, that the war is not their's but God's. Victory is certain, but — if they should get killed — they'll fly straight up to heaven. As Alastor leaves, he tells Charon to hurry back over the Styx: there are already 200,000 damned souls waiting to cross to Hell. The colloquy provoked an imperial "white paper" that blamed the work on Charles V's enemies. Vives was later prohibited from translating it into Spanish.

691   ——.*The Collected Works of Erasmus.* Various eds. Toronto and Buffalo, NY: University of Toronto Press, 1974-. See **710**. See also **718** for updates on its progress.

692   ——.*The Colloquies of Erasmus.* Craig R. Thompson, ed. and transl. Chicago: University of Chicago Press, 1965.

The standard English edition of these works, which Erasmus started writing in 1497 as Latin exercises for his tutorials. He began to introduce characters and plots only in 1522. They were first collected for publication in 1518 and reached twelve editions by 1533. While Erasmus never really considered these works very important, they had an immense influence both for their pedagogical value and for their religious, social and political criticisms. Despite their eventual placement on the Index of Forbidden

Books, they influenced Rabelais, Shakespeare, and even Walter Scott. They remained a standard school text into the nineteenth century. Thompson published a shorter collection in **714**. This collection includes **704, 708,** and **713**.

693   ——.*The Complaint of Peace.* See **699**, 174-204.

This appeal to the power of the press and of the new public opinion that it unleashed quickly became a best seller after its publication in 1517. It blends the Sermon on the Mount with newly revived Greek and Roman views of war and peace, especially those of the Stoics. Peace is the law of the universe. It is reflected in the order of the solar system and the laws of physics and biology. Erasmus' cosmology contrasts sharply with that of nineteenth-century Darwinists: his universe is built on love, cooperation, mutual attractions and harmonies that cooperate to guarantee life and peace. Human nature shares this tendency to peace. Yet contemporary Christian society has been corrupted. Modern peace is merely a sham that hides corruption and violence. Monastic peace is simply a flight from the world, an inner calm that only realizes a part of true peace. Christian peace, instead, is the highest of all virtues, and Christianity the religion of peace.

The chief culprits in this decline from Christian virtue are Europe's rulers who destroy the works of peace: cities and rich farmlands, trade and learning. The just-war excuses of princes are shams. Wars are fought out of "anger, ambition, and stupidity." The causes of princes have little in common with the concerns of the common folk. Churchmen aid the princes in their destruction. But, Peace asks, "what does the Bible have to do with a shield?...What filth is the tongue of a priest who exhorts war, evil, and murder!"

By contrast, Peace urges positive peacemaking: Christians must refuse to cooperate with the warmongers and reject war propaganda. They must realize that wars destroy more than they are ever fought to gain and raise every private vice into a widespread plague.

694   ——.T. Paynell, transl. La Salle, IL: Open Court, 1974.

This is a reprint of the 1917 edition, which was itself reprinted from "a rare old English version," probably that of 1802. Still, the text is well printed and presented, and the translation seems to have been modernized. No introduction, notes, or bibliography.

695   ——.José Chapiro, transl., as "Peace Protests." See **687**.

A handy, contemporary translation.

696   ——.*Cyclops, or the Gospel Bearer.* See **714**, 120-29.

First published in 1529, this is a dialogue between Polyphemus, a soldier, and Cannius. Polyphemus claims to be a soldier of Christ: he carries a bible around and settles all disputes with his battle axe. Asked whether he recalls Christ's command to turn the other cheek, Polyphemus replies "I've read that, but it slipped my mind."

697   ——.*The Education of a Christian Prince.* Lester K. Born, ed. New York: Columbia University Press, 1968.

First published in 1516, Erasmus' Prince is the antithesis of Machiavelli's, written in 1513. It was an immediate success, going through 18 editions in Erasmus' life alone and over 40 all together. Its influence on

English education was immense. The work focuses on the connection between Christian leadership, liberty, and peace. Such leadership must always be exercised in full consciousness of the Christian liberty of the princes subjects, which is both spiritual and political. The prince who exercises tyranny reduces his subjects to the level of animal slavery and is no legitimate Christian ruler. Consensus and restraint should be the tools of Christian rule.

But if the prince is to rule as a Christian, what models should he follow? Erasmus' purpose here is to demythologize militarism, to redirect princely education. First, the prince must reject pagan models: the false dreams of military glory, the bloodthirsty examples of Alexander, Xerxes, Caesar, Arthur, and Lancelot. These were all world robbers, tyrants drunk with ambition. The military class at peace is no better than at war: they live off the work of others, squander wealth on luxuries, produce no useful products.

Erasmus then outlines his education for peace and justice, the duties and responsibilities of the prince. In one chapter alone, Eleven, is waging war considered as a real possibility. Here, however, the Humanist details the risks and evils of war and contrasts them to the greater benefits of peace. While canon law, Augustine, and Bernard of Clairvaux may sometimes appear to approve of war, Christ teaches against it. "He rejoices to be called the Prince of Peace; may you do the same."

'98   ——.*Erasmus Against War.* See **689**, 308-53.

Included in the 1515 edition of the *Adages*, it is an expanded version of his *Letter to Anthony Bergin* (**706**) written in 1514. Also known as *War is Sweet to Those Who Do Not Know It (Dulce Bellum Inexpertis* or *Bellum*

Erasmi). This is an open letter to Europe's leaders, pleading for peace and analyzing the nature of war and individual responsibility for it. Aristotelian philosophy and Roman law have so corrupted Christian revelation that the meaning of true Christianity is lost. Most Christians honestly believe that their religion condones meeting force with force, accumulating wealth and honor, and fulfilling only external obligations.

War is the ultimate corruption of true religion, and military service nothing but banditry and barbarism in disguise. Even the just-war provision of war as a punishment for wrongdoing and the right to defend national sovereignty are shams. In a true court a wrongdoer is convicted by judge and jury before punishment. In war each side prosecutes the other, and the ones punished are chiefly the innocent: the old, women, and children. Even the claim of defense must collapse before the facts: when princes go to war it is the people who suffer. It is they who ultimately give sovereignty, and it is their interests that are harmed in the end.

Even the war against the Turks would be a mistake, for if Christians put away their cross of nonviolence, they themselves become Turks. The best way to conquer the enemies of Christ is to gird the spiritual weapons of the Gospels: the sword of the Word, the helmet of salvation, the shield of faith. True Christianity can be regained by the simple imitation of Christ as revealed in the Gospels.

Erasmus then presents several arguments against war: the Stoic, of universal brotherhood; the naturalist, showing the harmony and peace of the universe; the medical, which compares war to an epidemic; the practical and legal, focusing on the injustices of war; and the religious, the truths of Christian revelation. Christianity is truly a religion of peacemaking; true Christian lives must be devoted to this not only in words but also in action.

699 ——.*The Essential Erasmus*. John P. Dolan, ed. New York: Mentor-Omega, 1964.

This is an excellent, and convenient, collection of several of Erasmus' most enduring works, including the *Handbook of the Militant Christian* (**703**), *The Praise of Folly* (**711**), and *The Complaint of Peace* (**693**), and *On Mending the Peace of the Church* (**709**). Dolan's introduction is also very helpful. He notes at the outset that criticisms leveled against Erasmus for what the 1980s branded "secular Humanism" are wrong. The scholar was sincerely motivated by a Christian desire for peace and charity: these were the essential themes of all his works. Dolan briefly reviews his youth and education, his literary career and travels throughout Europe, his troubles during the Reformation, his final refusal of a cardinal's hat, his death, the later fate of his works at the hands of the Counter Reformation, and their continued modern appeal.

700 ——.*The Funeral*. See **714**, 92-112.

First published in 1526, this colloquy is a satire on the "art of dying" literature of the late Middle Ages. A respected general, Balearicus, is on his deathbed. Two witnesses exchange gossip, revealing how the general has grown rich from defense contracts and other "robberies, sacrileges, and extortions."

701 ——.*The Grub Pursues the Eagle*. See **689**, 229-65.

On the true nature of military heroism.

702   ——.*Guerre et paix dans la pensée d'Erasme.* Jean-Claude
        Margolin, ed. Paris, 1973.

        A collection of Erasmus' works on war and peace.
        While the texts are translated into French, this remains a
        useful guide.

703   ——.*The Handbook of the Militant Christian.* See **699**, 24-
        93.

        Written in 1501 to convert an arms manufacturer, this
        is Erasmus' earliest work condemning the glorification of
        war. It is a lengthy commentary on St. Paul's exhortation
        to Christians to become real soldiers of Christ, armed with
        the spirit and the true weapons of learning and piety. See
        also **707**.

704   ——.*The Ignoble Knight.* See **692**, 424-32.

        This appeared in 1529. Harpalus ("grasping,"
        "greedy"), the braggart soldier, encounters Nestor, the
        urban swindler. Harpalus seeks Nestor's advice on how
        to buy an aristocratic title and life. Nestor replies that his
        brand of nobility involves the company of high society
        expensive clothes, empty conversation, absurd coats of
        arms, and pedigrees. A noble reputation is greatly helped
        by syncophantic writers and publishers who prostitute
        themselves to honor the soldier. Nestor tells Harpalus that
        the basic principles of knighthood come down to this:
        robbing travelers and merchants, spreading threats of
        death and destruction, of total war, intimidating the
        peaceful into acquiescence. At all costs the soldier must
        avoid the poets, people like Erasmus: whatever they write
        is quickly spread around the world to confront the lies of
        soldiers.

705   ——.*The Julius Exclusus of Erasmus*. Paul Pascal, transl.
       Bloomington, IN: Indiana University Press, 1968.

The authorship of this tract has long been the object of
great debate, and well it might be, since it is a contemporary attack, in the most savage satire imaginable, of
Pope Julius II, the warrior pope who had recently died.
Pascal accepts Erasmus' authorship, fixes its writing to
1513/14 and its publication to 1517.
The title is a play on the pope's name and means
Julius Excluded from heaven. In this dialogue Pope Julius
arrives at heaven's door leading an army of Christians
freshly slain in the European wars that he has led or
instigated. He is met by St. Peter, who refuses him entry.
A heated debate ensues in which Julius recounts his
military exploits, his magnificent building programs, his
wealth and splendid court, his treaties made and broken
according to the need of the hour, his bloody wars and
warrior triumphs (one of which Erasmus witnessed first-
hand in Bologna in 1506).
To Peter's reply that heaven's gates open only for the
works of mercy, praising Saints Francis and Benedict,
Julius counters that his methods have long been used by
Catholic popes. He begins to rant about his absolute
power within the church, to mock Christian poverty, toil,
and nonviolence. By this time Peter has had enough and
closes the gates, and the dialogue, abruptly.

706   ——.*Letter to Anthony of Bergen*. Peter Mayer, ed. *The
       Pacifist Conscience*. Harmondsworth: Penguin
       Books, 1966, 53-59.

This dates from March 1514 and ranges over the
darkening political situation in Europe. The crusade

against the Turks is once again in the air. Erasmus
expresses his doubts over the possibility of ever waging a
just war. If one looks at past wars every one would be
disqualified using the strict just-war criteria. The history
of the Roman Empire with its endless list of pretexts of
legal grievances to justify its conquests is a case in point.
No, on final analysis, all the wars of kings are fought on
flimsy pretext. "Our wars, for the most part, proceed
either from ambition, from anger and malice, and from the
mere wantonness of unbridled power, or from some other
mental distemper." The real causes of war are "the
private, sinister, and selfish motives of princes." This is
the embryonic form of his *Erasmus Against War*. See
698.

707   ——.*Letter to Paul Volz*. John C. Olin, ed., *Desiderius
        Erasmus: Christian Humanism and the Reformation.*
        New York: Harper & Row, 1965, 107-33.

This first appeared as the preface to the 1518 edition of
the *Handbook of the Militant Christian* (**703**). With Pope
Leo X's bull calling for a crusade against the Turks
Erasmus remarks that a crusade against Christian vice is
certainly needed, but that such a crusade against Turks
was on shaky moral grounds. He notes ironically that
even if a few Turks should survive the Christian
onslaught, the divisions and hatreds of Christians for one
another, and their tyrannies, vices, and lusts would
dissuade even those survivors from converting. Erasmus
urges, instead, a pamphlet war and propaganda campaign
to convert the Turks before any military option. He
complains that if anyone should deter men from war, he is
marked out as an enemy of Christianity and a heretic. Yet
those who urge men on to killing are not seen as enemies
of the teaching of Christ and the Apostles.

708   ——.*Military Affairs.* See **692**, 11-15.

First published in 1522, this is a dialogue between Hanno, a civilian, and Thrasymachus (Bold Fighter), named after Plato's "might-makes-right" spokesman in the *Republic.* To Hanno's naive questions on the attractiveness of the military life, Thrasymachus answers honestly: rapine, butchery, theft, sacrilege, and moral cowardice. When pressed to explain how he ever entered such a life, the soldier replies that " a preacher declared from the pulpit that war is just." After Hanno condemns the profession of "burning houses, looting churches, violating nuns, robbing poor people, murdering harmless ones," Thrasymachus expressed fears that Hanno might change his conscience from clear to cloudy, a disagreeable prospect.

709   ——.*On Mending the Peace of the Church.* See **699**, 327-88.

Dolan calls this "the last will and testament of Erasmus." Written in 1533 at the height of the Reformation struggle, and only three years before his own death, the work continues to shine with the same themes that had dominated his life: conciliation, compromise, forgiveness of enemies. For many years after his death it remained a program for his Humanist followers throughout a divided Europe.

710   ——.*Paraphrases on Romans and Galatians.* Robert D. Sider, ed. John B. Payne, Albert Rabil, Jr. and Warren S. Smith, Jr., transl. See **691**, vol. 42, 1985.

Not seen.

711   ——.*The Praise of Folly.* See **699**, 94-173.

This is Erasmus' best-known work, still a best-seller today as it was when first written in 1509. It is a wide-ranging satire covering the contemporary moral, social and political scene, mocking abuses of every kind and of every social class and profession. "Folly," the hero and chief speaker, becomes a foil for the "folly of Christ," the simple life of Gospel imitation.

While a wise man has no place in war, the Fool finds full employment there. Bandits and all sorts of sociopaths are its true leaders. Even the church, built on the blood of the martyrs, now has its full share of warrior popes and bishops, as well as priests only too eager to urge on bloodshed and destruction. True Christians, those who practice Christ's nonviolence, are a minority and are considered mad fools by the world at large.

712   ——.*Sileni Alcibiades.* See **689**, 269-300.

Written in 1515, this is an attack on the just-war theory, a mockery and a pretext created by rulers to rob the people.

713   ——.*The Soldier and the Carthusian.* See **692**, 127-33.

First published in 1523. A monk encounters a former acquaintance who has returned home from a life as a mercenary — broken, impoverished, and diseased — his soul "as pure as the Paris sewer."

714   ——.*Ten Colloquies.* Craig R. Thompson, ed. Indianapolis and New York: Bobbs-Merrill, 1957.

See **692** for introduction. Includes **690**, **696**, and **700**

715   ——.*Ultissima consultatio de bello Turcis inferendo (A Most Useful Brief On Waging War Against the Turks)*, in *Opera Omnia*, ed. J. Clericus, Leyden, 1703-6, 5: 345-68.

Here is one of Erasmus' most difficult works, written in 1530 during a period in which he was under attack as a "clandestine Lutheran" for his pacifism, following the publication of Luther's *On War Against the Turks*. See **643**. It is an attempt to answer his critics, to refute the Lutheran claim that the Turkish threat was a divine punishment for the sins of Christians, and to spell out clearly his attitudes toward the crusade against the Turks, the only possible just war for him.

Erasmus makes no mistake that he considers the Turks rapacious, tyrannical, impious, and degenerate. He denies that he has ever embraced total pacifism. The charge is "so absurd that one hardly needs to refute it." A true Christian crusade, led by the Emperor and joined by a united Europe, waged in a Christian way, with as little bloodshed as possible, and with a true intent to convert the Turks, is acceptable. He rejects Luther's call to "resist not evil," and reminds his readers that Christians must indeed resist evil, but urges that Christians first reform their own spiritual and material lives. A truly Christian Europe would persuade the Turks to convert willingly, while the lack of reform will insure Christian failure. If Christians think they can lead a Christian life by slitting Turkish throats, they mock Christ and quickly turn into Turks themselves.

While accepting the theory of the just war, then, Erasmus seems to indicate that such a war is impossible in reality. He urges Christians instead to fight the Turk within them all. This important work has yet to be translated into English.

716   ——.reprint of 1643 ed., as *Consultatio de bello Turcis inferendo*. Athens: Karavia, 1974.

717   ——.*You Have Conquered Sparta, Now Govern It*. See **689**, 300-308.

The relationship between just rule and prowess in conquest is not always so straightforward. The former is far preferable, and should be enough to occupy any prince.

718   *Erasmus in English*.

A newsletter published by the University of Toronto Press on its continuing, English edition of his collected works. See **691**.

719   Fernandez, J.A. "Erasmus on the Just War," *Journal of the History of Ideas* 34 (1973): 209-26.

Erasmus continued in the mistaken perception that war was a problem of individual morality, not, as we moderns know, a prerogative of the state. His works thus aimed to awaken individual moral responses. The notion that war can be blamed on individual morality "displays the fundamental poverty of the Christian humanist purview," which Fernandez calls "disgracefully corrupt." Nevertheless, Erasmus' dismissal of almost all wars as unjust, and his question in the *Christian Prince* "if there really is any war which can be called just" strikes Fernandez as "prevarication and evasiveness," a stance that Erasmus shares with the entire Christian pacifist tradition from Tertullian on.

In response to Erasmus' declaration in his *War Against the Turks* (**715, 716**) that the proposition that he might be considered an absolutist pacifist "is too absurd to deserve refutation," Fernandez declares triumphantly, "so much for Erasmus' pacifism!" and considers the entire question settled except for one or two fine points. This treatise, he argues, is the most thorough defense of the just war until Vitoria. See **823** to **849**.

Fernandez then asserts that the very acceptance of the state by a Christian "is the doom of pacifism," since the state is made to wield the sword of magistracy, and this equals the sword of war, which it can wield "even [against] the unanimous consent of all the citizens." Discussing Fernandez's analysis of Erasmus' politics, James Tracy notes "what is 'flimsy' is not Erasmus' conception of the state, but Fernandez' understanding of Erasmus." See **735**.

720   Friedrich, C.-J. "Guerre et paix d'après Erasme et Kant." See **686**, 1: 277-83.

Erasmus was one of the "two most dogmatic pacifists in the intellectual history of Europe." Friedrich seems to equate moral stands with dogmatisms, and pacifism with an intellectual, not an ethical or activist tradition. Nevertheless, he does excuse the Humanist for making war a problem of individual morality, since the modern state, which we know is the real cause of all war, did not exist in his time.

721   Halkin, Léon-E. "Erasme et la politique des rois." See **652**, 109-18.

Erasmus wrote almost one hundred of his three thousand letters to statesmen: Charles V, Ferdinand of Austria, François I, Henry VIII, James V, Sigismund, Jão III and others. They all follow certain rhetorical forms appropriate to their royal audiences and reflect Erasmus' profession as moralist, not politician. Throughout the letters, however, Erasmus' historical perspective is clear, as is his moderation, even when expressing his pacifism.

722   Hardin, Richard F. "The Literary Conventions of Erasmus' *Education of a Christian Prince:* Advice and Aphorism," *Renaissance Quarterly* 35 (1982): 151-63.

There is no real contradiction between Erasmus' reputation as the "scourge of princes" and his position as a councilor to the Holy Roman Emperor Charles V. Erasmus saw both sin and the possibility of its reform. This willingness to live with human inconsistency gave rise to the "detached wit" that was a hallmark of both himself and Thomas More. Critics' charges of naiveté, simplicity, and primitiveness concerning politics are unfounded in light of the prevailing political theories of the age.

His *Education* shares the same themes as his earlier work, such as the *Panegyric* of 1504, the 1515 *Adages,* or the *Complaint of Peace,* but it expresses the interdependence between peace and responsible rule most clearly. The work is based on two medieval genres, the "advice to princes" and the *de casibus,* the fall of princes. The entire work is actually a collection of aphorisms, a series of separate observations and themes that he constructed to make a portrait of the ideal prince. He used the technique of two-part aphorism, contrasting the ideal political form with its visible sham. Yet Erasmus' work is neither innocuous cliché nor flattery. He adheres strongly to the democratic tradition of the Flemish city republics and reinforces this with an appeal to the liberty of the Christian: the spiritual freedom that God gave to each person that is inconsistent with unlimited monarchy.

Hardin sees Erasmus' analysis and prescriptions as fully consistent with his Humanist faith in the educability of the individual and of society. He dismisses cynical readings of the Humanist and his colleagues as mere self-advertising.

723   Herding, Otto. "Humanistische Friedensideen am Beispiel zweier Friendenklagen." See **652**, 7-34.

The intellectual tradition that preceded the *Complaint of Peace.*

724   Huizinga, Johan. *Erasmus and the Age of Reformation.* New York: Harper & Row, 1957.

This biography shares much in common with Bainton's (**681**). It traces his life and work in their historical context in a well illustrated and handy edition, this one supplemented by a selection of Erasmus' letters translated into English. Huizinga's view of Erasmus as a Humanist, reformer, and a man have long been controversial, however. Huizinga first published this book in 1924, when Europe was still reeling from the great passion of World War I, and after Huizinga himself had written that masterpiece portrait of cultural decline, *The Waning of the Middle Ages.*

For him Erasmus was ever the alienated intellectual, keeping to his Latin texts and language, ashamed of his native Holland, afraid to commit himself to the world around him, even when this might only involve the use of his mother tongue. Erasmus was naive about the real evils of his Catholic church, lacked any real spirituality, and did not realize the promise of the Reformation. When this came, Erasmus' true cowardice emerged. Rather than chose one side or the other, he temporized, justifiably heaping the scorn of both sides on his head. Erasmus was the pure creation of the printing press, and most of his late output was simply a journalism of attack and self-defense.

Ultimately he was a detached, self-interested, and only half-hearted scholar with little backbone for real commitment. Genuine loyalty and gratefulness were alien to him. Politically Erasmus was at his most naive, especially when espousing his pacifist views. Here he did not even realize their truly revolutionary content, concentrating on the goodness of human nature and its perfectibility. At the end of his life, when finally forced to make hard choices, Erasmus chose the path of reaction. In the end he was too moderate for the "heroic" sixteenth century, too "smooth" for his times. He was a tragic character, unable to act on his knowledge and convictions.

725   Hyma, Albert. *The Youth of Erasmus*. Ann Arbor, MI: University of Michigan Press, 1968.

Still one of the best, and sympathetic, treatments of Erasmus' intellectual and moral background. Hyma places Erasmus fully in the context of late medieval reform: the *Devotio Moderna* of the Brethren of the Common Life, by whom he was educated, the tradition of Thomas à Kempis. See **638, 639**.

726   Massaut, Jean-Pierre. "Humanisme et spiritualité chez Erasme." *DSAL* 7, fasc. 46-47, 1006-28.

Erasmus' pacifism was not simply moral, Utopian, or sentimental but derives from Christian ethical views and the imitation of Christ. It is founded on trinitarian Christological and ecclesiological mysteries and revealed through the sacraments. The Mystical Body lies at the center of his notion of peace and unity. See also **686** and **727**.

727   McConica, James K., C.S.B. "Erasmus and the Grammar of Consent," See **734**, 2: 96-99.

On Erasmus' attitude to Luther and the issues of conscience and authority. Erasmus faced the question of addressing religious dissent and formulated a response based on essentially orthodox, doctrinal, Christian norms. His attitude was not secular and ethical toleration, as Eugene Rice and others contend.

At the heart of Erasmus' notion of the church is the Mystical Body, which unites all Christians in Christ and his peace. Yet the faith of the church resides not in a pope, or council, or hierarchy but in all Christians. Therefore consensus must rule and define dogma. Theological disputes with Luther are not to be solved by the yes or no of authority but by the careful consideration by Christians acting in a spirit of peace and concord.

728   ——."Erasmus and the 'Julius': A Humanist Reflects on the Church," in Charles Trinkaus and Haiko Oberman, eds. *The Pursuit of Holiness in Late Medieval and Renaissance Religion.* Leiden: Brill, 1974, 444-77.

An excellent analysis of this work from an ecclesiological point of view: the themes of liberty, authority, and tyranny within the church set against McConica's close reading of the text. See **705**.

729   Olin, John C. "The Pacifism of Erasmus," in *Six Essays on Erasmus.* New York: Fordham University Press, 1979, 17-31. A revised version of the article in *Thought* 50, 199 (December 1975): 418-31.

Introduces Erasmus specifically as a *Christian* Humanist. His hopes for reform of the present life were based on the pure sources of Christian and pre-Christian learning and wisdom and were expressed clearly and consistently through his continuing efforts to make peace. Stresses that Erasmus' peacemaking was not merely a sentimental, ethical attitude but was fundamental to his theological understanding of the nature of God, the world, humanity, and the church. Reviews the pacifist themes of Erasmus' *Bellum Dulce Inexpertis* and *Complaint of Peace.* Useful annotations.

730   Padberg, Rudolf. "Pax Erasmiana. Das politische Engagement und die 'politische Theologie' des Erasmus von Rotterdam." See **734**, 2: 301-312.

Reviews the historiography on Erasmus as a peacemaker and his relevance to the post-World War II world. Recent research concludes that Erasmus' peace ethic was based on his life situation and that his political engagement was a result of his reform desire, which is the result of his Christian beliefs.

731   Payne, John B. "Erasmus, Interpreter of Romans," *Sixteenth-Century Essays and Studies* 2 (1971): 1-35.

Not seen.

732   Philips, Margaret Mann. *Erasmus and the Northern Renaissance.* London: English Universities Press, 1967.

This handy little volume offers a good survey of his life and works around several themes: the revival of ancient literature and learning, the "philosophy of Christ," Erasmus' cultural and religious criticisms, his political views, and his role in the Reformation. Brief bibliography, good index.

733   Rummel, Erika. "A Reader's Guide to Erasmus Controversies." See **718**, 12 (1983): 13-19.

Among these is the campaign against Erasmus as a "clandestine Lutheran" waged by Noel Beda of the University of Paris for his pacifism. See also **643**.

734   *Scrinium Erasmianum.* 2 vols., Leiden: E.J. Brill, 1969.

Includes **727**, and **730**.

735   Tracy, James. *The Politics of Erasmus: A Pacifist Intellectual and His Political Milieu.* Toronto: University of Toronto Press, 1978.

The political milieu was one in which the heads of the new nation-states could mobilize their subjects for war on a level never before imagined. While most Humanists did not question the military ambitions of their princely patrons, among those who did, Erasmus and his circle were certainly prominent. Erasmus' role in this critique has long been acknowledged as central. Yet debate still rages as to whether his outlook was realistic or naive, whether he or Machiavelli really understood the modern state. Tracy argues that Erasmus was quite correct in placing the blame for all the calamitous wars of the sixteenth century squarely on the dynastic and personal ambitions of these new monarchs, even given our post-Hegelian view of deeper social and economic processes. Whatever the judgment of historians on this score, Erasmus certainly did exercise significant influence on the modern debate over human violence. The question that he asked: is violence innate, or is it socialized, is still being asked by followers of Freud or Lorenz.
    Tracy follows Erasmus' political career. His first attempts to gain patronage displayed a naiveté about the

politics and factions in the Netherlands, but by 1503 his *Panegyric* to Philip, duke of Brabant, revealed the themes that were to remain part of his writings for the rest of his life: that human vice and virtue are taught, that humans are by nature peaceful, that rulers, especially Christian rulers, should use the means of peace, that consensus should govern, that civil and not military glory was the proper province of the prince, that even an unjust peace is preferable to an unjust war.

Tracy reviews Erasmus' major works, including his *Julius Exclusus* (705) and *Praise of Folly* (711), and concludes that he was "if not visionary, radical in his perception of the moral demands made by faith in Christ." His pleas for peace and condemnations of war were not based solely on literary forms, but from his own experience of war and its effects. His deep religious convictions put the Humanist peacemaker at odds with the political situation of his day. Even when appointed councilor to the young Prince Charles, soon to become Holy Roman Emperor, Erasmus used his *Education of the Christian Prince* to make clear the connection between the continued state of war and the loss of civil liberties at home and the destruction of all human endeavors. Tracy sees this work as essential to understanding Erasmus' political ideas.

The book also examines how Erasmus' pacifism dovetailed with the political interests of the peace party in the Netherlands. Even his anti-chivalric themes were more than literary exercises, since they furthered the cause of those in the imperial household opposed to the war party.

On the whole, Tracy concludes, Erasmus was well informed on the politics and personalities of his day and region. His works grew out of this political knowledge as much as from his biblical and Humanist impulses to peace. While this understanding, and his political criticisms, may have been wrong at times, on the whole he correctly understood the trends of the time: given the nature of politics in his age his appeal to the moral judgment of the prince was well placed.

* *
*

CHAPTER 10: *Missionary Peacemaking, 1500-1800. Peace and Justice in the New World*

Introduction

736   Cespedes, Guillermo. *Latin America: The Early Years.* New York: Alfred A. Knopf, 1974.

A structuralist history of institutions, economy, and society, pays attention to intellectual and religious currents. Pages 81-99, "The Quest for Utopia," summarize the career of Antonio de Montesinos and his efforts to fight Spanish exploitation of native Americans.

737   Davenport, Frances G., ed. *European Treaties Bearing on the History of the United States and its Dependencies to 1648.* 4 vols. Washington, D.C.: Carnegie Institution, 1917-1937; reprint, Gloucester, MA: Peter Smith, 1967, 1: 56-78.

For the text of *Summus pontifex* and *Inter caetera,* which arbitrated colonial rivalries in the New World and set precedents for later papal calls for peace and justice in Latin America. Davenport prints both Latin texts and English translations of documents.

738   Gibson, Charles. *Spain in America.* New York: Harper & Row, 1966.

For a general, balanced introduction to the events, cultures, and institutions of the Spanish conquest and colonization. Of particular use here are Gibson's discussions of the *encomienda* system, of the establishment of missions by Cardinal Ximénez, and the influence of Erasmian Humanism on their spirit and methods. Gibson briefly notes the careers of several of the best known defenders of the Americans, including Bartolomé de Las Casas (**761** to **778**), Juan de Zumárraga, and Vasco de Quiroga, and discusses the effects of More's *Utopia* on their thought and action. Well indexed, with an annotated bibliography useful for earlier work.

739   Keen, Benjamin. "Recent Writings on the Spanish Conquest," *Latin American Research Review* 20, 2 (1985): 161-71.

Reviews recent scholarship in the field. This includes work of the revisionist school, seeking to correct exaggerations in the Black Legend; anthropological and ethnological studies of native American cultures, including native use of the Spanish legal system to protect their rights; the history of colonial society; military history, once more in vogue; and studies examining the effects of colonial society on modern Latin America.

740   Kirkpatrick, Frederick A. *The Spanish Conquistadors.* 2nd ed. New York: Barnes & Noble, 1967.

For a political and military history.

741   Lockhart, James, and Stuart B. Schwartz. *Early Latin America.* New York: Cambridge University Press, 1983.

For socio-economic history, with little attention to cultural and intellectual trends. A fine annotated bibliography.

742   Parry, J.H. *The Establishment of the European*

Hegemony. New York: Harper & Row, 1966.

For general background of European exploration and expansionism.

743 ——."The New World, 1521-1580." See **634**, 562-90.

The Spanish both wittingly and unwittingly effected the genocide of the original peoples of Latin America. Disease, war crimes, and the rigors of forced labor under the *encomienda* system drastically reduced their numbers. The main check on this process of extermination and exploitation was the work of the Spanish missionaries. Trained in a radical evangelical Christianity and in the Christian Humanism of Erasmus' circle, and aided by free access to the Spanish court, they launched a campaign to protect and to educate the native Americans and to fill the spiritual and material gap left by the destruction of their cultures. Zumárraga and Las Casas were among the most important of these missionaries. Their efforts resulted in the Council of the Indies' applying strict new checks on the conquistadors and, eventually, in the New Laws and the Ordinances on Discoveries, which forbade even theoretically just wars against the Americans and became models for human rights in the New World. As usual with the *CMH,* the articles lack bibliography.

744 ——."The Spaniards in the New World, 1493-1521." See **633**, 430-44.

Useful background for events and institutions. As early as Columbus' voyages the Spanish were using the system of *repartimiento.* Although this later evolved into the *encomienda* system, both basically imported a medieval manorial form of economic serfdom: forced tributes and labor in exchange for conversion and "protection." With the arrival of Montesinos and Las Casas to the New World, however, the struggle for peace and justice was under way.

745   Picón-Salas, Mariano. *A Cultural History of Spanish America.* Irving A. Leonard, transl. Berkeley, Los Angeles and London: University of California Press, 1962.

This is cultural history in the broadest sense of the word: it includes religious, intellectual, and political trends and theories across a broad range of events and personalities. While not specifically a history of Liberation Theology or nonviolence, Picón-Salas' account shows the fundamental influence of Las Casas, Montesinos and the New Laws in the struggle against the worst aspects of the Spanish conquest. The book uses extensive quotation from primary sources to illustrate points. The author fits the missionary role of nonviolent prophesy firmly within the tradition of Erasmus and Ximénez.

Among the most important peacemakers he discusses are Juan de Zumárraga, Pedro de Gante and the other Franciscans of the first generation: Toribio de Benavente, called Motolinía, Bernardino de Sahagun, and Vasco de Quiroga. Picón-Salas traces the influence of these missionaries into the seventeenth century, discusses the Utopian dreams of the Jesuits in Paraguay and analyzes the decline of the church and of its influence in the late seventeenth and eighteenth centuries. Despite this decline, Picón-Salas' evidence shows that there remained a strong tradition of Latin American peacemaking. The popular imagination was stirred by the adventures of the "Saints of Action," missionaries who braved all dangers in the continent's wilds and in the North American west to spread the Gospel.

Under the influence of Humanism and the Enlightenment, new critics of the Spanish conquest emerged who revived the European debate over the enslavement of the native Americans and pressed for the recognition of universal human rights. Such writers as José de Acosta, Diego de Avendano, Felipé de Jesus, Antonio Ruiz de Montoya, Luis Bocaños, Pedro Claver, Francisco Solano, Francisco Falcon, Polo de Ondegardo, Francisco Xavier Clavijero, Andres Cano, Andreas de Guevera y Basoazabal, Pedro José Marquez, and Francisco Xavier Alegre all condemned Latin American racism, the caste system, educational deprivation and discrimination. They also encouraged the defense and preservation of pre-Columbian cultures, languages, and civilizations as the equals of European forms. In all these activities they not only helped prepare for revolution and independence but also continued the tradition of liberation in Latin America.

While Picón-Salas concentrates on the elite's point of view, his work is a treasure-house of personalities and movements that provide essential background for any analysis of nonviolence in Latin America.

746   Simpson, Lesley Byrd. *The Encomienda in New Spain.* Berkeley, Los Angeles and London: University of California Press, 1966; reprint 1982.

This is the best introduction to the history, nature, and effects of this Spanish form of colonial exploitation. Simpson provides a chronological account of the system that includes the efforts of Las Casas and other missionary peacemakers to end or reform it. He appends his text with many of the most important documents.

747 Todorov, Tzvetan. *The Conquest of America*. Richard
Howard, transl. New York: Harper & Row, 1984.

This is a new rehashing of familiar accounts of the
Spanish atrocities in the New World accompanied by a
somewhat over-stylish, new-literary, critical approach to
events and personalities. Todorov's slant is to examine
European culture's encounter with the "other" as both
physical and phenomenological reality. A careful reading
will reveal very little original that has not been discussed
by historians of the period.

The Religious Roots of Liberation

748 Attwater. *Saints*. See **1**.

While the age is known chiefly for its conquistadors
and colonial empire-builders, it also produced many
dedicated to nonviolent conversion and liberation of non-
Europeans. Among those recognized with sainthood by
the Catholic church are Luis Bertrand, Jean de Brébeuf,
Jão de Britto, Pedro Claver, Anthony Daniel, Charles
Garnier, René Goupil and Jean Lalande, Isaac Jogues,
Gabriel Lelement, the martyrs of Japan, and Francis
Xavier.

749 Bataillon, Marcel. *Erasme et l'Espagne*. Paris: Droz, 1937.

Traces Erasmus' influence on the Spanish Humanists,
discusses translations of his works, and follows his persecution and condemnation by Spanish ecclesiastics of the
Counter Reformation. Useful for tracing his influence
through the Humanists and the court of Cardinal Ximénez
to the missionary orders, including the Franciscans and
Dominicans whom the crown sent out to evangelize and
protect the native Americans.

750 ——."Évangelisme et millénarisme au Nouveau Monde," in *Courants réligieux et Humanisme à la fin du xvᵉ et au début de xviᵉ siècle.* Paris: Centre de Recherches de l'Institut d'Études Hispaniques, 1965.

Not seen.

751 Cragg, Gerald. *The Church and the Age of Reason 1648-1789.* New York: Penguin Books, 1981.

Catholic influence in missionary activity during the period was, on the whole, shallow and precarious. Except for the Jesuits in Paraguay, Catholic missions tended to stagnate.

752 Dussel, Enrique. *A History of the Church in Latin America: Colonialism to Liberation 1492-1979.* 3rd. ed. Alan Neely, transl. Grand Rapids, MI: Eerdmans, 1981.

The best historical account for Catholic peacemaking in Latin America, and one of the best ever written for peacemaking anywhere. But Dussel's book is more than this. It is a theology of liberation written through history, with careful attention to historical fact and accuracy, for only through the "praxis" of history can the church fully appreciate the meaning of liberation.

The book's four parts include a hermeneutical introduction on the theology of domination and liberation; Latin American culture, and relations between church and culture; Christendom in the West Indies from 1492 to 1808, which covers both chronological narrative and thematic analysis of evangelization; the neocolonial period from 1808 to 1962 examined from historical, structuralist-institutional, social, cultural, and theological viewpoints;

and finally a survey of the church and Latin American liberation from 1962 to 1979, including a description of recent events: the national security state, violence, bourgeois elites and the masses, the church's evolution in councils and in praxis, and the theological significance of these events.

Dussel's work is often difficult for the nontheologian, all the more so since Liberation Theology depends so much on drawing its data from the living world of Catholic practice and application to real social and political conditions. The reader is thus often faced with interpretive schematizations of the events narrated that compel reevaluation of accepted methods of viewing Latin America and its history. Nonetheless, the result is well worth the effort. Dussel's historical processes are dialogues between world views that have not yet ended, not Marxist dialectical confrontations between classes or economic systems that must end in the victory of one or the other. His analysis of pre-Columbian cultures pinpoints the truly devastating effect of the Spanish conquest and lays the groundwork for understanding all further European efforts either to conquer or convert and protect the native Americans. He also reminds the reader of the limitations of the Spanish culture that came to dominate the region: its authoritarianism, its feudal concepts of land, work, and personal relations; and the cultural shock inflicted on the native Americans by Spanish technology, society, and theological universe.

Along with Dussel's analyses comes a continuous narrative of Catholic efforts at liberation from the time of Antonio de Montesinos through the career of Bartolomé de Las Casas (**761** to **778**), the Franciscans, Dominicans and Augustinians, the New Laws and the New Law bishops, reform church councils that attempted to redress the atrocities of the conquistadors and emphasize the Christian nature of the conversion process. Dussel claims that Las

Casas and these other clerics are the true fountainhead of
Liberation Theology: their efforts to protect the native
Americans and to restore to them their human dignity is
based directly on the Gospels and the Old Testament
books of liberation and prophetic protest.

Dussel's major theme for the neocolonial period is the
struggle between the church and the colonial aristocracy
over the survival of the feudal *patronato,* the system under
which the native Americans had been subjected to a feudal
serfdom worse than slavery. In this light Dussel cites the
efforts of the Jesuits and the other missionary orders.
Despite the decadence of the Bourbon period (1700-1808)
and its legacy of deserted missions, accommodation, and
an ensuing anticlericalism, Dussel stresses that an active
lay spirituality survived and made new strides in the nineteenth and twentieth centuries. While this was not always
in keeping with strict Tridentine orthodoxy, it did lay the
groundwork for the activist approach of Latin America's
peoples and gave rise to Liberation Theology as understood today.

753 ——.*History and Theology of Liberation: A Latin American
Perspective.* John Drury, transl. Maryknoll, NY:
Orbis Books, 1976.

Essentially a distillation of much of his *History of the
Church.* See **752.**

754 Hanke, Lewis. *The Spanish Struggle for Justice in the
Conquest of America.* Philadelphia: University of
Pennsylvania Press, 1949.

Two factors inherent in the Spanish colonial system
helped establish a basis for the struggle for peace and
justice in the New World. Spanish legal formality thor-

oughly saturated every aspect of Spanish European and colonial life far beyond the legal fiction of the *requerimiento* used as a pretext for aggressive wars of conquest. A widespread freedom of speech was also encouraged by the Spanish monarchy, within the bounds of religious orthodoxy, and open discussion and movement of news from America was a vital aspect of Spanish policy.

There were, therefore, elements of Spanish culture that worked in favor of Bartolomé de Las Casas and the other missionary peacemakers in the New World. From Montesinos on a series of denunciations of Spanish colonial leadership was not only voiced heroically in America, but also faithfully transmitted and reported to the Spanish court. This made possible the commissions of inquiry that followed up charges made in the letters and writings of the missionary peacemakers. The open and often heated debates that these reports produced resulted in the Laws of Burgos, the New Laws, the appointment of the New Law bishops to implement royal reform decrees, and the termination of many of the most onerous of the Spanish colonial oppressions.

Hanke details the workings of an entire "Indian lobby" at the Hapsburg court that did much to persuade Charles V, and Philip II later, to check the greed and brutality of the colonial aristocracy. Perhaps the most dramatic example of this combination of legalism and free speech was the Valladolid debate between Las Casas and Juan Ginés de Sepúlveda in 1550/51 over the basic human rights and nature of the Americans. The debate decided in Las Casas' favor and resulted in the Royal Council's openly questioning the justice of wars against the native Americans and, ironically, the banning of Sepúlveda's views in Spain. A basic work in the area.

755 Latourette, Kenneth Scott. *Three Centuries of Advances,*
A.D. 1500-A.D. 1800. New York: Harper & Row,
1939. See **369**, vol. 3.

This remains the best single work on missionary
activities in the early modern period. This volume surveys
the general movement of missionary activity and details the
lives of many of the most important missionaries and
peacemakers in the Americas and what is now the Third
World. These include Bartolomé de Las Casas (**761** to
778), the Jesuits and the Flemish Franciscans in Mexico
and California, Luis Cancer de Barbastro in Florida,
Alfonso Sandoval and Pedro Claver in Colombia, Francis
Xavier in the Orient, Robert de Nobili in India, and Diego
de Herrera and Domingo de Salazar in the Philippines.
Very useful reference material.

756 Muldoon, James. "A Fifteenth-Century Application of the
Canonistic Theory of the Just War." See **615**, 467-82.

For a brief introduction to the legal issues involved in
the conquest and colonization. Focuses on the debate
arising over the Christian conquest of the Canary Islands
and the rights of colonial powers to wage any kind of war,
just or unjust, against peoples who were hitherto free and
whose conquest could not be seen as a defensive war.
Reviews theories that claimed that Christians had a natural
right of dominion over "heathens."

757 ——."Papal Responsibility for the Infidel. Another Look at
Alexander VI's *Inter caetera,*" *Catholic Historical*
Review 64 (1978): 168-84.

The bull *Inter caetera* was not so much a treaty

designed to divide up the world between colonial powers
as a statement of future Christian-infidel relations. Here
the papacy intervened to protect and to convert the infidel
whom war was bringing under Christian dominion. The
bull ultimately resulted from Eugenius IV's intervention in
the Canary Islands to stop further expansion and to
implement measures for the spiritual and material education
of the islanders. Alexander VI's use of this precedent in
Inter caetera may not have hindered the brutal Spanish
conquest, but it did provide a legal precedent for the
protests of Las Casas and his colleagues that the Spanish
court had to heed.

758   ——.*Popes*. See **519**, 8-24.

Reviews Las Casas' attack on the legal fiction of the
requerimiento that underpined the entire Spanish conquest
as a just war.

759   Neill. *History*. See **41**, 140-449.

Traces the early modern missions of the Catholic
church, among others, from Nicholas V's *Romanus
pontifex* in 1454, through the bulls of demarcation of
Alexander VI, and the activities of the missionary orders in
the New and Third Worlds. Surveys the lives of Francis
Xavier and the Japan missionaries and martyrs and traces
the progress of the Jesuit and Ursuline missions in
Canada. Neill sets the Latin American missions in the
context of Spanish genocide, the *encomienda* system, and
the missionary peacemakers who campaigned to stop
them. These include Antonio de Montesinos, Bartolomé
de Las Casas, and Bishop Zumárraga of Mexico. Neill
also traces the reaction against the creation of an
indigenous clergy under Gregory XIII and in a series of

councils in the New World through the sixteenth century.

By the time of Francesco Ingoli's tenure over the Propaganda, however, the church had again begun to move away from the political domination of the colonial powers and to insist on peaceful persuasion as the chief means of conversion. Later chapters provide useful background material for Catholic missions into the twentieth century. The researcher needs to remember that these missions were, almost without exception, nonviolent attempts to spread Christianity and to protect non-Europeans from the exploitation of their colonial masters. At times, especially on pages 140-240, his account seems to rely heavily on Latourette. See **755**.

760   Verlinden, Charles. "La 'Requerimiento' et la 'paix coloniale' dans l'empire espagnol d'Amerique." See **48**, 397-414.

Not seen.

Bartolomé de Las Casas

761   Biermann, Benno M. "Bartolomé de Las Casas and Verapaz." See **764**, 443-84.

Traces Las Casas' attempt to demonstrate the effectiveness of peaceful conversion in an area in modern Guatemala's Tuzutlan that had repulsed all Spanish attempts at violent conquest so thoroughly that it was called *Tierra del Guerra* (Land of War). Ignoring the advice of conquistadors that he would be slaughtered, Las Casas entered the jungles in 1537. After winning over the tribal chiefs through trading missions, his company was able to preach the Gospels unprotected by the military. By 1544 his success had earned him royal support and colonial hatred for his *Tierra del Vera Paz* (Land of True Peace).

762   Fernandez, Manuel Gimenez. "Fray Bartolomé de Las
         Casas: A Biographical Sketch." See **764**, 67-125.

A useful survey of his life and the main issues and
events that shaped it, with careful attention to chronology.
Fernandez reminds us of Las Casas' connection with
Adrian of Utrecht, Cardinal Ximénez de Cisneros, and
others of Erasmus' circle at the Spanish court. He thus
sets Las Casas' work for peace and justice in the New
World within the context of Spanish court politics and the
rivalries of the various religious orders conducting missions in America. The article also discusses papal efforts
to defend native Americans.

763   Friede, Juan. "Las Casas and Indigenism in the Sixteenth
         Century." See **764**, 127-234.

Friede summarizes much of his theory that the actions
of Las Casas and other defenders of the native Americans
stemmed as much from economic self-interest as from any
morality. Las Casas' efforts grew out of the need to
organize the new colonies both politically and economical-
ly and to protect the work force put at the friars' disposal
by their "reforms."

764   Friede, Juan and Benjamin Keen, eds. *Bartolomé de Las
         Casas in History.* DeKalb, IL: Northern Illinois
         University Press, 1971.

An excellent collection of essays by prominent
scholars of the Spanish conquest and early colonial period
Includes **761** to **763**, **771**, and **776**.

765   Hanke, Lewis. *All Mankind Is One.* DeKalb, IL: Northern
         Illinois University Press, 1974.

Studies the debate between Las Casas and Juan Ginés de Sepúlveda, a theologian and opponent of Erasmus, held in the presence of the royal Spanish court at the palace at Valladolid in 1550/51. The debate centered on Sepúlveda's adherence to the Aristotelian view that all barbarians, i.e. non-Europeans, were naturally inferior and thus just objects for conquest and enslavement, being less truly human than civilized peoples. Las Casas' arguments for the God-given equality of all peoples and of the injustice of the Spanish conquest won the day and resulted in important reforms of the colonial administration. This book is of fundamental importance for the study of Las Casas and peacemaking in the colonial era. A full and excellent bibliography. See also **766**.

766   ——.*Aristotle and the American Indians*. London: Hollis & Carter, 1959.

Focuses on the Valladolid debate of 1550/51 between Bartolomé de Las Casas and Juan Ginés de Sepúlveda. Hanke traces the sources of Sepúlveda's theory and contrasts them to the words and actions of many Catholic missionaries in the New World, such as Juan de Zumárraga and Motolinía, whose strong condemnations of Spanish exploitation implicitly bore a rebuttal of Aristotle's theory. See also **765**.

767   ——.*Bartolomé de Las Casas*. The Hague: Nijhoff, 1951.

This is still the best single volume available for an introduction to Las Casas. Hanke divides his study into three parts: Las Casas' struggle for justice during the Spanish conquest; his achievement as a political theorist and historian, analyzing his writings and their impact; and

Las Casas as an anthropologist, that is, his attempts to understand the culture of the native Americans and to translate the message of Christianity into a form they could accept and adopt.

768   ——.*Bartolomé de Las Casas, Bookman, Scholar and Propagandist.* Philadelphia: University of Pennsylvania Press, 1952.

On his work as a historian and apologist for the native Americans.

769   ——."More Heat and Some Light on the Spanish Struggle for Justice in the Conquest of America," *Hispanic American Historical Review* 44 (1964): 293-340.

Hanke notes that the Spanish conquest is already the most highly debated topic in Latin American history. Here he answers objections of Friede's "Indigenista" theory (763) and those of Ramon Menendez Pidal that Las Casas was a paranoiac, grossly exaggerating the abuses against native peoples and inflating his own role as their embattled defender.

770   ——.*Spanish Struggle.* See 754.

771   Keen, Benjamin. "Approaches to Las Casas, 1535-1970." See 764, 3-63.

On historiography. Las Casas himself was a major source of the "Black Legend" of Spanish atrocity and injustice in the New World. His accounts made vivid reading and effective propaganda against the Catholic Monarchy when used by Protestant reformers and later Dutch rebels and English competitors. At the same time these external attacks helped reduce Las Casas' popularity in Spain, as he began to be seen as a turncoat. In the Enlightenment, however, he again became a hero of humanity against the forces of violence and injustice. In revolutionary Europe sentiment for him was so strong that a movement was launched to have him canonized, while he became the nemesis of conservatives and reactionaries. Keen sums up American opinion and then warns that there is a real danger of a "White Legend" growing up around Las Casas and his associates that over-stresses their efforts for peace and justice and leads us to ignore the grim reality behind the "Black Legend."

772   Las Casas, Bartolomé de. *Apologetic History*. Lewis Hanke, transl. and ed. *All The Peoples of the World Are Men*. Minneapolis, MN: University of Minnesota, 1970.

Hanke's title refers to the debate within Spain as to whether the native Americans were even human beings. He traces Las Casas' evolving notions of universal kinship and human rights, first in defense of the native Americans and, later, in defense of the freedom of black slaves. Hanke concludes that Las Casas' message is in exactly the same spirit as that of John XXIII's *Pacem in Terris*. See **954**.

773   ——.*The Devastation of the Indies: A Brief Account*. Herma Briffault, transl. New York: Seabury Press, 1974.

Here is the chief source of the "Black Legend," the history of Spanish genocide in the New World. While historians may question Las Casas' statistics of the number of native Americans actually killed by the Spanish, his record of war, massacre, atrocity, abuses of basic human rights, torture, and enslavement are more vivid than anything until the Holocaust. The book caused a sensation and immediate royal investigations into the conduct of their colonial empire in the New World. It has been used as a weapon against the Spanish and Catholic treatment of native Americans ever since. Las Casas' goal was quite different, however: to awaken the consciences of his compatriots to the grim reality behind their new-found wealth and empire.

774   ——.*History of the Indies.* Andrée Collard, transl. and ed. New York: Harper & Row, 1971.

Las Casas was among the first generation of New World colonists, and his first-hand sources go back to the voyages of Columbus, which he also recalled. His work is thus a fundamental source for the period of discovery and conquest. More than this, however, it is Las Casas' narrative of the struggle of the missionary peacemakers, including himself at center stage, for peace and justice in America. Much of what we know of this struggle comes from Las Casas, but his account seems reliable on most points. A good English edition.

775   ——.*In Defense of the Indians.* Stafford Poole, C.M., transl. and ed. DeKalb, IL: Northern Illinois University Press, 1974.

Las Casas' examination of native American culture, its importance and its dignity, and its right to be protected against the depredations of the Spanish conquerors.

776   Losada, Angel. "The Controversy between Sepúlveda and Las Casas in the Junta of Valladolid." See **764**, 279-307.

Among the issues debated were Sepúlveda's contention that pacifism disappeared after the age of Constantine, that the just war was the only acceptable Christian response in this new age, and that Aristotle and the Old Testament had stressed the difference between Jew and Gentile, Greek and barbarian. Traces Las Casas' successful rebuttals. See also 765 and 766.

777   Pennington, Kenneth. "Bartolomé de Las Casas and the Tradition of Medieval Law," *Church History* 39 (1970): 149-61.

Attempts to study Las Casas as a canonist and concludes that he actually may have agreed with Sepúlveda that the Spanish had just dominion over the New World.

778   Zavala, Silvio. "Nuevas datos sobre Bartolomé de las Casas, obispo de Chiapas," *Cuaderno Americano* 43 (March-April 1984): 129-38.

On a manuscript in the Library of Congress in Washington containing a petition from the bishop to Charles V concerning ecclesiastical jurisdiction in Chiapas.

Individual Mission Areas

779   Burrus, Ernest J. "Alonso de la Vera Cruz (+1584), Pioneer Defender of the American Indians," *Catholic Historical Review* 70, 4 (Oct. 1984): 531-46.

De la Vera Cruz was a lawyer at Salamanca and a friend of Vitoria (823 to 849) who left Spain in 1536 to join the Augustinian mission in Mexico. He quickly became a strong defender of native American rights against the conquistadors, emphasizing their God-given human rights and allying with Las Casas to fight for justice. While de la Cruz was far more moderate in his defense than Las Casas, between 1562 and 1573 he was able to use his position at the Spanish court to protect the rights of both American and Philippine peoples.

780   Caraman, Philip. *The Lost Paradise: The Jesuit Republic in South America.* New York: Seabury, 1976.

A fascinating account of the Jesuit attempt in what is now modern Paraguay to save their native American converts from the depredations of conquistadors and slave traders. After failing at attempts at itinerant missions, they accepted a commission from Philip II to convert the Indians by nonviolent means, without exploitation. They proceeded to set up a colonial state, a series of *reduciones* complete with secular and religious institutions: church, schools, hospitals, courts, and — eventually — a strong military force that kept aggressors at bay in a series of bloody battles. They combined this with journeys to the colonial capitals to preach against the injustices of the Spanish regime or to liberate prisoners from Brazilian slave traders. Ultimately, however, the Jesuit experiment was a failure. Their paternalistic control provided the Americans with little skill in self-government or ability to resist colonial exploitation. In the end the *reduciones* melted away into the forests. This is fascinating adventure reading combined with sobering lessons in the nature of political and cultural liberation.

781   Deck, Allan F. *Francisco Javier Alegre. A Study in Mexican Literary Criticism.* Rome: Jesuit Historical Institute, 1977.

Alegre was one of the expatriot Mexican Jesuits who

carried on a running criticism of Latin American tyranny from the salons of Enlightenment Europe. His works helped build the foundations for the political liberation of the region. While Deck does not deal explicitly with Alegre's criticisms of Spanish colonial rule and his enlightened Humanism, he does provide some biographical and intellectual background and a thorough and useful bibliography.

782   Geiger, Maynard, O.F.M. *Franciscan Missionaries in Hispanic California 1769-1848: A Biographical Dictionary.* San Marino, CA: Huntington Library, 1969.

The Spanish missionaries in California were adventurous heroes committed to nonviolent conversion. Their lives gripped the popular imagination of New Spain and provided a counterbalance to the tales of the conquistadors. Geiger's book provides a useful reference guide to the lives of many of these adventurers.

783   Gutierrez, Lucio. "Domingo de Salazar, O.P., First Bishop of the Philippines (1512-1594): A Defender of the Rights of the Filipinos and the Spanish Contact," *Philippiana Sacra* 20 (Jan.-April 1985): 62-79.

Not seen.

784   Kennedy, J.H. *Jesuit and Savage in New France.* New Haven: Yale University Press, 1950.

The Jesuit mission in Canada was a marriage of the Order's thorough grounding in Christian Humanism and its members' willingness to accommodate to the languages, customs, and culture of the Americans. Despite this intellectual preparation, however, the Canadian mission was still an act of martyrdom, both in the conditions imposed on these Europeans and in their physical deaths, which the Jesuits saw as an imitation of Christ. For the Jesuits the New World offered them the opportunity to return to the first centuries of the church, to the poverty and suffering of the first age, among a people morally and intellectually equal to the Europeans but untouched by the centuries of religious decline.

785 McNaspy, C.J., S.J. *Conquistador without Sword: The Life of Roque Gonzalez, S.J.* Chicago: Loyola University Press, 1984.

On the most important founder of the Jesuit *reduciones* in Paraguay.

786 ——.and Jose Maria Blanch, S.J. *Lost Cities of Paraguay.* Chicago: Loyola University Press, 1982.

A history of the Jesuit *reduciones* of Paraguay.

787 Phelan, John Leddy. *The Millennial Kingdom of the Franciscans in the New World.* Berkeley and Los Angeles: University of California Press, and London: Cambridge University Press, 1956; revised, 1970.

Focuses on the life and often contradictory thought of Geronimo de Mendietta, O.F.M. (1525-1604), a Spanish missionary in Mexico. Mendietta's life is as interesting for his theories as for the missions that grew out of them. Through Mendietta's own *Historia eclesiatica indiana (Ecclesiastical History of the Indies)* and his biography by Juan de Torquemada, O.F.M. it emerges that Mendietta saw the Spanish Empire as the universal millennial kingdom of the last days that would bring all the peoples of the world to Christianity. While much of his historical thought derived directly from the apocalyptic Joachimism of Cardinal Ximénez de Cisneros and his Franciscan circle (545 to 557), Mendieta agreed with Sepúlveda and other just-war theorists in seeing war as a valid means of bringing this universal monarchy about. He saw the Spanish conquest in the light of the Old Testament wars of the Israelites and Cortes as a new Moses.

If the time of Cortes was the Golden Age of the New World, one of unspoiled purity that was close to the life of the primitive church, his own age was closer to the Apocalyptic time of troubles that preceded the coming of the New Jerusalem. His own Franciscan Order had pointed the way to the restoration of the primitive church, and the native Americans were the true children of this age in their poverty, simplicity, and humility. Yet the Franciscans had therefore to protect them from the moral pollution and greed of their European overlords. In order to guarantee their "evangelical liberty" the Franciscans would therefore have to reeducate the Indians to form their own commonwealth. Mendietta thus opposed any policy that would force the Hispanization of indigenous peoples and stressed that existing social and cultural structures that did not clash with Christianity must be retained.

While he was therefore very much a man of his times in accepting the role of force in the conquest of the New World, he looked forward to some aspects of Liberation Theology in stressing that the Hispanization of Latin America did not equal its Christianization, and that, in fact, it might be the very opposite. He thus, paradoxically, opposed all efforts to force them to conform to Spanish institutions, including the *encomienda*.

Phelan's work is remarkable both for its early appreciation of the role of Joachimite prophesy in the religious thought of the time and in his discernment of a theology of liberation at work in colonial Latin America.

788   Ricard, Robert. *The Spiritual Conquest of Mexico, An Essay on the Apostolate and Evangelizing Methods of the Mendicant Orders in New Spain, 1523-1572.* Berkeley and Los Angeles: University of California Press, 1966.

While the special emphasis of the mendicants — Franciscans, Dominicans, Hieronymites, and Augustinians — in converting the New World may have differed somewhat from order to order, their basic outlook was essentially the same: the creation of a safe refuge for both body and soul from exploitation and brutality, education to create a native elite, instruction in new trades and crafts, a religious cycle and liturgy that would build on the remnants of pre-Columbian practice and world view. The mendicants hoped that these methods of nonviolent persuasion, would attract the Americans to the Christian life with a deep-rooted appreciation for its truths.

789   Ronan, Charles E. *Francisco Javier Clavijero, S.J. (1731-1787), Figure of the Mexican Enlightenment.* Rome: Institutum Historicum; Chicago: Loyola University Press, 1977.

Clavijero was another of the Mexican emigré intellectuals who carried on a campaign against the political and cultural tyranny of late colonial Latin America. See **781**. His *Ancient History of Mexico* picks up where Las Casas left off, combining a deep understanding of pre-Columbian civilization with criticism of the Spanish conquest. His ultimate goal was to show native American culture and individual status as the equal of the European and so press for full human rights in the New World.

CHAPTER 11: *The Ebb Tide of Catholic Peacemaking, 1500-1800*

General Introduction

790   Breunig, Charles. *The Age of Revolution and Reaction, 1789-1850*. New York: W.W. Norton, 1971.

A good introductory survey.

791   Dunn, Richard S. *The Age of Religious Wars, 1559-1689*. New York: W.W. Norton, 1970.

A good historical survey of the period, with ample attention paid to religious aspects.

792   Krieger, Leonard. *Kings and Philosophers, 1689-1789*. New York: W.W. Norton, 1970.

A useful survey, with background information and bibliography on all aspects of eighteenth-century culture and life.

The Religious Background

793   Berenger, Jean. "The Austrian Church." See **796**, 88-105.

Popular spirituality was carefully molded by the Jesuits and other orders in this land newly won back from the Protestants. The religion of the people was now restricted to communion and mass, pilgrimages and processions, and Marian devotions. Important background to understand the disappearance of any widespread Catholic peace movement and the laity's acceptance of the increasingly authoritarian nature of the church.

794   Bokenkotter. *History.* See **5**, 248-339.

In the post-Tridentine Catholic church no room was allowed for the laity's participation in administration. Doctrinal definitions were narrowed, and the Inquisition and Index ferreted out any dissent and heterodox thought. The Council of Trent also strengthened episcopal control over dioceses, and bishops were quick to stamp out any "challenge to orthodoxy or uniformity." The church became a "rigorist and authoritarian institution," highly centralized, negative, and defensive to the outside world. This state-of-siege mentality opposed all the new democratic and liberal trends of the modern world and stamped out any popular movements, including those for peace. An excellent survey of the trends and ideas that have shaped the modern church until Vatican II.

795   Callahan, William J. "The Spanish Church." See **796**, 34-50.

Traces the growing rift in class background, education, and interests between lower clergy and the hierarchy. The latter came almost exclusively from the nobility, shared its morality, and worked closer and closer with the crown. Cites several examples of high clergy humiliated and hounded out of office for their oppostion to state interests. "In the end, the hold of the church over the masses depended on the ceremonial and placatory aspects of religion." One can easily see the great difficulty of building any form of peace witness under such circumstances.

796   Callahan, William J. and David Higgs, eds. *Church and
       Society in Catholic Europe of the Eighteenth Century.*
       New York: Cambridge University Press, 1979.

       The early modern church was more rigid in every way
       than the medieval, pre-Tridentine one. All forms of popu-
       lar spirituality and expression were thoroughly controlled.
       All dissent was systematically wiped out. Though it does
       not discuss the Catholic peace tradition, this collection of
       essays provides excellent discussion of this rigidification.
       Includes **793, 795, 801, 802,** and **807.**

797   Chadwick, Owen. *The Reformation.* New York: Penguin
       Books, 1979.

       Reprint of the 1972 edition. A good, popular, single-
       volume history of the period. Excellent background
       material. Good general bibliography.

798   Cragg. *Age of Reason.* See **751.**

       This is a good survey of all religious developments
       during the seventeenth and eighteenth centuries. Cragg
       shows how papal influence fell to an all-time low during
       the period, and how the churches gradually fell under the
       control of nation-states and served the interests of
       monarchies. They became powerless against new eco-
       nomic and political forms as all reform impulses were
       subordinated to raison d'etat. Bishops, drawn increas-
       ingly from the aristocracy, lost sight of the spiritual and
       material needs of their congregations and remained content
       with the church's servitude to the state.
       The Enlightenment's distrust of all deep religious
       convictions and of popular spirituality as crass superstition
       reinforced the decline of genuine religious movements
       from the people. Jansenism also contributed to this dis-

trust of activism in its hostility to a theology of good
works and its opposition to Jesuit Humanism and
rationalism. Quietism's spiritual passivity and its avoidance of external demonstrations of piety also helped create
an atmosphere of religious passivity that equated peace
solely with the inner contemplation of the godhead.

On the other end, parish clergy received increasingly
poorer educations, while their efforts to join the laity in
protesting abuses were silenced by the bishops. In short,
the spirituality of the age flowed from the top down;
dissent in all forms was swiftly silenced by the apparatus
of the state and by the Inquisition and episcopal controls.
The evidence that Cragg assembles shows that this was
not an age for widespread, popular peace movements.

799   Greaves, R.W. "Religion," *NCMH* 7: *The Old Regime,
        1713-1763.* J.O. Lindsay, ed. New York: Cambridge
        University Press, 1966, 113-40.

        Good background and introduction.

800   Heyer, F. *The Catholic Church from 1648 to 1870.*
        London: Black, 1969.

        A useful survey.

801   Higgs, David. "The Portuguese Church." See **796**, 51-
        65.

        The Portuguese experience paralleled that of other
        Catholic countries in the age. As the gap between higher
        and lower clergy widened, and the needs of the poor
        majority receded into the background, the hierarchy and
        monarchy imposed ever tighter controls on all forms of
        popular expression both secular and religious. The
        Inquisition set up an almost secret police to ferret out

dissenters, popular religious festivals and processions were suppressed, the laity was excluded from the pulpit and other forms of expression. The result was the separation of the hierarchy from popular spirituality in urban centers and the de-Christianization of large portions of the countryside. Clearly not the conditions required for a thriving Catholic peace movement.

802   Hufton, Olwen. "The French Church." See **796**, 13-33.

Popular spirituality declined throughout the eighteenth century to such an extent that in certain areas fifty percent of the population had abandoned the church. Religious observance was reduced to the level of ritual externals, with the result that Catholicism became a paganized religion in rural France. Replacing the Christian structures for the young, military service now became a normative influence. The intellectual forces of the church were, meanwhile, devoted to combatting the Philosophes, to the disregard of the moral education of most Catholics.

803   McManners, J. "Religion and the Relations of Church and State," *NCMH* 6 (1970): *The Rise of Great Britain and Russia, 1688-1715/25.* J.S. Bromley, ed., 119-53.

A good introduction to the broad trends of the period.

804   Moose, G.L. "Changes in Religious Thought," *NCMH* 4 (1970): *The Decline of Spain and the Thirty Years War, 1606-48/59.* J.F. Cooper, ed., 169-201.

Traces the major developments during the period: Roman Triumphalism, or the church militant coming to dominate all aspects of life in an alliance with political power; the rise of new spiritualities, including Jansenism and Quietism; and new forms of a socially activist Catholic piety, exemplified by Francis de Sales (1567-1622), Vincent de Paul (1580-1660), and others.

805   Noel, Charles C. "Missionary Preachers in Spain: Teaching Social Virtue in the Eighteenth Century," *American Historical Review* 90, 4 (Oct. 1985): 866-92.

Focuses on four famous preachers, whose themes were all in the Renaissance Humanist tradition of Christian virtues. To this the preachers added a lively criticism of capitalism, business, and economic exploitation. Among the sermons were some that extolled social justice and reconciliation of enemies.

806   O'Connell, Marvin R. *The Counter Reformation, 1560-1610*. New York: Harper & Row, 1974.

An excellent volume, in the Rise of Modern Europe series, that synthesizes much recent research. Pages 32-82, "The Catholic Peace," is an apt description of the Triumphalist definition: the church in alliance with power coming to dominate society and to combat its enemies with all the force made available to it. This is the peace of order and stability achieved by crusade abroad against Protestants, Moslems, and pagans in the New World and enforced at home through repression and Inquisition. O'Connell also provides excellent introduction to the Council of Trent, religious forms, and the beginnings of religious war and rebellion. Excellent bibliography

807   Rosa, Mario. "The Italian Churches." See **796**, 66-76.

The church began to rely more and more on state intervention to put its post-Trent reforms into practice.

Thus Catholic religious life fell more and more into line with governments' aspirations for social and political order. Popular devotion and other religious expression were tightly controlled or suppressed, while greater and greater reliance was placed on internal piety, sacramental devotion, and the spiritual life of the individual family. Social definitions of peace and justice thus fell into disuse.

808   Vidler, Alec R. *The Church in an Age of Revolution*. New York: Penguin Books, 1961.

    A good introduction.

809   Walsh, John. "Religion: Church and State in Europe and the Americas," *NCMH* 9 (1965): *War and Peace in an Age of Upheaval, 1793-1830*. C.W. Crawley, ed., 146-78.

    A good introduction.

810   Whiteman, Ann. "Church and State," *NCMH* 5 (1964): *The Ascendancy of France 1648-88*. F.L. Carsten, ed., 122-48.

    A good introduction.

The Peace Tradition in Early Modern Europe

811   Bainton. *Attitudes*. See 2.

    This is not a satisfactory survey for the period. Pages 122-89 identify the Catholic tradition almost exclusively with the just war and give short shrift to such positive contributions as Las Casas'. While the period produced Rabelais' satires on just-war theory, Bainton contends that most plans for world peace written by Catholics were not essentially Christian but based on natural law. Eimeric Crucé's plan for a world assembly is an example.

812   Brock, Peter. *Pacifism in Europe to 1914*. Princeton: Princeton University Press, 1972.

Takes the Protestant leap over the Middle Ages from the early church to the Czech Brethren and then focuses on Protestant peace churches for the rest of his account.

813   Constantinescu-Bagdat, Elise. *Études d'histoire pacifique.* 2 vols. Paris: Les Presses Universitaires de France, 1924-1925.

This work is uneven and stems from the pacifist reaction in between-war France. Here pacifism can mean anything from Erasmus in Volume 1 to such "pacifists" as Sully and the military engineer Vauban in volume 2. Anyone remotely interested in providing international, or domestic, order, by almost whatever means, seems to fit this definition of pacifism. Yet while there is a great deal of chafe to plod through, there is also some wheat in this broad field. Saint-Pierre's projects for international peace is one example.

814   Lammers. "Ethics." See **33**, 93-103.

While pacifism might be a viable alternative at present, it was never in the mainstream of Catholic moral or ethical philosophy. This was so especially after the Reformation, when the Catholic church rejected the Protestant pacifist sects and saw the unity of the Old and New Testaments threatened by Protestant emphasis on the New. Instead, Roman Catholic ethics turned to natural-law philosophy and the Greco-Roman just-war tradition. Early forms of Catholic international law also deliberately rejected religious justifications and turned to these natural-law solutions. Lammers also contends that, since the Reformation, pacifism has been misunderstood as upholding conscience above just authority, whereas Catholic teaching always subordinated the conscience of the soldier to the decisions of political leaders. True pacifism was thus an aberration in the Catholic tradition. A rehashing of Catholic views familiar in the pre-Vatican II church.

815   Souleyman, Elizabeth V. *The Vision of World Peace in Seventeenth and Eighteenth Century France*. New York: G.P. Putnam's, 1941.

This is one of the most important books for tracing the Catholic peace tradition, and the best available for the early modern period. Includes detailed discussion, with lengthy quotations, of Dubois (**862**), Crucé (**869**), La Bruyère, Fenelon, Guez de Balzac, Pascal (**822**), Saint-Pierre (**878**), and Raynal, among others. Topics include early seventeenth-century proposals, the critics of Louis XIV, strictly religious attitudes to war, the free thinkers, political plans for world order, the thought of the Philosophes, Rousseau and the moralists, and the physiocrats and financiers. Balanced and useful. Excellent bibliography and notes.

The Humanist Tradition

Rabelais

816   Costa. *Irenic Apocalypse*. See **546**.

Pages 107-38, "Daily Bread, the Horrible Mysteries of Rabelais," discuss Rabelais' superabundance of words and images as a true apocalyptic metaphor for the process of fulfillment in the end time. Aside from direct parallels to the text of the *Apocalypse,* which Costa analyzes, Rabelais' subtext is a discourse on the essential non-violence required for the apocalyptic transition to fulfill-ment. Violence in pursuit of the millennium, in fact, will only postpone its coming. Individual episodes also highlight Rabelais' Erasmian concern for peace and his parodies of France's war preparations. Excellent biblio-graphy on apocalyptic literature.

817   Rabelais, François. *The Histories of Gargantua and Pantagruel.* J.M. Cohen, transl. Baltimore: Penguin Books, 1969.

Rabelais was an unabashed disciple of Erasmus. His book is fully in the Humanist tradition of social and political satire and, like the *Praise of Folly* (711), touches on every aspect of contemporary life. Rabelais' age was one of increasing rigidity and ideological war, however, and both his impact and the reaction to it were far more bitter. Book One, "Gargantua," presents — among many other things — the story of Picrochole's invasion of Grandgousier's kingdom. In Rabelais' satire of the just war, the conflict is caused by an argument over some sweet cakes and by Picrochole's bad advisors and personal madness. Yet Grandgousier defends his king-dom only with the most just means — if, of course, we ignore the help of his son, the giant Gargantua.

In the course of the campaign Rabelais is able to paint vivid mockeries of chivalrous encounters, but his condemnations of war (spoken by the victors) are straightforward, if also a bit overblown: war is contrary to Gospel teachings and imitates the exploits of pagan heros — the Alexanders, Scipios, and Herculeses of the world. "What the Saracens and Barbarians of old called deeds of prowess we now call robbery and wickedness."

Book Three includes a satire on the just wars of colonial expansion first hinted at by More in *Utopia* and now being waged around the world. Pantagruel and his companions' conquest of Dipsodia is a direct attack on the methods of European colonization. Rabelais' criticism of the warrior also takes on an interesting modern note when he explicitly equates war with sexual aggression, declaring the codpiece "the first piece of harness in the arming of a warrior." Cohen provides a good introduction to Rabelais' life and work.

818   Stapfer, Paul. "Les idées de Rabelais sur la guerre," *Bibliothèque Universelle et Revue Suisse* 3rd. ser., 40 (1888): 367-79.

Detailed discussion of Picrochole's invasion of Grandgousier's realm in Book One, the devastation of the peasants' lives, of the warrior monks, and of the contrast between Gospel precepts and the deeds of Hercules, Alexander, Hannibal, and Caesar. Stapfer shows how Grandgousier attempts to prevent war out of a sense of humanity and insists that Rabelais' intent here is quite serious. Stapfer also discusses Pantagruel's peaceful transplanting of the Utopians to Dipsodia in Book Three and concludes that Rabelais intended this to contrast sharply with Charlemagne's forced resettlements of the Saxons and Flemings.

Montaigne

819   Armaingaud, N. "Montaigne et la guerre," *Revue Politique et Parlementaire* 98 (1919): 81-86, 186-96, 304-15.

A survey of Montaigne's views on peace drawn from his essays. A good introduction.

820   Montaigne, Michel Eyquem de. *The Complete Essays.*
        Donald M. Frame, transl. Stanford: Stanford University Press, 1958.

These essays cover a great span of time and subject matter. One must be wary, therefore, of selecting only those that provide evidence for peacemaking to the detriment of an overall understanding of the man. While Montaigne was no pacifist, he was an important spokesman for the Erasmian tradition of Humanism in sixteenth-century France. Both his political career and his writings demonstrate an unswerving commitment to toleration and the peaceful settlement of conflicts. For this he was named as an arbiter in several of the Protestant-Catholic conflicts of the period and was condemned by extremists on both sides for his efforts. Montaigne's classicism and his intellectual skepticism, both similar to Erasmus', allowed him to strip through the pious myths and sentimentalism of war and the warrior ethic. While he called on the warrior to fight honestly, he saw the just war as a mere pretext for aggression and condemned all wars of religion and violence against religious dissenters. Like Erasmus, he also used comparisons to the animal world for his sociology of violence, declaring that war makes humans far more savage than beasts.

While Montaigne can praise Caesar as the ideal soldier in one essay, in another he observes that ancient history is full of stories of great heroes who were nothing more than bloodthirsty and lecherous men bent on plunder: Caesar, Augustus, Alexander, the Trojans and Greeks. In the modern world kings show little better motive: war is caused by personal whims, a lust for glory, and flattery. War must be judged on the same moral level that we judge individual actions. Frame is an acknowledged master of this field. His biographical and introductory materials are first rate.

Pascal

821   Pascal, Blaise. *Pensées.* T.S. Eliot, intro. New York: Dutton, 1958.

      A good, handy edition. See especially the essays numbered 291-294, 300-301, and 538.

822   Souleyman. See **815**, 56-58.

      In his *Pensées,* Pascal declares that all wars are abominations and that peace is the highest blessing. This and other truths are not confined by national boundaries, and it is absurd to kill another man simply because he lives on the other side of a boundary line. Just wars are an absurdity.

Francisco de Vitoria and International Law

823   Aguilar, Jose Manuel de. *The Law of Nations and the Salamanca School of Theology.* Washington, DC: Spanish Embassy, 1947.

      The Catholic tradition of international law had precedents in Roman law, in Isidore of Seville, and in Thomas Aquinas and the Scholastics. With Vitoria and his colleagues the law of nations evolved into a hybrid of natural and positive law, which includes custom but is also based on Scripture, Aristotle, Cicero, and St. Augustine. This tradition states that civic life is natural and involves mutual obligations and rights. Basic human rights stem from the natural foundations of international law and the inherent unity of humanity. Nation-states have legal validity only so long as they respect these basic principles of human unity and rights.

From these principles stem international customs, such as the inviolability of ambassadors, and the basis for international agreements on the law of nations. While Vitoria implies that a supranational authority is needed to implement the natural-law rights and obligations of individuals and peoples, he does not really ever define one. War is a just instrument of this world order, like the force used by the police, but such wars can only be just if waged to implement world order and not the policies of individual princes or nations. The individual prince or state cannot act as both plaintiff, judge, and executioner. In these attitudes Vitoria, and not Grotius, emerges as the true founder of modern international law.

824   Benson, Robert L. "Medieval Canonistic Origins of the Debate on the Lawfulness of the Spanish Conquest." See **826**, 1: 327-34.

The basis of Indian rights, justness of wars of conquest, and compulsion in canon law.

825   Brière, Yves de la. "Conceptions du droit international chez les théologiens catholiques." In C. Dupuis. *Les grands systèmes de politique internationale*. Paris: Carnegie Endowment for International Peace, 1930.

Not seen.

826   Chiappelli, Fredi, ed. *First Images of America: The Impact of the New World on the Old*. 2 vols. Berkeley and Los Angeles: University of California Press, 1976.

A collection of essays. Includes **824** and **831**.

827   Dalmau, J. "Suarez, Francisco," *NCE* 13: 751-54.

     A good introduction.

828   Eppstein John. *The Catholic Tradition of the Law of
     Nations.* Washington, DC: Carnegie Endowment for
     International Peace, 1935.

     Surveys the intellectual tradition of such writers as
Vitoria and Fenelon.

829   Foriers, Paul. "L'organisation de la paix chez Grotius et
     l'école de droit naturel." See **48**, 275-376.

     Reviews Grotius' antecedents in the Spanish school of
international law.

830   *Francisco de Vitoria. Addresses in Commemoration of the
     Fourth Centenary of his Lectures "De Indis" and "De
     Iure Belli" 1532-1932.* Washington, DC: Catholic
     University, 1932.

     A collection of essays, including **838, 845,** and **849.**

831   Grisel, Étienne. "The Beginnings of International Law and
     General Public Law Doctrine: Francisco de Vitoria's
     De Indis prior." See **826**, 1: 305-25.

     The *De Indis* emerged as a series of lecture notes. In
the course of these lectures, analyzing all the pros and cons
of an argument in true Scholastic style, Vitoria touched on
the native Americans' rightful dominion to the New
World, Spain's illegitimate claims, and its legitimate titles
to possession. Among these legitimate claims were
peaceful trade, natural association of peoples, Christian
missionary activity, alliances and aid to the Americans,

combating the tyranny of Indian lords, the voluntary submission of tribes at war with others, and their inability to rule themselves. Thus Spain's titles were based on divine, natural, and some positive laws. Most important are the divine and natural laws that govern international relations between hitherto unrelated peoples. In this, Grisel argues, Vitoria was fully in the tradition of Erasmus and Vives. (See **680** to **735, 677** to **679.**) While Vitoria's theories may seem to justify Spanish conquest, they also stress the full human rights of the Americans and the essential unity of all humanity.

832   Hamilton, Bernice. *Political Thought in Sixteenth-Century Spain: A Study of the Political Ideas of Vitoria, De Soto, Suarez, and Molina.* Oxford: Clarendon Press, 1963.

This is an extremely useful and well documented survey, and it includes good biographical information and much material of use for the peace tradition in early modern Europe. The Salamanca theologians had fundamental influence on the development of the law of nations. Despite his arguments supporting the Spanish rights of colonization, for example, Vitoria was also instrumental in establishing the rights of the native Americans as full and equal human beings in the context of international law. Vitoria rejected coercion and stressed the rights of non-Christians. Natural law gave native peoples legitimate rights to rule the New World, and he refuted Sepúlveda's arguments that they were inferior beings and thus rightfully enslaved. See **756, 757, 776.** Even the rule of Christ himself is not enough to justify conquest of the New World. Instead, peaceful conversion must be attempted. "War is not an argument for the truth of Christianity. The Indians cannot be made to believe by war, only to pretend to believe and to receive the Christian faith, which would be horrible and sacrilegious."

While Spanish rule is thus seen as a trusteeship over new converts, the Salamanca theologians do argue that Christ did not approve total pacifism and in founding the Gospel law did not abolish natural law. Both Vitoria and Molina agree, however, that war can be justified in defense of peaceful settlements, their colonists or converts, or to redress injuries. In detailing the nature of these defensive wars the Salamanca theologians are led to spell out the criteria for just wars. These expand the thought of medieval Scholastics (609 to 618) and include legitimate power, just cause and reason, proper conduct, including proportionality throughout.

Of great importance to the later just-war and pacifist traditions is Vitoria's discussion of the rights of individual soldiers to question the orders of superiors in the course of a war or preparations for one. On the whole, he notes, the soldier should rely on the judgment of his superiors. This stems from the ignorance of the common folk, their lack of power to stop wars, as well as from the contempt in which rulers hold their subjects. Yet, Vitoria adds, a war can commonly be judged unjust by popular opinion. In this case subjects are not bound to obey. Even if a war is commonly judged just, however, the rights of conscience must be exercised if the individual subject is convinced that the war is wrong, and he ought not to fight if so ordered. "The corollary of this is that whether a war is just or unjust, if a subject's conscience tells him that it is wrong, he must not fight in it."

The influence of these theorists was immense. Not only did they teach thousands of students, but in their own time they also advised Charles V and Philip II on the charges made by Bartolomé de Las Casas (761 to 778) and others against the conquistadors. Their support of the missionaries helped persuade the kings to drastically change Spanish royal policy in the New World.

833   Hanke. *Spanish Struggle.* See **754.**

        While Vitoria insisted that the Spanish had a legal right
to settle in the New World and to carry on missionary
work, even to defend these against attack, he made clear
that neither king, nor emperor, nor pope had any inherent
right over non-Christian lands. In fact, the indigenous
peoples had the right to resist any attempts at conquest,
since natural law made them the full equals of Europeans.
In the end, however, Vitoria's influence on the course of
events was questionable.

834   Johnson. *Ideology.* See **613.**

        Pages 150-71 are especially useful for the Spanish
tradition of International Law, just-war theory and the
contributions of the Spanish legists and theologians to this
discussion.

835   Kamen, Henry. "Clerical Violence in a Catholic Society:
        The Hispanic World 1450-1720." See **53,** 201-216.

        On Spain's militant clergy in theory in action both in
the New World and in Spain. The essay is part of a
collection that emphasizes the church's links to the state
and its warmaking. Nevertheless, Kamen does acknowl-
edge the role of the Salamanca school, of Las Casas, the
Franciscans and Dominicans in forming a "peace lobby" at
the Spanish court. This lobby had a strong influence on
royal policy and was able to alter the brutality of the
Spanish in the New World.
        Such efforts were, however, overcome by events, and
Kamen cites the paternalism of the Franciscans in Mexico
and the Jesuits in Paraguay and their resort to violence as
evidence. The last part of the essay focuses on clerical
crime and violence in Spain.

836   Lange. *Doctrine pacifique.* See **654**.

The title is a misnomer. Includes sections on Saint Pierre, Crucé, and on Sully's Grand Design for peace, all of which were internationalist plans for world confederations with military forces to impose international peace and internal stability. A good example of the intellectual confusion concerning the true nature of nonviolence.

837   ——.*Histoire de l'internationalisme.* See **655**.

A good survey, including sections on Dubois (**852** and **856**), Wolsey's Universal Peace project of 1518 (**850**), Rabelais (**817-818**), Montaigne (**819-820**), Vitoria, Suarez, Grotius, the anonymous *Apologie de la Paix,* Guillaume Postel and his hopes for millennial conversion, Tommaso Campanella and his universal monarchy, Crucé (**866-869**), and Sully's *Grand Design.*

838   McKenna, Charles H. "Vitoria and His Times." See **830**, 13-24.

A good introduction to his life, works, and times.

839   ——."Vitoria, Francisco de." *NCE* 14: 727-28.

A good brief introduction.

840   Muldoon, James M. "The Contribution of the Medieval Canon Lawyer to the Formation of International Law," *Traditio* 28 (1972): 483-97.

A good survey.

841   ——.*Popes.* See **519**.

Vitoria helped found the intellectual opposition to the conquest of the Indies on moral, not legal, grounds.

842   Onclin, Willy. "L'idée de la société internationale en Europe occidentale avant Grotius." See **48**, 219-40.

The medieval and Renaissance origins of the concepts of international order and law.

843   Scott, James Brown. *The Catholic Conception of International Law.* Washington, DC: Georgetown University Press, 1934.

Its origins in the medieval traditions and into the Salamanca school.

844   ——.*The Spanish Conception of International Law and of Sanctions.* Washington, DC: Carnegie Endowment for International Peace), 1934.

Focuses on the Salamanca school.

845   ——."Vitoria and International Law." See **830**, 37-43.

A brief examination of his concepts and their place in the development of the modern system.

846   Suarez, Francisco. *A Work on the Three Theological Virtues: Faith, Hope and Charity.* In James Brown Scott, ed. *The Classics of International Law. Selections from Three Works of Francisco Suarez, S.J.* Oxford: Clarendon Press, 1944.

Presents the text of this important work.

847 Truyol y Serra, Antonio. "La conception de la paix chez Vitoria et les classiques espagnols du droit des gens." See **48**, 241-73.

The age of Vitoria saw vast new dislocations: the new discoveries, the rise of the nation-states, religious division and the end of Christendom, and the pressing problem of war and peace. The emerging theory of international law therefore drew on church, scholastic, and Humanist traditions to address these problems. Excellent biographical and bibliographical materials on Vitoria and nearly a dozen other Spanish legal thinkers.

Much of the article focuses on Vitoria, however, and seeks to explain his internationalism in terms of a common human republic that allows for a pluralist structure. Truyol y Serra sees the roots of this concept in classical political theory: Aristotle, Cicero and the Stoics, underscored by biblical injunctions to "love your neighbor as yourself." Unlike the Stoics and the medieval tradition, however, Vitoria's human unit is not bound by a universal monarchy but by a community of independent states harmonized by the *ius gentium,* the law of nations, that is based on natural law and provides all humans with the same human rights and states with the basis for independence and cooperation. Natural law, and not divine right, is also the basis for political legitimacy. This therefore gives non-Christians fully equal rights against conquest and subjugation.

848 Vitoria, Francisco de. *De Indis et De Iure Belli relectiones.* Ernest Nys, ed.; John P. Bate, transl. Washington,

DC: Carnegie Institution, 1917; reprint, Dobbs Ferry, NY: Oceana, 1964.

Still a good edition, with facing English and Latin texts. Nys' English introduction precedes the texts translated by Bate. Pages 299 to 471 print a facsimile of the 1696 edition.

849   Wright, Herbert. "Vitoria and the State." See **830**, 25-38.

Not seen.

Plans for World Peace

850   Adams. *Better Part of Valor*. See **9-16**.

Spurred by ambitions to the papacy, Cardinal Wolsey launched an all-out campaign to have ratified a treaty of universal peace among European rulers. Such a treaty was signed on October 2, 1518 to the lavish praise of the Humanists. While broken almost immediately, the treaty does show that sentiment for some form of international control over conflicts did survive from the medieval idea of Christendom and could be converted into the political language of early modern Europe.

851   Alighieri, Dante. *On World Government (De Monarchia)*. Herbert W. Schneider, transl.; Dino Bigongiari, intro. Indianapolis and New York: Bobbs-Merrill, 1957.

The same love of peace and order that infuses so much of the *Divine Comedy* is also apparent here. Yet, while the great poem focuses on the social anarchy of the Italian city states, the *De Monarchia* tries to offer a solution in the unity brought about through the rule of a single government over the peninsula and over Christendom as a whole

Humanity, Dante argues, needs unity for peace and tranquility. Unity is the nature of God and of humanity, and divine rule in heaven should be mirrored by monarchy on earth. Only with a unified rule can peace, justice, and individual liberty be fulfilled. The Roman Empire was marked by special divine favor. Now, however, the papacy and the clergy argue that rule derives through the church, and clerical usurpation of the laity's power has brought great havoc to the world. Christ's sword is that of spiritual rule, and the church must concentrate on its spiritual mission.

Dante is not preaching Christian quietism, but an active political role for the laity written in the language of the times. His vision of peace is highly influenced by medieval Scholastic notions of order and justice: each in his or her own place properly fulfilling his or her function unhindered by the violence or oppression of others, each one's place guaranteed by a strong government.

852   Attiya. *Crusade.* See **411**.

Pages 47-73 offer a good introduction to Pierre Dubois' life and his plans for a new international order.

853   Davis, Charles T. "Remigio de' Girolami and Dante: A Comparison of Their Conceptions of Peace." *Studi danteschi* 36 (1959): 105-36.

Not seen.

854   Dubois, Pierre. *The Recovery of the Holy Land.* Walther I. Brandt, transl. and ed. New York: Columbia University Press, 1956.

Brandt provides a good introduction to Dubois' life and the context of his works, and then goes on to analyze the *Recovery*. The work presents two major themes: the genuine desire for a crusade that would serve to strengthen the position of his master, King Philip IV of France, and the reform of church and society at home as prelude to this crusade. This second theme has interest for the student of internationalism.

Dubois' reform themes have their roots in Scripture, Roger Bacon (524, 525), and Ramon Lull (534 to 544), medieval scholastic and canonist theory, and in Aristotle. This expedition would be planned by a general council of Christendom and would presuppose unity among Christian princes, peace in Christian hearts, and a single Christian commonwealth in which internal war was outlawed. The pope and hierarchy bear the chief responsibility for waging this campaign against war. Language schools devoted to training missionaries and physicians to convert Moslem courts would be established throughout Christendom.

While Dubois gives much attention to plans for the crusade, he states outright that war in itself is wicked. Most princes fight them for their own sake, peace is never their goal, despite their claims. No war can ever be fought against fellow Christians. Instead of through war, disputes between states are to be settled by impartial arbiters, with final appeal to the pope. Sanctions include economic and political: confiscations, embargos, and exile. War can be used only as a last resort, and then only with a heavy heart. Universal peace is the aim of these policies.

855   ——*Summaria brevis et compendiosa doctrina felicis expedicionis et abreviacionis guerrarum.* H. Kampf, ed., in *Quellen zur Geistesgeschichte des Mittelalters und der Renaissance.* Vol. 4. Leipzig-Berlin, 1936.

Not seen.

856 Gatto, Ludovico. "La pace nel pensiero politico di Pierre Dubois." See **449**, 113-53.

While Dubois is known for his ideas on total war, his ideas on making peace are far more important. In fact, his works, including *De recuperatione* and *De abreviatioine guerrarum,* focus on making peace in Europe, with the Crusade to the Holy Land only the occasion for his writing.
Gatto briefly reviews peace writers of the preceding century, as well as Dubois' contemporaries. These include Adam Marsh and Guibert de Tournay, Roger Bacon, and Ramon Lull. He then reviews the content and themes of the *De recuperatione* and emphasizes the originality and importance of Dubois' call for an international assembly (general council) to resolve Europe's conflicts and establish the mechanism for a permanent peace. We must wait until the sixteenth century, in Erasmus' *Querela pacis* (See **693** to **695**) for a discussion of a general peace plan as well thought out.

857 Hemleben, Sylvester John. *Plans for World Peace Through Six Centuries.* Chicago: University of Chicago Press, 1943.

A good, introductory, review of many of the best known Catholic internationalists, including Pierre Dubois, Dante Alighieri, the peace plan of the Congress of Cambrai in 1513, Cardinal Wolsey's plan for universal peace of 1518, Eimeric Crucé's *New Cyneas,* the Spanish internationalists, and Charles Irenée de Saint-Pierre. See also **868** and **871**.

858   Marsiglio of Padua. *The Defender of Peace (The Defensor
        Pacis)*. Alan Gewirth, transl. and ed. New York:
        Harper & Row, 1967; reprint, Toronto: University of
        Toronto Press with the Medieval Academy of
        America, 1980.

        Peace meant much the same to Marsiglio as it meant
        for Dante, or for most thinkers trained in the scholastic
        tradition: harmony and order, and a justice that gave each
        person his or her proper place in the universe. Marsiglio's
        analysis covers the foundations of the state in natural law,
        the origin and development of the church, and the church's
        usurpation of the powers of the state, with the resulting
        civil war and social anarchy that it entailed. True peace, he
        argues, will come about only when the papacy renounces,
        or is made to renounce, its claims to supremacy and
        assumes a spiritual leadership, leaving the state to lay
        leadership. Only when Christendom has one head can the
        order and justice required for peace be built. Marsiglio
        also discusses the nature of this unified rule and concludes
        that it resides with the people themselves. The *Defender of
        the Peace* was immediately condemned by the pope.
        Gewirth provides a good introduction to Marsiglio's life.

859   Reeves. *Influence*. See **554**, 295-508.

        An intrinsic element of Joachite millennial thought in
        the Middle Ages and early modern period was the role
        given to a Last World Emperor or Angelic Pope in the las
        apocalyptic days. At this time the world would be
        converted to Christianity and brought under universa
        peace and harmony by the rule of a divinely appointed
        agent. Depending on the sources and tradition, this was
        either to be a secular or a religious ruler. At various time
        the Hapsburg or Valois kings, at others a pope, or even a
        leader of the Spiritual Franciscans or another dissiden

group was the likely candidate. While the sources are not consistent in discussing the agency of this universal conversion and peace, most attribute it to divine intervention without the need for human effort in crusades and other wars. In fact, the nonviolent suffering of the elect in imitation of the early church is an important element in many prophesies of the Joachite tradition.

860   ——.*Prophetic Future.* See **555**, 59-82.

This is essentially a distillation of **554** in paperback form.

861   Russell, Joycelyne G. "The Search for Universal Peace: The Conferences at Calais and Bruges in 1521," *Bulletin of the Institute of Historical Research* 44 (1971): 162-93.

The Renaissance inherited at least the propaganda notion that peace could be concluded on a universal scale by leaders of nations acknowledging that they were all part of a single Christendom.

862   Souleyman. See **815**, 2-8.

Detailed discussion of the life, career, and works of Pierre Dubois and his plans for an international order.

863   Vasoli, Cesare. "La pace nel pensiero filosofico e teologico-politico di Dante a Ockham." See **449**, 27-67.

On medieval theories of general human rights and politics. Dante's political views were not based simply on a reading of Aristotle but also derive from his first-hand

experience of the spiritual and political crisis of his time.
He held that the state is built on humanity's natural
cooperativeness and expresses itself best in city life, in
which no one is sufficient without another's help. From
this, however, the desire for more territory leads to war,
which introduces discord into the state and reduces it to a
base level. Dante therefore looks to the *Imperium*, politica
authority writ large, to restore peace and justice on a local
basis. Only with this tranquility, guaranteed by order, can
true justice be found. This is the ability of each to fulfill
the potential for perfection. This "peace" is also the
starting point for Marsiglio of Padua, who held that all
human groupings must be informed by universal
principles of justice that form communities and lead to
peace, which is the health of the body politic.

Ockham, on the other hand, predicated his political
theory on the doctrine of the fall and the need for human
institutions to check evil human nature and thus guarantee
peace as order and justice. Ockham also acknowledged
the theoretical universality of imperial authority, but based
his writing on the reality of states and principalities, all o
whom have the authority and duty to guarantee peace. His
work clearly shows the shift in the fourteenth century
away from universalist theories, such as those of Dante
and Marsiglio.

864   Vesnitch, R.M. "Deux précurseurs français du pacifisme
et de l'arbitrage internationale," *Revue d'Histoire
Diplomatique* 25 (1911): 23-78.

Reviews the life and thought of Pierre Dubois and
Eimeric Crucé. Superceded by Souleyman (**862** and **869**
and others.

865   Wright, Robert F. *Medieval Internationalism*. London
Williams and Norgate, 1930.

The subtitle reads "the contribution of the medieval church to international law and peace." Topics include canon law, papal sovereignty as expressed through international assemblies and arbitrations, theories of international or universal government, papal diplomacy, international finance and commerce, treaties, and marriage alliances. Also discusses the restraints on war provided by the just-war theory, chivalry, the Truce of God, and sanctuary.

Wright attempts to explain away the Crusades by noting that, while they may be condemned by our standards, in the Middle Ages they represented an attempt to bring peace to Europe by exporting war.

Eimeric Crucé

866   Crucé, Eimeric. *Le Nouveau Cynée*. Thomas W. Balch, transl. and ed. Philadelphia: Allen, Lane & Scott, 1909.

The work's five parts discuss the causes of war, the international foundations of peace, the principles of just government, freedom of commerce, and the means used for gaining international peace.

Crucé proposes a form of world confederation meeting regularly at a chosen city through permanent embassies, where international differences are to be settled by a general assembly, with more weighty attention given to a separate, smaller assembly of the representatives of the great republics. The confederation would prevent both international aggression and internal rebellions. Despite Crucé's authoritarianism, however, his peace depends on good government and laws, social justice for the poor, a civil service based on merit, just taxation, and other innovations.

867   ——."A Holy Resolve." See **39**, 68-70.

    This excerpt from *Le Nouveau Cynée* focuses on
Crucé's pacifism more than on his plans for international
order.   Peace, Crucé says, far excels the triumphs of
Alexander, Hannibal, Caesar, or Sertorius.   The honor
that princes gain from peace is not that gained from
tyranny, slaughter, or pillage but entails consistent government and lawful and regulated power.   Differences
between Turk and Persian, French and Spanish, Chinese
and Tartar, Christian, Jew and Moslem are only political.
"Geography does not weaken the ties of blood."

868   Hemleben. *Plans.* See **857**.

    Reviews Crucé's life, career, and works.   Crucé's life
has revealed few details, and his *New Cyneas* exists in
only three copies, of two editions, the 1623 and 1624.   Yet
his analysis of war clearly shows the Erasmian tradition
surviving into the seventeenth century.   His plans for
world peace, on the other hand, look forward to the
internationalism of the nineteenth and the twentieth.
Briefly outlines the work.

869   Souleyman. See **815**, 9-19.

    A good introduction to his thought.   This includes a
strong pacifism that saw even the just war as causing more
harm than it is fought to remedy.   Crucé declares that war
has had its day and that, instead, arbitration must now
determine international conflicts.   He therefore proposes a
World Council of Representatives that relies on moral
compulsion over force.

Saint-Pierre

870 Hayden, J.M. "Saint-Pierre, Charles Irenée Castel de," *NCE* 12: 942.

A brief review of his life and works, with some bibliography.

871 Hemleben. *Plans.* See **857**.

Traces the diplomatic career and writing of Saint-Pierre, especially his *Memorandum for Achieving Perpetual Peace in Europe* of 1712. Hemleben follows the work's different editions and influence and then briefly reviews its major themes.

872 Jacob, M.C., ed. *Peace Projects of the Eighteenth Century.* New York: Garland Publishing, 1974, 1-61.

This is actually a reprint of the *Memorandum* bound together with other works on peace, with the separate paginations of the original editions. Saint-Pierre's plans include a European confederation that would foster unity in political and economic spheres and would insure the internal stability of any member state. While states that refuse to join should be considered enemies, war itself is renounced as an instrument of foreign policy among member states. With disarmament the official policy of members, disputes are to be settled by a commission of arbitration permanently housed in a City of Peace.

873 Laborie, Lanzac de. "L'Apôtre de la paix perpetuelle: l'Abbé de Saint-Pierre," *Revue haebdomadaire* (May 1919).

Not seen.

874   Lacroix, Lucien. "Un Apôtre de la paix: l'Abbé de Saint-Pierre," *La Grande Revue* (May 1919).

        Saint-Pierre as an exponent of international order.

875   La Fontaine, Henri. *Histoire sommaire et chronologique des arbitrages internationaux 1794-1900.* Brussels, 1902.

        Not seen.

876   Lange. *Doctrine.* See **836**, 303-10.

        A good, brief introduction.

877   ——.*Internationalisme.* See **837**, 2: 196-213.

        A good introduction.

878   Souleyman. See **815**, 78-90.

        Saint-Pierre paid a heavy price for his opposition to Louis XIV's wars: dismissal from the French Academy, disgrace at court, and mockery for his adherence to a new international order. His *Project for Perpetual Peace* called for a permanent League of European States and a Federal States of Europe. He provided a detailed list of articles for such a confederation, which Souleyman summarizes in detail.

                    *   *
                       *

CHAPTER 12: *The Lessons of the Twentieth Century*

Introduction

879   Bokenkotter. *History.* See **5**, 301-67.

A very useful introduction to the social and intellectual currents in the Catholic church in the nineteenth and twentieth centuries. These include Christian Democracy, Social Catholics, worker welfare associations, the Catholic workers and Catholic labor union movements, which all had mass appeal and sought to instill traditional Catholic ideas of social justice into the new capitalist world of the nineteenth century. Decentralization and individual responsibility were also cornerstones of the movements. Good background for the foundations of modern Catholic thought on peace and justice.

Bokenkotter also provides a very useful comments on the popes of the twentieth century and notes that they followed a consistent policy that contained an increasingly strong criticism of capitalism and that stressed the rights of the poor and the oppressed. The major work of the modern papacy for peace has been in the realm of world order and internationalism, including limitations on national sovereignty and its efforts for disarmament.

880   Geany, D.J. "Catholic Action," *NCE* 3: 262-63.

This refers to the organized movement of Catholic lay people directed by the church hierarchy. Pius X was the first pope to use the modern concept, and Pius XI gave it definition. By the time of Pius XII it was already being replaced by the term "lay apostolate." John XXIII played down the formal hierarchical elements in the institution. Primarily aimed at issues of personal, familial, and social mores — secondarily at social and economic issues — Catholic Action focused on those aspects on modern liberal societies that the hierarchy was uncomfortable with or incapable of addressing. The movement never really became political in the sense that it opposed the status quo or sought to change fundamental political, economic, or social structures and had little effect on the rise of Fascism, Nazism, or European militarism. Demonstrates the limitations of Catholic work for peace and justice in the early twentieth century.

881   Holmes, J. Derek. *The Papacy in the Modern World.* New York: Crossroad, 1981.

An excellent survey of the twentieth century, including detailed discussion of Benedict XV and World War I; Pius XI and Fascist Italy and Nazi Germany; Pius XII, the Nazis, Soviets, and World War II.

882   Rhodes, Anthony. *The Power of Rome in the Twentieth Century: The Vatican in the Age of Liberal Democracies 1870-1922.* New York: Franklin Watts, 1983.

This and **883** provide an excellent introductory history of the papacy in the twentieth century. This volume begins with the reign of Pius IX, and discusses the Kulturkampf in Germany, Leo XIII and the new Catholic social message, and Benedict XV and World War I.

883   ——.*The Vatican in the Age of the Dictators, 1922-1945.* New York: Holt, Rinehart & Winston, 1974.

Discusses the equivocal attitude of Pius XI toward the Italian Fascists and their invasion of Ethiopia, his ultimate support of Franco in the Spanish civil war, and his gradual withdrawal of support for Catholic political parties, all in the interests of harmony with the secular state. Rhodes views the Reich Concordat of 1933 in much the same light, an attempt to preserve church liberties from the secular state and to ally with the state against the threat of "godless socialism." He also traces Pius XI's progressive disillusionment with the Nazis, culminating in his explosive condemnation in the bull *Mit Brennender Sorge*.

884   Vidler, Alec. *A Century of Social Catholicism*. London: S.P.C.K., 1964.

Traces the movement as a reaction to the industrial revolution and as an attempt to interpret the new methods of work and production in the light of traditional Catholic social teaching. Pages 125-29 and 143-47 examine *Rerum Novarum* of Pope Leo XIII.

Catholic Peacemaking in the Twentieth Century

885   Bainton. *Attitudes*. See 2.

While the peace movements of the nineteenth century stemmed from the international peace societies, both Catholic and Protestant mainline churches tended to avoid contact with them.

886   Beales, Arthur C.F. *The History of Peace*. London: G. Bell, New York: Dial, 1931.

For a general introduction to Catholic peace history in the twentieth century. This focuses on the peace societies in Europe and the United States with brief introductions on pacifism, internationalism, papal arbitration, Catholic and Christian peace societies, and worker's peace groups. Beales notes the suspicion with which papal peace initiatives were met, but records the brilliant record of Benedict XV, who was a pacifist in both theory and practice. Useful survey.

887   Biocca, Dario. "Il nuovo pacifismo e il dibattito sulle consequenze economiche dell'imperialismo e della guerra: 1913-1915," *Nuovo Rivista Storica* 66 (5-6, 1982): 547-63.

Not seen.

888   Cooper, Sandi E. "The Guns of August and the Doves of Italy: Intervention and Internationalism," *Peace and Change* 7, 1-2 (1981): 29-44.

Focuses on the debate among the middle class and intellectuals over maintaining Italy's neutrality during World War I, with Italian peace societies leading the way. Until the 1890s liberal internationalism was the central theme of Italian peace societies. Such internationalists were not pacifists, however, and they opposed Tolstoy's and the Quakers' opposition to military training. Even while militarism became a central concern during the 1890s, with the invasion of Belgium in World War I the peace societies shifted decidedly in favor of military intervention. A good introduction to liberal, secular peace movements that are not pacifist and have no particularly inherent opposition to war.

889   Jougnelet, Suzanne. "Un pacifiste dans la Grande Guerre.

Les letters de Roger Martin du Gard de 1914 à 1918,"
Revue de Bibliothèque Nationale 1, 2 (1981): 99-107.

Not seen.

Papal Peace Efforts

890   Brière, Yves de la. *L'organization international du monde
      contemporain et la papauté souveraine.* 3 vols. Paris:
      Editions S. Spes, 1924-30.

      Papal peace efforts, stemming from the pope's
      position as the universal pastor. Typical of the inter-
      nationalist "pacifism" between the world wars.

891   ——.*L'église et paix.* See **7**.

      While the church has always professed a doctrine of
      peace and has always worked for the "pacification of
      peoples", its peacemaking was "not a sentimental pacifism,
      confused and lacking in judgment, but indeed a positive
      concept, realistic and fertile, in harmony with all the
      postulates and all the just scruples of patriotism." For de
      la Brière these include the military requirements of defense
      and war.

892   Fernessole. *La papauté.* See **581**.

      Begins with a good historical survey of papal peace
      activity before Gregory XVI, and then divides his main
      study into the era before World War I, including Pius IX,
      Leo XIII, and Pius X. Then devotes a separate chapter to
      Benedict XV and to Pius XI.

893   Flannery. *Pattern for Peace.* See **26**.

This is probably the most useful collection of papal documents on papal peacemaking in the twentieth century. Includes writings of every pope from Leo XIII to John XXIII, including documents from papal secretaries of state. This work is indispensable for Catholic peace history.

894   Guerry, Émile M. *The Popes and World Government.* G.J. Roettger, transl. Baltimore: Helicon, 1964.

Focuses on Pius XII's internationalism under a variety of topics, including the community of nations, international order, natural law, the rights and duties of states, obstacles to a community of nations, the disruptions of war, and the church's role in forging a community of nations.

895   Herberichs, G. *Théorie de la paix selon Pie XII.* Paris: A. Pedone, 1964.

Not seen.

896   Koenig, Harry C., ed. *Principles of Peace: Selections from Papal Documents, Leo XIII to Pius XII.* Washington, DC: National Catholic Welfare Conference, 1943.

Like Flannery's (**893**) this is an excellent collection of papal letters, addresses, radio broadcasts, and encyclicals covering the popes of the twentieth century to World War II.

897   Schaefer, Mary C. *A Papal Peace Mosaic 1878-1936. Excerpts from the Messages of Popes Leo XIII, Pius*

X, Benedict XV, and Pius XI. Washington, DC: CAIP, 1936.

A brief collection of excerpts from papal writings on war and peace.

898 Sweeney, Francis, S.J., ed. *The Vatican and World Peace: A Boston College Symposium.* Gerrards Cross: Smythe, 1970.

Here is a collection of congratulatory essays by learned and powerful men, handsomely bound and printed, expounding the merits of the internationalist system. "Twenty copies of this book," the reader is reassured, "have been specially bound in full vellum." Includes **901** and **913**

899 Wright, J.J. "Peace: Modern Papal Teaching," *NCE* 11: 41-45.

Pages 41-42 offer examples of papal texts ranging from Leo XIII to Pius XII that demonstrate that modern Catholic teaching of peace as the work of justice has characterized papal thought throughout the twentieth century.

Pius XII

900 Blet, P. "Pie XII et la France en guerre." *Revue de l'Église Française* 69 (July 1983): 209-32.

Briefly reviews the career of Mgr. Pacelli as a papal diplomat in France and his efforts to reconcile both European powers bent on war and factions within France during and after the struggle.

901   Cardenale, Archbishop H.E. "The Contribution of the Holy See to World Peace in the Areas of Diplomacy, Development and Ecumenism." See **898**, 79-121.

Pius XII's record with the Jews has not gotten a fair hearing. He wrote at least 124 letters to the German bishops condemning atrocities against the Jews, and in 1942 publicly condemned German genocide of Jews in Poland. While the allies did nothing to save the Jews, Pius XII's quiet work through church agencies saved 860,000 throughout Europe.

902   Conway, John S. "The Silence of Pope Pius XII." See **903**, 79-108.

The dispute over Pius XII's complicity with the Nazi regime's atrocities.

903   Delzell, Charles F., ed. *The Papacy and Totalitarianism Between the Two World Wars*. New York: John Wiley, 1974.

Includes **902, 905**.

904   Duclos, P. *Le Vatican et la seconde guerre mondiale*. Paris, 1955.

Not seen.

905   Ellsberg, Patricia Marx. "An Interview with Rolf Hochhuth." See **903**, 108-24.

Hochhuth's play, *The Deputy*, became an overnight sensation and revived the controversy over Pius XII's complicity through silence with the Nazis. Hochhuth discusses the play, his characters, and his critics.

906   Falconi, Carlo. *The Silence of Pius XII*. Bernard Wall,
        transl. Boston: Little, Brown, 1970.

        There were many areas in which the pope knew of
        German atrocities and war crimes: against the Jews, in
        Poland, and Yugoslavia. Even though he was often urged
        to speak out, the pope chose to remain silent. Falconi
        maintains that this was not from fear but from "respectable
        if inadequate motives."

907   Friedlander, Saul. *Pius XII and the Third Reich*. New
        York: Alfred A. Knopf, 1966.

        A collection of documents on papal diplomacy. The
        pope's silence in relation to the Holocaust and the war is
        one of the main themes of the collection. Good back-
        ground material.

908   Gonella, Guido. *The Papacy and World Peace: A Study of
        the Christmas Messages of Pope Pius XII*. London:
        Hollis and Carter, 1945.

        Commentaries on the messages of Christmas 1939,
        1940, and 1941, with excerpts from the Christmas mes-
        sages of 1942, 1943, and 1944. Gonella prefaces this
        collection with remarks that papal peacemaking for Pius
        XII was the "work of justice" and that international peace
        could only be achieved through justice on a world scale.
        Pius repeatedly called for an international organization that
        would have the legislative and judicial powers of the
        League of Nations but that would also have stronger
        powers to compel nation-states to order. The rights of
        minorities, of the oppressed and poor, arms control and
        disarmament, the rights of conscience, and the law of
        nations were also constant themes of the pope's messages.

909   Halecki, Oscar, with James F. Murray. *Eugenio Pacelli:
        Pope of Peace.* New York: Creative Age Press, 1951.

        Traces Pacelli's early life and career, his early papacy
        and World War II, his first peace efforts, and the pope's
        five-point peace plan outlined in *Summi Pontificatus.*
        Then follows his relations with Hitler and Stalin, postwar
        reconstruction, the pope's attitudes to the communists, and
        his encouragement of the United Nations.

910   Hehir. "Just-War Ethic." See **29.**

        By the end of World War II, Pius XII had reduced the
        classic just-war criteria of defense, avenging evil, and
        restoring violated rights to only one: defense from unjust
        attack. While pacifism remained unacceptable to the pope,
        his narrowing of just-war causality helped move the
        church closer to a pacifist stance.

911   Holmes. *Papacy.* See **881.**

        Reviews the large amount of research on Pius XII and
        the Holocaust and notes that the pope received many letters
        of thanks after the war from Jewish groups for his saving
        hundreds of thousands from the Nazis. Holmes examines
        the issues of Pius' silence raised in Rolf Hochhuth's
        controversial play, *The Deputy.* Holmes notes that the
        playwright based his portrait of Pius' complicity with the
        Nazis on a letter deliberately sent to deceive Berlin about
        his real efforts. In so doing he has clouded the pope's
        record and memory. In the end, however, Pius' exercise
        in restraint in an effort to avoid even greater evil played
        into the cynical hands of the Nazis. His efforts to save
        individuals ultimately cost him his reputation.
            With the end of the war Pius became a fervent
        proponent of a new international system and gradually

came to view all the old moral categories of defense as outmoded in light of new weapons, including nuclear ones.

912   Rhodes. *Dictators.* See **883**.

Examines the problems of Pius XII's reign: the German Catholic support of the Nazi war effort, papal opposition to the Italian war effort, Catholic resistance in France and Belgium, and Catholic complicity with the Nazis in such areas as Croatia. Rhodes surveys all literature on Pius XII's silence over the Holocaust and concludes that open opposition would have resulted in the pope's murder at the hands of the Nazis and even greater persecution of Jews and Christians alike. Open excommunication of the Nazis, he argues, would not have prevented the atrocities of Hitler's regime.

913   Walsh, Michael, P., S.J. "Introductory Remarks." See **898**.

Walsh sums up papal peace efforts as a "question of fulchrums and levers." "Stalin asking the question, 'The Pope — how many divisions has he?' was missing the point."

German Catholics, Nazis, and World War II

914   Chickering, Roger P. "The Peace Movement and the Religious Community in Germany 1900-1914," *Church History* 38 (1969): 300-311.

By 1900 internationalism had come to replace personal nonviolence as the meaning of pacifism. Societies for disarmament and international law were at their peak in the years just before the first world war. In Germany such peace societies tended to be predominantly Protestant and middle class, and to be closely monitored by the state. Pacifist groups had no influence at all and were derided by every group in German society, including the church, which was one of the groups' most strident critics. In the end the internationalist "pacifists" failed utterly to prevent war.

915   Claver, Henri. "Une résistance allemande à l'hitlerisme," *Revue d'Histoire et de Philosophie Réligieuse* 62 (July-September, 1982): 261-68.

Not seen.

916   Conway, John S. "The Struggle for Peace Between the Wars: A Chapter from the History of the Western Churches," *Ecumenical Review* 35 (Jan. 1983): 25-40.

Examines the World Alliance of Churches for Promoting International Friendship founded in Constance in August 1914 with the support of the Carnegie Endowment. The movement was predominantly protestant and middle class until 1918 when the devastation of the war forced it to realize that its amateur and sentimental approach had been totally ineffective. Only then was a new emphasis put on individual conscience and Gospel morality.

917   Gallin, Mary Alice. "German Resistance to Hitler; Ethical and Religious Factors." Ph.D. dissertation. Washington, DC: Catholic University, 1961.

On the resistance in general. Very few pages devoted to Catholics per se.

918   Graml, Hermann, H. Mommsen, H. Reichhardt, and E.
        Wolf, eds. *The German Resistance to Hitler.*
        Berkeley: University of California Press, 1970.

        Emphasizes the political resistance. Church resistance
        is covered by **925**.

919   Helmreich, Ernst C. *The German Churches Under Hitler.*
        Detroit: Wayne State University Press, 1979.

        An excellent study of the attitudes of all churches to
        the Nazi regime. Sections on the Catholic response are
        very useful to a study of Catholic peacemaking during the
        period. Analyzes the background of German Catholicism
        in the nineteenth and twentieth century, the Nazis fear of
        possible Catholic resistance, and Catholics' early criti-
        cisms of the Nazi Party as anti-Christian. Yet Helmreich
        also carefully delineates the conflict within German
        Catholicism between this criticism and the desire among
        German Catholics to prove their loyalty to the state. He
        asserts that churchmen were also naive about the true
        intent of the Nazis and glossed over their own anti-
        Semitism.
        Traces Catholics' loyalty to the Center Party in the
        1933 election that brought Hitler to power and their
        continued opposition to the SA and SS. Follows events
        from the Reich Concordat between the Vatican and Hitler's
        government in 1933, the years of conflict over church
        freedoms and moral criticism of the Nazi program, and
        Pius XI's strong condemnations of the Nazi government.
        Helmreich demonstrates that German Catholics did not
        give absolute obedience to the German state. Many, in
        fact, suffered for their opposition. With World War II,
        however, Catholic laity and clergy alike rallied around the
        German nation and people. Unlike the Protestant
        churches, however, Catholic support was conditional, and

Catholics continued to protest many of the Nazis domestic policies, in some cases causing Hitler to back off for fear that increased Catholic resistance would hurt the war effort.

Helmreich observes through carefully assembled evidence that although Catholics did suffer in large numbers for their opposition to certain Nazi policies, all in all "there were no conscientious objectors" to Hitler's wars. He also remarks that in the end German Catholics must share the blame of their country for anti-Semitism, the Holocaust, and the other disasters of the war. Having said this, however, he notes that the German churches stood almost alone in criticizing the Nazi state.

920   Koebner, Thomas. "Vom 'Pazifismus' der dreissiger Jahre: Der Aktivismus deutscher Intellectueller im Exil (1933-1945), *Parlament* 33, 40-41 (1983): B9-B16.

Not seen.

921   Lewy, Guenter. *The Catholic Church and Nazi Germany.* New York: McGraw-Hill, 1964.

This is an excellent study of the church's relations to Hitler and his regime. Traces developments from church relations to the Center Party, Hitler's election and early rule, the Reich Concordat, and the Fulda Bishops' Conference and its warnings against the Nazis. Then traces the shift in Catholic attitudes supporting the Reich in the political sphere, but its continued opposition to the Nazis' "moral" and "religious" neopaganism: the conflicts over eugenics and euthanasia, over church privileges and liturgical practices. Lewy then examines the role of the church in World War II, the bishops' support of the war effort, the role of the papacy in the war and the Holocaust.

Lewy observes that the Nazis feared the church's

strength and asserts that had it leveled excommunications and interdicts upon the Nazis it could have been effective in halting the regime's brutality. After the war Pius XII claimed that there had been an active Catholic resistance, yet the record, and the bishops' own condemnation of any revolt against the Reich, must make this role minimal.

922   Littell, Franklin H., and Hubert G. Locke. *The German Church Struggle and the Holocaust.* Detroit: Wayne State University Press, 1974.

A collection of essays, including **927**.

923   Von Oppen, Beate Ruhm. *Religion and Resistance to Nazism.* Princeton: Center for International Studies, Princeton University Press, 1971.

This address surveys the general problem of church resistance. Von Oppen notes that, according to surviving secret police reports, Catholic resistance was better defined and more vocal than Protestant and gave the Nazis far greater trouble. Many examples survive of Catholic denunciations of anti-Semitism and other racial policies. The paper also gives several individual examples of Catholic resistance to Nazi war and social policies, including that of the Catholics Franz Jaegerstaetter (**933, 941** to **944**), Archbishop von Gallen, and Bernhard Lictenberg.

924   Walker, Lawrence D. "Priests vs Nazis in the Diocese of Limbourg, 1934: The Confessional Factor," *Historical Social Research-Historische Sozialforschung* 23 (July 1982): 55-65.

The bishop encouraged political dissent against the Nazis and made his diocese a center of protest. Such protest stemmed naturally from the Catholic tradition of opposition to the secular state and was a legacy of the Kulturkampf of the nineteenth century.

925   Wolf, Ernst. "Political and Moral Motives Behind the Resistance." See **918**, 193-234.

A general survey of all church resistance. Catholics are discussed on pages 224-26. Catholic resistance was based on an opposition to the Nazis "un-Christian naturalism" and grew reluctantly. At heart church leadership feared the destruction of hierarchical structures and thus the self-destruction of the church itself. They therefore backed away from any total break with the Nazi government. There were, however, many notable individuals who did protest. These included Franz Reinisch, Max Josef Metzger, and A. Delp. Since the war, however, these isolated individuals have been built up to create a legend of Catholic church resistance.

926   Zahn Gordon. "The Case for Christian Dissent." See **930**, 243-63.

With rare exceptions German Catholics cooperated with the Nazi war effort. Individual resisters included Franz Reinisch and Max Josef Metzger. More significant, however, was the radical shift among the hierarchy from active support of such peace groups as the German Peace League after World War I to avid support of the Nazi war effort. Such a collapse of the peace movement was due as much to the extreme nationalism of many German Catholics as to the brutal suppression of the peace groups by the Nazis immediately after they came into power. Authoritarian interpretations of the just-war theory, excluding the layperson from any competent evaluation of the war's justice, also contributed to the demise of a peace movement. Zahn notes that the "presumption of justice" on behalf of the state's ability to wage war and of the individual's incompetence to question this justice is a true wild card for the state, a joker in the deck of the just-war theory.

927   ——."Catholic Resistance? A Yes and a No." See 922, 203-37.

During the postwar Adhenauer years in Germany, largely as a result of leftist revisionism, there grew up in Germany the postwar myth of church resistance to Adolf Hitler. While such claims of church resistance have often been exaggerated, in the final analysis the church remained the only institution in German society that mounted any effective opposition to the Nazis. This opposition had a paradoxical nature, however, what Zahn terms the "patriotism-and-protest" dynamic. The church as an institution, an *ecclesia*, was jealous of its freedoms and privileges and made every effort to maintain them. It did so, however, within the context of the Reich Concordat and traditional arrangements between church and state in German society. It protected the realm of God: liturgy, popular devotion, moral issues, such as euthanasia and eugenics, the immunity of clerics from military and other service; while it left what was Caesar's — war and peace, and political policy — entirely to the state and urged obedience on church members. The hierarchy also had to compete with the fanatical nationalism of the Catholic laity, with the cult of the nation and of the new German "manliness."

When it came to the duty of Catholics to serve their country, however, the Catholic hierarchy displayed an ultra-nationalism that equated service to Christ with service in Hitler's armies and that never questioned the legitimacy of the Führer himself. Thus whatever social and moral opposition the church had mounted beginning in 1934 crumbled with the coming of war in 1939.

Zahn then asks the logical question to these findings: did the German bishops underestimate the potential for resistance of 30 million Catholics? Protest against Nazi domestic issues had drawn thousands to the bishops' standards, and this should have assured them that withdrawal of support was a real possibility, yet the hierarchy continued to give the Nazis their full loyalty. Zahn concludes that the bishops themselves truly believed in the Reich, thus leaving the Nazis to choose the terms of the debate. "If there is any single overriding lesson to be learned from this, it would seem to be that the religious community must never become so enmeshed in its support for a given socio-political order that it looses its potential to be a source of dissent and disobedience."

928   ——*German Catholics and Hitler's Wars: A Study in Social Control.* New York: Sheed and Ward, 1962.

This is a scholarly, well argued and well annotated study of the problem of Catholic complicity with the Nazi war effort. Zahn summarizes much of the research he presents in other articles. See **926, 927, 929**. The book traces the shift from the strong support by Germany's Catholic bishops for the German Peace Union immediately after World War I to the nationalistic support they gave to the Nazi war effort. The bishops, and most German Catholics, Zahn notes, were willing to give the text "render to Caesar" as broad an interpretation as possible, equating the "Good Catholic" with the "Good German," the "soldier of Christ" with the defender of the German Fatherland against the Bolsheviks. Official Catholic thought sided decisively against social upheaval and made the strongest presumption in favor of the state's right to decide on the justness of its own wars. Such active association of the church with the secular state thus eliminated all questioning and dissent.

929   ——."The German Catholic Press and Hitler's Wars." See **930**, 204-29.

The German Catholic press had clear and definite criteria to judge the justice of Hitler's wars. The question is: did they? Zahn concludes that the Catholic press shared the extreme nationalism of German Catholics. While they generally opposed many of the Nazis' domestic programs, they were decidedly in favor of their wars, and emphasized that Catholics should continue to do duty to Folk and Fatherland. After the suppression of independent Catholic papers in 1935, the remaining official diocesan papers not only failed to condemn Hitler's wars, but by caving in to censorship in order to continue publishing they also became, wittingly or not, an arm of Goebbel's propaganda machine.

930   ——.*War, Conscience and Dissent.* See **57**.

A collection of Zahn's essays, including **926, 929,** and **941**.

Individual Witness

931   Fahey. "Pax Christi." See **22**.

Relates the story of Bishop Pierre-Marie Théas of Lourdes, who was arrested by the Nazis in 1944 and imprisoned for his vocal opposition to the occupation of France and the persecution of the Jews. After the war

Théas founded Pax Christi as an act of reconciliation with his former German enemies. "To make peace," he has said, "one must learn to forgive, for to forgive is to make peace."

932   Gill, Eric. *Autobiography.* London: Cape, 1940.

Gill was an innovative English engraver, book designer, sculptor, and intellectual whose art and life pursued a return to the community and life of the pre-industrial age while simultaneously contributing to the new style of expression of the 1930s and 1940s. His circle included many of Great Britain's leading Catholic peacemakers. At Capel-y-ffin in Wales Gill, his wife, and their associates formed a modern monastic community, a precursor to artistic communes of the 1960s and Lanza del Vasto's Community of the Ark in France (See **997** to **1017**).

Gill linked his nonviolence to an acute interest in the pursuit of social justice as an antidote to the exploitation that he found in the modern capitalist world.

933   Merton, Thomas. "An Enemy of the State." See **40**, 134-38.

Merton's reflections on Franz Jaegerstaetter and the publication of Gordon Zahn's *In Solitary Witness* (**944**). Merton declares that the single individual enjoying God's grace is greater than the whole church without God's grace (a view shared by the medieval Franciscan Spirituals. See **619** to **632**). Jaegerstaetter understood that nonviolent resistance involved giving rather than taking life, and that only spiritual weapons could prevail against the great Anti-Christ. Merton concludes by declaring that after the

Second Vatican Council no Catholic can escape the obligation to refuse obedience to unjust commands.

934 ——."Danish Nonviolent Resistance to Hitler." See **40**, 165-67.

A very important appreciation of courageous and effective noncooperation, illustrating the role of the Danish *nation* in nonviolence that converted even the SS from exterminating the Jews. Merton recounts how, when the Jews of Denmark were forced to adopt the yellow star, the king immediately took to wearing one in public. He was soon joined by most of his subjects. This and other acts of nonviolent resistance finally persuaded the Nazis that to continue their deportations would lose them the cooperation of the people and would require vast allotments of troops to keep an entire population at bay.

935 ——."A Martyr for Peace and Unity: Father Max Josef Metzger (1887-1944)." See **40**, 139-43.

Reflections on the Catholic priest executed by the Gestapo for preaching Christian unity and nonviolence.

936 ——."Passivity and Abuse of Authority." See **40**, 129-33.

An extended meditation on Ignace Lepp's *Christian Failure*. Merton examines individual clergy and laity whose popular spirituality bore witness to Christian truths when learned and powerful churchmen were lost in moral confusion and complicity with the warmakers. Merton's words recall the ideas of medieval Franciscan Spirituals who declared that when all else in the church fails, truth may abide in one person alone, such as the Virgin Mary alone at the foot of Christ's cross. See **619** to **632**.

937   Origo, Iris. *A Need to Testify*. Orlando, FL: Harcourt
       Brace Jovanovich, 1984.

       A series of portraits of nonviolent opponents to
       Mussolini. These include Lauro de Bosis, Ignazio Silone,
       Ruth Draper, and Gaetano Salvemini.

938   Riesterer, P. *Father Rupert Mayer, S.J.* London, n.d.

       Not seen.

939   Shen, Lucia Simpson. "A Martyr's Voice," *America* 152
       (March 2, 1985): 171-74.

       On anti-Nazi priest A. Delp. Reviews his life, con-
       version to Roman Catholicism at 14, his work as editor of
       the Jesuit magazine *Stimmen der Zeit,* and Nazi suspicions
       of him for his writings there. Nazi censorship only
       increased Delp's resistance, his help to Jews and his
       activities in the Kreisau Circle, an interfaith and interclass
       group aimed at reconstructing Germany after the war.
       With the assassination attempt on Hitler, the Circle, though
       not linked to the plot, was destroyed and its members,
       including Delp, condemned to death.
       His prison experiences only heightened his Christian
       witness as we learn from his *Prison Meditations,* smug-
       gled out on scraps of paper. Shen concludes the article
       with a summary of Delp's sermon on the feast of St.
       Elizabeth of Hungary, stressing that the saint was a peace-
       maker; that she gathered around her the powerless, poor,
       and sick; and that Christians must protect life. "And woe
       to those who have destroyed a human life, who have
       desecrated an image of God."

940   Steinfels, Peter. "Appointment with Hitler," *Commonweal*
       (July 12, 1985): 395.

Asks once again the popular question for pacifists: what would you have done about Adolf Hitler? Answers pacifists that the just war must sometimes be considered.

941   Zahn, Gordon. "Conscientious Objection in Nazi Germany: Martyrdom, 1943." See **930,** 177-91.

A summation of his research on Franz Jaegerstaetter, who had his own answer on what to do about Hitler, with parallels to the trials of conscience in contemporary America.

942   ——.*Franz Jaegerstaetter: Martyr for Conscience.* Erie, PA: Pax Christi, n.d.

An abbreviated version of **944,** with reflections on the situation in modern America.

943   ——."In Praise of Individual Witness: F. Jaegerstaetter's Refusal to Serve in the Nazi Army," *America* 129 (Sept. 8, 1973): 141-45.

Traces the spread of the Jaegerstaetter story since the publication of *In Solitary Witness* **(944).** Focuses on the story as a plea for the rights of conscientious objection and a call for amnesty for the opponents of the Vietnam War.

944   ——.*In Solitary Witness. The Life and Death of Franz Jaegerstaetter.* Collegeville, MN: Liturgical Press, 1964; reissued, 1977; reissued, Springfield, IL: Templegate, 1986.

Franz Jaegerstaetter was an Austrian farmer, family man, and sexton of his village church who had a simple grammar-school education and the popular spirituality of his day. With the coming of the Anschluss in Austria, however, and the almost universal support among Austrians for Hitler's annexation of their country, Jaegerstaetter began to express serious reservations about the morality of the Nazis. When finally drafted to serve in the German army, he refused, earning the ridicule and contempt of neighbors, local clergy, and even the diocese of Linz. Finally arrested and taken to prison in Berlin, the farmer was urged repeatedly by friends, priests, even Nazi officers who has come to admire his courage, to accept noncombatant service. He refused, basing his conscientious objection firmly on the Gospel injunctions against killing, on love of enemies, and in imitation of Christ's own nonviolence. Finally, in 1943 he was executed in his Berlin prison.

The story of Jaegerstaetter's opposition would have disappeared along with the records of so many other resisters to Hitler had it not been for a series of his letters from prison, the smuggled prison statement he wrote shortly before his execution, his *Commentaries* (a collection of his short essays on moral and political issues), and for Zahn's patient reconstruction of testimony from surviving witnesses. Zahn presents English editions of all Jaegerstaetter's writings as appendices.

This is a fascinating and emotional story that verges on hagiography, yet it is also a thoroughly professional work of modern sociology and oral history, thoroughly researched and clear in its sources and interpretations. This synthesis is a model, and a testimony to the true value, of professional research when tied to peace studies.

*   *
*

CHAPTER 13: *European Peacemaking from Vatican II to Solidarity*

Vatican II and Papal Encyclicals

945   Abbott, Walter M. and Joseph Gallagher, eds. *Documents of Vatican II.* New York: Guild, America, and Association Presses, 1966.

The best collection for Vatican II available. Presents all the texts for the entire council, including *Gaudium et Spes* (The Pastoral Constitution on the Church in the Modern World, **950**), with comments by respected theologians and scholars, among them Donald R. Campion, S.J. and Robert McAfee Brown.

946   "The Agenda for 1983." *America* 148 (Jan. 1-8, 1983): 3.

The pope's World Day of Peace Message. War and peace are primary issues. Nations and peoples must overcome fear, distrust, and ideologies to meet the common danger: nuclear war.

947   "Conditions of Peace; Concerning John XXIII's Recent Encyclical." *America* 109 (July 13, 1963): 38.

John XXIII appeals to both sides in the Cold War. Editorial seems to miss the point that the encyclical spoke to peoples as well as to governments.

948   Cornell, Thomas. "The Catholic Church and Witness Against War." See **51**, 200-213.

A Catholic Worker's recollection of the evolution of Catholic peacemaking from World War II to the present, and the American peace community's role in Vatican II.

949   Finn, Thomas M., C.S.P. "Peace, War and the Vatican Council," *Catholic World* 203 (August 1966): 270-75.

"The Church in the Modern World" gives a key, new emphasis to U.N. internationalism.

950   *Gaudium et Spes (The Pastoral Constitution on the Church in the Modern World).* See **945**, 183-316; **962**, 178-284.

Essential reading. The central peace document of Vatican II, including its condemnations of war in the modern world and its call on Catholics to become peacemakers. Along with *Pacem in Terris* (**954**) this is the constitution of modern Catholic peacemakers. The document's discussion of peace is divided into three parts: a theology of peace (arts. 77-78), restrictions on war (79-82) and the conclusion of the theology of peace (83-90). It presents a new positive approach to peacemaking that goes beyond the absence of war to the positive works of charity and justice. It follows John XXIII's appeal to individual conscience and calls on governments to provide for conscientious objection to military service. Most important, it heeds the call of *Pacem in Terris* to look at war "with an entirely new attitude," rejecting the balance o terror of nuclear deterrence and calling for a "conversion to peacemaking."

951   Graham, R.A. "Vatican Peace Initiatives," *America* 114 (March 26, 1966): 416.

Paul VI's world-wide efforts.

952   Gremillion, Joseph. *The Gospel of Peace and Justice:*
       Catholic Social Teaching Since Pope John. Maryknoll,
       NY: Orbis Books, 1976.

       Discusses the global political community, inter-
       nationalism, and the Catholic peace movement.
       Documents include *Mater et Magistra, Pacem in Terris,*
       Gaudium et Spes, Populorum Progressio, the Medellin
       documents, and *Evangelii Nuntiandi,* among others.

953   Holmes. *Papacy.* See **881**, 203-34.

       Good background for the lives and pontificates of
       John XXIII and Paul VI.

954   John XXIII, Pope. *Pacem in Terris.* See **962**, 117-70.

       With *Gaudium et Spes* (**950**), this is the fountainhead
       of all modern Catholic thinking on peace. The pope calls
       on all people to become peacemakers. The basis of a
       positive "theology of peace" rather than a negative
       "theology of war." Individual conscience plays a key role.
       The pope's words set off a revolution in modern
       Catholic thinking about war and peace. While often
       misinterpreted to apply to nuclear war alone, his cate-
       gorical statement, "in an age such as ours which prides
       itself on its atomic energy, it is contrary to reason to hold
       that war is now a suitable way to restore rights which have
       been violated," actually questions the justness of any
       modern war. Even more important, the pope appeals to
       individual conscience, not government good will or
       power, as the foundation of real peace. All authority is
       based on moral law, and if governments should command
       anything contrary to divine law, the individual is bound to
       obey divine law over human law. In the end peace is

God's gift and challenge to make peace and justice in the world. Catholics must now "undertake an evaluation of war with an entirely new attitude."

955   ——."Road to Peace, Address of Dec. 23, 1959," *Vital Speeches* 26 (Jan. 15, 1960): 195-98.

Reprints the entire text of his Christmas peace message.

956   ——."Pope John and True Peace," *America* 102 (Jan. 9, 1960): 412.

On his Christmas Broadcast for peace in 1959. See **955**.

957   Lammers. "Catholic Social Ethics." See **33**.

Traces post-World War II trends in the acceptance of pacifism as a valid Catholic position, one impossible since the Counter Reformation.

958   MacEoin, Gary. "The European Church and the War." See **1335**, 151-62.

There was strong opposition to the Vietnam War from all segments of the European church, including many Catholics, and shock at Cardinal Spellman's support for the war.

959   McSorley, Richard, S.J. "The Pope's Call for a Day of Peace," *Commonweal* 87 (Feb. 2, 1968): 519, 547.

The U.S. press has distorted Pope Paul's call for a day of peace and his condemnation of "pacifism." The pope condemned passive acquiescence to evil, not conscientious objection or nonviolence. We need to consult the Latin text.

960   Molnar, Thomas. "The French Bishops' Bomb," *National Review* 36 (Jan. 27, 1984): 40, 65.

On the reaction to the U.S. bishops' pastoral. Notes that the German bishops believe that the policy adopted by their American brethren would make war and the subjugation of Europe more likely. For their part the French bishops have responded with the November 8, 1983 pastoral, "To Win the Peace," largely the work of Msg. Jacques Jullien, the vicar of the armed forces.

The bishops begin from a Cold-War premise not used since Pius XII: that the Soviets are bent on conquest and only nuclear weapons check their desire. The West's materialism must be protected against the East's materialism. Rejecting even the teachings of John Paul II, the letter states that individual morality is not the same as national morality. Pacifism, it asserts, is passivism and exposes the individual — and the nation — to aggression. Contradicting John XXIII, the bishops assert that war is possible in the nuclear age, and trumpet the old "Better Dead than Red" slogan that the choice is between "annihilation and slavery," between "Finlandization and the Gulag."

The author, whose own views seem to color the article, concludes that the letter has caused rejoicing in the Elyssés Palace, toughened President Mitterand's hand, and "strengthened the West." Should one imply that the author believes that the U.S. bishops' letter has betrayed the West?

961   Mullay, Camilla. "Peace Forever — and Now. John Paul
        II's Teaching on Peace and Peace Making." *Vital
        Speeches* 49 (April 1, 1983): 373-77.

        A good, if often equivocating, summation of the
        pope's thoughts, using his World Day of Peace, 1983,
        Message. On the whole it appears that the pope's concept
        of peace is more often of the pre-Vatican II variety than
        not. Peace as world order predominates; and the right of
        national self-defense is stressed. The pope seems highly
        influenced by his Polish experience. Peace efforts must
        recognize the reality of national sovereignty, which is a
        good. Disarmament is also a good, but must not be
        unilateral; deterrence is still morally acceptable.
        On the other hand, peace is not acquiescence to evil,
        or passivity, or cowardice. While he seeks to underpin the
        needs of the state for self-defense, the pope stresses that
        public and private morality are the same; that individual
        conversion must precede peacemaking, and that peace
        cannot be achieved through violence.

962   O'Brien and Shannon. *Renewing the Earth.* See **42**.

        Extremely useful collection for documents in Catholic
        peacemaking from John XXIII's *Mater et Magistra* to
        Vatican II, Medellin, and statements by U.S. Catholic
        bishops. Includes good editions of *Pacem in Terris* (**954**)
        on pages 117-70 and the *Pastoral Constitution* (**950**) on
        pages 171-284.

963   Paul VI, Pope. "Christmas Message — Paul VI Address,
        Dec. 22, 1966," *Vital Speeches* 33 (Jan. 15, 1967):
        194-96.

        "Goodwill: The Key to Peace" stresses that true peace

is the result of order, justice, and harmony in the world. It is not complacent serenity but the result of constant struggle. Vietnam is a tragedy.

964   ——,"No to Violence, Yes to Peace; Pope Paul's Message," *America* 138 (Jan. 7, 1978): 4.

His Christmas message condemns both terrorism and war.

965   ——,*Paolo VI per la pace.* Luciano Bergonzoni, ed. Bologna: Patron, 1970.

Not seen.

966   ——."'Peace and Justice in the World: The Church's Contribution,' Paul VI Address to Diplomats," *Vital Speeches* 38 (Feb. 15, 1972): 258-60.

Chapter 76 of *Gaudium et Spes,* from Vatican II, is the church's policy.

967   ——,"Pope and Peace: Appeal Against Pacifism," *Christian Century* 85 (Jan. 3, 1968): 3.

The pope condemned "passivism," not "pacifism," calling for an activist approach to the problems of peace and justice.

968   ——."Pope Paul's Christmas Plea for Peace," *America* 114 (Jan. 8, 1966): 35.

The pope deplores the Cold War.

969   ——.*Populorum Progressio (On the Development of Peoples)*. See **962**, 307-346.

This papal encyclical is the starting point of Latin American and other Third World liberation theologies. Peace is inextricably bound to social justice and the economic progress of all peoples, especially those of the developing world. In fact, development is the new name for peace. One cannot condemn violent revolution, while not simultaneously condemning the violence of repressive injustice.

970   "Popes on Peace. Pius XI, Pius XII, John XXIII," *Commonweal* 75 (Dec. 29, 1961): 352-53.

Brief excerpts from their speeches.

971   Riga, Peter. *A Guide to Pacem in Terris for Students*. New York: Paulist Press, 1964.

A fine, simple explanation of the document, which stays close to the text and follows traditional Catholic moral and political theory, with a definite liberal slant. While it puts the arms race clearly in the context of the development of the modern world, it glosses over the encyclical's call to obey God above man and passes gingerly through John's condemnation of war in the modern world.

972   Rostow, Eugene V. "The Vatican and its Role in the World Order." See **898**, 17-26.

Papal peacemaking is based on the Vatican's international organization, its long experience and diplomatic expertise, and its neutrality, which is the key to conciliation. *Pacem in Terris* has now severely limited the just-war theory, and the papacy has pressed this point. It also is a strong advocate of the U.N. and of disarmament and has become a leader of world opinion.

973   Schuijt, William J. and René Coste. "History and Commentary of Gaudium et Spes, pt. II, chap. V." See **975**, 328-69.

An excellent analysis of the controversy surrounding the framing of *Gaudium et Spes* and the issues of conscientious objection, military service, and total war in the age of nuclear weapons.

974   Swiezawski, Stefan. "Excursus on Article 90: The Commission 'Iustitia et Pax'." See **975**, 382-83.

A brief history of the commission and the role of Mgr. Joseph Gremillion in framing the council's call for a new approach to peacemaking.

975   Vorgrimler, Herbert, ed. *Commentary on the Documents of Vatican II.* Vol. 5: *Pastoral Constitution on the Church in the Modern World.* New York: Herder & Herder, 1969.

An excellent companion to the documents of the council, including both detailed discussions of the political aspects of the council and of the doctrinal issues involved in each. Includes **973** and **974**.

976   Wright. "Peace." See **899**.

Peace is the power of reconciliation. Peacemaking is a positive action, the "fruit of love," and "a loving service to the world." Peace is "the work of justice."

Conscientious Objection in Europe

977   Borgese, E.M. "Vatican II: Anathema Upon War: Cases of
        Italian Conscientious Objectors," *The Nation* 202
        (April 11, 1966): 415-21.

        The impact of Vatican II on Catholic peacemaking, the
        case of conscientious objector Giuseppe Gozzini, and the
        famous trial of Fr. Ernesto Balducci, who came to his
        defense using traditional Catholic moral theory. The
        "Balducci Case" encouraged thousands of Italian CO
        claims and won the attention of the bishops assembled at
        Vatican II and their support after the publication of *Pacem
        in Terris*. With the trial and acquittal of both Balducci and
        Don Lorenzo Milani, conscientious objection became an
        established principle in Italian law. Essential reading.

978   Davidon, A.M. "International War Resisters: Spain,"
        Progressive 40 (October 1976): 8-9.

        The cases of José Luis (Pepe) Buenza, Jesus Viñas
        Cirera, and other members of GOCE awaiting trial as
        conscientious objectors in violation of Spain's defense
        laws.

979   Deedy, John G. "At Ease: Status in West Germany,"
        Commonweal 103 (June 4, 1976): 354.

        The relaxation of requirements for conscientious
        objector status brings a flood of applications.

980   Farnsworth, Elizabeth, and Stephen Talbot. "Italy: Pax
        Romana?" *The Nation* 234 (April 17, 1982): 454.

        "Peace Catholics" are a big surprise here. Even more

surprising is the widespread anti-nuclear sentiment among Italians. In the fall of 1981 over one-half million Italians demonstrated against U.S. cruise missile basing. "Priests" were actively involved in the demonstration planning; and the offices of Rev. Gianni Novelli, editor of *Nuovi Tempi,* served as headquarters. The majority of moral theologians in Italy have condemned nuclear weapons, their teaching "resurrected from a 17-year-old document." The authors mean article 80 of *Gaudium et Spes,* the *Pastoral Constitution* enacted at Vatican II. Reflects the *Nation's* often anti-Catholic and anti-religious prejudices.

981   Fiedeler, Beate, and Ulrike Ladwig. "Women and the Peace Movement in the Federal Republic of Germany," *Frontiers* 8, 2 (1985): 59-64.

        Not seen.

982   Heneghan, T. "COs or Cheap Labor: West Germany," *Commonweal* 105 (Jan. 6, 1978): 5-7.

        About 2,000 Catholic conscientious objectors serve with *Caritas* in programs for the elderly and disabled. The image of the CO has changed drastically from that of the shirker to the social idealist. In 1977 alone 50,000 Germans applied for the status, and the demand rises for the services of this "social fire brigade."

983   "International C.O. Report: Italy," *CCCO News Notes* 36, 2 (Summer 1984): 3.

        An Italian court has ruled that factory workers may legally state their conscientious objection to war production and be assigned to nonmilitary production.

984   Kaza, J. "West Germany's COs," *New Leader* 61 (Feb. 27, 1978): 3.

Records the storm of protests from German conservatives over the easing of claims for conscientious objector status. There were 40,000 CO claims in five months in 1977.

985   Kimber, Brian. "Italian Objectors Face Confusing Treatment," *CCCO News Notes* 37, 2 (Summer 1985): 3, 16.

Even though Italian objectors have been granted legal status since December 1972, the law and its regulations are still confusing and vague. Though most recognized COs are religious, political objectors have also gained the status. The government has, however, acted arbitrarily, introducing and then withdrawing regulations as the number of objectors swelled (20,000 in 1983, for example). Focuses on the cases of several Italian objectors to illustrate its point.

986   Leiper, G.A. "Letter from Italy," *Christian Century* 79 (March 21, 1962): 359-60.

The political and religious controversy around the Italian government's censoring, and the Vatican's condemnation of, the French film, *Thou Shalt Not Kill,* and the Italian peace movement that defied them.

987   "Pacifists Win in France," *Christian Century* 79 (July 11, 1962): 856.

Due to the hunger strike of pacifist Louis Lecoin, the Pompidou government released 28 French conscientious

objectors and promises revision of defense laws to allow
this right.

988   Pancracio, Jean-Paul. "Le nouveau status des objecteurs
       de conscience," *Revue du droit publique* 101 (Jan.
       1985): 103-56.

       Not seen.

989   Paterson, Tony. "The Heat Is On," *New Statesman* (July
       8, 1983): 20.

       The crackdown on pacifism in West Germany in light
       of the campaign to base Pershing II and Cruise missiles on
       German soil. Outlines a series of measures intended to
       make nonviolence far more difficult in the future.
       Nonviolent "blockades" are now considered violence by
       the Kohl government; while new legislation proposes
       arresting both violent demonstrators and those, even
       nonviolent, demonstrators, found close to the violence.
       This last measure is opposed by the Socialists, Greens,
       and lawyers' and police groups.

990   Powers and Freeman. "Conscientious Objectors." See **45**.

       The individual Catholic cannot possibly understand all
       the reasons for his government's waging a war or judge its
       justice. His conscience is always poorly informed, and he
       therefore has no right to conscientious objection. A
       modern rehashing of theories hatched in the just-war
       tradition and widely used under Europe's absolutist
       monarchs and by the German bishops during World War
       II. Typical of pre-Vatican II attitudes.

991   Smyth, Philip. "Anti-War Feeling Growing in Belgium,"
        CCCO News Notes 35, 2 (Summer 1983): 3.

        Traces the growth of conscientious objection in
        Belgium from 134 objectors in 1964 to 2317, or 7.5% of
        all conscripts in 1980, and the 51% of all Belgians who
        oppose the draft.

992   ——."New Hope for Spanish COs," *CCCO News Notes*
        35:1 (Spring 1983): 3.

        Under the 1978 constitution conscientious objection is
        recognized as a legal right. A new bill allows alternative
        service in environmental and other dangerous services.

993   "Spain Incarcerates Catholic CO," *Christian Century* 88
        (May 12, 1971): 585.

        José Luis Buenza, sentenced to 15 months by a
        Valencia military court, is the first Spanish Catholic ever to
        claim conscientious objection. He based his defense on
        the call of Vatican II. Also surveys current status of
        Spain's CO legislation.

994   Wentworth, Cedric. "COs in France," *The Objector* 3, 2
        (October 1982): 5-6.

        Changes in laws governing CO status from 1958 to
        1982, the tightening of regulations due the the surge of
        applications in 1971, and the Mitterand government's
        plans to liberalize the laws.

995   ——."New Rights for French COs," *The Objector* 4, 1 (Sept.1, 1983): 3.

COs will now be allowed to join political parties and trade unions and to exercise their religion freely. By 1985, 25,000 COs will participate in some form of national service.

996   Wiegand, W. "Why There Is No Peace Movement in France," *Encounter* 61 (November 1983): 52-54.

A thought-provoking, if unsympathetic analysis. In the United States, Great Britain and West Germany the peace movement is generally not aligned with any one political party. Conservatives therefore cannot bash them for ideological reasons, but must contend with the myriad of motivations: religious and moral, ecological, economic and political, that they present.

In France, however, the three segments of the peace movement are isolated and impotent. The pacifists have never been able to dent the ultra-patriotism and militarism of French culture and France's bitter feelings over two invasions in recent history. In a predominantly agrarian society the ecologists have had little impact discussing the dangers of nuclear power, and their impact is confined to bohemians and other "subcultures." The politically motivated peace movement is so closely aligned with the Moscow-dominated Communist Party that it has little credibility.

Wiegand also introduces a factor that has great importance: the French police have always been para-military in function and outlook; they crush demonstrations unmercifully, without conscience. This, and their political clout, presents a great deterrence to nonviolent action.

Catholic Peacemaking in Europe

Lanza del Vasto

997   Hope, Marjorie and James Young. *The Struggle for Humanity*. Maryknoll, NY: Orbis Books, 1979, 41-70.

His life and teachings on nonviolence, based on interviews and first-hand observations of the life of the Ark at Cevennes, France, as well as a survey of recent nonviolent actions by the community of the Ark.

998   Lanza del Vasto, Joseph Jean. *Approches de la vie intérieure*. Paris: Éditions Denoël, 1962.

Not seen.

999   ——.*L'arche avait pour voilure une vigne*. Paris: Éditions Denoël, 1978.

Part of his spiritual autobiography. The pilgrim returns from India to begin the process of founding the Ark. Recounts the first nonviolent campaigns. Then discusses the constitution of the Ark, the seven vows, and Lanza del Vasto's teachings on openness and truth, the Bible, the Old Testament, religion today, and the prayers of the Ark.

1000   ——.*Commentario del Evangelio*. Enrique Pezzoni, transl. Buenos Aires: SUR, 1955.

Not seen.

1001   ——.*Dialogues avec Lanza del Vasto: Non-violence, Bible et communautés*. René Doumerc, ed. Paris: Éditions du Cerf, 1980.

The roots of his activist nonviolence in Gandhi and Catholic spirituality. A series of dialogues, monologues on his books and spiritual development, on nonviolence and the sacrifice it entails. Also discusses Vinoba, Gandhi's successor, history, progress, the kingdom of heaven, his biblical commentaries, poetry, prayer, inspiration, mediation and reconciliation, power, technology, and science. The collection also examines his notions on the salvation of the individual and the world, the Ark, and Chantarelle. Provides a good chronology of his life.

1002   ——.*Gandhi to Vinoba: The New Pilgrimage.* Philip Leon, transl. London: Rider, 1956.

The life and teachings of Vinoba, Lanza del Vasto's teacher and Gandhi's successor. Includes a selection of texts, prayers and songs on the spirit of nonviolence, action and prayer, etc.

1003   ——.*L'Homme et sa réalisation.* Eric Edelmann, ed. Paris: Beauchesne, 1980.

Interviews on a wide variety of topics. Lanza del Vasto covers pages 9-21. Focuses on his nonviolence, the Ark and its withdrawal from a world dominated by Moloch and Baal, awaiting World War III. Interesting insights into this remote patriarch of peacemakers.

1004   ——.*L'Homme libre et les âmes sauvages.* Paris: Éditions Denoël, 1959.

Not seen.

1005 ——.*Make Straight the Way of the Lord.* New York: Alfred A. Knopf, 1974.

A collection of his short essays and meditations on a wider variety of topics, including nonviolent life and action. Brief essays are grouped under the general headings In Search of the Self, God and Nature, Social Responsibility, Utopia, and the Kingdom of Heaven.

1006 ——.*Noé.* Paris: Éditions Denoël, 1965.

Not seen.

1007 ——.*La passion, mystère de Pâques.* Paris: Grasset, 1951.

Not seen.

1008 ——.*Pour eviter la fin du monde.* Jean-Guy Dubuc and Jean-Louis Morgan, eds. Montréal: Éditions La Presse, 1973.

On the occasion of his visit to Montréal to address a conference. Essays on liberty and law revealing Lanza del Vasto's patriarchal, mystical-dominant, authoritarian form of spirituality; as well as his basic Luddism, a rejection of all of the modern world's goods and bads. Most evil, in fact, is quite real in the world, and is chiefly associated with technology. Nevertheless there also shines through his active nonviolence, his stress that change in the world must begin with change within.

1009 ——.*Principles and Precepts of the Return to the Obvious.* New York: Schocken Books, 1974.

A series of meditations on poverty, pomp and its effects, chastity, youth, silence, old age, sickness, asceticism and the dignity of the body, God, reason, service, pleasure and pain, beauty and the life of simplicity, nonviolence, and a return to the sources of our spiritual life.

1010   ——.*Les quatres fléaux, 1959.* Paris: Éditions Denoël, 1959.

Not seen.

1011   ——.*Return to the Source.* Jean Sidgwick, transl. London: Rider, 1971.

A personal account of his conversion and awakening to his life's work via his wanderings in the mystical East. A brief review of his life and present activities at the Ark, his life of nonviolence.

1012   ——.*La trinité spirituelle.* Paris: Éditions Denoël, 1971.

Not seen.

1013   ——.*Viatique.* 9 vols. in 4. Paris: Éditions Denoël, 1970-1975.

Journals of his travels, both physical and spiritual. Portraits, memories, reflections on God, music, etc. Up to 1926.

1014   ——,*Warriors of Peace: Writings on the Technique of Nonviolence.* Michel Random, ed. Jean Sidgwick, transl. New York: Alfred A. Knopf, 1974.

Definitions of nonviolence; the seven axioms of nonviolence, and a review of the Arks tactics , including the appeal to conscience, fasts, including that in Rome staged by Chantarelle and other women. The Ark has taken nonviolent action against the use of torture, the bomb, internment camps, for conscientious objection and civilian service. Concludes with a very impressionistic review of nonviolence in the West in history and its practice in the world today.

1015   ——,and Arnaud de Mareüil. *L'orée des trois vertus.* Paris: Le Courrier du Livre, 1971.

A series of essays and meditations on conversion — of the mind, the flesh, and the heart. Maxims and meditations on faith, hope and charity; on justice, liberty and beauty. Includes essays on nonviolence.

1016   Mareüil, Arnaud de, ed. *Lanza del Vasto: Présentation, choix de textes.* Paris: P. Seghers, 1966.

Not seen.

1017   Random, Michel. *Les puissances du dedans.* Paris: Éditions Denoël, 1966.

Not seen.

Danilo Dolci

1018   Ammann, Walter. *Danilo Dolci.* Bern: Benteli, 1972.

A review of his life, with special focus on his nonviolent activities. Nicely illustrated with photos. Topics include Dolci, Sicilian life and culture, economy, history, including the Mafia. Briefly traces his career, highlighting the Partinico trial, his contest with the Mafia, and his debt to Gandhi. An excellent chronology up to July 1972.

1019 Capitani, Aldo. *Danilo Dolci*. Manduria: Lacaita, 1958.

Not seen.

1020 ——.*Revoluzione Aperta; Che cosa ha fatto Danilo Dolci?* Florence: Parenti, 1956.

The title continues, "on nonviolence, transformation of power, economy, nature, love for all, on the roads to the liberation of the people."

1021 Casarrubea, Giuseppe. *Una alternativa culturale dalla Sicilia occidentale*. Trapani: Celebes, 1974.

The grip of the Mafia on the region of western Sicily, and the need to organize to break this cycle of ignorance, exploitation and violence. Is Dolci a writer or a revolutionary? Conversations with associates, analysis of educational and organizational methods, of his writing and poetry, of the Education Center, his deep-seated anti-fascism. Includes a very useful bibliography of Dolci's works, their translations, articles and reviews on him.

1022 Dolci, Danilo. *Conversazioni*. Turin: Einaudi, 1962.

Not seen.

1023 ——.*Conversazioni con Danilo Dolci*. Giacinto Spagnoletti, ed. Milan: Mondadori, 1977.

Part One traces his youth, education, family life and friends; his career from the reverse strike at Partinico, the Iato Dam project, the struggle against the Mafia, the Russell Tribunal and his anti-fascist activities, his experiences in the United States on lecture tours, the Mirto educational center, his poetry, and points of controversy in his life.

Part Two provides selected source materials.

1024   ——.*Creature of Creatures. Selected Poems.* Justin Vitiello, transl. Saratoga, CA: Anma Libri, 1980.

Dolci's poems on the life of Sicily's peasants, their exploitation, the need for change, and for nonviolence. A good introduction to Dolci's life and career as a peacemaker.

1025   ——.*For the Young.* Antonia Cowan, transl. London: Macgibbon & Kee, 1967.

Answers letters from children who have written supporting his efforts. The letters come from all over Europe and the United States. Their constant theme is the "waste" of Sicilian lives. The points are often made through simple dialogues.

1026   ——.*Il limone lunare. Non sentite l'odore del fumo?* Bari: A. Laterza, 1972.

A combined edition of these two works. *Il limone lunare* (the lemon moon) is a poem for the radio aimed at western Sicily, where the newspapers are viewed with suspicion and the radio is the prime means of communication. It traces the life of the country people and is designed to raise the consciousness, and hopes, of the peasants and fishermen, to give voices to the voiceless by reminding them of the beauty and dignity of their lives. *Non sentite l'odore del fumo?* is a collection of poems on Auschwitz and the Holocaust and is intended to fight a resurgence of fascism in Italy. The title means "Don't you smell the odor of smoke?"

1027   ——.*The Man Who Plays Alone.* New York: Pantheon, 1968.

Two pieces of peasant wisdom typify the problem: in western Sicily *chi cammina solo, si trova sempre bene* (the man who walks alone always feels at ease) and *chi gioca solo non perde mai* (the man who plays alone never loses). Dolci's own recollections of his struggle to raise the consciousness of the Sicilian peasants to overcome their sense of isolated self-interest and to struggle nonviolently for basic human rights. The alienation of the Sicilian poor is expressed in hostility to any loyalty other than to self and to the closed circle of the family. The opposition of the church hierarchy to his efforts is not merely personal but official policy.

1028   ——.*A New World in the Making.* R. Munroe, transl. New York: Monthly Review Press, 1965.

An attempt to go beyond the moral laws of the past to find new answers for a new age. A new ethical system for a new united world. Studies efforts in the Soviet Union, Yugoslavia, Senegal, and Ghana to familiarize the West with different approaches.

1029   ——.*Non esiste in silenzio.* Turin: Einaudi, 1974.

A collection of dialogues between Dolci and the

inhabitants of Partinico, and his companions. An update to *Conversazioni* (**1024**) that includes a roving discussion on what it means to be a man or woman today, on war, military service, the meaning of life and death, justness of killing, infant baptism, and more.

1030   ——."Non-Violence vs the Mafia," *WIN Magazine*. Reprinted in Guinan, 55-58.

Not seen.

1031   ——.*The Outlaws of Partinico*. R. Munroe, transl. New York: Orion Press, 1963.

Dolci's account of the conditions around Partinico in western Sicily, its poverty, violence and alienation. Focuses on Dolci's group and their struggle against violence and examines the life of violence in the region. The book's heart is a portrait of these "outlaws," the fishermen and the poor peasants, their living conditions, lack of education, social life and values, and their sense of exploitation.

Part V of the book turns the term "outlaw" on its head by describing the "strike in reverse" by Dolci and the region's unemployed to begin work on a damaged section of road. They did so without government permission but in accordance with Article IV of the Italian Constitution guaranteeing the right to work to all citizens. Follows their nonviolent action, arrest, and trial. The book concludes with some notes from Dolci's Study Centers.

1032   ——.*Palpitare di nessi: Ricerca di educare creativo a un mundo nonviolento.* Rome: Armando, 1985.

The subtitle translates: research for creative education for a nonviolent world.

1033   ——.*Poema umano.* Turin: Einaudi, 1974.

Poems from various collections on war and peace, dignity and beauty, Hiroshima, the Holocaust, and other topics.

1034   ——.*A Policy for Full Employment (Una politica per la piena occupazione).* Turin: Einaudi, 1958.

Dolci's policy for full employment. He contrasts the scandal of Italy's army and defense budgets with its lack of a comprehensive employment policy. He then offers suggestions for the proper utilization of natural and human resources. Highlights the problems of illiteracy, the need for political reform, the lack of local industry, exploitation by the landowners, apathy, and the nostalgia of the educated for a more comfortable past.

1035   ——.*Il ponte screpolato.* Turin: Stampatori, 1979.

Basically on educational methods in western Sicily, but also on people's ability to overcome obstacles. Focuses on Partinico but also recounts experiences in the United States and Soviet Union, his work with Paolo Freire (See **1153**) and others on the "new education." Dolci shows how easy the tie is between these efforts and social activism, and thus with conflict with the Mafia and government corruption.

1036   ——.*Poverty in Sicily.* Harmondsworth: Penguin Books,
        1966.

The findings of a series of surveys among the poor
and unemployed in and around Palermo in western Sicily.
Responses to the question, "Do you think it is God's will
that you are unemployed?" show an almost pagan belief in
the unbridgeable gap between God and the world of
humans. God takes care of himself and leaves us to do the
same. He is not concerned with "social" issues. As one
informant remarked, "In my opinion God's got nothing to
do with unemployment."

1037   ——.*Report from Palermo.* P.D. Cummins, transl. New
        York: Orion Press, 1959.

In his introduction to this volume Aldous Huxley calls
Dolci, "one of these modern Franciscans with-a-degree"
who have attempted to apply modern sociological and
other professional skills to the problems of exploitation,
poverty and violence in a new age, but in the same spirit as
the medieval saint.
        This book is a study of the unemployed in the
province of Palermo. It relies on first-hand accounts
collected through questionnaires on such areas as
education, trade, means of support without work, self-
assessment of the situation, religious beliefs, social,
political views, opinions on corruption, and ideas for
action. Dolci prints the responses verbatim.

1038   ——.*Sicilian Lives.* New York: Pantheon, 1982.

Not seen.

1039 ——.*To Feed the Hungry.* London: Penguin Books, 1966.

Not seen.

1040 ——."Trial Statement," from *Outlaws.* See **39**, 391-401.

Recounting the events of the "reverse strike," the work-in to repair the roads at Partinico, his and his follower's arrest, and Dolci's apologia for nonviolent civil disobedience. While he and his group were found guilty, the judge passed light sentences in view of "the high moral value of Dolci's action."

1041 ——.*Waste: An Eye-Witness Report on Some Aspects of Waste in Western Sicily.* R. Munroe, transl. New York: Monthly Review Press, 1964.

This documents "waste" in all its forms: superstition, water pollution and waste, violence and murder, soil erosion, abject poverty and ignorance, waste of natural resources, of human labor and construction, poor housing, depopulation, infant mortality and more.
The book is compellingly illustrated with photos, maps, and charts.

1042 Fizzotti, Germana. *La divina folia: Danilo Dolci e il "Borgo di Dio."* Palermo: ABC, 1956.

Not seen.

1043 "The Gandhi of Sicily Continuing Crusade," *New York Times,* Oct. 30, 1977: 49, 1.

Brief biographical sketch and comment on his current

activities, continuing and expanding his nonviolent campaign against the Mafia and linking it to other issues of peace and justice.

1044   Grasso, Franco. *A Montelepre hanno plantato una croce.* Milan: Avanti!, 1956.

The cross is that of nonviolence planted in a region controlled by bandits and the Mafia.

1045   Hope and Young. *Struggle.* See **997**, 73-107.

Dolci's life and struggle for nonviolent change in Sicily, again based on interviews and first-hand observations by the authors.

1046   Mangione, Jerre. *A Passion for Sicilians. The World Around Danilo Dolci.* New York: William Morrow, 1968.

An excellent book. Dolci mentions God frequently in his early writings but not in his later ones. Has he given up belief? What is the nature of his nonviolence? What are his hopes for revolution and political change? Who is the man behind the legend? Mangione sets out to find some answers.

He first gives an interesting account of Dolci in the United States on a speaking tour and the hostility shown him by some Italo-Americans for the bleak picture he draws of Sicily and of Italian corruption. Mangione then travels to Italy where he encounters a marked hostility or bored disinterest in the man from many of Italy's most brilliant writers, thinkers and activists, who find that Dolci has outlived his usefulness. Even some of his former closest friends have now turned against him. Why?

Mangione travels to western Sicily, finds even

Sicilians living in the region ignorant of his efforts, finds intense opposition to the man even within his own organization. Much of the hostility stems from Dolci's trust in native Sicilians on his staff, for his "non-professional" staff and methods, for the lack of drama in his work at present. Many are bewildered over his commitment: is it religious, political, naive? Dolci does seem to have trouble as an organizer and in keeping the loyalty of his associates.

Most of Mangione's book is in the form of a journal, and this does recount several of Dolci's group actions, in Sicily, and in Rome.

1047   McNeish, James. *Fire Under the Ashes. The Life of Danilo Dolci*. London: Hodder & Stoughton, 1965.

The best and most complete biography of Dolci available in English.

1048   Melville, Harcourt. *Portraits of Destiny*. New York: Sheed & Ward, 1966.

Dolci is covered on pages 48-97. Focuses on his life, work in Sicily, the Centro Studi, his personality. A good, brief introduction.

1049   Peachment, Brian. *The Defiant Ones: Dramatic Studies of Modern Social Reformers*. Oxford: Religious Education Press, 1969.

Discusses Dolci.

1050   *Processo all'articolo 4 nella documentazione di Achille Battaglia et al*. Turin: Einaudi, 1956.

The Partinico trial.

1051   Steinmann, Jean. *Pour ou contre Danilo Dolci*. Paris: Éditions du Cerf, 1959.

       Not seen.

1052   Waller, Ross D. *Danilo Dolci*. Manchester: Manchester Library and Philosophical Society. Memoires and Proceedings, vol. 102, 1959-1960.

       Not seen.

Northern Irish Peace People

1053   Boyd, Andrew. "The 'Success' of the Peace People," *The Nation* 224 (April 16, 1977): 453-56.

       As of early 1977 the Peace People have been very successful with the media in the United States and Europe. But has all this had any effect? The IRA, Royal Ulster Constabulary and Loyalists keep up level records of butchery. The Peace People's effects seem to be far greater abroad than in Ireland. Even in Ireland there is more glitter than hope from the Peace People.

       Reviews the history of the movement and the personalities of its leaders. But who backs them? Where do they get their money? Boyd repeats suspicions that they are fronts for the British. Peace groups, he contends, are lots of empty verbiage, with their "prayers" and lists of empty platitudes. They don't do enough exposing of corruption, not enough condemnation of politicians; and there has not been a peace group in northern Ireland that has not been encouraged by the British. Therefore they must be government fronts.

Boyd's true feelings about peacemaking and his macho admiration for force come through: "The only people who can make peace are those who are making war." All the prayers in the world and all the nonviolent demonstrations and small-scale actions will not change the *real* men's minds; and these, of course, are the ones with the big guns.

1054 Deutsch, Richard. *Mairead Corrigan — Betty Williams.* Woodbury, NY: Barrons, 1977.

The best single source on the lives, motives, and careers of the Peace People. Begins with the first peace march, the situation in Ulster in August 1976, the lives, backgrounds and ideas of Mairead Corrigan, Betty Williams, and Ciaran McKeown. Then discusses the history of the peace marches, the Declaration of the Peace People, and four of the major rallies. Examines the program of the group in some detail, with full quotation from the "Strategy for Peace" and the "Model Constitution." Concludes with an examination of the crisis in the group caused by growth and a shift to low-key community organizing, the loss of media coverage, the opposition in Ireland, the personal dynamics among the three leaders, the effects of the Nobel Peace Prize, and some appendices. Foreword by Joan Baez.

1055 McDowell, Michael H.C. "Post-Nobel Decline: Peace People Fall on Hard Times," *Commonweal* 107 (March 28, 1980): 164-65.

Brief review of the movement, its present state of inactivity, the damaged credibility of Corrigan and Williams for keeping their Nobel Peace Prize money.

1056   O'Donnell, Dalry. *The Peace People of Northern Ireland.*
        Camberwell: Widescope, 1977.

        Not seen.

1057   Power, Jonathan. "Can the Peace People Bring an Irish
        Peace?" *Encounter* 48 (March 1977): 9-17.

        "Love your enemy" is at the root of Mairead
        Corrigan's actions; but hostility to the Peace People from
        the Irish themselves is very strong. Betty Williams is
        quicker, sharper, and less Christian in outlook. Ciaran
        McKeown has been a leader of the movement from the
        start.
        Reviews the work of the group, its marches and
        rallies, its Christian vocabulary, its strengths and
        weaknesses. Its truths do not appeal to the politicians o
        the media; but, like the civil rights movement in the U.S
        the movement feeds on adversity. To maintain their
        strength, however, the Peace People need continued
        opposition that makes big mistakes. It also needs clearly
        defined targets and goals. What can the British and Irish
        governments do to help? Expresses fears that Northern
        Ireland will become another Lebanon.

1058   "The Prize for Peace Doesn't Always Lead to It: Two
        Women of Ulster," *New York Times,* Oct. 21, 1984.

        Reviews the current activities of Corrigan and
        Williams. The Peace People survives as an organization
        despite the lack of publicity, and runs camps and athleti
        activities to bring together Catholic and Protestant youth.

1059   Tousley, Ben. "Small Candles of Peace in Northern
        Ireland," *Fellowship* 49, 12 (December 1983): 7-10
        22.

The Peace People succeeded in drawing people together. By 1977 their membership has been dwindling, but they have spurred many other grass-roots and religious groups.

Solidarity and Poland

1060 Bird, Thomas E. "The Pope and Poland: And Now What? Resistance, Not Rebellion," *Commonweal* 110: 13 (July 15, 1983): 390-92.

John Paul's visit unabashedly political, to urge Poles to nonviolent resistance. Solidarity is the most massive people's movement in the history of Europe.

1061 Bobinski, Christopher. "Polish Bishops: Talk, Don't Fight," *NCR* 18, 19 (March 12, 1982): 2.

Nonviolence and dialogue are not acquiescence to evil.

1062 *The Book of Lech Walesa.* New York: Simon & Schuster, 1982.

Collection of first-hand assessments of Walesa by friends and associates. Valuable materials on his Catholicism and nonviolence.

1063 Brandys, Kazimierz. *A Warsaw Diary.* Richard Lourie, transl. New York: Random House, 1984.

Reflections on a great many things, including the role of John Paul II in bringing hope to Poland. Solidarity is mentioned only in passing.

1064 Bratman, Fred. "A Triumph of Moral Force: Walesa

Discomforts the Communists by Winning a Nobel Prize," *Time* 122, 17 (Oct. 17, 1983): 50.

Walesa recognized as a force for nonviolent change.

1065   Brecher, John and Elaine Sciolino. "Poland: The Church vs the State," *Newsweek* 99 (Feb. 15, 1982): 39-40.

Pope John Paul is sympathetic with the hardliners in the Polish hierarchy who seek to challenge martial law regime through their moral influence.

1066   Cviic, Christopher. "The Church," in *Poland, Genesis of a Revolution*. Abraham Brumberg, ed. New York: Random House, 1983, 92-108.

A general survey of the Catholic church's role in Polish history, from 1945 to 1978, in alliance with Poland's dissidents, John Paul's visit, and the Solidarity period. While Solidarity finds its roots in Catholicism, it is not a "Catholic" movement.

1067   "Faith, Prayer — and Defiance," *Newsweek* 101 (June 27, 1983): 38-47.

A general account of the pope's visit and its meaning for Polish nonviolence.

1068   Hebblethwaite, Peter. "'Murder in the Cathedral' Echoes in Poland Plans," *NCR* 19 (Feb. 11, 1983): 7.

The martyrdom of Thomas à Becket in defense of Catholic liberty stands as a strong model for Poland's church under martial law.

1069 Jones, Arthur. "Warsaw: Walking in Walesa's Shadow," *NCR* 20, 10 (Dec. 23, 1983): 24.

> Polish priests are outspoken in their support of Solidarity and in their condemnation of Soviet oppression.

1070 Kohan, John. "Poland: A Nation Mourns a Martyred Priest," *Time* (Nov. 12, 1984): 58-59.

> Recounts the known events surrounding Fr. Jerzy Popieluszko's kidnapping and murder by Polish security agents. Lech Walesa's plea to the 400,000 mourners at his funeral that the authorities "wanted to kill the hope that it is possible in Poland to avoid violence in political life."

1071 ——."Poland: Marching Out of Step," *Time* (May 14, 1984): 36.

> The banned Solidarity's strong showing on May Day ceremonies in 1984 demonstrates the ongoing strength of nonviolence.

1072 ——."Return of the Native," *Time* 121 (June 27, 1983): 28-37.

> On John Paul's visit and his message: A victory through Christian means is part of Poland's heritage.

1073 Labedz, Leopold, ed. *Poland Under Jaruzelski: A Comprehensive Sourcebook on Poland During and After Martial Law.* New York: Charles Scribner's, 1984.

> Not seen.

1074   MacShane, Denis. *Solidarity*. Nottingham: Spokesman, 1981.

A good account of the movement, its background and motivations, its personalities and events.

1075   Persky, Stan and Henry Flam, eds. *The Solidarity Sourcebook*. Vancouver: New Star, 1982.

An excellent collection of primary sources on the history, personalities, and theory of the Solidarity movement.

1076   "Pope and Emperor," *New Republic* 189 (July 18, 1983): 7-9.

John Paul's visit and his sermon at Czestochowa have ended Cardinal Glemp's accommodation. The Catholic church plays a vital role in Solidarity's nonviolent resistance.

1077   Potel, Jean-Yves. *The Promise of Solidarity*. New York: Praeger, 1982.

Not seen.

1078   Sikorska, Grazyma. *Jerzy Popieluszko: A Martyr for the Truth*. Grand Rapids, MI: Eerdman's, 1985.

Chapters include discussions of the Catholic heritage of Poland through the Solidarity period, Jerzy's early years to 1972, his priesthood and allegiance to Solidarity members, even through the worst trials of the time, his activities after martial law was declared, and his outspoken condemnations of the government's repression.
Throughout his ministry Popieluszko continued to

stress nonviolence and reconciliation, reminding even the oppressors within the Polish government of their humanity. He had to contend with constant efforts by the police to provoke violence or pro-Solidarity demonstrations during his masses, and remained constantly vigilant against such methods.

The martyred priest based his actions and words consciously on Pope John Paul II and Cardinal Wyzsynski. He gained the support of the workers and local bishops but was condemned by the government for his opposition to communism and its materialistic nihilism. At first the government tried to silence him through church channels. When this failed, they resorted to violence and harassment.

The book concludes with a description of his kidnapping and murder, based on the later trial record. It includes the priest's own statement made in September 1984: "the state of the Church will always be the same as the state of the people. The Church is not just the Church hierarchy: it is all the people of God, a nation of millions, who constitute the Church in the greater sense, and when they suffer, when they are persecuted, the Church suffers."

1079   Singer, Daniel. "Poland Diary: Bitter Hope in a Cold Climate," *The Nation* 240, 24 (June 22, 1985): 760-64.

Continued economic troubles, the survival of Solidarity as a real presence, the country's mood after the amnesty of political prisoners and the trial of Jerzy Popieluszko's murderers. While active opposition may be on hold, this is only natural; great hope remains for economic and some political democracy, and the continued heroism of Lech Walesa, whose essentially religious motivation Singer now understands.

1080   Staniszkis, Jadwiga. *Poland's Self-Limiting Revolution.*
        Princeton: Princeton University Press, 1984.

        The Catholic influence on Solidarity has weakened a
        slow trend toward secularization; but the power of the
        Polish episcopate to negotiate with the government seems
        to be aimed at protecting institutional interests.

1081   Swomley, John M. "The Lessons of Solidarity,"
        Fellowship 51, 7-8 (July-August 1985): 15-16, 37.

        Solidarity is the most significant nonviolent movement
        to emerge within the Soviet bloc. Briefly reviews its rise,
        goals, and nature. This cuts across class, and ideological
        lines; the movement is not strictly religious, although it is
        deeply influenced by the Catholic church's social
        teachings; its nonviolence is tactical, not theological.
        Interviews several Protestant clergymen, as well as Paris-
        based journalist Daniel Singer to downplay the Catholic
        and religious nature of Solidarity's nonviolence. The
        Polish government and Soviets exercised great restraint.
        The pope and Polish hierarchy used fear of reprisal as a
        tool to restrain the movement's revolutionary impetus. "It
        is doubtful if there is enough consciousness in Poland of
        the theory and practice of nonviolence to build a continuing
        movement or even a mythology about nonviolence."
                Ironically the article is led off by a three-column photo
        of a Solidarity demonstration set in front of a huge poster
        of Pope John Paul II. In the midst of the demonstration a
        nun, in full habit, beams at the camera.

1082   Szajkowski, Bogdan. "The Catholic Church in Defense of

Civil Society in Poland," in *Poland After Solidarity: Social Movements Versus the State.* Bronislaw Misztal, ed. New Brunswick, NJ: Transaction Books, 1985, 67-84.

Using classic discussions of "civil society" in Hegel, Marx and Gramsci as a basis, he discusses the role of the church in moderating civil discourse and furthering Polish aspirations for truth, dignity and basic human rights. Good bibliography.

1083 Tischner, Josef. *The Spirit of Solidarity.* Marek B. Zaleski and Benjamin Fiore, S.J., transls. San Francisco: Harper & Row, 1982.

A collection of short, homily-like essays by Tischner, a Polish priest and spiritual leader of Solidarity. Solidarity is committed to peaceful action based on religious faith. Nonviolence is a key element in its program. The preface by Zbigniew Brzezinski is especially important in this regard.

1084 Touraine, Alain and others, eds. *The Analysis of a Social Movement; Poland 1980-1981.* New York: Cambridge University Press, 1983.

Useful as background, but fails to assess properly the religious nonviolence of the movement.

1085 Watson, Russell. "Has Walesa Been Dumped? The Pope Plays Politics in Poland," *Newsweek* 102 (July 11, 1983): 30-31.

The *L'Osservatore Romano* story and the Vatican's denial.

1086   Weschler, Lawrence. *The Passion of Poland.* New York:
        Pantheon, 1984.

        Excellent essays originally appearing in the *New
        Yorker,* based on interviews, printed and underground
        works, and first-hand observations of the situation in
        Poland from May 1981 to September 1983. Well anno-
        tated, with a useful chronology of Polish history. An
        excellent introduction to the Solidarity period.

1087   Will, James E. "The Power of the Polish Church,"
        Christian Century 99 (Jan. 6, 1982): 5-6.

        Fifty percent of Polish Communist Party members are
        practicing Catholics. The religious character of Solidarity
        is astonishing. Glemp has condemned martial law but has
        called for nonviolence and has refused to negotiate without
        Lech Walesa. Poland's bishops have condemned martial
        law and called for the release of Solidarity prisoners.

* *
*

CHAPTER 14: *The Third World, Catholic Peacemaking and Liberation*

South Africa

1088   Bosch, David J. "Currents and Crosscurrents in South
        African Black Theology." See **1092**, 220-37.

        Briefly traces the development of Black Theology in
        South Africa and then sums up the major elements of the
        theology: overcoming the slave mentality, eliminating
        white tokenism and the patronizing of white liberals. At
        the same time Black Theology calls for love of the White
        enemy, ecumenism, and a shift beyond the inner, pietistic
        elements of Christianity and toward an emphasis on the
        whole person.

1089   "Catholics Defy Banning," *Christian Century* 98 (July 15,
        1981): 729.

        In a direct challenge to South Africa's apartheid, the
        South African Catholic Bishops Conference named banned
        black priest Smangaliso Mkhatshwa as the group's general
        secretary.

1090   Cone, James H., and Gayraud S. Wilmore, eds. *Black
        Theology: A Documentary History 1966-1979*.
        Maryknoll, NY: Orbis Books, 1979.

        A collection of essays, including **1088, 1091,** and
        1146.

1091   ——."Black Theology and African Theology: Considera-
        tions for Dialogue, Critique, and Integration." See
        1092, 463-76.

        The basis of both theologies is the liberation theme in
        Exodus and the New Testament theme of Christ as
        liberator found in Galatians 5:1.

1092   Crowe, Sarah. "Clergy Stand Up, Cut Down with South
        African People," *NCR* 22, 18 (Feb. 28, 1986): 1, 25.

        The clergy, of all faiths, are playing a key role in
        avoiding even bloodier confrontations, but bringing their
        physical presence to funerals and other demonstrations and
        attempting to keep protestors and police apart and calm.
        Catholic clergy of all ranks from bishops down have been
        attacked, arrested, threatened, and deported. The South
        African Catholic Bishops' Council under Archbishop
        Denis Hurley has committed itself to an activist campaign
        of civil disobedience and nonviolent resistance. Res-
        ponding to the overwhelming call of Black unionists, the
        Catholic bishops are now moving to a forceful combina-
        tion of economic sanctions against their government. Yet
        the church is racing against time and political currents that
        could make its recent actions meaningless.

1093   ——."Episcopal Votes Pose Challenges to Race, Nuclear
        Policy Positions," *NCR* 22, 28 (May 9, 1986): 1, 17.

        Sanctions by other nations are approved by the South
        African Catholic bishops as the most effective nonviolent
        method these countries can use against apartheid.

1094   de Gruchy, John W. *The Church Struggle in South Africa.*
        Grand Rapids, MI: Eerdman's, 1979.

Not seen.

1095   Goodman, David L. "South Africa: Whites Who Won't
        Fight," *Progressive* 49,9 (September 1985): 29-31.

        On whites who refuse to serve in the Defense Force
        either to enforce apartheid or to fight in Namibia. The End
        Conscription Campaign was launched in October 1984
        and was an outgrowth of the conscientious-objector
        movement. Its strength has been increasing dramatically.
        In January 1984, 15,000 white males were called up for
        army duty. Of these 7,589 did not report. In fact only
        1,596 did report in all of 1984.
        This has caused a crisis in the apartheid government,
        since conscription has been used since 1961 as a major
        means of enforcing racial oppression. Since 1973 over
        5,000 men have been prosecuted for failing to report for
        duty; 6,000 left the service between 1973 and 1980; and
        2,000 a year currently leave. The first conscientious
        objectors were Jehovah's Witnesses. In 1976 the first
        mainline Protestant refused service on just-war grounds; in
        1983 the first political conscientious objector was jailed.
        The End Conscription Campaign has been made
        possible by the crucial role of women working within it
        and the impetus given by Black Sash, the women's group
        that has provided counseling on opposing the Pass laws.
        The ECC is also backed by Allan Boesak, Desmond Tutu,
        Nadine Gordimer, and others, including the ANC. It
        represents the major white nonviolent opposition to apart-
        heid, and the government has acknowledged its power by
        beginning a series of raids and threats against it.

1096   Herman, Beth. "South African COs Continue Witness,"
        Reporter for Conscience Sake 35, 8 (August 1981): 3.

        On May 11, 1981 Charles Yeats was sentenced to

twelve months imprisonment for his conscientious objection. Such objection is especially threatening to South
Africa's system of apartheid, since it relies on the
compliance of all eligible white males to military service to
enforce its system of repression. Conscientious objection
is thus an act of nonviolent rebellion.

1097   Hope, Marjorie, and James Young. *The South African*
          Churches in a Revolutionary Situation. Maryknoll,
          NY: Orbis Books, 1983.

          Examines the role of all the South African churches
today and devotes a good deal of attention to the Catholic
Church there. Catholicism entered South Africa as a
minority religion, pushed off to the margins. This, and its
linguistic and anthropological methods of evangelization,
brought it success among the oppressed Blacks and gave
root to the creation of an indigenous leadership. Not part
of the ruling establishment that created apartheid, it thus
has an easier time colliding with it.
          The Catholic church thus maintained school integration
after the Bantu Education Act of 1953 prohibited it, and it
continued its policy after the Group Areas Act of 1960.
Catholic bishops' condemnations of apartheid first
appeared in 1948 and were repeated in 1952, 1957, and
1960, when the hierarchy urged the Catholic laity to obey
God's law above human law. On the parish level, however, Catholics have been more hesitant to break with their
neighbors, but strong leadership, especially that of
Archbishop Denis Hurley of Durban, has begun to change
attitudes. In 1976 the bishops' announcement that they
would integrate the Catholic schools despite the law saw
lay and government opposition collapse. Catholics polled
were 85% in favor of integration.
          Within the church itself, however, things have been
slower to change, as few Blacks have won high positions.

In 1977, however, the bishops vowed to speed up this process.

Another of the church's most significant acts has been to urge the provision of a conscientious objector status for the military. This would, in effect, allow the young Catholic to refuse the military service that defends apartheid. The church has, significantly, thus put itself behind a nonviolent revolution among South African whites. Questions remain, however: what has the church's effect been among Blacks? Can nonviolence, a word looked on with scorn in South Africa today, win the race against apartheid's increasing oppression, and against the counterviolence of the oppressed?

1098 McCann, Owen Cardinal. "Letter from Rome," *Leadership South Africa* 2 (Autumn 1983): 50-57.

Not seen.

1099 Regehr, Ernie. *Perceptions of Apartheid: The Churches and Political Change in South Africa*. Scottsdale, PA: Herald Press; Kitchener, Ont. Between the Lines, 1979.

Outlines events and attitudes of the churches toward South African society and the state, with some attention to the Catholic church. While the church is not as actively opposed to injustice as in Latin America, it did begin to voice its protests as early as the 1950s, and in response to black pressures it began to speak out against bannings, restrictions, pass laws, and eventually for the nonviolent overthrow of the apartheid system itself. Despite this, the church still has much progress to make in a very short time. In a church overwhelmingly Black, Blacks still represent only a small minority of the church hierarchy.

1100   "Rights of Anti-Apartheid Objectors to Refuse Service
        Recognized," *UN Chronicle* 16, 66 (January 1979):
        66.

        The United Nations recognizes the right of the South
        African conscientious objector to refuse military or police
        service rather than enforce the racist and oppressive
        policies of the Pretoria regime.

1101   Walshe, Peter. *Church vs State in South Africa.*
        Maryknoll, NY: Orbis Books, 1983.

        Despite its open condemnations of apartheid in 1957,
        1960, and 1962, the Catholic church has a long, slow way
        to go in living up to its words. Only in 1973 were its own
        seminaries integrated, and Archbishop Denis Hurley has
        had to face the criticism of his own colleagues, clergy, and
        laity for his opposition to apartheid. Despite this, Hurley
        has called on fellow Catholics to join him in a nonviolent
        revolution to overthrow the South African system. This
        and other pressures, including the Soweto Massacre, have
        spurred the hierarchy to admit its own failure to pursue
        peace and justice actively enough and to commit itself to
        the poor and the oppressed, to ally with the Black
        consciousness movement, and to call for true conversion.
        Despite these moves, however, time continues to run out
        in South Africa.

The Philippines

1102   Bernas, Joaquin G. "Empowering the Powerless,"
        America 145 (Dec. 26, 1981): 414.

        Not seen.

1103   Broad, Robin, and John Cavanaugh. "The Philippines: Government Hits Church in Waves of Repression," *NCR* 19, 19 (March 4, 1983): 1, 8.

Both Filipino clergy and foreign missionaries have been subjected to harassment, public denunciations, arrest, torture, and murder under the Marcos regime because of their activities on behalf of peace and social justice. The church hierarchy has steadily moved toward a condemnation of Marcos' regime.

1104   "Church of Both Right and Left Suffers...Splits," *NCR* 19, 41 (Sept. 16, 1983): 6-7, 9.

Church people are in all camps of the Filipino struggle. The institutional church seeks to protect its vast holdings and stay in Marcos' favor, and the hierarchy remains largely ignorant about popular movements. In fact, fear of infiltration has caused many in the hierarchy to disown or end controversial church programs among the people. Cardinal Sin's "critical collaboration" does not satisfy many. In the meanwhile many in the "popular" church have taken up the call of basic Christian communities to conscienticize among the people. Some others have also taken up the more extreme aspects of Liberation Theology and have sided with Marxist rebels in an attempt to overthrow the government by force. The result threatens a great polarization of the church.

1105   Claver, Francisco F. "Free Even in Enslavement. The Philippines: Yesterday, Today, Tomorrow," *Commonweal* 111 (March 9, 1984): 141-45.

Reviews the Philippines situation from the declaration of Martial Law in 1972 and summarizes the results of Marcos' regime as militarization, insurgency, injustice, destruction of democracy, and the growing stranglehold of the multinational corporations. Either a military coup or communist counterviolence have become real possibilities. A return to democracy by nonviolent means is the most difficult path, but it is not impossible. Basic Christian communities show the true direction of change that is built slowly from the people, the grass roots upward.

1106   ——."Revolution, the Church and Nonviolence," *Fellowship* 51, 6 (June 1985): 9-11.

Is violence justifiable in the attempt to right the wrongs of Filipino society and in implementing justice? It is a question that has faced the church there since the early 1970s. Marxism, and its millennial promise has attempted to enlist Christians to fight violently for justice; and the temptation is great, for violence is used on the right and the left. Nonviolence is condemned as subversive by the government and as reactionary by the Communists. With the assassination of Benigno Aquino, however, nonviolence has been seen as an increasingly viable alternative. While Bishop Claver admits that violence could make sense in the abstract, if tied to the struggle for justice, in concrete terms in the Philippines, and in light of Christ's cross, one must hesitate to use it. Yet what must one say to the desperate victims of violence? Claver urges the folly of Christ's cross, the slow, patient revolution in society that will not pitch peasant against peasant and make them the only victims of evolutionary violence. Yet nonviolence is more than a mere tactic: it is the end of the struggle itself. As one peasant farmer told him: " We seek the peace and love of the kingdom through justice. Our justice must therefore be in full accord throughout with that peace and love. Otherwise, we destroy what we seek. We destroy ourselves." Admirable testimony to the long, slow process of conscientization to active nonviolence that Claver and others are achieving in the Philippines.

1107 ——."Prophesy or Accommodation. The Dilemma of a Discerning Church," *America* 142 (April 26, 1980): 354-56.

The basic question for the church has become: how does it play its prophetic role in the face of martial law? Because of the extreme suffering of the Filipino people this action has increasingly become as choice between "critical collaboration" with the power of the "national security state" or with that of violent revolution. But since the 1950s the church's definition of its mission has begun to find a third path. It has begun to shift from passive and indirect support of "Catholic action" in unions and cooperatives to concerns of a more direct nature: economic and political clout. These have merged with the new Liberation Theology and the push to conscientization that Marcos' martial law may, in fact, have been designed to halt. This theology, already developing in the Philippines independently, saw the salvation of the soul as the salvation of the whole person, body and soul, thus necessitating all the freedoms of the Christian essential for both. This has led to a true "option for the poor" expressed in social action.

At the same time the church's response to this martial law grew gradually but strongly. In the process of change that was to overthrow the dictator, the role of the Catholic religious and laity was central, eventually reversing the process by which change flows through the church itself and influencing the hierarchy to declare itself against Marcos.

1108   ——.*The Stones Will Cry Out.* Maryknoll, NY: Orbis
         Books, 1978.

         A collection of letters from this bishop to his diocese
         on the conditions of oppression within the Philippines, the
         injustices and brutalities of their lives under tyranny. It
         focuses on the faith of the Philippines Christians, and the
         work of the Basic Christian Communities in bringing hope
         in the midst of this darkness.

1109   Deats, Richard Baggett, "The Philippines: Islands in
         Ferment," *Fellowship* 51, 6 (June 1985): 3-7.

         Reviews the current situation in the Philippines in the
         wake of the Aquino assassination. Focus on the key role
         of the Basic Christian Communities in this overwhelm-
         ingly Catholic country, their process of conscientization,
         and the growing "politics of nonviolent action." Yet the
         process is fraught with dangers: the growing militarization
         of society, aided and abetted by the U.S. Reagan adminis-
         tration, the open brutalities of Marcos' paramilitary
         squads, and the desperation of a people that leads them to
         violence to redress their ills.

1110   Digan, Parig. *Churches in Contestation. Asian Christian
         Social Protest.* Maryknoll, NY: Orbis Books, 1984.

         An excellent introduction to Christianity in Asia.
         Digan's account includes background on the origins and
         nature of Christianity there as a marginal, if not tenuous,
         Western cultural import. Tied to authoritarianism and
         colonialism, the church's passive role merged well with
         the lack of an Asian tradition of protest. By the late
         twentieth century, however, this very marginality and
         Christianity's base among the poor and oppressed had

combined with an older Christian tradition of prophetic
protest to forge a new Asian movement that began to fight
against the "national security state" and its institutionalized
oppression.

By the 1960s Asian bishops had begun organizing and
launching programs for conscientization and social action
that merged with the efforts of Vatican II and the emerging
Liberation Theology in its option for the poor, influenced
by Marx, Mao, Gandhi, and Martin Luther King. This
has led to a theology that also borrows from the Asian
tradition of Buddhist nonviolence but that also sees
violence as inevitable under certain conditions of
oppression.

Digan then goes on to offer several examples of this
new Christian activism at work in South Korea and in the
Philippines. In the latter, under Jaime Cardinal Sin, the
church has moved from its condemnation of revolutionary
violence and reluctant support of oppressive state violence
to a rejection of both. It acts, however, in a race against
time between the communists and national security state
and in fear of either communist infiltration of its work in
the basic Christian communities or of government
repression of these efforts.

1111   Drinan, Robert F., S.J. "Passiontide for the Philippine
        Church," *America* 152 (March 16, 1985): 209-212.

In preaching the preferential option for the poor and
for basic human and political rights the Catholic church has
become a major force against Marcos. The main impetus
comes through Basic Christian Communities. There are
now 2,000 of these throughout the country with over
600,000 members.

Marcos has therefore set out to infiltrate or disrupt
these; and government spokesmen like Juan Ponce Enrile
have stressed the need for fight against communism on all

levels. It has therefore launched a campaign of illegal
arrests, disappearances and murders against churchpeople
and members of the Basic Christian Communities.

1112   Evans, J.H., and Jack Epstein. "The Philippines: Manila
       Resembles Managua of Past," *NCR* 20, 2 (Oct. 28,
       1983): 8.

The atmosphere after the assassination of Benigno
Aquino resembles that of Nicaragua shortly before the
downfall of Somoza.

1113   "Filipino Bishops Approve Boycott of Election," *NCR* 20,
       14 (Jan. 27, 1984): 3.

Catholic bishops urge their congregations to ignore the
Philippines' compulsory election law and to participate
only according to the dictates of their own consciences,
repeating their stance in the 1981 election.

1114   Gaspar, Karl. *How Long? Prison Reflections from the
       Philippines.* Maryknoll, NY: Orbis Books, 1985.

In march 1983 Gaspar, a lay theologian and church
worker, was kidnapped by forces directed by Juan Ponce
Enrile. He was held without charge for two years and
repeatedly interrogated on suspicion of being a communist
leader.
   This book is a collection of his letters that, together,
form a diary of life in prison amid physical and mental
deprivations, boredom, beatings and torture. Gaspar's
hopes and physical condition were kept alive, however, by
the quick work of friends and organizations who got wind
of his disappearance and continued to pressure the government for his eventual release.

1115   Giordano, Pasquale T., S.J. "The Philippine Church:
       Exercising Her Prophetic Role to a Nation in Crisis,"
       New Catholic World 226 (Sept.-Oct. 1983): 226-28.

Since Vatican II the church has been involved in an
"integral evangelization," to portray the Gospels not only
in words but also in promoting the development and
liberation of peoples. This process is now at work in the
Filipino church. There are problems, however: the
shortage of clergy and the continuing suppression of
human rights, of violence and counterviolence, that
emerged under the Marcos regime.

1116   Hunt, Chester L. "Liberation Theology in the Philippines:
       A Test Case," *Christianity Today* 26 (March 5, 1982):
       24-26.

A negative assessment. Sees Liberation Theology as
Marxist, pro-violence, class war and revolution, anti-
Western, anti-rational, and ideological. Only one-third of
the Filipino clergy are really opposed to Cardinal Sin's
"critical collaboration." In fact, most of the Liberation
Theology emerging in the Philippines is pressed on the
native clergy by foreigners. Yet these discontents have
failed in their attempts to stir up anti-American feeling.
Conscientization is similar to the Alinsky technique of
exacerbating grievances to bring on the revolution.
"Liberation theology brings the frustrated Filipino
intellectual and the expatriate clergy together. It combines
the usual Marxist views with long-standing nationalist
grievances." Written at a period when it looked as if the
forces of reaction would succeed in silencing the new
theology.

1117   MacEoin, Gary. *The Inner Elite*. Kansas City, KS: Sheed, Andrews & McMeel, 1978.

Biographies of major contenders in the college of cardinals to succeed Paul VI. Jaime Cardinal Sin is profiled.

1118   Martin, Earl S. "Cardinal Opposes Repression, Revolution," *NCR* 16, 37 (Aug. 15, 1980): 7.

Jaime Cardinal Sin seeks to maintain his friendship with Ferdinand Marcos as his "parishioner," thus influencing policy from the top, and he has rejected any support from mass demonstrations or other expressions of the popular church. By late 1980, however, one-quarter of Filipino bishops were openly opposed to martial law. While rejecting violent revolution, the October 1979 bishops' conference had to admit that the causes of violence in Filipino society lay in the "inequalities among countless poor, the use of force — both overt and subtle — to preserve the privileges of wealth and status; the denial and frequent violation of basic human rights."

1119   "Message from the Philippines," *America* 151 (Oct. 20, 1984): 219-20.

On the efforts of Cardinal Sin to bring all segments of Filipino society, including business and professionals, into the struggle against Marcos. Marcos is still a friend of the United States, but he has warned of the dangers of keeping Marcos in power.

1120   Neumann, A. Lin. "Dictator Roulette: Philippine Vote Sparks Bishops' Resistance Call," *NCR* 22, 17 (Feb. 21, 1986): 1, 4, 8.

The Filipino Bishops' Conference labeled the February 1986 election results a fraud and called on the Filipino people to "nonviolent struggle" and resistance. Reprints text of their letter.

1121   ——."It Was the Grace of God That Enabled Us. Philippine Church Plays Key Role in Political Transition," *NCR* 22, 19 (March 7, 1986): 1, 22.

As the Army, dissident troops, and the people stood on the verge of violent confrontation, priests, friars, nuns, and laity pushed themselves into their midst and with great physical bravery created a human shield that prevented bloodshed and sealed the downfall of the Marcos government. Cardinal Sin's intervention, blasting the papal nuncio for his lingering support of Marcos, and calling on the Filipino people to complete their nonviolent revolution, was also key.

1122   ——."Pressures Forced Church Break with Marcos. Philippine Bishops Squeezed Between Forces Left and Right," *NCR* 22, 22 (March 28, 1986): 9.

Traces the gradual evolution in the position of the Catholic hierarchy from accommodation with Marcos and martial law in the early 1970s, to their open condemnation of his regime in early 1986. Bishop Francisco Claver, the author of the bishop's letter in February 1986, has been a key force in describing, and furthering, this process of conversion.

1123   Ostling, Richard N. "Mission to the East," *Time* 117 (March 2, 1981): 34-36.

A good summary of Pope John Paul II's mission to

the Philippines. In preparation for the visit Marcos lifted
the eight-year martial law, but the pope still openly
rebuked him for abuses. At the same time he also rebuked
the clergy for participating in revolutionary activity and
stressed that political action is the sphere of the laity. The
poor must be liberated, but this cannot be done through
violence or hate.

1124   "Papal Postponement Political," *NCR* 16, 37 (Aug. 15,
       1980): 14.

By delaying his trip to the Philippines John Paul II
hoped to warn Marcos about his repression and main-
tenance of martial law.

1125   "Philippines," *NCR* 19, 41 (Sept. 16, 1983).

A special issue.

1126   Rosenthal, Peggy. "The Precarious Road: Nonviolence in
       the Philippines," *Commonweal* 113, 12 (June 20,
       1986): 364-67.

What was the process that led up to the Philippines'
nonviolent revolution in February 1986? One of the
answers lies ion the unheralded activities of the Goss-
Mayrs, champions of nonviolence around the world.
They themselves were invited to the Philippines in August
1984 to organize a nonviolent revolution, but give much of
the credit to Benigno Aquino,who underwent his own
conversion to nonviolence, Corazon Aquino, Cardinal
Jaime Sin, and to the Basic Christian Communities in the
Philippines, and Radio Veritas, with whom they worked to
create the AKKAPKA, the nonviolent resistance
movement that finally toppled Marcos. Yet the story goes
beyond these individuals and groups, to the first non-

violent resistance organized by Bishop Francisco Claver in
the early 1970s, and looks forward to the fulfillment of the
promise of the February Revolution.

1127   Steif, William. "Philippines' Sin Says Marcos Must Go to
        Halt Gains by Extremists," *NCR* 22, 13 (Jan. 24,
        1986): 1, 26-28.

Sin calls for Marcos' election defeat in order to stem
the rising tide of Communist revolution. Examines Sin's
personality, his life, and his role in the nonviolent revolution.

1128   Veneroso, Joseph R., M.M. "The Gathering Storm,"
        Maryknoll 80, 2 (February 1986): 3-11.

Catholic missionaries attempt to carry on their work
amid rising violence from both government and
insurgents. The article briefly reviews the government's
murder of clergy and church workers among the Basic
Christian Communities. Meanwhile the church is increasingly lining up against Marcos.

Latin America

1129   Bamat, Thomas. "The Catholic Church and Latin
        American Politics," *Latin American Research Review*
        18, 3 (1983): 219-26.

A review article. The church's activities throughout
Latin America are the single most important development
since the Cuban revolution.

1130   Bokenkotter. *History*. See 5, 455-56.

Brief but useful introductory material to the church in

Latin America that puts it firmly within the broad context of developments of the church in the twentieth century. Bokenkotter also gives attention to some of the continent's most important peacemakers, including Archbishop Helder Camara of Brazil, Cardinal Silva Henriquez of Chile, and Archbishop Silvero of Paraguay. With ninety percent of the population at least nominally Catholic, recent decades have seen the church as the only institution that can stand up to the dictators and the military.

1131   Brown, Richard C. "Liberation Theology in Latin America: Its Challenge to the United States," *Conflict* 4 (1983): 21-58.

This is a leftist ideology whose major thrust poses a threat to U.S. interests.

1132   Comblin, José. *The Church and the National Security State*. Maryknoll, NY: Orbis Books, 1979.

This is a work of theological observation and reflection. It begins with a discussion of forms of theology, academic and liberation, European and Latin American. It then reviews the influence of Marx and the methods of modern social science on Catholic thought and goes on to outline a new "theology of revolution." Comblin then briefly traces the history of Latin America from colonialism to modern times, the creation of the National Security State and the role it plays in worldwide geopolitics and as a bolster to local elites. The doctrine of the National Security State has, in effect, become a new theology, since it underpins the elite rule of military dictatorships with supposedly Christian sanctions and goals. Comblin next discusses the role of the church as the subservient tool of the state, its growing criticism, and ensuing conflict. This conflict is expressed in new

theologies, in new practice of organization and evangelization, and in new divisions between a true church of
the people and the false myths and brutal force of the
political ideology of the state.

1133   Dahlin, Therrin C. and others. *The Catholic Left in Latin
        America: A Comprehensive Bibliography.* Boston:
        G.K. Hall, 1981.

An excellent introduction to the materials available,
including both violent and nonviolent movements for
change.

1134   Dipboye, Carolyn Cook. "The Roman Catholic Church
        and the Political Struggle for Human Rights in Latin
        America 1968-1980," *Journal of Church and State* 24
        (Autumn 1982): 497-524.

Not seen.

1135   Dussel, Enrique. "Current Events in Latin America." See
        1137, 77-102.

Follows events from the council of Sucre in 1972 to
that of Puebla in 1979, characterizing this as a reactionary
period in the history of church and state in Latin America.

1136   ——.*History.* See **752**, 117-255.

The Latin American church entered the twentieth
century as truly marginal: impoverished, powerless, and
cut off from European Christendom. At the same time,
from the 1930s a reawakening among the laity and the
survival of collegiality among the region's hierarchy
insured that the church would become a strong force for

change, especially after Vatican II (See **945** to **976**) and in the face of the "national security state's" brutal defense of "Western Christian Civilization" in the 1960s and 1970s.

Traces the immense impact of Vatican II, of Paul VI's *Populorum Progressio,* of CELAM (The Conference of Latin American Bishops), of the Medellin Conference, and emerging Liberation Theology. Follows the events of the 1960s and 1970s in Brazil, Argentina, Peru, Paraguay, and Cuba. Then examines the examples of several individuals, including Helder Camara, Leonidas Proaño and Fr. Camilo Torres as an introduction to the problem of violence in Latin America today and the quest for an appropriate "vocabulary of peace" that will match the risk and the challenge of nonviolence.

Dussel also traces the reaction to Liberation in North America, in the reign of terror unleashed against the church by the National Security State between 1973 and 1979 (which created more martyrs for the church than the past 500 years combined) and at the councils of Sucre and Puebla. Surprisingly, however, Puebla ended as a triumph for the "People of God," endorsed Liberation Theology, and put the church in Latin America clearly back in the tradition of Montesinos and Las Casas. See **761** to **778**. The church thus declared decisively that it sought not to replace one oppressor with another, not the rule of elites over the masses, but to take up the role of teacher and prophet to lead the people themselves to their own liberation. Liberation Theology thus reembraced the peaceful apocalyptic of the Catholic tradition as an understanding of the mysteries of history and a process of gradual revelation, leading the people from the womb of the present into a new age.

1137   Eagleson, John, and Sergio Torres, eds. *The Challenge of Basic Christian Communities.* Maryknoll, NY: Orbis Books, 1981.

Articles by Sergio Torres, Dussel, Gutierrez, Boff, Sobrino, d'Escoto, and others.

1138 Lange, Martin and Reinhold Iblacker, eds. *Witnesses of Hope*. William E. Jerman, transl. Maryknoll, NY: Orbis Books, 1981.

Documents the sufferings of Christians under the National Security State in Latin America between 1968 in the wake of the Medellin Conference and 1980. During these years over 1,500 bishops, priests, nuns, religious lay workers, numerous Indians and poor campesinos were imprisoned, tortured, murdered, and "disappeared" precisely because of their witness as *Christians* in seeking peace and justice according to the call of Medellin and Vatican II. The editors cite many examples from around the region, ranging from Archbishop Oscar Romero (See 1238 to 1243) and the American religious women martyred in El Salvador (See 1244 to 1248), to the plight of the poor and oppressed in Chile, to Indians exterminated in Brazil. This often recalls the Acts of the Christian Martyrs. It should. Foreword by Karl Rahner, S.J.

1139 Lernoux, Penny. *Cry of the People*. New York: Penguin Books, 1982.

In minute, often painful detail, this journalist and expert on Latin American political and religious affairs narrates the sufferings of the Latin American people under the National Security State of the 1960s and 1970s. Her theme is the concerted U.S. policy of supporting military coups and dictatorships, and their rampages of arrest, torture, disappearances and murders against those struggling for human rights, most especially the Roman

Catholic church. The church itself underwent a dramatic change from conservative bulwark of the status quo to the most dynamic force for change in the region in the period after Vatican II and Medellin, and it consequently suffered more martyrdoms than at any time since the Roman Empire.

Sometimes reading like the acts of the martyrs, sometimes like pure investigative reporting, sometimes like war correspondence, Lernoux's narrative is riveting and emotionally packed. Her research is meticulous, based on first-hand interviews, newspaper and magazine accounts, church and government documents. The book covers the rise of the new dictators, the church's response, and numerous examples of the repression that this response invited, including ones from El Salvador, Chile, Mexico, and Brazil.

It then documents the role of the U.S. in training and motivating the Latin American officer corps that has unleashed this persecution, the doctrine of the National Security State, designed to protect U.S. "development" and regional elites, the role of U.S. multinationals, and the work of the CIA. Also examines the new ideology of "family, tradition, and property" that has been the rallying cry of oligarchs and death squads throughout the region. Lernoux also details European and U.S. funding for the repression.

The book then examines the role of the Catholic church in resisting this repression, the divisions within the church's hierarchy and between hierarchy, lower clergy, and laity in working out a new "option for the poor," and finally the U.S. role in supporting the church's progressives and reactionaries in Latin America. This work is a shocking eye-opener for any North American who is concerned with U.S. government and church policy toward Latin America, and it is an indispensable introduction to events there.

1140 ——."The Long Path to Puebla." See **1150**, 3-27.

An excellent introduction to the historical, political, and religious events that led to the Puebla conference and to the church's confirmation of the importance of Liberation Theology. This can be used as a brief introduction to the entire process of Catholic peacemaking in the region from first colonization to the 1970s.

1141 Levine, Daniel H. *Religion and Politics in Latin America: The Catholic Church in Venezuela and Colombia.* Princeton: Princeton University Press, 1981.

Religion is a vital and important factor in Latin America today; it is not a vestige of the past. These two countries provide case studies of the church's influence and the forms that it takes. The work tends to focus on the hierarchy, however, and devotes little attention to the Basic Christian Communities. It also links Liberation Theology to Marxist and socialist political aims.

1142 "Nonviolence and Social Change in Latin America," *Maryknoll* 79, 8 (August 1985): Special Issue.

Seven articles from throughout South and Central America on religious peacemaking.

1143 Skidmore, Thomas E., and Peter H. Smith. *Modern Latin America.* New York and Oxford: Oxford University Press, 1984.

A political and socio-economic account, that traces modern structures from the colonial period, and views

Latin American history in terms of this neo-colonial "dependency." Good, up-to-date bibliography.

1144   Smith, Brian H. *The Church and Politics in Chile: Challenges to Modern Catholicism.* Princeton: Princeton University Press, 1982.

How can the church as a whole implement the aims of Vatican II? Marxist analysis seems a valuable tool; yet on the whole the church in Chile is hesitant to take up its prophetic role unless its own hierarchical structures are threatened. A sociological approach based on extensive field research.

Theological Reflection in Latin America

1145   Berryman, Philip E. "Latin American Liberation Theology." See **1174**, 20-83.

A solid, and sympathetic introduction to the subject.

1146   "Black Theology and Latin American Liberation Theology." See **1092**, 510-15.

Reflections by Paolo Friere, Assman, Cone and others. Attempts at dialogue between the two religious traditions in the face of European assertiveness.

1147   Boff, Leonardo. "Christ's Liberation via Oppression: An Attempt at Theological Construction from the Standpoint of Latin America." See **1156**, 100-132.

The book of Exodus and Christ's temptations in Luke 4:1-13 serve as the model for the new Christian who rejects both the power and despair of the world in doing God's will.

1148   Colonnes, Louis M. *Conscientization for Liberation.* Washington, DC: U.S. Catholic Conference, 1971.

Not seen.

1149   Dussel, Enrique. "Historical and Philosophical Presuppositions of Latin American Theology." See **1156**, 184-212.

Liberation Theology grows out of praxis, from the experience of Latin America from Bartolomé de Las Casas (**761** to **778**) on. While Liberation Theology must be understood in the context of the universal Catholic church, the voice of that church is not a monologue. Latin American theology is the child of both European and Amerindian cultures, not only of European Christendom. Its tasks are therefore suited to the conditions of Latin America. It must serve to foster independence from authoritarianism and to unmask exploitation, as Christ and Las Casas did.

1150   Eagleson, John and Philip Scharper, eds.; John Drury, transl. *Puebla and Beyond.* Maryknoll, NY: Orbis Books, 1980.

For the council of Puebla, Mexico in 1979, which conservatives in the church had intended to mark the end of Medellin's influence and of Liberation Theology. The council was attended by important clerics and laity from around the world, including such Latin American bishops as Oscar Romero and Helder Camara. Press attention focused on the debates between conservatives and radicals within and outside the council, especially since Pope John Paul II attended the meetings and confirmed its conclusions. To the surprise of conservatives, the pope actually endorsed the thrust of the church's new "option for the poor" and for nonviolent change in Latin America, while he also applied its theory to liberation struggles in other parts of the world. As the result of a church council, the final document is now part of the official teaching of the Catholic church throughout the world.

The editors present the entire final document, the pope's major addresses, and commentaries by leading theologians and observers of the Latin American scene.

1151   Ellacuria, Ignacio. *Freedom Made Flesh. The Mission of Christ and His Church*. John Drury, transl. Maryknoll, NY: Orbis Books, 1976.

Like Christ himself, who lived and died in the real world of political repression and liberation, his church today must take up its mission of liberation, even if this again involves the cross of suffering and death. Christ's salvation is not purely spiritual — he came to save the world, which means flesh and blood as well as spirit. Examines the problems of discussing a political ideology of salvation, the political and social elements of Jesus' mission, his relationship to the state and political movements of his time, and then relates these to the situation of the church in Latin America.

Part Three: Violence and the Cross, examines the problems of aggressiveness and violence, finds their roots in human nature, and examines the choices open to Christians in pacifism (Charles de Foucauld), nonviolence (Martin Luther King) and revolutionary violence (Camilo Torres), and concludes that Christianity is too rich and multifaceted to be restricted to one attitude toward violence. Ellacuria carefully avoids passing judgment on any of these forms.

1152   "The Final Document: International Ecumenical Congress of Theology, Feb. 20-March 2, 1980, São Paulo,

Brazil." See **1137**, 231-46.

On the theological and practical life of the basic Christian communities.

1153   Freire, Paolo. *Pedagogy of the Oppressed.* Myra Bergman Ramos, transl. New York: Seabury Press, 1970; reprinted Continuum, 1981.

On the process of conscientization. This is the fundamental book that has inspired much of the methods of Latin American Liberation Theology and the basic Christian communities.

1154   Galilea, Segundo. "Liberation Theology and New Tasks Facing Christians." See **1156**, 163-83.

Reviews the accomplishments of the Medellin and Sucre church conferences. Then outlines the tasks that face Liberation Theology: cultural liberation and conscientization. The new theology must also pursue liberation from violence, both the institutionalized and subversive types. Yet this cannot be overcome by human means, or through violence, but only through the Cross. Christians must shoulder the burden of prophetic proclamation, of denunciation of power and injustice, and the announcement of solidarity with the poor and oppressed, of repentance and reconciliation. "Christian liberation, then, implies reconciliation; hence Liberation Theology implies a *theology of reconciliation.*"

1155   ——.*Theology and the Church, A Response to Cardinal (Joseph) Ratzinger.* New York: Seabury Press, 1985.

A pointed rebuttal to Cardinal Ratzinger's attack on

Liberation Theology as a "potential negation" of Christian teaching. Segundo defends the use of Marxist analysis and distinguishes this from Marxist-Leninist atheistic ideology. He notes, in fact, that even Pope John Paul II is using Marxist terminology when he speaks of "alienation" as the modern condition of sin. Marxism, however, is not the point of issue in the attack on Liberation Theology. Segundo goes right to the heart of Ratzinger's instruction and sees it as an attack on Vatican II and the Pastoral Constitution that put an end to the dualistic split between inner spirituality and Christian activism for social justice and peace.

1156   Gibellini, Rosino, ed. *Frontiers of Theology in Latin America.* John Drury, transl. Maryknoll, NY: Orbis Books, 1979.

A collection of essays by the region's leading intellectuals, including Boff (**1147**), Dussel (**1149**), Galilea (**1154**), Gutierrez (**1158**), Segundo (**1171**), and Vidales (**1175**).

1157   Goodman, Walter. "Church's Activist Clergy: Rome Draws Line," *New York Times,* Sept. 6, 1984.

On growing papal criticism of Boff and Gutierrez.

1158   Gutierrez, Gustavo. "Liberation Praxis and Christian Faith." See **1156**, 1-33.

A basic summation of Liberation Theology.

1159   ——*A Theology of Liberation.* Caridad Inda and John Eagleson, transls. and eds. Maryknoll, NY: Orbis Books, 1973.

This is dense, often difficult, but fundamentally important reading for Catholic liberation and nonviolence, not only in Latin America, but around the world. The controversy that surrounded Gutierrez' works, the attempt of Cardinal Ratzinger's Holy Office to silence Gutierrez and Boff, and Pope John Paul II's embrace and eventual vindication of Liberation Theology have made it the most important theological and *practical* movement in the church today. This book is the key text of that theology.

The church has finally entered an era that calls for a return to earlier Christian traditions: that faith is expressed through charity, that the church must raise a voice of prophesy, and that theology must once again flow from *praxis,* its working in the world, to illuminate the world and become the agent of the world's transformation. The sources of Liberation Theology are papal documents, such as Paul VI's *Populorum Progressio* (See **969**), *Gaudium et Spes* of Vatican II (See **950**), the Medellin Conference, and most importantly, the Bible. Key biblical texts include Galatians 5:1, Luke 4:1-13, and Exodus.

The major characteristics of this theology are the centrality of building the Kingdom of God that rejects the old dualism between personal, inner salvation and the institutional action of the church in Constantinian alliance with the powers of the world. Salvation is now seen as integral, that is, the church saves not only souls, but complete persons; it liberates both the oppressed and the oppressors from sin and from the poverty, alienation, exploitation, and oppression that define sin. Its emphasis on change is thus radical and integral, a rejection of older models of change, such as Western-style development, that impose it from the top down, the work of elites either clerical or governmental. Instead, change must come from the poor and the oppressed themselves, first through "conscientization," then through denunciation of sin, and then through the proclamation of liberation.

In this process the structure of the church plays an essential part, for the church must manifest the new society of peace and justice by changing its own life, opting for the poverty of the oppressed, changing its structure to reflect the voice of the humble, rejecting its alliance with power, while defying the threats of the secular state that it is "meddling in politics" when it speaks out for the oppressed. Yet just as Christ refused to despair or to hope in the forces of this world by casting himself down from the temple, the new theology refuses to despair. Neither does it seek utopian solutions to the problems of the world, for these utopias are the works of humans and of ideologies; while the kingdom of God, though implemented by men and women, is really the work of God, and it builds new men and women, not new societies. As such it demands individual conversion, not compulsion or the leadership of enlightened elites.

The church, then, is the visible manifestation of God's kingdom in the world and in history. The church exists not for itself, for its own structures and power, then, but for the world; it is the self-reflective part of the world. It is truly the sacrament of Christ's liberation in history and time. All history, then, is sacred history, the history of salvation, and the growth of God's kingdom is the process of liberation in the world. Only by forging social justice and love, therefore, can the individual and the church know God, and the type of knowledge one has of God through love and action ("orthopraxis") far excels that of intellectual knowledge of God through "orthodoxy."

Just as the new theology shifts emphasis from orthodoxy to orthopraxis, so too the sacramental and liturgical life of the church must focus away from individualistic piety and empty cultic worship and to a renewed emphasis on the Eucharist and Christ as the source and symbol of this new solidarity.

Much has been made of the "Marxist" and revolutionary elements of Liberation Theology. Here Gutierrez emphasizes that liberation must be the work of love and not of hate, but at the same time he recognizes that the oppressor is the enemy, and that physical poverty and oppression are real evils that must be combatted.

1160   ——,*We Drink From Our Own Wells. The Spiritual Journey of a People.* Matthew J. O'Connell, transl. Maryknoll, NY: Orbis Books, 1983.

The working of Liberation Theology in praxis, in the lives of the poor in Latin America. Part One discusses the contextual experience of Latin American liberation, the region's oppression, alienation, and poverty. Part Two examines forms of Christian spirituality based on biblical paradigms. Part Three traces the actual developments in contemporary Latin America, blending theological reflection with the recollection of events as concrete manifestations of Christian faith, hope, and love.

1161   Kamm, Henry. "Friar Defends Views at Vatican Session," *New York Times,* Sept. 8, 1984.

On Cardinal Ratzinger's silencing of Liberation Theologian Leonardo Boff and the friar's inquisition on the "Marxist" elements of his theology.

1162   ——."Vatican Censures Marxist Elements in New Theology," *New York Times,* Sept. 4, 1984:

On certain aspects of Boff's and Gutierrez' writings perceived by Cardinal Ratzinger and his Holy Office as Marxist, political teachings of class hatred and struggle.

1163 "Liberation Theology: Thy Kingdom Come, Here and Now," *Economist,* Oct. 13, 1984.

Critical of Boff and other Liberation Theologians for their insistence that sin and salvation apply to the body as well as the soul.

1164 "Light in the Latin Darkness," *Time* 116 (Oct. 27, 1980): 75.

Not seen.

1165 McCann, Dennis P. *Christian Realism and Liberation Theology.* Maryknoll, NY: Orbis Books, 1981.

Basically suspicious of the role of basic Christian communities and of individual Christians taking action that can be characterized as "political." In the tradition of Rheinhold Niebuhr, McCann asserts that the Christian must leave the problems of the world to political solutions worked out by secular agents. Briefly reviews the leading Liberation theologians, asserting that Gutierrez, for example, has stretched Medellin's option for the poor as a full endorsement of his position, that Segundo rejects "pacifism" as contributing to the status quo and calls for a liberating violence whose religious basis is illusionary, that he says the manipulation of the masses by a revolutionary elite dedicated to liberation is justified, and that he believes "the end justifies the means."

1166 O'Brien and Shannon. *Renewing the Earth.* See **42**, 539-79.

Includes an introduction to Liberation Theology and the documents of the Medellin Conference on Justice and Peace, as well as the Conference's Message to the Peoples of Latin America. The Medellin Conference was the second general meeting of the Conference of Latin American Bishops, held in Medellin, Colombia from August 24 to September 6, 1968. As such it was an official church council, and its final documents are part of the official teaching of the Catholic church around the world. These final documents are the Latin American response to Vatican II and Pope Paul VI's *Populorum Progressio,* and they form the theological and ecclesiological basis for the church's nonviolent struggle for liberation. Medellin has become the central event for Latin American Liberation theologians and is the cornerstone of all later reflection, just as it was the summation of previous practice and theory. These documents are essential to any study of Latin American events and theory in the 1970s and 1980s.

1167 Ostling, Richard N. "*Si* to a Demanding Friend," *Time,* Feb. 11, 1985: 76.

On John Paul II's Latin American tour and his support for a nonviolent version of Liberation Theology strained of its Marxist elements. The pope fully supports the goals of peace as social justice embodied in the new theology.

1168 Pasca, T.M. "The Vatican Flops in Latin America," *The Nation* 240, 3 (Jan. 26, 1985): 76-79.

On the failed attack on Liberation Theology and the Vatican's accommodation with Nicaragua's Sandinistas.

1169 Ratzinger, Joseph Cardinal. *Instruction on Certain Aspects of the "Theology of Liberation."* Rome: Sacred Congregation for the Doctrine of the Faith; Washington, DC: U.S. Catholic Conference, 1984.

Assumes immediately a sharp distinction between liberation from sin, which he asserts to be purely spiritual, and liberation from "servitude of an earthly and temporal kind." Ratzinger thus a priori condemns what he has set out to examine, since the unity of spiritual and temporal sin lies at the heart of Liberation Theology. One cannot speak of physical oppression, political tyranny, or economic exploitation without defining them as sins against God and humanity, the Liberation Theologians contend, yet Ratzinger would stress the pre-Vatican II assumption that one can be saved from sin individually and internally while one ignores the injustices and calamities of the world around.

Ratzinger does, however, then go on to examine the origins of Liberation Theology in the praxis of Latin America and the Third World, to review its biblical foundations, and the "voice of the Magisterium," that is the church's own pronouncements on the process of liberation as found in *Mater et magistra, Pacem in terris, Populorum progressio,* and *Evangelii nuntiando.*

Ratzinger then goes to what he considers the heart of the problem, the confusion among good-intentioned clergy and laity to adopt "Marxist" analysis to further the process of liberation. While many currents exist within Marxism, its "pure" form notes "class-struggle" and this is not compatible with Christianity. One must avoid treating Marxism as if it were a scientific analysis to reality and not simply a sympathetic language. Ratzinger rejects what he considers the fundamentally violent interpretation of class-struggle and implies that this colors all of Liberation Theology, although he is careful to note that it is explicit in "certain of the writings." He then goes on to stress that this identification is incompatible with Vatican II.

What also seems to disturb Ratzinger is what he sees as a sinister perversion of Christian doctrine into a "real system" complete with a rival "church of the poor, a rival liturgy of struggle, that rejects the true sacramental nature of the Eucharist, a questioning of the hierarchical structure of the church, and a "radical politicization of faith's affirmations" which is a priori bad. Pure Liberation Theologians, he asserts, stress that whoever disagrees with them are a priori members of the oppressor class. These people hold church social teaching in disdain, attempt a political re-reading of Scripture, and make the Kingdom of God an earthly goal. Even the assertions of complete faith in Christian creeds and doctrines espoused by the Liberation Theologians are mere shams, and the Jesus of struggle that they preach denies the Incarnate Word, "God made Lord and Christ." True liberation is baptism, not "the political liberation of a people."

In conclusion Ratzinger asserts that he is not for earthly oppression and calls on all clergy to dialogue with the "Magisterium of the Church," to reject "blind" violence, to seek for the roots of injustice in the hearts of men, and to reject the temptation to seek solutions in structural change. He also dismisses Basic Christian Communities as misinformed and ignorant, if "generous," sessions in which these false doctrines are spread.

By his stress of what he begins by saying are "certain aspects" of Liberation Theology: Marxism, class-division, violence, un-Christian Christologies, Ratzinger raises so many red herrings that the reader who is not also familiar with the basic texts of Liberation Theology will come away believing that these "certain aspects" are the root and heart of the theology. In fact, it is not entirely clear if this is not what the cardinal has in mind, or whether he himself has not fully understood the texts and intent of these works.

1170   Russell, George. "Taming the Liberation Theologians," *Time,* Feb. 4, 1985, 56-59.

On Cardinal Ratzinger's Holy Office investigation of aspects of the works of Liberation theologians Boff and Gutierrez.

1171   Segundo, Juan Luis. "Capitalism Versus Socialism: Crux Theologica." See **1156,** 240-59.

Liberation theology is a whole theology that speaks to the reality of Latin America. This reality is not dominated by the struggle between the U.S. and U.S.S.R. but derives from the plight of the vast majority of its people.

1172   Swomley, John M. *Liberation Ethics.* New York: Macmillan, 1972.

The theory and methods of nonviolent change and revolution. The moral conversion of the individual to liberation is necessary before such change can begin. Recent history offers many examples of successful nonviolent change in Latin America. These include the nonviolent revolutions in Chile in July 1931, in Guatemala in 1944, and in El Salvador in 1944. All involved the withdrawal of consent from the dictators by the majority of the people across all classes and professions, often in the face of violent attempts at repression.

1173   ——.*Liberation Politics.* Elgin, IL: Brethren Press, 1984.

Not seen,

1174   Torres, Sergio and John Eagleson, eds. *Theology in the Americas.* Maryknoll, NY: Orbis Books, 1976.

A collection of essays by the leading theologians in both continents.

1175   Vidales, Raul. "Methodological Issues in Liberation Theology." See **1156**, 34-57.

A discussion of Liberation Theology and its roots in theory and praxis. Summarizes its historical base and stresses that faith can only be understood via action. The basic features of Liberation Theology include solidarity with the exploited, a joyous unity among brothers and sisters, its operation in the midst of conflict, and a basis in Christian faith that is above all Christocentric.

Individual Witness

Dom Helder Camara and Brazil

1176   Bruneau, Thomas C. "The Church and Politics in Brazil: The Genesis of Change," *Journal of Latin American Studies* 17 (Nov. 1985): 271-93.

Follows the transformation of the Catholic church in Brazil under the influence of Vatican II. CELAM and the statements of Medellin have been fundamental. Reviews developments and research in the field, statements of the hierarchy, the retreat from new commitments after the coup, but their reassertion in different form during the military's rule. The church, in fact, weakened the political and economic grip of the generals. In return its own structures have changed. The church emerging now in Brazil will be far less institutionally oriented.

1177   ——.*The Church in Brazil: The Politics of Religion.* Austin:

University of Texas Press, 1982.

Examines the 60,000 Basic Christian Communities throughout Brazil. These are the outcome of the church's new approach to evangelization: the work through the people. The communities were begun between 1950 and 1964 and consolidated between 1964 and 1974, despite state repression. While the "MEBs" have not been as successful as hoped in true evangelization, they have presented a real challenge to Brazilian authoritarianism.

1178   Camara Helder. *Church and Colonialism.* London: Sheed & Ward, 1969.

Not seen.

1179   ——.*The Conversions of a Bishop: An Interview with José de Broucker.* Hilary Davies, transl. London and Cleveland: Collins, 1979.

A biography of the bishop through a series of interviews in 1975 and 1976. Camara is quite outspoken here about many of the personalities in his life. He offers his thoughts on the struggle of a united people toward liberation, not by guerrilla war or violent revolution but through nonviolence, or "the violence of pacifists," as he prefers to call it. He sharply distinguishes this with "passivism."

1180   ——.*The Desert Is Fertile.* Dinah Livingstone, transl. Maryknoll, NY: Orbis Books, 1982.

Active nonviolence is a force as strong as nuclear energy. It is the power of love and justice. Camara discusses his half-failure; his six-year attempt to make his

Action for Justice and Peace succeed as an organized pressure group. He eventually realized, however, that institutions as such are incapable of bringing about change.

Camara condemns the U.S., U.S.S.R. and EEC for their exploitation and their continued arms race. He rests his hopes on the "Abrahamic minorities" who work in the darkness against all hope to create change.

1181 ——.*Hoping Against All Hope*. Matthew J. O'Connell, transl. Maryknoll, NY: Orbis Books, 1984.

Camara goes beyond a disgust with poverty, the arms race, waste, materialism, and overspecialization to see hope that this disgust among people will be turned to positive energy to *change*. All these troubles in the world are "signs of God."

This is a theological approach and underpining to his activist life. It is based heavily on Vatican II, Medellin, and Teilhard de Chardin's teleological approach. Abraham's "hope against all hope" is a model for groups practicing "active nonviolence." These are the "Abrahamic minorities."

1182 ——.*Race Against Time*. Della Couling, transl. London: Sheed & Ward, 1971.

Camara's profound Christianity is the root of his concern for economic and social justice in Brazil. Examines the injustice and oppression of Brazilian society, discusses the need for change, the role of the institutional church, or capitalism and neo-colonialism, of the U.S.A.

Camara calls for a revolution, among the universities and intellectuals especially here, and he declares his hopes despite the dehumanizing trends in science and technology. Teilhard de Chardin is an inspiration.

1183   ——.*Revolution Through Peace*. Ruth Nanada Anshen,
        ed.; Amparo McLean, transl. New York: Harper &
        Row, 1971.

The now retired archbishop of Recifé, Brazil, Camara
lays out the basic tenets of his revolution: neither capitalism nor communism will work in the Third World to cure
the violence of poverty or exploitation, for which the U.S.
and the U.S.S.R. are largely responsible both through
their own economic exploitation and through the vast
amounts they spend on arms while millions starve. Both
nations, in fact, put the world in danger of extermination,
while the U.S.'s emphasis on communism as the supreme
evil of the world ignores the real evils suffered by the poor
every day.
     What, then, are the solutions to the Third World's
problems? Development as practiced by the North
American and European technocrats certainly is not. This
is change imposed from above for the benefit of oligarchs.
Instead, Camara urges a gradual process, first of conscientization among the people, and then once the people
have taken their lives into their own hands, a movement
for true peace, which is based on justice, truth, charity,
and dialogue.   While violent revolutionaries have
attempted to redress the violence of poverty and repression
by armed struggle, Camara refuses to condemn their
sacrifices, but he insists that "only love can build. Hate
and violence only destroy."

1184   ——.*Spiral of Violence*. London: Sheed & Ward, 1969.

A description and analysis of violence, repression and
counterviolence. Is there a solution? Camara describes

his Action for Peace and Justice, its objectives, problems, modes of action, audience, and appeal.

1185 ——.*A Thousand Reasons for Living.* José de Broucker, ed., Alan Neame, transl. Philadelphia: Fortress Press, 1981.

Not seen.

1186 Castro, Marcos de. *Dom Helder, O'bispo da esperança.* Rio de Janeiro: Graal, 1978.

Camara's profoundly religious approach is based on the hope of God's grace. His development away from integralism to a struggle for justice via nonviolence. Examines his close ties to Pope Paul VI.

1187 Cirano, Marcos. *Os caminhos de Dom Helder (1964-1980).* Recifé: Editora Guararapes, 1983.

On the persecution of Camara and government attempts to keep him from the public eye. They have accused him of being a demagogue, a communist agitator, and a subversive. Reviews the press's attacks on him, with a complete bibliography of articles written about him.

1188 Cuneen, Sally. "The Good News from Latin America," *Christian Century* 98 (Jan. 7, 1981): 5.

On the occasion of Camara's visit to the Fellowship of Reconciliation in the U.S. Traces the steps of John Paul II's visit to Brazil and his physical embrace of the banned Camara on Brazilian television, and the coverage given to the pope's invitation to Camara and Cardinal Aloisio Lorscheider, another proponent of nonviolent change, to ride in his open car from the airport. Camara declares that nonviolence stems from conviction and from the certitude that violence would be suicidal.

1189   De Broucker, José. *Dom Helder Camara. The Violence of a Peacemaker*. Herma Briffault, transl. Maryknoll, NY: Orbis Books, 1970.

Traces Camara's personality and his daily routine, reviews the poverty and injustice of northeastern Brazil, the church's role in the struggle for justice, and the state's response in repression. Then goes on to analyze Camara's own nonviolence and his emerging reputation as the Voice of the Third World. Concludes with a portrait of Camara's life as a bishop in the Catholic church in Latin.

1190   Filius, Jan, and Jan Glissenaar. *Helder Camara in Nederland*. Utrecht: Bruna & Zoon, 1971.

On the occasion of Camara's 1970 visit. The warm welcome, the media coverage, the debates.

1191   Goss-Mayr, Hildegard. "Choosing Means Toward a Just End," *Fellowship* 49, 10-11 (Oct./Nov. 1983): 5, 27.

Contrasts the commitments to revolution of Helder Camara and Camilo Torres, the Colombian priest who went underground to emerge with Marxist guerillas devoted to the armed overthrow of the government. Camara admires the courage and sacrifice that Torres made in giving up his life, and dislikes the word nonviolence to describe what he himself does. He finds it too passive.

1192   Hall, Mary. *The Impossible Dream. The Spirituality of Dom Helder Camara*. Maryknoll, NY: Orbis Books, 1980.

A spiritual biography based on interviews and the author's observation of his daily life. Discusses his work, the difficulties, and constant reminders of the brutal government repression.

1193 Hebblethwaite, Peter. "Harsh Letter to Brazil Bishops Repeats 'Stay Out of Politics'," *NCR* 17 (May 15, 1981): 5.

Not seen.

1194 Hope and Young. *Struggle*. See **997**, 109-44.

Reviews Camara's life and early rise through the hierarchy in alliance with Brazil's political and economic establishment, his subsequent conversion following Vatican II, and his embrace of the cause, and life, of the poor and the oppressed. Camara was subsequently removed from power and influence, banned from appearing in the media, and subjected to constant denunciation, harassment, and violent attack on his staff and friends.

Camara rejects both capitalist development and communism, both of which empower the elite even further and ignore the real needs of individual development and liberation. Change must begin with the people themselves, through conscientization and basic Christian communities. Its impact on society must be nonviolent, aimed at converting both the oppressed and oppressor. Yet "nonviolence" is too weak a word. Camara refuses to condemn the sacrifices of a Che Guevera or a Camilo Torres, but he argues that such violence, while altruistic, only pits the oppressed against the oppressed. Still, one cannot condemn the violence of terrorism without first condemning the violence of injustice.

1195   "Just Look Around a Bit," *Time* 116 (July 14, 1980): 58.

        On John Paul II's trip to Brazil.

1196   Mainwaring, Scott. "The Catholic Church, Popular
        Education, and Political Change in Brazil," *Journal of
        Interamerican Studies and World Affairs* 26 (February
        1984): 97-124.

        On the conversion of the church hierarchy from an
        alliance with the dominant class and the state to its link
        with the poor. The military government attempted to
        repress the tendencies proclaimed by Medellin, but the
        church remained the main opposition between 1968 and
        1974. The influence of the Basic Christian Communities
        in this regard was strong.
        Article analyzes the strengths and weaknesses of the
        MEBs, the important role of intellectuals in these changes
        and processes. Good bibliography.

1197   Matta, Fernando Reyes, ed. *Universidad y Revolucion.*
        Santiago: Ediciones Nueva Universidad, 1969.

        A collection of documents, including Camara's
        "University and Revolution," and an examination of press
        coverage of the bishop on a wide variety of topics.

1198   Moosbrugger, Bernard. *A Voice of the Third World: Dom
        Helder Camara.* New York: Paulist Press, 1972.

        Often in the bishop's own words, this discusses his
        road to the bishopric, the poverty, hunger, ignorance and
        unemployment, the "silent fatalism" of the north. Reviews
        Camara's appeals for justice and peace in Latin America,
        the United States, and Europe, and his hope that inter-
        national big business can still be made responsible. He

retains faith that human institutions — religious, political, economic — can solve problems. His greatest hope rests on youth.

1199   "The Pope in Brazil," *America* 143 (July 5, 1980): 4.

    Not seen.

1200   Schumacher, E. "Tireless Friend of the Dispossessed," *New York Times Biography Service* 11 (October 1980): 1455-56.

    A competent, brief biography.

Adolfo Perez Esquivel and the Mothers of the Plaza de Mayo

1201   "Adolfo Perez Esquivel," *Current Biography Yearbook.* New York: H.H. Wilson, 1981, 321-24.

    A good introduction to his life, written after his winning the Nobel Peace Prize for 1980, for which he had been nominated by Irish Peace People Mairead Corrigan and Betty Williams. (See **1053** to **1059**.) A good supplement to Esquivel's own writing. See **1205**.

1202   Amador, Miguel. "Silent Accomplices," *Christian Century* 97 (Dec. 3, 1980): 1180-81.

    Traces Esquivel's activities since 1971, and his work as coordinator of the Service for Peace and Justice. On the news of Esquivel's winning the Nobel Peace Prize, the bishops of Argentina quickly disassociated themselves from him, while the Mothers of the Plaza de Mayo greeted him with ecumenical services. In the end, while some Catholic bishops congratulated the work of the Service for Peace and Justice, most remained silent, in tacit complicity with the generals.

1203 "An Interview with Adolfo Perez Esquivel," *Fellowship*
51, 7-8 (July-August 1985): 9-11.

Nonviolence is not nonaggression but a respect for life
and the individual. It is not an aim, not a tool, but a way
of life. In the very process of changing their lives of
oppression and ignorance in real ways people must be
conscientizied to their harmony with the essence of life,
their histories of war and heroes must be replaced by a
history of peoples to teach the story of human cooperation
and creativity. In this process both the great thinkers and
the great activists have a part: Thomas Merton as well as
Francis of Assisi. Yet even the "mystics" did not live with
their eyes rolled up to heaven but energetically partook of
the world and its problems. Without this, spirituality,
even devout churchgoing appears empty.

In the end, however, the theory of nonviolence is a
waste of time; only by putting principles into practice is it
real. Working on the small, local, and limited scale,
within one's capabilities is the best way to solve the "big"
world problems, which otherwise seem overwhelming.
Hope is the best food and advice for peacemakers.

1204 Drinan, Robert F. "Human Rights in Argentina," *America*
145 (Oct. 10, 1981): 198-200.

On July 15, 1981 seventy Catholic bishops issued a
74-page statement charging the government with illegal
repression in their "dirty war." While the bishops
condemned "revolutionary violence," they also strongly
condemned such institutional and repressive violence.
One of the strongest manifestations of Catholic
nonviolence are the Mothers of the Plaza de Mayo, who
gather every Thursday to protest the disappearance of their

loved ones. While, at the time of Drinan's writing, there was no open persecution of the Catholic church in Argentina, there was considerable hostility to the outspoken, such as Adolfo Perez Esquivel.

1205 Esquivel, Adolfo Perez. *Christ in a Poncho*. Charles Antoine ed.; Robert R. Barr, transl. Maryknoll, NY: Orbis Books, 1983, 117-34.

A collection of essays on various aspects of Esquivel's life and work for nonviolent change in Latin America. Traces his life, organizing efforts, and the events of Argentine history in the 1970s that led to his arrest, imprisonment, and torture under the generals. Esquivel notes that his major influences have included John the Baptist, Gandhi, Thomas Merton (**1305 to 1326**), Francis of Assisi (**454 to 465**), Ernesto Cardenal (**1216 to 1237**), Helder Camara (**1176 to 1200**), Lanza del Vasto (**997 to 1017**), the Medellin Conference's declarations on Liberation Theology (**1166**), among others. While he is committed to nonviolent change, he rejects "do-gooder" social work aimed at patching the current system and seeks to build a new community from the grass roots up, through such forms as the Basic Christian Communities.

"Nonviolence" is a bad word in Latin America, since for so many it connotes passivity, yet no better word has yet been found. While Liberation Theology has not yet evolved a complete critique of violence, and liberation reached through armed struggle is not to be condemned, such victory is not efficacious: one cannot cure evil by using it. Instead one merely replaces one oppressor with another. Nonviolence, instead, must be built on a broad and popular base, it must be the result of people acting in trust and solidarity, whose own nonviolence renders the violence of the oppressor useless. Not even Nicaragua's revolution succeeded through violence, but by the long nonviolent campaign that pushed the Sandinistas into power.

Esquivel rejects both communism and capitalism, and he sees the arms race as linked essentially to the materialism of both the U.S. and U.S.S.R. Therefore the work of the peacemaker must also be to awaken the consciences of those who make, profit from, or remain comfortable with, an arms race that starves the rest of the world.

The collection then goes on to examine several examples of active nonviolence at work in Latin America: the victory of nonviolent strikers and the efforts of Bishop Leonidas Proaño in Peru; the Latin American Charter of nonviolence; and the Mothers of the Plaza de Mayo.

The Mothers are the sisters, daughters, cousins, wives, and mothers of the up to 30,000 men, women, and children who "disappeared" during the "dirty war" waged by Argentina's generals in the years between their coup in 1976 and the restoration of democracy in 1983. They first began in isolation, seeking information about their relatives, but they soon organized to hold weekly protest vigils in Buenos Aires' main square, not only demanding to know what the military had done to the disappeared but demanding justice for all of Argentina's poor and oppressed.

Their original inspiration was nourished by Esquivel's Peace and Justice office. They reject all forms of violence in favor of a Gospel form of peacemaking. The Mothers have been willing to suffer accusations of being subversives and communists; they have even been willing to face martyrdom for their witness to the truth that the Argentine generals' defense of "Western Christian Civilization" was a sham. They continue to declare that only through the broad-based, nonviolent methods of the people — boycotts, strikes, noncooperation, civil disobedience, hunger strikes, etc. — can the field be taken from the enemy and his own tools of elitism and violence overthrown.

1206   "Forum: Adolfo Perez Esquivel," *NCR* 22, 19 (March 7, 1986): 9-11.

A wide-ranging interview on apartheid in South Africa, the connection between the arms race, the Latin American debt, and the rise of the dictatorships in Latin America. Esquivel also pins the blame for the dictatorships and their reign of terror directly on the U.S. and their capitalist interests. President Carter was an exception to this, and his struggle for human rights is recognized, yet the Reagan administration has only worsened matters. Reagan's "freedom fighters" kill women and children, destroy crops and wreak havoc on a people; at stake is U.S. hegemony over Central America.

Esquivel also sees the pope as too conditioned by his Polish experience and its anti-Communism. He does not understand the situation in the Third World or the full meaning of Liberation Theology. He also ignores, or is misinformed about the many Christian martyrs being made in Latin America today as an expression of Christian faith. Liberation involves the while person, and therefore it is possible for Christians and Marxists to enter into dialogue over practical issues. In Nicaragua, both Marxist and Christian, violent and nonviolent responses are being made. One need only think of Foreign Minister d'Escoto's nonviolent fast that brought world attention to U.S. aggression to get the point. Archbishop Obando y Bravo, on the other hand, urges draft resistance while refusing to condemn *contra* atrocities: his is a political, not a religious opposition.

Esquivel advises his North American friends that peace is not the absence of conflict, but an activism to human relations. Too often North American peace movements take only a passive resistance. He urges North Americans to actively seek out the facts about Latin America, to know U.S. policy, and to bring the policy of their government into line with their own wishes.

1207   Lernoux, Penny. "In Peru, Argentina: Bishops Hit Government Acts," *NCR* 17 (Aug. 28, 1981): 3.

Not seen.

1208   Lundy, M. "Interview: Adolfo Perez Esquivel," *America* 143 (Dec. 27, 1980): 427-30.

Not seen.

1209   "Nobel Laureate Pleads Missing Children's Case," *NCR* 17 (Sept. 18, 1981): 6.

Esquivel attempts to get answers for the parents of the "disappeared."

1210   "The Prize for Peace Doesn't Always Lead to It: Outlasting Oppression," *New York Times,* Oct. 21, 1984.

Briefly reviews Esquivel's activities since the prize.

1211   "Self-Amnesty. A Military Pardon," *Time* 122 (Oct. 3, 1983): 40.

Despite the optimism that the Falklands defeat would bring in a renewed democracy, the Mothers of the Plaza de Mayo continue to demonstrate, demanding a final answer to the disappearance of thousands in the "dirty war."

1212   Simpson, John, and Jana Bennett. *The Disappeared and the Mothers of the Plaza: The Story of the 11,000*

Argentinians Who Vanished. New York: St. Martin's, 1985.

This book gives ample credit and fine documentation to the Mothers. It stresses the internal dynamic and initiative of the Mothers themselves. The story of the disappeared, which the authors call the closest thing to Nazi Germany after 1933, is based on hundreds of interviews. The Mothers organized under constant threat, attack, even murder and kidnapping. Their demonstrations were harassed and broken up violently throughout 1978. By 1979 they had almost stopped completely. Finally they decided they had nothing to lose. Their act of courage broke the entire well-laid plan of the generals to commit mass murder via secret means. By 1980 they had turned the tide and had once again begun demonstrating in public.

The authors notes the almost total silence of the Argentine hierarchy to the atrocity, except in cases where clergy were the targets. Surprisingly, the role of Esquivel in this drama is ignored almost completely, except for the authors to remark that he also was imprisoned and that he may have invented his story of torture (pp. 281-82).

Bishop Leonidas Proaño

1213   Esquivel. *Christ in a Poncho.* See **1205**, 71-91.

Recounts the bishop's alliance with the Indians of Toctezinin in Chimborazo province of Ecuador. Together they fight against the corruption of government officials in league with wealthy landowners who seek to end land reform and take the small farmers' lands from them. The small farmers and the diocese's pastoral teams aiding them have faced smear campaigns, accusations of being communist subversives, threats and physical violence from the landlords' thugs, police, and army; but they have rejected all forms of violence as wrong and counterproductive. In a newspaper interview Proaño has called on the inspiration of Bartolomé de Las Casas (See **761** to **778**), the Medellin Conference (See **1166**), and Helder Camara (See **1176** to **1200**) and has declared, "there are only two invincible forces in the twentieth century — the atom bomb, and nonviolence."

1214   Gudorf, Christine. "The Quiet Strength of Liberation Theology," *Commonweal* 111, 12 (June 15, 1984): 365-67.

Reviews the situation in Peru: the Vatican's investigation of theologian Gustavo Gutierrez at the instigation of Archbishop Lopez-Trujillo, the deadlock among Peruvian bishops on the issues of Gutierrez and Liberation Theology, and the activities of the church among the people, including the work of "pastoral agents." Despite the hierarchy's opposition and active repression by the government, the popular church has faith that the hierarchy will come over to its side and has no intention of causing a schism. Since the people *are* the church they expect to infuse the church with their efforts.

1215   Proaño, Leonidas. "The Church and Politics in Ecuador." *Concilium* 71 (1972): 99-105.

Not seen.

Central America

1216   Barreno, Mano. "Is There a Future for Nonviolence in Central America? A Latin American Response," *Fellowship* 49, 10-11 (Oct./Nov. 1983): 7.

Nonviolence is a capitalist ploy to keep the people down. Just revolution was wedded to liberation by the Medellin Conference.

1217   Belli, Humberto. "Nicaragua's Bishops: A Response to Gary MacEoin," *America* 152 (Feb. 23, 1985): 145-46, 148.

Gary MacEoin's attack on Nicaragua's Catholic hierarchy (**1230**) is one-sided. The bishops' response to the Sandinistas has been a delicate one. The hierarchy, especially Archbishop Obando y Bravo, played a brave role in resisting Somoza. Since 1974 he refused to attend any Somoza inaugurations and in October 1978 called on Somoza to resign. In fact, he was called "commando Miguel" by the Somozista press and as early as 1972 was the object of their defamations. The Sandinistas acknowledged this role in 1980.

MacEoin reduces support or opposition for the Sandinistas to a simplistic one of class. Yet the clergy in Nicaragua has not divided along class lines. For example, Obando y Bravo is from a poor background, while many of the clergy in the Sandinista government are from the elite, as are Ernesto Cardenal and Miguel d'Escoto. Some are even foreign-born intellectuals. In addition, the Nicaraguan priests who are from the working class tend to be opposed to the Sandinistas.

Belli also disputes CELAM-CIA-Reagan links made by MacEoin and asserts that he whitewashes the Sandinista record. They are anti-Semitic, they are carrying out an unprecedented arms buildup, they have abandoned the poor, they are warring against the Miskito people, they are developing a Marxist economy. "There is genuine civil war in Nicaragua, with more rebels fighting the government than in El Salvador."

1218   Berrigan. Daniel. *Steadfastness of the Saints. A Journal of Peace and War in Central and North America.* Maryknoll, NY: Orbis Books, 1985.

An account of Berrigan's journey from the U.S. via the Plowshares trials and the madness of North American fixation on mass destruction to Central America. In El Salvador he encounters on-going, internal church politics, the refugee camps, the death squads, the Mothers of the Disappeared (yes, even here), theologians and pastors like Jon Sobrino and Medardos Gómez, and all over the Basic Christian Communities, the reservoirs of martyrdom and of hope. A tour through the desolate ruins of the State University, destroyed by the military in a crackdown on student protestors, the spirit of Oscar Romero, still alive.

Nicaragua is like day to El Salvador's night. Here Witness for Peace members from North America are welcomed in a country threatened by their own government. Yet here are also signs that the rigors of revolution and of defense are taking their toll: the government's hesitation to grant conscientious objector status, the offensive prevarications of government spokesmen like Ernesto Cardenal, an old friend in whom Berrigan does not hide his disappointment. Yet here too is a thriving Christianity among base Christian communities and the very real threat of the *contras.* Berrigan is also troubled by the conflict between the Nicaraguan state and church and by the dilemma of the priests within the government.

This journal also ranges over his rejection of violence, even that called just by revolution, on this previous exile to Latin America in 1965, on Thomas Merton, and on the strength and joy his companionship in the Jesuits gives him.

1219   Berryman, Philip. *Inside Central America: The Essential*

Facts Past and Present on El Salvador, Nicaragua, Honduras, Guatemala, and Costa Rica. New York: Pantheon, 1986.

A short paperback highlighting the main issues involved in Central America today and providing information on the origins of the conflicts there, the U.S. attempt to confront revolution, U.S. policy and the terms of debate, the actual results of U.S. policy in the region, and the regionalization of the conflict. Also examines the outlook for accommodation and negotiation in the context of U.S. ignorance of the situation there and the wide gap and stalemate between North Americans working for human rights and those obsessed with U.S. national security considerations.

1220 ——.*The Religious Roots of Rebellion. Christians in Central American Revolutions.* Maryknoll, NY: Orbis Books, 1984.

This is a huge, and very important, work chronicling Christians' activities, violent and nonviolent throughout the region. Essential introduction.

1221 Cabestrero, Téofilo. *Blood of the Innocent: Victims of the Contras' War in Nicaragua.* Robert R. Barr, transl. Maryknoll, NY: Orbis Books, 1985.

This is a powerful collection of first-hand testimony on the death threats, murders, rapes, beatings, kidnappings, tortures, massacres, destruction of property of individuals and cooperatives carried out by President Reagan's "freedom fighters." Victims include Nicaraguans, North Americans, Europeans, men, women, and children. Cabestrero prints his accounts exactly as they were reported to him.

1222   ——.*Ministers of God, Ministers of the People*. Robert R.
         Barr, transl. Maryknoll, NY: Orbis Books, 1983.

Detailed, first-person accounts of the Christian's
response to the Nicaraguan revolution by some of its best-
known leaders, including Ernesto Cardenal, the priest,
poet, friend of Thomas Merton and Daniel Berrigan,
founder of Solintiname, and Nicaragua's Minister of
Culture; Fernando Cardenal, S.J., his brother, former
Jesuit priest and coordinator of Nicaragua's successful
literacy program; and Miguel d'Escoto, Maryknoll priest
and now Nicaragua's foreign minister.

All three men have much in common, most especially
their support of the "just revolution" against the Somoza
government; their belief that as priests they had something
unique to add to Nicaragua's revolutionary government;
their subsequent conflict with Pope John Paul II and his
command to them to choose either service to the church or
service to the government. These are all highly articulate,
sensitive, and intelligent people, deeply committed to their
Christianity and to the Nicaraguan revolution. While they
accept the role of violence in that revolution, they also
hope that their presence in it and the influence of many like
them will Christianize the revolution. They hope not that
the church might rule in alliance with power once again,
but that the influence of Christians might truly make the
revolution one for the people, imbued with human and
religious ideals of the highest order.

1223   ——.*Revolutionaries for the Gospel*. Philip Berryman,
         transl. Maryknoll, NY: Orbis Books, 1986.

The subtitle reads, "Testimony of Fifteen Christians in

the Nicaraguan Government." This is an important, eye-opening collection that will cause even the most skeptical to wonder. Those interviewed are in high- and middle-level positions in the government: the President of the Supreme Court, Comptroller General, Minister of Education, General Secretary of Housing, managers of the ports, energy, libraries and archives, judges, and social planners. They are well educated, with more or less solid Christian educations, many at Catholic universities in Central and North America. They are deeply committed to the ideals of Vatican II and its gospel of justice, yet they have almost all accepted the necessity of the revolution, if not of the revolution's violence.

These Christians are aware of the conflict between Christianity and the state on one level, and are careful not to compromise their Christianity for the sake of the revolution. They are also people who believe in civil government, not military dictatorship. They stress that their conflict is not with doctrine, or with the hierarchical church, but with certain bishops and priests.

These are also *practicing* Roman Catholics, some with a traditional orthodoxy, many with a profound spirituality. Biblical citations flow naturally in their conversation, and sections of the Gospels are conscious models for policy. They assert, however, that if Marxist goals are not incompatible with Christian goals and means, they will cooperate fully in the revolution.

1224 Dear, John, S.J. "El Salvador: A Reference Point for Life," *Catholic Peace Fellowship Bulletin*, Autumn 1985, pp. 1, 5-6.

A brief, sparse, but chilling account of this young Jesuit scholastic assignment as a worker in a refugee camp. Amid the constant threats of violence and the visible scars of bullet holes on church buildings, the Jesuit experiences both the degradation of the refugee camps and the great hope born of a feeling of unity with the oppressed. The church workers in the camp were constantly the objects of arrests, threats, and intimidation by the Army. Here even to possess a photo of slain archbishop Oscar Romero is considered subversive, to visit the grave of the women martyrs: Ita Ford, Maura Clarke, Dorothy Kazel, and Jean Donovan, enough to be brought in for questioning. Meanwhile the people of El Salvador live in constant terror of the Army, whose searches of homes and buses could lead to arrest or death at any time. Yet Dear also learned that only by forgiving those who commit the atrocities, in El Salvador and in the U.S. can one redeem one's own humanity and that of one's enemies and begin to bring Christ's solidarity into the world.

1225   De Mott, Stephen T., M.M. "Central America's Suffering People," *Maryknoll* 80, 4 (April 1986): 3-11.

Testimony gathered during this Maryknoll missionary's visit to Guatemalas, Honduras, and Nicaragua. Throughout the region the Army and right-wing death squads have burned down villages, killed and raped and tortured peasants, forced citizens into refugee camps, while U.S. corporations control up to 80% of the commerce of a country like Honduras, the U.S. uses the region as a base for its attacks on Nicaragua, and the vast majority of the people live it shacks without water, electricity, or the the most basic sanitation. Instead of building houses, hospitals and schools these governments buy guns and helicopters and ignore. In Nicaragua, meanwhile, vital programs of public health, education, and land reform are threatened by the *contras* and by a virtual U.S. embargo in equipment and supplies. Problems do exist: the most serious are the military draft and the poor economy. Both Latin America and the U.S. know that Nicaragua is the keystone to change in the entire region. Much hangs in the balance.

1226 *El Salvador: Background to the Crisis.* Cambridge, MA: Central America Information Office, 1982.

A good, general introduction. Covers the history, the military, the Indians, land and its poverty, urbanization and industrialization, women, the international economy, the Catholic church, human rights, the death squads, agrarian reform, U.S. military and economic aid. The book also provides a chronology, glossaries, bibliography.

1227 "El Salvador's Search for Peace," *America* 151 (Oct. 27, 1984): 42-46.

Since 1979, 50,000 civilians have been killed in El Salvador. On March 6, 1983 Pope John Paul II called for peace talks there. This editorial notes optimism surrounding President Duarte's offer to meet with rebels.

1228 Gettleman, Marvin E., Patrick Lacefield, Louis Manache, David Marmelstein, and Ronald Radosh, eds. *El Salvador: Central America in the New Cold War.* New York: Grove Press, 1982.

Excellent introduction to the contemporary political, economic, social, and religious situation in the region. See also **1234** to **1236**, and **1241**.

1229 Hunt, G.W. "Of Many Things," *America* 151 (Dec. 22, 1984): 412.

On Dec. 21, 1984 Fernando Cardenal, S.J. was

dismissed from the Jesuits for his insistence on remaining in his position on the Nicaraguan government. Notes the long process of negotiations surrounding the order to leave one or the other and Archbishop Obando y Bravo's opposition to the Sandinistas. Review's Cardenal's achievement in planning and carrying out the Sandinista literacy campaign. While Cardenal had to leave the Jesuits for breaking his vow of obedience, he remains a priest.

1230   MacEoin, Gary. "Nicaragua: A Church Divided," *America* 151 (Nov. 10, 1984): 294-99.

Religion is central to the current struggle in Nicaragua. At first the bishops supported the revolution and the ideals of the Sandinistas. By mid-1980, however, conflict had begun; and it reached its climax with the March 1983 visit of Pope John Paul II to the country. This conflict stems from both vested interest and opposition to the revolution and differing ecclesiologies, from both the legacy of Spanish Christendom in confrontation with developments in modern Latin America and from class struggle.

MacEoin reviews episcopal documents between 1971 and 1979 and asserts that they left the people defenseless against tyranny and oppression. Archbishop Obando y Bravo acted in overt complicity with the Somoza regime. Only in 1979, when Somoza was clearly on his way out, did the bishops make any sign of opposition, in their pastoral praising the revolution. In retrospect this seems a political ploy.

Since 1972 the Latin American bishops' conference, CELAM, has been dominated by reactionaries and in the 1980s has been in league with the U.S. Reagan administration to turn back the tide of Liberation Theology. In this Reagan's and John Paul II's interests dovetail.

Within Nicaragua the Sandinistas enjoy truly wide support, but the clergy is divided, with the best orders —

the Jesuits and Dominicans — supporting the Sandinistas and opposing the *contras* and the U.S. The "people's church" is really a matter of ecclesiology, not Christian doctrine. Charges of Sandinista persecution of the church, of Jews, and others are unfounded. For a rebuttal see **1217.**

1231   Montgomery, Tommie Sue. "Cross and Rifle: Revolution and the Church in El Salvador and Nicaragua," *Journal of International Affairs* 36 (Fall/Winter 1982-83): 209-22.

A comparison of the church's relation to the revolution in Nicaragua and El Salvador, and an examination of divisions within the church: theological, political, and ecclesiological. Montgomery notes the role of Central American universities and of the Basic Christian Communities.

The article concludes that the church has been a very important variable in the revolutionary process and makes two central observations. Despite repression and violence the church cannot be killed, and the church has always had a tradition of being opposed to the state, even when this opposition was not revolutionary.

1232   ——.*Revolution in El Salvador*. Boulder, CO: Westview, 1982.

An excellent introduction to the economic, social, political, and religious roots of rebellion, and to the progress of that process. The book will demonstrate that the problems of El Salvador and of Central America are native grown and not the product of East-West superpower conflicts.

1233   Randall, Margaret. *Christians in the Nicaraguan Revolution.* Vancouver: New Star, 1983.

The people whom Randall interviews here, intellectual elite, middle class, poor and semi-literate, are for the most part Christians deeply committed to the revolution in Nicaragua. They all embrace what can be loosely described as the "just-revolution" theory, an outgrowth of the just-war theory; and they still maintain that this revolution must be defended by the gun if their work as Christians is to be maintained. Their language is that of the Crusades, of dying "like Christ, to end the injustices that we have in Nicaragua." They maintain that it is the Gospel that has told them to kill for Christ and the revolution. They emphasize the split between a true church of revolutionaries, who have read and understood the Gospels correctly, and a reactionary hierarchy that continues to distort the words of the Gospel in favor of oligarchs and reactionaries in Nicaragua and in North America.

A true synthesis of Marxism and Christianity can be achieved, they contend. If it cannot, the Nicaraguans interviewed here seem to favor a Christianity that is colored by Marx for the ends of the revolution. Some, in fact, favor a gradual discarding of formal Christianity once either Christian "values" have infused the revolution or once these values prove to be incompatible with it. In the end these Nicaraguans feel that the revolution can only be led by a small committed elite, that most "peasants" are too passive to lead their own revolution, and that it is up to this enlightened elite to pick who will fight, who will kill, and who will die in defense of the revolution. Nonviolence, in the end, is passivity. "Christ was a guerilla fighter."

1234   Riding, Alan. "The Cross and the Sword in Latin

America." See **1228**, 189-98. First published in *New York Review of Books*, May 28, 1981.

Traces the Catholic church's evolving attitude as one of the decisive elements for change and revolution in Central America. The centuries-old alliance of the cross and the sword in Latin America is now finally falling apart. "The metamorphosis of the Church is the most significant political development in Latin America since the Cuban revolution."

1235   Rivera y Damas, Archbishop, and Radio Vinceremos. "The Church in Salvador: Which Side Are You On?" See **1228**, 203-6.

Riveras is criticized by Radio Vinceremos for accommodation to the oligarchs. Rivera contends that he is following in the footsteps of Oscar Romero, but Radio Vinceremos says he is now backing down.

1236   "A Sign of Resurrection in El Salvador." See **1228**, 206-10.

Outlines the theory of just-revolution emerging in El Salvador. Church groups, both hierarchical and popular, approve of violent revolution as a last resort.

1237   Williams, Philip J. "The Catholic Hierarchy in the Nicaraguan Revolution," *Journal of Latin American Studies* 17 (November 1985): 341-69.

The presence of Christians in the Nicaraguan revolution is a clear sign of profound changes. The bishops' middle path rejecting both violence and accommodation has proven futile. At the same time the revolution has brought with it radical priests; and the distance between the hierarchy and the revolution is widening. Even so, the bishops' distancing themselves with the traditional Constantinian alliance with the state has some wisdom. Analyzes events surrounding the March 1983 visit of Pope John Paul II. Good bibliography in notes.

Oscar Romero

1238	Brockman, James R. *The Church Is All of You: Thoughts of Archbishop Oscar Romero.* Minneapolis: Winston Press, 1984.

Not seen.

1239	——.*The Word Remains: A Life of Oscar Romero.* Maryknoll, NY: Orbis Books, 1983.

Oscar Romero was the archbishop of San Salvador in El Salvador. On March 23, 1980 he called on the army of El Salvador to lay down their arms, to stop the brutal repression of their fellow citizens, and to embrace the peace and justice of their religion. The next day he was slain while saying mass by a gunman set on him by the ruling oligarchy. Oscar Romero's life symbolizes the progress of the church in Latin America today.

Raised in the conventional spirituality of the early twentieth century, with its emphasis on internal piety and obedience to authority in alliance with the secular state, Romero rose quickly through his church's hierarchy and became a staunch defender of orthodoxy and political order as the rebellion in El Salvador spread. Soon after his election as archbishop of San Salvador, however, he began to turn away from the government's harsh repression of dissent, its corruption, constant attacks on campesinos and those who would help them, its death squads, tortures, disappearances.

As he saw friends assassinated and unarmed farmers slaughtered, he quickly turned against his former friends in the oligarchy, condemning the violence of repression as well as that of rebellion. He began to forge a new image of the church as the sacrament of salvation that must save both the body and the soul, and embracing the new Liberation Theology. In the course of this journey Romero gained the support of Pope John Paul II, of Catholic hierarchy and laity around the world, and a nomination for the Nobel Peace Prize for his call for nonviolent revolution against the forces of tyranny.

This is the best account of this martyr to Catholic peacemaking. Brockman bases his account on Romero's own papers, numerous interviews with witnesses to the events described, newspaper accounts, and church documents. He also gives a great deal of attention to Salvadoran church politics, which are as important today to the progress of liberation as the doctrines and actions of the clergy and laity actively making peace in the region.

1240   Erdozain, Placido. *Archbishop Romero. Martyr of Salvador*. Maryknoll, NY: Orbis Books, 1985.

Not seen.

1241   Lacefield, Patrick. "Oscar Romero: Archbishop of the Poor." See **1228**, 198-203.

An interview with the archbishop first published in *Fellowship* in November 1979.

1242   Pyes, Craig. "Who Killed Archbishop Romero? D'Aubuisson's Role," *The Nation* 239, 11 (Oct. 13, 1984): 337, 350-54.

Traces the guilt from the assassin — a psychopathic killer acting on a taunt and for cash — up the ladder of El Salvador's military and paramilitary and into the channels of the ruling oligarchy, ending with D'Aubuisson himself as the man who ordered the archbishop shot.

1243   Sobrino, Jon, S.J. "A Voice Still Heard," *Maryknoll* 80, 4 (April 1986): 49-51.

Since Archbishop Romero was killed more than 50,000 have also been assassinated, most by the government; 5,000 have disappeared, and 15,000 have been killed and wounded in battle. This, as the U.S. and Salvadoran governments boast a return to democracy and peace. More than a half-million have fled the country as kidnappings and murders on both sides, but mostly the government's continue. Almost 50% of the government budget is for war, wages have not risen since 1980, while prices have risen constantly. Unemployment is 50%. Yet aid from the U.S. totals more than $1 million a day.

The Woman Martyrs of El Salvador

1244   Allman, Timothy. "Rising Rebellion," *Harper's* (March 1981).

Not seen.

1245   Carrigan, Ana. *Salvador Witness*. New York: Simon & Schuster, 1984; Ballantine/Epiphany, 1986.

A biography of Jean Donovan, one of the American Catholic missionary workers raped and murdered by the Salvadoran military on the outskirts of San Salvador in December 1980. The other three were Ita Ford and Maura Clarke, Maryknoll missionary sisters; and Dorothy Kazel, an Ursuline missionary. The biography traces Donovan's conversion from the daughter of North American affluence, to business executive, lay missionary, and martyr for peace and social justice in Central America during the last days of Archbishop Oscar Romero. Called subversives by the government in El Salvador for their protest against repression and genocide and for their aid to the poor and dispossessed, the missionaries were brutally slain precisely because of their Christian witness and work. Their murders were largely ignored by the Reagan administration in the United States until public outrage, the pressure of the Catholic church, the victims' families, and the courageous witness of former U.S. ambassador to El Salvador, Robert White, forced an investigation.

This account is told in a crisp, journalistic style. It is based on extensive interviews with friends, family and acquaintances from all phases of Donovan's life, as well frequent quotations from Donovan's diary and letters.

1246   Dear, John, S.J. *Jean Donovan: The Call to Discipleship.* Erie, PA: Pax Christi, 1986.

Dear moves from a brief introduction on El Salvador (5 million citizens, 500,000 refugees within the country, 600,000 abroad, 60,000 killed since 1979, $1.5 million a day spent by the U.S. on military equipment used against the people by their own government), to the monuments to Oscar Romero and to the four American women martyrs on a road outside the capital where they were raped, murdered and hastily buried by the army.

Jean Donovan's story is one of conversion, retracing the choice of the rich young man and deciding to give up all her riches and connections in the United States for the path of Christ and martyrdom. This little booklet traces her life with drawings and photographs, first-hand

accounts of family and friends both in the U.S. and in El
Salvador as a Maryknoll lay missionary. There her life
became closely tied to the mission and fate of Archbishop
Oscar Romero and all the church workers dedicated to
bringing the Gospel to the poor and oppressed. Despite
the dangers, and the increasing death threats for her work
with poor refugees, or simply for burying the bodies of
the dead and mutilated left by the army, Donovan
continued to stress her sense of mission and to refuse
friends' offers and advice to leave the country.

Jean Donovan and her coworkers — Ita Ford, Maura
Clarke, and Dorothy Kazel — are martyrs of our time who
accepted God's call. She and her companions have
followed Jesus' call to follow him; and their life and death
invites others to follow in their steps. Her inner tranquility
and outer commitment is the true meaning of peace.

1247   Jacobsen, Patricia. "God Came to El Salvador."   See
       1138, 141-53.

       Sparse, impressionistic, reflective, prayer-like bio-
       graphies of the slain women missionaries that read like
       eulogies and that wrench the emotions in the same way.

1248   Noone, Judith M., M.M. *The Same Fate As the Poor*.
       Maryknoll, NY: Maryknoll Sisters Publications, 1985.

       This account begins with the grim details of the four
       church-women's kidnap, rape, and murder by El
       Salvador's army. It then recounts the story of their lives,
       professional, solidly middle class and very mainstream,
       yet touched by a compassion for the worst of the world.
       Ita Ford's reaction to Oscar Romero's assassination, that
       "his death will bear fruit," reminds us of the early martyrs.
       And so it should, for in this book we realize that those of

us, main stream, middle class, comfortable North Americans, who reach out to "share the same fate as the poor," may share it in its truest, most Christ-like sense.

* *
*

CHAPTER 15: *Catholic Peacemaking in America*

General Introduction

1249   Bokenkotter. *History*. See **5**, 378-96.

      A good, brief, introduction to the problems of the immigrant church: prejudice, Catholic defensiveness, Catholic hostility to American liberalism, and the Catholic commitment to social justice as expressed in such forms as the labor movement.

1250   Dolan, Jay P. *The American Catholic Experience. A History from Colonial Times to the Present.* New York: Doubleday, 1986.

      An excellent survey, including much recent work, told from the "bottom up," from the viewpoint of social history.

1251   Ellis, John Tracy. *American Catholicism*. Rev., 2nd ed. Chicago: University of Chicago Press, 1969.

      Useful for the history of American Catholicism from the colonial era through the nineteenth century. Among the topics discussed are the motives of Catholic immigration, the prejudice Catholics encountered on their arrival, their resulting defensiveness, Catholics' cultural and religious ties to their countries of origin, Catholic suspicion of American culture, and opposition to the Civil War and the Spanish American War.

1252   ——.*Catholics in Colonial America.* Baltimore: Helicon, 1965.

A good survey.

1253   ——."United States of America," *NCE* 14: 425-48.

A brief summary of the American church.

1254   Greeley, Andrew M. *The American Catholic. A Select Portrait.* New York: Harper & Row, 1977.

This is an excellent, and often surprising, survey of American Catholic life and attitudes. These attitudes include those to war and peace, and Greeley uses statistical studies and surveys to show that Catholic attitudes have never been quite so conservative and uncritical as most observers, including Catholic ones, have long believed. Among the most fundamental Catholic attitudes that help foster a frequent inclination to peacemaking are the Catholic tendency to stress personal conversion over institutional reform and the fundamental assumption of Catholic social thought that people can work together in cooperation to create a humane society. Greeley also notes Catholic thought's rejection of Hobbesian models of forceful constraint and universal struggle.

1255   Hennessey, James, S.J. *American Catholics. A History of the Roman Catholic Community in the United States.* New York: Oxford University Press, 1981.

An excellent historical and social survey.

American Catholics and Peace

1256   Brock, Peter. *Pacifism in the United States from the Colonial Era to the First World War.* Princeton: Princeton University Press, 1968.

     Brock's main emphasis, and rightly so here, is on the traditional Protestant peace churches for the early period, and on more secular and political motivations through the nineteenth century. Little attention is paid to Catholic peacemaking.

1257   Chatfield, Charles. *For Peace and Justice; Pacifism in America, 1914-1941.* Boston: Beacon Press, 1973.

     A collection of essays on opposition to war in all its forms, motives, and perspectives.

1258   Conley, J.J. "Catholic Pacifism in America," *America* 131 (Dec. 14, 1974): 381-83.

     Traces the development of a strong Catholic peace movement from Roger LaPorte's self immolation in November 1965 (See **1344**) to the very conspicuous Catholic presence in the early 1970s. Abortion, civil violence, and capital punishment remain key issues facing Catholic peacemakers. At the same time, renewed activism requires a new scholarship into the Catholic tradition that will challenge the supremacy of the just-war theory. Conley then briefly discusses some Catholic peacemakers in the United States, including Orestes Brownson during the Civil War, John Dunn during World War I, and Dorothy Day and the Catholic Worker.

1259   Conlin, Joseph R. *American Anti-War Movements.* New
        York: Macmillan, 1970.

        Not seen.

1260   De Benedetti, Charles. "Peace History in the American
        Manner," *History Teacher* (Long Beach) 18
        (November 1984): 75-110.

        Not seen.

1261   ——.*The Peace Reform in American History.* Bloomington,
        IN: University of Indiana Press, 1980.

        Not seen.

1262   Ellis, John Tracy. "American Catholics and Peace: A
        Historical Sketch." See *The Family of Nations.* James
        S. Rauch, ed. Huntington, NY, 1970.

        Not seen.

1263   Fine, Melinda, and Peter M. Steven, eds. *American Peace
        Directory 1984.* Cambridge, MA: Ballinger, 1984.

        Not seen.

1264   Flannery. *Pattern.* See **26**.

        Includes the following pastorals of the U.S. bishops:
        "The Crisis of Christianity" (November 1941),
        "International Order" (November 1944), "᾿Between War
        and Peace" (November 1945), "Man and the Peace"
        (November 1946), "The Dignity of Man" (November
        1953), "The Hope of Mankind" (November 1956),

"Discrimination and the Christian Conscience" (November 1958), and "Freedom and Peace" (November 1959). A careful reading of these letters will reveal a gradually changing tone from full and almost unquestioning support of the state, to doubts and questions concerning both peace and social-justice issues in America and around the world.

1265   Howlett, Charles F., and Glen Zeitzer. *The American Peace Movement: History and Historiography.* Washington, DC: American Historical Association. Pamphlet 20, 1985.

The article's glossary calls peace, "The absence of war; a condition marked by tranquility and governed order, within the international public community." The pamphlet reflects the limitations of this outlook: peace is a passive state of order, at best internationalism arranged by elites.

1266   Josephson, Harold, ed. *Biographical Dictionary of Modern Peace Leaders.* Westport, CT: Greenwood, 1985.

Not seen.

1267   Kreider, Alan. "Christian Views on American Wars," *Fides et Historia* 16 (Fall-Winter 1983): 87-93.

Not seen.

1268   Lammers. "Catholic Social Ethics." See **33**, 93-103.

Notes that pacifism has gained a new legitimacy due to the nature of modern war and from papal and conciliar statements. The Vietnam War marked the real shift in thinking among American Catholics, who emerged from it

with a new concept of peace as distributive justice and a
shift away from a natural-law ethic to one based on
Christian biblical roots. Twentieth-century pacifism is not
that of witness, as in the early church, but one of
resistance, an activist approach that not only opposes war
but also seeks to build a just society without lethal force.

1269   Long, Edward L. *War and Conscience in America.*
        Philadelphia: Westminster, 1968.

Examines all religious and moral backgrounds in
opposition to conventional and nuclear war, its ethics, and
the imperatives of individual conscience. The Catholic
view is represented by the just-war and the Crusades. It is
summed up by Archbishop R.E. Lucey of San Antonio:
"It is necessary to use force...and the man [sic] who
doesn't believe in force will be a slave. You cannot have
peace in the world without force because there are evil men
in the world."

1270   Marchand, C. Roland. *The American Peace Movement
        and Social Reform 1898-1918.* Princeton: Princeton
        University Press, 1973.

On social and political opposition to war. Very few
pages on Catholic peacemaking.

1271   McNeal, Patricia. *The American Catholic Peace Movement
        1928-1972.* New York: Arno, 1978.

Originally a dissertation, and reprinted, this work is
indispensable for any study of American Catholic peacemaking and, despite some inadequacies and inaccuracies,
should be more widely known and used. McNeal bases
her study on a wide knowledge of secondary sources and
on many interviews and personal memoirs of those

involved with the events she describes. The book covers the origins of the Catholic peace movement, Dorothy Day and pacifism, Catholic dissent during World War II, the period between World War II and Vatican II, the Catholic peace movement of the 1960s, the Berrigans and the Catholic Left of the 1970s. The book is well annotated and contains a bibliography and appendix of CAIP pamphlets. See also **1301**.

1272   Morison, Samuel Eliot, Frederick Merk, Frank Freidel. *Dissent in Three American Wars*. Cambridge, MA, 1970.

Not seen.

1273   Riley, Paul. "American Catholicism and Conscientious Objection from 1776 to 1924." Ph.D. dissertation. Philadelphia: Temple University.

Not seen.

1274   Wittner, Lawrence. *Rebels Against War: The American Peace Movement 1941-1960*. New York: Columbia University Press, 1969.

While this has very little on the Catholic peace tradition per se, it provides an excellent overview of the American peace movement and has an excellent bibliography.

Catholic Association for International Peace (CAIP)

1275   "Farewell to CAIP," *America* 120 (May 24, 1969): 609-10.

An obituary and a sad farewell to the Catholic internationalist group that had come to fully identify with the foreign policy aims of the United States and thus discredited itself in the 1960s.

1276   Flannery, Harry W. "Catholic Association for International Peace (CAIP)," *NCE* 3: 264.

Reviews its history from its founding in 1927 by John A. Ryan and Fr. Raymond McGowan.

1277   McCloskey, P.W. "CAIP: What is its Future?" *Commonweal* 87 (Nov.17, 1967): 194-95.

Notes that most of CAIP's leadership and membership are academics and just-warriors. John Courtney Murray, the Jesuit intellectual, is typical.

Dorothy Day and The Catholic Worker

1278   *The Catholic Worker.*

The famous monthly, published continuously since 1933, including regular columns by Dorothy Day, Peter Maurin, Paul Furfey, Ammon Hennacy, Robert Ludlow, Tom Cornell, Eileen Egan, and others.

1279   Day, Dorothy. *By Little and Little: The Selected Writings of Dorothy Day.* Robert Ellsberg, ed. New York: Alfred A. Knopf, 1983.

Including such essays as "The Use of Force" (1936), "Our Country Passes from Undeclared to Declared War; We Continue Our Christian Pacifist Stand" (1942), "We Are Un-American; We Are Catholics" (1949-1953), "The Fear of Our Enemies" (1960), "War Without Weapons" (1963), "A Prayer for Peace" (1965), and "In Peace is My Bitterness Most Bitter" (1967). Day's essays confronted the prevailing sentiments of the time and stressed the consistent themes of Christian unity, nonviolence, and justice.

1280 ——.*Loaves and Fishes*. San Francisco: Harper & Row, 1983.

This is devoted more to the Catholic Worker movement than to Day herself, and it describes her meeting Peter Maurin and founding of the Worker and the newspaper, the establishment of the Houses of Hospitality, the communal farms, the Catholic Worker during World War II, the personalist philosophy of Peter Maurin, and the arrival and achievements of Ammon Hennacy.

1281 ——*The Long Loneliness*. New York: Harper & Row, 1952, reissued San Francisco: Harper & Row, 1983.

This traces Day's early life, describes her parents and childhood, her student days, life on the East Side of New York, her journalism career, and first jail terms for peace activism, her free-lance work, searching, marriage, baby, and ultimate conversion to Roman Catholicism. It then describes her meeting Peter Maurin, the founding of the Catholic Worker, the community houses, and concludes with some personal observations, a discussion of her pacifism, and Peter Maurin's death.

1282 Egan, Eileen. *Dorothy Day and the Permanent Revolution*. Erie, PA: Pax Christi, 1983.

A brief, well-illustrated booklet by one who knew, and worked with, her, told as part history, part personal reminiscence. It follows her life from her divorce from

Forster Batterham, the father of her daughter, her
conversion and meeting Peter Maurin, the founding of the
movement, the success of the *Catholic Worker* newspaper,
and follows the Worker's peacemaking from the 1930s to
the 1970s. It concludes with some reflections on the
Catholic Worker and recent trends in American Catholic
peacemaking, in which Egan is centrally involved.

1283   Forest, James. *Love Is the Measure.* New York: Paulist
Press, 1986.

A biography of Day written by a former Catholic
Worker who worked closely with her.

1284   Klejment, Anne, and Alice Klejment. *Dorothy Day and* The
Catholic Worker. *A Bibliography and Index.* New
York: Garland Publishing, 1986.

A chronological listing of all articles to appear in the
Catholic Worker, followed by a complete bibliography of
works by Dorothy Day. The third part contains a selected
listing of works about Day and the Catholic Worker
arranged by author. Four indexes. Not annotated. Well
illustrated with much of the *Worker's* original art.

1285   LeBrun, John L. "The Role of the Catholic Worker
Movement in American Pacifism, 1933-1972." Ph.D.
dissertation. Cleveland: Case Western Reserve
University, 1973.

Not seen.

1286   Miller, William D. *Dorothy Day: A Biography.* San
Francisco: Harper & Row, 1982.

Despite Day's eventual opposition to a biography, this

is as close to an authorized version as one is likely to find. This attractive, and lengthy, volume covers Day's entire life. It contains much first-hand material from Day's friends and associates, and draws heavily on Miller's personal friendship with Day, his own recollections, and much of his previous work on the Catholic Worker movement (See **1287**). Well indexed.

1287 ——.*A Harsh and Dreadful Love: Dorothy Day and the Catholic Worker Movement*. New York: Liveright, 1973.

Chapters deal with Peter Maurin, Dorothy Day, the personalist philosophy and the life of poverty, the spread of Maurin's ideas, pacifism and World War II, the retreat of the Catholic Worker movement during the war years, the death of Maurin, the post-war period, the Cold War and the emergence of new leadership: Robert Ludlow, Ammon Hennacy, and the Catholic Worker in the 1960s.

1288 Piehl, Mel. *Breaking Bread: The Catholic Worker and the Origin of Catholic Radicalism in America*. Philadelphia: Temple University Press, 1982.

This is a well annotated and documented study, with an excellent bibliography and index. It deals with Day herself, the social and religious context of the movement, the *Catholic Worker* newspaper, the nature of the Catholic Worker's radicalism, its relations to liberal, mainstream Catholicism, its work for peace, and concludes with a fascinating examination of the Catholic Worker as an agent for radical change within American Catholicism. A good complement to **1287**.

1289   Quigley, Margaret, and Michael Garvey, eds. *The Dorothy Day Book: A Selection of Her Writing and Reading.* Springfield, IL: Templegate, 1985.

Select excerpts.

1290   Roberts, Nancy L. *Dorothy Day and the Catholic Worker.* Albany: State University of New York Press, 1984.

A concise study of the first fifty years of the *Catholic Worker* newspaper, well annotated, and based on much archival material. Roberts also offers a good thematic analysis of the paper, stressing its pacifism. This book has been criticized as too concerned with Dorothy Day and not enough with the personalist philosophy of Peter Maurin, and for underestimating the achievements of the other figures in the Catholic Worker's history.

1291   Sicius, Francis J. "Karl Meyer, the Catholic Worker, and Active Personalism," *Records of the American Catholic Historical Society of Philadelphia* 93 (1982): 107-23.

Not seen.

1292   Vishnewski, Stanley, ed. *Meditations — Dorothy Day.* Ramsey, NJ: Paulist Press.

Not seen.

1293   ——.*Wings of the Dawn.* New York: Catholic Worker, 1984.

Stories on the Worker's first decade.

1294   West, Mary. "How Far Does the Line Go Back," *America*
        152 (March 9, 1985): 189-91.

        On the activities of the Worker in Detroit.

Peter Maurin

1295   Ellis, Marc. *Peter Maurin: Prophet of the Twentieth
        Century.* New York: Paulist, 1981.

        Traces his early life in France, his wanderings, the
        development of his Christian personalism, his arrival in
        New York, and his work with Dorothy Day in the Catholic
        Worker. The book concludes with an examination of
        Maurin's legacy in the Worker movement itself, in
        American Catholicism, and in American culture in general.
        The book is full of anecdotes and lengthy quotations from
        Maurin's friends and associates, and it makes frequent use
        of Maurin's own works and words. Well annotated.

1296   Maurin, Peter. *Easy Essays.* New York: Sheed & Ward,
        1936; reissued Chicago: Franciscan Herald Press,
        1977.

        These are a series of very personal reflections on
        contemporary events, social and economic conditions, and
        biblical texts, the full effect of which is to give the reader
        an understanding of what Maurin's "personalism" was all
        about.

1297   Sheehan, Arthur. *Peter Maurin: Gay Believer. The
        Biography of an Unusual and Saintly Man.* Garden
        City, NY: Hanover House, 1959.

        A modern hagiography.

Ammon Hennacy

1298   Hennacy, Ammon. *The Autobiography of a Catholic Anarchist*. New York: Catholic Worker, 1954.

Divides his life into his childhood and youth (1893-1916), his anti-war agitation (1917-1919), marriage (1920-1930), social work (1930-1942), income tax resistance and life as a laborer (1943-1947), his life with the Hopi (1947-1949), and his activities in the 1950s, with Dorothy Day, on the Hiroshima Fast, his tax refusal, and final conversion to Roman Catholicism.

1299   Lynd, Staughton. *Nonviolence in America: A Documentary History*. Indianapolis: Bobbs Merrill.

Selections from Ammon Hennacy.

World War II and Conscientious Objection

1300   Catholic Pacifist Association. *Blessed Are the Peacemakers*. Toronto, Ont. Catholic Pacifist Association, 1944.

Not seen.

1301   McNeal, Patricia. "Catholic Conscientious Objectors During World War II," *Catholic Historical Review* 61 (April 1975): 219-42.

Much of this material is similar to that found in **1271**. While World War I claimed four Catholic COs out of 3,989, and World War II 135 out of 11,887, by 1969 there were 2,494 Catholic COs out of a total of 34,255, making Catholics the largest single group among religious denominations represented.

1302   Zahn, Gordon. *Another Part of the War: The Camp Simon Story.* Amherst, MA: University of Massachusetts Press, 1979.

An excellent account of the lives and routines of the Catholic conscientious objectors during World War II sent to a series of work camps for the duration, written by one of them. Examines the motivations, behavior, and forms of pacifism of the interned objectors. The book also recounts anecdotes about life in the camps and the characters of the men that provide the reader with a very good picture of "real-life" pacifists.

1303   ——."Catholic Conscientious Objection in the United States." See **57**, 145-59.

A study of 135 men in the Civilian Public Service camps. No one really knows the total number of Catholic COs who served. Much of this material appears in **1302**.

1304   ——."The Social Thought of the Catholic Conscientious Objector." See **57**, 160-76.

A survey of the opinions of the men in the CPS camps during World War II, examined in **1302**. Zahn concludes that although the forms ranged from Christian anarchism to Thomist just-war pacifism, in effect most of the inmates were total pacifists.

Thomas Merton

1305   Breit, Marquita, ed. & compiler. *Thomas Merton: A Bibliography.* Metuchen, NJ: Scarecrow, 1974.

An excellent introduction to the materials available on the man and his writings.

1306   ——, and Robert E. Daggy. *Thomas Merton: A Comprehensive Bibliography*. 2nd ed. New York and London: Garland Publishing, 1985.

Revised edition of **1305**.

1307   Forest, James. "Thomas Merton's Struggle with Peacemaking." See **1325**, 15-54; reprinted Erie, PA: Pax Christi, n.d.

Follows Merton's progression from an acceptance of the just-war tradition as the only valid Catholic position, to his realization that we now live in a post-Christian era where such distinctions are meaningless, to his insistence that peace must involve "a complete change of heart and a totally new outlook on the world of men." Forest traces Merton's role in founding the Catholic Peace Fellowship and his crisis of conscience after the suicide of Roger LaPorte in 1965.

1308   Furlong, Monica. *Merton: A Biography*. San Francisco: Harper & Row, 1980; reprinted 1985.

An excellent biography. Merton's nonviolence is examined in particular detail on pages 252 to 269, but his life as a whole was one of peacemaking, of finding the voice of the Christian in the modern world and raising it against its injustices and violence.

1309   Merton, Thomas. "The Answer of Minerva. Pacifism and Resistance in Simone Weil." See **40**, 144-49.

The peace movement needs a metaphysic that will bring it beyond the passivity of pacifism and enable it to confront the myths of the warmakers.

1310   ——."Breakthrough to Peace." See **40**, 76-81.

The challenge to peacemakers is to overcome the despair that leads to the wish for self-destruction. We must renounce passive irresponsibility and fatalistic submission to violence.

1311   ——."Christian Action in World Crisis." See **40**, 219-26.

We live in an apocalyptic age, but is it one of death or of new birth? The problem of the age is not the beast of the apocalypse, but our own paralysis in the face of such evil, our own hatred and evil. In this Merton echoes the words of Thomas More or Erasmus in placing the real evil in ourselves. See **670-671** and **715**. He also recalls Erasmus in saying that the problem now is that we live in a world saturated by the Christian message, in a world tired of hearing it, in fact. We must therefore now *live* the Christian life.

From the time of Pius XII Catholic thought has declared war out of date. Nuclear war cannot possibly be just, and the Christian must reject it, as has Dorothy Day. The essay reflects Merton's rapid approach to "nuclear pacifism."

1312   ——."Christian Ethics in Nuclear War." See **40**, 82-87.

Nuclear war, in fact even such conventional techniques as saturation bombing aimed at civilian centers, has been condemned by Pope Pius XII. Such action is not permissible under the just-war criteria followed by the church. Yet such statements are ignored by Catholics. In the end Christians cannot be passive; they must work actively for peace.

1313   ——."Faith and Violence." See **40**, 185-207.

This is a troubled work reflecting Merton's grappling with nonviolence in the late 1960s and his movement toward a "theology of resistance." The state is without any justice; it is, in fact, St. Augustine's great band of robbers. Society condemns the isolated, individual violence of criminals while it participates fully in corporate and technological violence in war, and in the violence of poverty. True peace cannot be order alone.

Was Camilo Torres, the Colombian priest turned guerilla, right in his use of force? Is there a valid theology of revolution? Is force to be used if Christianity fails? Merton remains troubled by these questions and calls for the development of a theology of resistance, an activist nonviolence that seeks to bring justice and real peace, while avoiding the moral aggression of self-righteousness.

Merton then turns to contemporary events and declares the Vietnam War an overwhelming atrocity tied to America's suicidal drive to self-destruction. He condemns the draft law as unjust and illegal, as the forced acting out by the young of the manias of their political leaders. In the Civil Rights movement Merton believes that nonviolence may be dead and is not effective. He upbraids white liberals and calls on them simply to act as witnesses, not to attempt to lead the movement. He concludes by praising the "Death of God" theology for freeing religion from the restraints of institutionalism and ambiguity.

1314   ——.*The Hidden Ground of Love: The Letters of Thomas Merton.* William H. Shannon, ed. New York: Farrar,

Straus & Giroux, 1985.

Not seen.

1315   ——."The Machine Gun in the Fallout Shelter." See **40**,
        103-6.

Uses the image of the occupant of the post-nuclear
fall-out shelter defending his right to survive from those
locked outside as a metaphor for contemporary American
society, with its passive notion of morality and order.
While he condemns violence, Merton remains uncomfortable here with pacifism, equating it with passive acquiescence. He calls, rather, for an active resistance to evil that
he terms true nonviolence and concludes that, contrary to
the ethic of the fall-out shelter, true Christian love may
entail sacrificing one's own life for one's neighbor.

1316   ——."Man Is a Gorilla with a Gun." See **40**, 168-71.

A sharp criticism of Robert Ardrey's then popular
African Genesis, an example of the anthropology of re-
ductionism that concludes that the human being is simply a
sophisticated animal fighting for the same imperatives of
survival and domination. Merton notes that this supposedly scientific analysis is couched in the semantics of
violence that presupposes what it sets out to prove: the
innate violence of human nature and of the world. His
rebuttal recalls the peaceful anthropology of Erasmus and
the Humanists. See Chapter 9.

1317   ——."Peace: Christian Duties and Perspectives." See **40**,
        12-19.

A rebuttal to theories of determinism and a call to

Christians to assume the individual responsibility for good
and evil. Christians also have a duty to resist the evil that
is overcoming the world's leaders in their temptation to
mass suicide. In the face of nuclear holocaust we have all
fallen prey to a moral numbness that must be resisted.

Merton goes on to declare that there can be no just war
with modern technology, and that the Christian must
refuse consent and pursue nonviolent resistance in
disobeying evil authority, even if this means death.

1318   ——."Peace: A Religious Responsibility." See **40**, 107-28.

Merton questions the morality of nuclear war and
states that moral truth is not a sentimental luxury of
intellectuals but a necessity of our survival as human
beings. The policy of nuclear deterrence reduces all values
to one — survival — and is thus a totalitarian form.

He then goes on the note that there are hidden forces at
work in these apocalyptic times, a Manichaeism that
separates the physical from the spiritual world in such
declarations as "Better Dead Than Red!" This Merton
says, is tantamount to saying that it is permissible to
destroy God's physical creation in favor of some
ideology, or life style, of the moment. He condemns
Augustine's similarly Manichaean dichotomy that one can
kill an enemy while still loving him. Nuclear war is a
resort to magic, an ultimate solution fostered by frustrated
minds who despair of God's plan. Nuclear war itself is a
second crucifixion to which the Christian must refuse
consent. Real Christians have a duty to form their
consciences on these issues, and then to act on them. A
pacifism in regards to nuclear war is necessary.

1319   ——."Peace and Protest: A Statement." See **40**, 67-69.

The current moral climate is one of violence and reaction. We must therefore think calmly to make a positive and constructive witness to peace. Peacemakers must overcome the desperation and hopelessness that leads to war.

1320 ——."Peace and Revolution: A Footnote to *Ulysses*." See **40**, 70-75.

The Cyclopes episode and Bloom's passivity in Joyce's novel is a metaphor for the modern idea of "pacifism." This position is one of chiché-ridden platitudes, of ideas incapable of being put into practice. An excellent criticism of what peacemaking is *not*.

1321 ——."Preface to the Vietnamese Translation of *No Man Is An Island*." See **40**, 63-66.

Since all peoples are brothers and sisters, in loving we love the other and ourselves, in hating, we also hate ourselves. Being itself is grounded in love, and love is founded on the will to build, to forgive, to be reconciled.

1322 ——."Target Equals City." See **40**, 94-102.

Nuclear war, or any war aimed at mass destruction, is terrorism and is clearly unjust. Merton's criticisms anticipate those of the Bishops' Pastoral (**1457** to **1485**) by two decades.

1323 ——."A Tribute to Gandhi." See **40**, 178-84.

Nonviolence must begin with internal conversion. Gandhi's approach, his *satyagraha*, or active devotion to truth, was inseparably both religious and political.

1324   Mott, Michael. *The Seven Mountains of Thomas Merton.*
        Boston: Houghton Mifflin, 1984.

        A biography.

1325   Twomey, Gerard, ed. *Thomas Merton: Prophet in the
        Belly of a Paradox.* New York: Paulist Press, 1978.

        A collection of essays by many who knew him and
        worked with him in the Catholic peace movement. See
        1307 and **1326**.

1326   Zahn, Gordon. "Thomas Merton: Reluctant Pacifist." See
        1325, 55-79.

        This is essentially the same material as Zahn's
        introduction to **40**.

The 1960s: Vatican II and Vietnam

1327   Deedy, John G. "The Catholic Press and Vietnam." See
        1335, 121-31.

        The course of the war saw the Catholic press convert
        from avid support of the war effort, to a call for
        negotiations consistent with the policies of Pope Paul VI.
        On the whole, however, the Catholic press could not be
        stereotyped according to any political or moral position.
        Editorial stances ranged from the *Catholic Worker's*
        pacifism, to *America's* hawkishness. Such an important
        lay paper as *Commonweal* eventually saw the war as
        indecent and immoral, and called for civil disobedience
        against it.

1328 Forest, James. "No Longer Alone: The Catholic Peace Movement." See **1335**, 139-49.

Over the period the the Vietnam War Catholic peacemakers have found that their position was not as isolated and condemned as it first appeared.

1329 Gaylin, Willard. *In the Service of Their Country.* New York: Viking, 1970.

Not seen.

1330 Gray, Francine du Plessix. *Divine Disobedience: Profiles in Catholic Radicalism.* New York: Alfred A. Knopf, 1970.

Reviews the life and careers of Daniel and Philip Berrigan and others.

1331 Furfey, Paul Hanley. "The Civilian COs." See **51**, 188-99.

The general U.S. population gradually came to oppose the war in Vietnam on just-war grounds.

1332 O'Brien, David J. "American Catholic Opposition to the Vietnam War: A Preliminary Assessment." See **51**, 119-50.

A good narrative survey of the changing position of American Catholics from super-patriotic support to opposition and to the recognition of pacifism and the emerging "just-revolution" position among many Catholics. O'Brien actually notes that despite the popular media image, surveys show that American Catholics were no more or less anti-communist or pro-government than the general U.S. population. He also traces the change in attitudes in the Catholic press, among the hierarchy, and in activist groups such as the Catholic Peace Fellowship, and the nonviolent thought and action of Dorothy Day, Gordon Zahn, Thomas Merton, and the Berrigans.

1333   "*Pacem in Terris* and Vietnam," *Christianity Today* 12 (Jan. 5, 1968): 39.

Not seen.

1334   Powers, Thomas. *The War At Home: Vietnam and the American People, 1964-1968.* New York: Grossman, 1973.

This is an excellent, left-leaning account that is comprehensive in scope. Included are sections on Catholic activities set in the context of the peace movement as a whole. Among them are the activities of the Catholic Worker in the draft-card burnings of 1965 and 1967.

1335   Quigley, Thomas E., ed. *American Catholics and Vietnam.* Grand Rapids, MI: Eerdman's, 1968.

A collection of essays, including **1327** and **1330**.

1336   Schuijt and Coste. "History." See **973**, 344-46.

While *Gaudium et Spes* finally moved the church away from the just-war tradition, a group of American bishops led by Cardinal Spellman opposed Chapter V as too radical. They opposed any stigmatization of nuclear weapons, arguing that one cannot have a legitimate defense without them, and that they preserve the freedom of the world. In the end the American bishops involved showed little knowledge of the true meaning of the

Constitution of the Church, especially in view of the U.S. involvement in Vietnam at the time. In the end, however, even these bishops came over to the majority side.

1337   U.S. Catholic Conference. *In the Name of Peace: Collective Statements of the United States Catholic Bishops on War and Peace 1919-1980.* Washington, DC: U.S. Catholic Conference, 1983.

Includes **1338, 1339, 1373,** and **1374.** A superlative collection.

1338   ——.*Peace and Vietnam.* Washington, DC: U.S. Catholic Conference, 1966. See **1337,** 27-28.

The war in Vietnam must be fought within the limits of the just war: no civilian targets, a limitation of the means used, it must be in the national defense, with provision for conscientious objection, and with the full confidence of the American people in their leaders. Therefore, "it is reasonable to argue that our presence in Vietnam is justified." Yet the bishops add, "while we can conscientiously support the position of our country in the present circumstances, it is the duty of everyone to search for other alternatives."

1339   ——.*Resolution on Southeast Asia.* Washington, DC: U.S. Catholic Conference, 1971. See **1337,** 59-62.

Written only five years after **1338,** the letter declares, "At this point in history it seems clear to us that whatever good we hope to achieve through continued involvement in this war is now outweighed by the destruction of human life and of moral values which it inflicts. It is our firm conviction, therefore, that the speedy ending of this war is a moral imperative of the highest priority." The letter stresses that the church must embrace a new attitude to war and a new theology of peace. It must help rebuild Southeast Asia, strengthen the U.N., and bring forgiveness and reconciliation within the United States.

1340   Yzermans, Vincent A., ed. *American Participation in the Second Vatican Council*. New York: Sheed and Ward, 1967.

Examines the background and debates over the Pastoral Constitution and Schema XIII. American activity at the council sessions on war and peace focused on two issues: conscientious objection and the morality of nuclear war. Excellent account of the political maneuvering and the conflict of personalities and ideologies among the American bishops on these issues.

Conscientious Objection: Vietnam to the Present

1341   "American Catholic Bishops Support Selective Conscientious Objection," *Christian Century* 88 (Nov. 10, 1971): 1320.

Based on the just-war criteria that demands that the individual inform his or her conscience as to the morality of a certain war, and then refuse participation if that war is unjust.

1342   Baskir, Lawrence M., and William A. Strauss. *Chance and Circumstance. The Draft, the War and the Vietnam Generation*. New York: Vintage Books, 1978.

The best interpretive and statistical source available for the types, numbers, motivations, and actions of those who resisted or avoided the draft during the Vietnam War. Discusses conscientious objection and gives some, but not much, specific information on Catholics.

1343 "Bishops, the COs and Amnesty," *America* 125 (Sept. 4, 1971): 108.

The ending of the Vietnam War has seen the U.S. hierarchy converted to the principle of Vatican II, that objection to war is now a valid Catholic option. They now look forward to the healing of the war's wounds and the reconciliation of all Americans.

1344 "Catholic Worker, R.A. LaPorte Burns Self to Death," *Newsweek* 66 (Nov. 22, 1965): 71.

In a protest against the U.S. involvement in Vietnam, and in imitation of its Buddhist monks, this 22-year old, loosely associated with the Catholic Worker, committed suicide in an attempt to call attention to the death and destruction in Southeast Asia. Lapsing into a coma after his self-immolation, LaPorte died 33 hours later. He told an ambulance attendant, "I am a Catholic Worker. I'm against war, all wars. I did this as a religious action."

1345 Coffman, J. "CO and the Draft; Bibliography," *Library* 94 (May 15, 1969): 2059-65.

Useful for the 1960s.

1346 Connery, J.R. "Law and Conscience," *America* 122 (Feb. 21, 1970): 178-81.

Examines conscientious objection to war as one example of the interaction of moral and legal dynamics. Discusses the criteria for conscientious choice, erroneous conscience and truly informed conscience.

1347   Cooney, Robert, and Helen Michalowski. *Power of the People: Nonviolence in the United States.* Culver City, CA: Peace Press, 1985.

Not seen.

1348   Cornell. "Catholic Church." See **51**, 200-213.

A brief review of the Catholic pacifist movement in the United States. Discusses the background in the Catholic Worker through the 1960s, the Catholic role in the Fellowship of Reconciliation, Catholic pacifism and the war in Vietnam, the Catholic Peace Fellowship, the Berrigans, and Pax Christi.

1349   ——."Twenty Years of the Catholic Peace Fellowship," *Fellowship* 51, 6 (June 1985): 16-17.

A review of this peace organization from its founding in 1965, the work of the Catholic Worker, Thomas Merton, A.J. Muste, the Berrigans, Jim Forest and John Heidbrink in bringing it about. Recalls the early days, the formulation of a plan to counsel Catholic COs, the first educational publications, and the first few years.

1350   Dougherty, James E. "The Christian and Nuclear Pacifism," *Catholic World* 198 (March 1964): 336-46.

The pacifist must follow his or her conscience, but this must not usurp the magisterium of the church, which has long upheld the just-war tradition. Dougherty seems comfortable with Niebuhr's Christianity in which prophesy is no substitute for "rational control systems, underwritten by the consensus of experienced analysts and politically acceptable to both sides." In the end Dougherty concludes that it is too bad, but nuclear weapons exist, and they must be made to serve both Christ and country in the cause of peace.

1351   Egan, Eileen. *The Catholic Conscientious Objector: The Right to Refuse to Kill.* Chicago: Pax Christi, 1981.

This booklet examines the issues of conscience and war, some historical antecedents, the just-war theory, modern Catholic statements, including *Pacem in Terris* and Vatican II, *Human Life in Our Day,* and U.S. bishops' statements on conscientious objection, registration, conscription, and the statements of Pope John Paul II. It also lists resources, including Pax Christi, the Catholic Peace Fellowship, NISBCO, and the Fellowship of Reconciliation. Includes a list of readings.

1352   Forest, James. *Catholics and Conscientious Objection.* New York: Catholic Peace Fellowship, 1981.

A brief pamphlet places peacemaking in the context of the twentieth century: Vatican II and the holocausts of World War II. Forest then briefly traces the history of Christian pacifism, from the early church, skipping from the fourth to the twentieth century, then discussing Franz Jaegerstaetter, Thomas Merton, recent church teaching, and the process of forming one's own conscience, choosing a course of action, and finding support. Lists helpful peace and counseling groups, and selected readings.

1353   Frazier, Paul. *Catholic College Students and the Draft.* New York: Catholic Peace Fellowship, 1981.

Gives a brief historical introduction to the history of conscription, the procedures of the Selective Service System, and the various alternatives open to a Catholic of draft age: conscientious objection, deferments and exemptions, noncooperation, the armed forces, and emigration. Includes a good list of counseling and information resources and a good bibliography.

1354   Gorgen, Carol. *Catholic Conscientious Objectors.* San Francisco: Allied Printing, 1963.

Not seen.

1355   Henriot, P.J. "American Bishops and Conscientious Objectors," *America* 120 (Jan. 4, 1969): 17-19.

The bishops' pastoral of November 15, 1969 approves selective conscientious objection. Denying that Catholics can be total pacifists, this stresses that Catholics can refuse participation in certain wars only on just-war criteria.

1356   Jennings, James R., ed. *Just War and Pacifism: A Catholic Dialogue.* Washington, DC: U.S. Catholic Conference, 1973.

Not seen.

1357   Meehan, Francis X. "The Catholic Conscience Faces the Military Draft," *Catholic Mind* (September 1980).

Not seen.

1358   Newman, Judy. "CO and International Law," *The Objector* 6, 2 (October 1985): 6-7. See also **1474**.

Discusses the issue of nuclear pacifism, based on just-war criteria, stemming from the Bishops' Pastoral, and the fears in military circles that this just-war rejection has inspired.

1359   Palms, C.L. "Peace and the Catholic Conscience," *Catholic World* 203 (June 1966): 145-52.

A rambling look at the foremost Catholic peacemakers of the time, including Dorothy Day and the Catholic Worker, James Forest, Gordon Zahn, Tom Cornell and David Miller. All these stress the Gandhian aspects of peacemaking, an activism that goes beyond pacifism, and their courage is apparent.

1360   Pax Christi Reflection Guide. *Conscience and Civil Disobedience.* Cambridge, MA: Pax Christi, 1985.

Pacem in Terris reminds us that when the call of the state conflicts with the call of God, "God has more right to be obeyed than men." Bibliography and resources.

1361   ——.*Conscience and Nonviolence.* Cambridge, MA: Pax Christi, 1985.

A brief pamphlet, keyed to the text of the bishops' pastoral. Good, short, bibliography.

1362   ——.*Conscience and Reverence for Life.* Cambridge, MA: Pax Christi, 1985.

A short pamphlet. Violence in the oppression of the poor, sexism, exploitation, abortion, are all linked to the violence of war and must be overcome by peacemakers just as strongly. Keyed to the bishops' pastoral. Brief bibliography and resources.

1363   ——.*Conscience and Tax Resistance.* Cambridge, MA: Pax Christi, 1985.

The Pentagon enters all our lives through the 1040 form. Are we to render to Caesar or to God? A brief discussion. Short bibliography. Resources.

1364   ——.*Conscience and War.* Cambridge, MA: Pax Christi, 1985.

The relationship between the individual conscience and the demands of the state. Short pamphlet keyed to the Bishops' pastoral. Bibliography and resources.

1365   Pisani, J. "Conscientious Objection: No Longer Un-Catholic," *Christian Century* 88 (July 21, 1971): 876-78.

The bishops have given their support to Catholic objectors.

1366   Polner, M. "No Jew nor Catholic Need Apply," *Commonweal* 90 (June 20, 1969): 386-87.

On the hostility and prejudice met by young Catholics and Jews seeking conscientious objector status before local draft boards during the Vietnam War. These young people, members of mainline religious groups, were not associated with traditional peace churches, and therefore had a very difficult time proving the sincerity of their beliefs and a consistent tradition of peace in their religious backgrounds.

1367   Prasad, Devi and Tony Smythe, eds. *Conscription: A*

World Survey. London: War Resisters International, New York: WRL, 1968.

Also surveys resistance to the draft and conscientious objection around the world.

1368   Riga, P.J. "Selective Conscientious Objection: Progress Report," *Catholic World* 211 (July 1970): 161-65.

There is difficulty proving that the just-war is truly a "traditional religious teaching" of the Catholic church. Yet eminent Catholic theologians have endorsed it. Thomas Aquinas stressed the binding force of the conscience in deciding on the justness of a war, and the just war has been accepted implicitly by Catholic tradition. Vatican II supported it, and the teaching will pave the way for Catholics to selectively object to specific wars.

1369   Rigali, Norbert J. "Just War and Pacifism," *America* 150 (March 31, 1984): 233-36.

The recent Bishops' Pastoral reveals irreconcilable differences between the two traditions.

1370   "Selective Objectors and the Court," *America* 123 (July 11, 1970): 6.

The situation is still not favorable.

1371   Sheerin, J.B. "Must Conscientious Objectors be Pacifists?" *Catholic World* 206 (January 1968): 146-47.

This editorial focuses on the problems of Catholics who oppose the war in Vietnam. A provision for selective conscientious objection is needed, but the government is

hesitant to provide it, fearing a groundswell of objectors.
Catholics must therefore protest the inadequacy of the draft
law.

1372   U.S. Catholic Conference. *The Catholic Conscientious
        Objector.* Washington, DC: U.S. Catholic Conference,
        1969.

The right of the Roman Catholic to claim this status is
confirmed by the bishops.

1373   ——.*Declaration on Conscientious Objection and Selective
        Conscientious Objection.* Washington, DC: U.S.
        Catholic Conference, 1971.

All Catholics are bound to observe the dictates of their
consciences.   Furthermore, Vatican II has approved
Catholic conscientious objection. "In the light of the
Gospel and from an analysis of the Church's teaching on
conscience, it is clear that a Catholic can be a conscientious
objector to war in general or to a particular war 'because of
religious training and belief.'"   The church must now
encourage education in this teaching and must provide
opportunities for alternative service. Selective conscientious objection must be legalized, in reaffirmation of the
call of *Human Life* in 1968. See **1337**.

1374   ——.*Statement on Registration and Conscription for
        Military Service.* Feb.14, 1980. See **1337**, 83-86.

The state has a right to self-defense, but not to blind
obedience. While registration for a draft is permissible,
the state must show convincing reasons for its implemen-
tation. The bishops oppose conscription at present, and
any conscription for women, and call for provision for

both conscientious objection and selective conscientious objection under any new draft. They urge a program of draft counseling for Catholic schools and agencies.

1375 Yoder, John Howard. *When War Is Unjust: Being Honest in Just-War Thinking.* Minneapolis: Augsburg Publishing, 1984.

When rightly applied, just-war theory is as stringent as pacifism in its rejection of modern war.

1376 Zahn, Gordon. "The Draft: Occasion of Sin?" *America,* August 2-9, 1980.

Not seen.

1377 ——.and others, eds. *John Timothy Leary: A Different Kind of Hero.* Erie, PA: Pax Christi, 1983.

A small booklet on this young man, a staff member of Pax Christi, compiled shortly after his sudden death. Essays and poems by Gordon Zahn, John Marsh, John Botean, and Daniel Berrigan reveal what it means to be a peacemaker, and how and why the community of peace works in the world.

1378 Zaroulis, Nancy, and Gerald Sullivan. *Who Spoke Up? American Protest Against the War in Vietnam, 1963-1975.* Garden City, NY: Doubleday, 1984.

Discusses the activities of Catholic peacemakers in the context of the anti-war movement as a whole, noting the quite early appearance of the Catholic Workers as opponents of U.S. involvement. While they received little publicity, Catholic Workers Chris Kearns and Tom

Cornell were picketing the Vietnamese mission to the U.N. as early as the summer of 1963. On the other hand, Cardinal Spellman's support of the war was very well publicized and overshadowed the criticisms of Catholic papers, such as *Commonweal.*

Toward a Theology of Peacemaking

1379   "Catholics and Peace," *Commonweal* 95 (Jan. 7, 1972): 315-16.

For perspectives on the Catholic peace movement since Vietnam. While there was widespread Catholic indifference to the early phases of the Vietnam War, things began to change by the early 1970s, as a new awareness seemed to be arriving.

1380   Cornell, Thomas. "The Catholic Church and Witness Against War." See **51**, 200-213.

A personal recounting of the evolution of Catholic peacemaking since World War II.

1381   Deedy, John G. "Pax Romana: The 'Peace Catholics' Speak Out," *The Nation* 234, 11 (March 20, 1982): 338-40.

The days of Cardinal Spellman, waving the flag in World War II, Korea and Vietnam are past. More and more Catholics, laity and hierarchy, have turned against both nuclear and conventional war. Outspoken bishops, groups like the Catholic Peace Fellowship and Pax Christi, and a multitude of Catholic conscientious objectors are now an accepted Catholic fact. Why? John XXIII, John Paul II, the Berrigans, the realization that we cannot have both guns and butter have all begun to convert Catholics.

There are still some hawks among the Catholic hierarchy, but the bishops are still far out ahead of most Catholics.

1382   Dozier, Carol T. "Peace: Gift and Task. A Pastoral Letter," *Commonweal* 95 (Dec. 24, 1971): 289, 294-300.

Reviews the peace tradition in the church from Christ and the early church, through the Middle Ages (just war, crusades, and nonviolence), then reminds readers of the Catholics who came to America in the nineteenth century to avoid conscription. During World War II Christian sensitivity was almost completely extinguished, but *Pacem in Terris* rekindled Catholic peacemaking. Dozier concludes by declaring that the Vietnam War is not justified and by extending his personal pledge of support to any conscientious objector against the war.

1383   Fahey, Joseph. "Toward A Theology of Peace," *Catholic World* 213 (May 1971): 64-68.

This is based on our knowledge of God, who is transcendent and a god of love, whose very being opposes all violence and war. The church must now move away from thinking of ways to justify, limit, or referee war — a theology of war — and toward the positive acts of peacemaking, which translate as the works of justice bringing God's presence to the world.

1384   Ferber, Michael. "Politics of Transcendance: Religious Revival on the Left," *The Nation* (July 6/13, 1985): 9-10, 12-13.

The revival of the religious right has been matched by an equally impressive revival of left and liberal religious

groups, focusing on issues of peace and justice. In this
work Catholics play a prominent part, especially in the
Sanctuary Movement, an outgrowth of the activities of the
Berrigans and other Catholic activists during the Vietnam
War. In these activities the churchpeople are reclaiming
moral and ethical issues that have been ignored or forfeited
to the forces of reaction.

1385   Finn, James. "Pacifism and Justifiable War." See **51**, 3-
          14.

Pacifists have had little comfort from the Catholic
hierarchy in modern times. As recently as the 1960s they
had to contend with Pope Paul VI's condemnation of
pacifism as an escape from the responsibility of peacemaking. Despite this, the hierarchy has been moving
slowly toward a new criticism of war. In 1976 the Detroit
"Call to Action" conference of U.S. bishops called for a
condemnation of the production, possession, and threatened use of nuclear weapons, and in 1979 their pastoral
"To Live in Jesus Christ," condemned even the existence
of the nuclear deterrent.

1386   Gallagher, Michael. "Clergy and Laity Concerned:
          Opposition to War Sparks Group's Birth," *National
          Catholic Reporter* 20 (Sept. 7, 1984): 6.

Not seen.

1387   Gumbleton, Thomas J. "The Role of the Peacemaker."
          See **51**, 214-29.

The peacemaker is blessed, not the peaceful. Like the
medieval Joachites and other peaceful apocalyptics,
Gumbleton discusses peacemaking in the imagery of the
womb and of birth, the seed that will blossom into a new

age of peace. The history of peacemaking is one of progression or moral consciousness, "developing the understanding of justice, harmony, and true religion." Peacemaking is both the process and the result of this developing understanding.

1388　Haessly, Jacqueline. *Peacemaking: Family Activities for Justice and Peace.* New York: Paulist Press, 1980.

One of the Paths of Life series. Focuses on peace-making within the family for use in daily situations, especially in families with children in school. Examines the roots and causes of violence and injustice, beginning within the family. The book's aim is to help children "develop the awareness and the skills necessary to respond creatively as a just people in our society."

1389　Hehir. "Just-War Ethic." See **51**, 15-39.

Delineates all the modern criteria for the just war and notes that, despite the pacifist statements of Pope John XXIII and his successors, the just war is still a legitimate Catholic position. The just war, in fact, forms the basis of Vatican II's condemnation of war in the modern nuclear age. Whether Vatican II also condemned deterrence is still not clear, however. In the final analysis, the just-war theory is tied to the concept of the church as an activist, formative force in the world.

1390　Hutchinson, B. "Christians in an Immoral World," *America* 150 (Jan. 28, 1984): 51-52.

Not seen.

1391　Kownacki, Sr. Mary Lou, O.S.B. *Imagine....* Erie, PA: Pax Christi, 1982.

An imaginary scenario in which some future (?) pope is moved by a vision of the world's suffering to declare a fast until the two superpowers agree to a nuclear freeze. The fast gains the attention of the world's media, apparently by the skillful design of the pope and his followers, as the leaders of Catholic liberation and of other religions around the world assemble at Rome to speak in support of the pope's action.

Despite cynicism and consternation in the centers of power, gradually even the world's political leaders, first on the peripheries, in the Third World, come to the pope's side. As the pope approaches death, the leaders of the U.S. and U.S.S.R., moved by tremendous world pressure, finally came to Rome to sign the treaty. After that it is only a matter of time before the peoples of the world realize that the power of consent really does reside with them. General disarmament follows soon thereafter.

1392   MacEoin, Gary. "Gospel of Change," *The Progressive* 49, 12 (December 1985): 30-33.

The religiously motivated have moved into the vanguard of the peace movement. The recent history of the Plowshares, Witness for Peace in Central America, and the Sanctuary movement has shown that the ancient prophetic tradition still has strength. These changes are most visible and dramatic in the Catholic church.

A marked increase in the laity's involvement in peacemaking has been matched by a new theological interpretation of the church's role in society and by unprecedented government surveillance. Nevertheless, these religious activists are still only a small elite. Mass organization and an ideological base are still to come.

1393 McManus, Philip. "Refusing to Disappear," *Fellowship* 51, 7-8 (July/August 1985): 12-13, 37.

The Catholic peace movement.

1394 Nicholl, D. "Ecumenical Risk for an Academy of Peace," *America* 149 (Nov. 19, 1983): 310-11.

Not seen.

1395 O'Brien, David J. "Catholic Peace Movement Lives!" *America* 130 (May 4, 1974): 342-43.

Examines the regional meeting of the Catholic Peace Fellowship at Holyoke, Massachusetts in March 1974, attended by James Forest, Gordon Zahn, Bishop Thomas J. Gumbleton, and others. Also discusses the pioneering work of the Maryknoll Order for peace and justice in the Third World.

1396 Reese, T.J. "Strike for Peace," *America* 149 (July 9-16, 1983): 24.

Not seen.

1397 Stahel, T.H. "Gift of Peace," *America* 130 (May 11, 1974).

Not seen.

1398 Thompson, Charles S., ed. *Morals and Missiles: Catholic Essays on the Problem of War Today*. London, 1979.

Not seen.

1399   Toton, S.C. "Peacemaking Put in Context," *America* 149
        (Aug. 6-13, 1983): 67-69.

        Not seen.

1400   True, Michael. "Persisters for Peace: Catholic Peace
        Movement," *Commonweal* 100 (April 26, 1974): 180-
        81.

        On the meeting of the Catholic Peace Fellowship at
        Waterbury, Connecticut and in Holyoke, Massachusetts.
        Bishop Thomas J. Gumbleton set the theme of the
        meetings in his call for a conversion of the church to an
        authentic tradition of nonviolence. Issues addressed
        included poverty in the Third World, Vietnam and political
        prisoners, the UFW boycott, tax resistance, and alternative
        life styles.

1401   U.S. Catholic Conference. *A Call to Action: An Agenda
        for the Catholic Community.* Washington, D.C.,
        1976.

        Includes a radical call for disarmament, selective
        conscientious objection, and penance for our creation of
        nuclear arms.

1402   ——.*Human Life in Our Day.* Washington, DC: U.S.
        Catholic Conference, 1968. See **42,** 421-67.

        This pastoral was a response to both Paul VI's
        Humanae Vitae and to U.S. involvement in Vietnam.
        Controversial among liberals and radicals for its

condemnations of birth control and abortion, the letter is consistent in its pro-life stance that included growing doubts about the Vietnam War. Relying strongly on the just-war tradition, the pastoral condemns all aggressive wars outright, as well as unlimited war, but does concede the justness of defensive wars, but only as a last resort. While military service, properly fulfilled, can be a work of peace, peace is not simply the ending of war or imposed order: it is charity and the workings of justice in the world.

Quoting frequently from *Gaudium et Spes* (See **950**), it condemns the arms race and the continued stockpiling of nuclear weapons. Turning to the draft, it repeats Pope Benedict XV's opposition to a peacetime draft (See **886**). Concerning Vietnam, it asks if the U.S. has already crossed the point where the means being used are proportional to the just end being sought, and it questions whether the conflict has provoked inhuman dimensions of suffering. It concludes that the war may be teaching a moral lesson that military power and technology do not suffice to restore order or to accomplish peace and justice, that evils like malnutrition, economic frustration, social stagnation, and political injustice are best attacked and corrected by non-military means.

Turning to individual duty, the letter notes that conscientious objection, even selective conscientious objection, can have a basis in the teachings of the church, and that unquestioning obedience is not necessarily in conformity with the mind and heart of the church. It therefore recommends changes in Selective Service System rules to allow objection to unjust wars. It further advises Catholics that they must follow their own consciences, even if the Selective Service System does not allow such objection. In effect, the bishops are approving disobedience to human law in obedience to divine law.

1403   ——.*Statement on Central America.* Washington, D.C.,
         1982.

      The bishops affirm the legacy of Vatican II, Medellin,
Puebla, and the theology of liberation. They mourn the
martyrdoms of Archbishop Oscar Romero and the four
American churchwomen in El Salvador (See **1238** to **1248**)
and confirm the special tie of U.S. Catholics to their
brothers and sisters in Central America. The bishops
refute U.S. government contentions about communist
infiltration in the region and declare that the church there is
neither naive nor complacent. The basic threat is from
hunger, poverty, and political tyranny.

1404   Zahn, Gordon. *An Alternative to War.* New York: CRIA,
         1963.

      Zahn's reflections on peacemaking past and present.

1405   ——."Future of the Catholic Peace Movement,"
         Commonweal 99 (Dec. 28, 1973): 337-42.

      Many tasks await the movement: post-war recon-
ciliation, rebuilding, the freedom of South Vietnamese
political prisoners, amnesty for draft resisters, a reexam-
ination of the war on just-war grounds. While little
foundation for a future movement exists, still there is better
preparation for one than in the wake of World War II. The
peace movement had suffered from a diffusion and
confusion of issues, issues often quite different from those
of real peacemaking. The Catholic peace movement must
now reach out to that great majority of Catholics, lay and
clergy, "who are not yet alert to the pacifist implications of
their religious tradition."

Such a new movement must avoid the "crusade-a-week" syndrome, it should be Catholic, with an institutional alignment, it must accept Catholic leadership and its restraints, and it must reach out to change hearts and minds. At the same time the movement must avoid scandalizing other Catholics, it must avoid elitism, and live up to a high moral standard, perhaps accepting the necessity of the "Caesar's wife syndrome."

Pax Christi

1406   "Catholic Pacifism: Pax Christi," *America* 131 (Dec. 14, 1974): 379-80.

A brief introduction.

1407   Dodaro, Robert, O.S.A., and Julie O'Reilly. *Pax Christi, USA. Reflection/Discussion Guide.* Chicago: Pax Christi, 1985.

Questions and suggestions for study inspired by the Bishops' Pastoral.

1408   Fahey, Joseph. "Pax Christi." See **51**, 59-71.

An excellent summation of the group's history and current positions. It was born out of a French desire for reconciliation with their former German enemies in 1945 and won papal approval in 1947 and 1948. Today there are chapters in eleven European countries, in the U.S. and in Australia. The group has very close ties to the institutional church and focuses on disarmament, the primacy of conscience, peace education, contacts with the Eastern Bloc, and a continuing critique of worldwide arms sales.

Pax Christi/USA was founded in 1973, and includes

both pacifists and adherents of the just-war theory. Its general aims are to explore the ideal of Christian nonviolence. It seeks to implement the general principles of Pax Christi by attempting to replace ROTC and JROTC with programs for peace and justice, to help formulate a peace theology in the light of Vatican II, and to carry on a continuing criticism of the policies of nuclear deterrence and weapons.

1409   Gilhooley, J.J. "Pax Christi/U.S.A.: Out of the Ashes; National Assembly," *America* 133 (Dec. 27, 1975): 458-60.

Examines the convention held in Dayton, Ohio in November 1975. Sessions focused on conscientious objection, registration, recruitment, the possibility of the just war in the modern world, the role of women as peacemakers, and the role of the community as an agent of peace. Leaders of the Catholic peace movement were much in evidence: Gordon Zahn, Dorothy Day, Tom Cornell, James Finn, Archbishop James Dozier, Joseph Fahey. Yet the assembly spent much time searching for a common denominator that would bring all the diverse forces of Catholic peacemaking into unity.

1410   Graham, R.A. "Pax Christi," *NCE* 11: 34-35.

The organization was founded in 1945 by French Catholics to bring reconciliation between French and Germans. Reviews the early years of the movement under Archbishop Pierre Théas of Lourdes and Cardinal Maurice Felton. As an organization Pax Christi seeks to avoid any stances that will alienate by controversy. It seeks to forge a new consensus for peacemaking through education and traditional forms of Catholic piety, including pilgrimages and prayer. It seeks the pacification of the world through new international order.

1411 Jones, Arthur. "Pax Christi Conference Records Historic Change," *The Reporter for Conscience Sake* 38, 12 (December 1981): 1-2.

The organization is at last beginning to draw support and to have its influence felt both among the laity and in the hierarchy. It is setting new, active goals.

1412 *Pax Christi.* Erie, PA: Pax Christi. Quarterly.

News of Pax Christi activities and members, interviews with prominent peacemakers around the world, book reviews and articles by some of the country's best-known peacemakers

1413 *Peaceweaving.* Erie, PA: Pax Christi. Bi-Monthly.

A pamphlet of prayers and meditations, with news briefs and notices of activities.

1414 *PXI Bulletin.* Erie, PA: Pax Christi. Quarterly.

On the International activities of Pax Christi.

1415 Van Allen, R. "Pax Christi in Dayton: International Peace Movement," *Commonweal* 102 (Dec. 19, 1975): 612-14.

A review of the conference held at the University of Dayton in November 1975, with some background information on Pax Christi.

1416 Zahn, Gordon. "Carrying Our Weight in the Catholic Peace Movement," *America* 133 (Sept. 20, 1975):

143-46.

On the importance of Pax Christi and of aims at renewing it on as broad a base as possible. Such a base would allow pacifists and just warriors to work together, thus not alienating large numbers from the peace movement while converting the church gradually to peace. Pax Christi must, therefore, respect the church, its traditions, and its sensibilities; it must not scandalize others with an "avant-garde" elitism.

These recommendations are really a compromise for the time, not a general set of principles, and outline a course of action preferable to a split within Catholic peace ranks. Zahn's ultimate hope for the church is "converting it into the effective vehicle for peace it ought to be." Pax Christi's programs should therefore focus on nuclear arms, the national budget, and arms traffic.

The Berrigans and Plowshares

1417   Berrigan, Daniel, S.J. *The Trial of the Catonsville Nine.* Boston: Beacon Press, 1970.

The play, with poetry, based on the trial of these nine Catholic activists, who in May 1968 destroyed Selective Service files in Catonsville, Maryland before surrendering themselves to the police.

1418   ——.*The Discipline of the Mountain. Dante's Purgatorio in a Nuclear World.* New York: Seabury-Crossroad, 1979.

Reflections on the great moral poem, written as a series of passages through the seven vices, encountered by the modern poet, who seeks to ascend the mountain of wisdom, with Dante as his guide. Berrigan's poetry alternates with his own meditations. "Enmity and Love," pp. 50-58, deals with war and peace directly.

1419 ——.ed. *For Swords into Plowshares, The Hammer Has to Fall.* Piscataway, NJ: Plowshares Press, 1984.

A series of essays covering the history of the Plowshares, first arrested for their entry into the General Electric plant at King of Prussia, Pennsylvania and "disarming" Mark 12A nuclear warheads. Contributions by Archbishop Raymond Hunthausen, Elizabeth McAlister, Sidney Lens, Petra Kelly, Meridel LeSueur, Berrigan himself, and others on the necessity to halt the nuclear arms race and to free humanity from their idolization of the "gods of metal" and their love of death. The name "Plowshares" comes from the biblical text (Is. 2:4, Micah 4:3): "They shall beat their swords into plowshares, and their spears into pruning hooks."

1420 ——.*Steadfastness of the Saints.*

See **1218**.

1421 ——.*The Words Our Saviour Gave Us.* Springfield, IL: Templegate, 1985.

Not seen.

1422 Catonsville Nine — Milwaukee Fourteen Defense Committee, ed. *Delivered Into Resistance.* New Haven: Advocate Press, 1969.

A collection of documents, including the Statement of the Catonsville Nine, the Meditation of the Nine, the

Statement of the Milwaukee Fourteen, and essays by James Forest, Staughton Lynd, Barbara Deming, William Kunstler, Robert Shaull, and Daniel Berrigan. Includes a good reading list.

1423   Deedy, John G. *Apologies Good Friends. An Interim Biography of Daniel Berrigan.* Chicago: Fides Claretian, 1981.

Not seen.

1423a   Fowler, Robert Booth. "Prophetic Religion in the United States," *Humanities in Society* 6 (Winter 1983): 5-70.

Not seen.

1424   Grace, Tom. "Living on the Front Lines," *Fellowship* 49, 4 (April 1983): 11-13.

On the life and commitments of Philip Berrigan. Reviews the Baltimore Courthouse, Catonsville 9, and Harrisburg 8 trials, his marriage to Elizabeth McAlister and excommunication. Berrigan discusses American materialism, its kinship to the U.S.S.R., and the desire of both systems for economic domination. The U.S. needs a nonviolent revolution, but this, Berrigan sees, is not coming. The American political process, instead, keeps us snared by its promise of material riches.

1425   Jones, Arthur. "Pershing Plowshares Eight on Freedom Road," *National Catholic Reporter* 22, 28 (May 9, 1986): 7.

On the release of Paul Mango, the last imprisoned member of the Pershing Plowshares to be freed to half way houses or to probation, two years after their conviction for damaging nuclear missile equipment on Easter 1984. Like most of the Pershing and other Plowshares members, Mango will be returning to activist life, as a member of the Catholic Worker.

1426 Keerdoja, E., and W. Slate. "Berrigans, Still Marching," *Newsweek* 93 (March 26, 1979): 16.

A brief look at the life of Philip and Elizabeth McAlister in Baltimore's Jonah House community, a peace commune, and their speaking tours against the U.S. "death trap."

1427 Klejment, Anne. *The Berrigans. A Bibliography of Published Works by Daniel, Philip, and Elizabeth McAlister Berrigan.* New York and London: Garland Publishing, 1979.

The entries, without annotation, are arranged by person, chronologically up to 1979. With indexes by titles, first line, and authors. Not surprisingly, most of the materials are by Daniel Berrigan. The collection is introduced by a brief essay and a chronology.

1428 McAlister, Elizabeth. "On Civil Disobedience," *Pax Christi* 10, 2 (June 1985): 16-17.

Not seen.

1429 Meconis, Charles A. *With Clumsy Grace: The American Catholic Left 1961-1975.* New York: Seabury-Continuum, 1979.

An excellent history.

1430　O'Rourke, William. *The Harrisburg Seven and the New Catholic Left.* New York: Crowell, 1972.

　　　A complete history of the pre-trial, jury selection process, and trial for this alleged conspiracy by the "Catholic Left" to kidnap Secretary of State Henry Kissinger and to bomb heating facilities in Washington, DC. While all defendants were acquitted, the trial tied up the "Catholic left" for years.

1431　"Plowshares Actions," *CPF Bulletin,* May 1984, 4-5.

　　　Brief synopses of the Plowshares 8 appeal process, the AVCO (July 14, 1983) Plowshares trial, the Griffiss Plowshares case (Thanksgiving 1983), and the Pershing II Plowshares actions.

1432　"Plowshares Update," *The Nation* 240, 2 (Jan. 19, 1985): 45.

　　　Briefly reviews the Plowshares 8, Trident 2 Plowshares, Griffiss Plowshares, and Pershing Plowshares cases, characterizing them, favorably, as "Luddism against the war machine."

1433　"Vindication," *Christian Century* 101 (March 7, 1984): 242.

　　　On the overturning of the conviction of Plowshares members because of trial irregularities.

The Sanctuary Movement

1434　Boteler, William, M.M., and Luise Ahrens, M.M. "Editorial: Support for the Sanctuary Movement," *Maryknoll* 79, 8 (August 1985): 28-29.

The need for justice both within the U.S. and toward the poor and displaced of the world.

1435 Bruning, Fred. "The Church Against the State," *Macleans* (March 11, 1985): 9.

Not seen.

1436 "Church Alien Aid Defended in Trial; Lawyers for Group Sheltering Fleeing Latins Tell Court of Religious Motives," *New York Times,* Nov. 20, 1985: 7.

A review of Tucson case.

1437 "Crackdown on the Sanctuaries," *Time* (Jan. 28, 1985): 17.

The INS has decided to move against the movement .

1438 Drinan, Robert F., S.J. "The Sanctuary Movement on Trial," *America* (Aug. 17, 1985): 81.

Not seen.

1439 Ebert-Miner, Allan. "The Politics of Asylum," *The Progressive,* 49,8 (August 1985): 23.

Salvadoran refugees are "economic," not "political" according to the State Dept.

1440 Frame, Randy. "Churches Violate Federal Law to Shelter Illegal Aliens," *Christianity Today* (March 16, 1984): 31.

Conscience confronts human law.

1441   Golden, Renny, and Michael McConnell. *Sanctuary: The New Underground Railroad.* Chicago: Guild Books, Maryknoll, NY: Orbis Books, 1985.

The best introduction and survey available.

1442   Hansell, Dean. "Sanctuary Movement Worker Convicted in Texas," *Fellowship* 50, 7-8 (July/August 1984): 34.

Focuses on the Catholics in the movement.

1443   Hentoff, Nat. "Snoops in the Pews," *The Progressive* 49,8 (August 1985): 24-26.

Ecumenical efforts of Roman Catholics, Quakers, mainline Protestants, and Jews who defy the government through their underground railroad. Reviews the central issue in the Tucson trial of Sanctuary workers: government bugging of Bible-study classes in Arizona. Hentoff compares the tactic to those of the Gestapo agents who sat in on church sermons in Nazi Germany and the government informants used in the U.S.S.R. and Czechoslovakia.

1444   Jorstad, Eric. "No Routine Smugglers: Reverberations from the Sanctuary Trial," *Commonweal* 113, 17 (Oct. 10, 1986): 522-25.

Reviews the legal case of the Tucson Sanctuary trial, procedural problems in the judges instructions to the jury, questions the ethics and legality of Federal evidence gathering, discusses the guilty feelings of the jurors who convicted eight of the eleven defendants, reviews states and cities that have declared themselves sanctuary zones. Concludes that the situation is now at a stalemate.

1445   King, Wayne. "When Is a Criminal Conspiracy Also an
       Act of Conscience? The Sanctuary Movement on
       Trial," *New York Times,* Nov. 24, 1985: E1.

       The conflict between the dictates of religious
       conscience and U.S. law forbidding the aiding of illegal
       aliens entering the country. The trial of Sanctuary
       defendants pits these two outlooks against one another.

1446   McCarthy, Tim. "Mixed Sanctuary Verdicts End Contro-
       versial Six-Month Trial," *NCR* 22, 28 (May 9, 1986):
       1, 19-20.

       Eight of the eleven defendants were convicted for
       smuggling aliens into the United States. The federal
       prosecutors argued that the altruism of the Sanctuary
       people was irrelevant to the case, since this was simply a
       matter of immigration law. The sentences were considered
       extremely harsh. Both government prosecutors and right-
       wing critics have long attempted to remove the movement
       from its essentially religious motives and roots, Federal
       prosecutor Reno calling it an "evil unto itself" and a "threat
       to society."
       Essentially the government has attempted to hide the
       real truth, that these immigrants are refugees from
       persecution, from the threats of death squads, survivors of
       massacres, relatives of the disappeared in the U.S.-backed
       holocaust of Central America. In response the churches
       have come together to cry out for justice and to bear
       witness to this truth that the government would conceal by
       physically aiding the victims find sanctuary in the United
       States.

1447   McGrath, Ellie. "Bringing Sanctuary to Trial; A Tucson
       Case Provides a Major Test of Church Against State,"

Time (Oct. 28, 1985): 69.

A review of the issues.

1448   "Politics Mixed with Prayer," *U.S. News & World Report* (Dec. 30, 1985): 115.

Not seen.

1449   "Religious Liberalism Revived," *America* (July 20, 1985): 23.

The Sanctuary movement reveals that despite the age of Reaganism, there remain forces within the church dedicated to social justice.

1450   Quammen, N. "Keepers of the Flame," *Esquire,* June 1985, 253.

Not seen.

1451   "Sanctuary Movement — A National Debate," *Nuestro,* September 1985, 12.

Not seen.

1452   Scherer, Peggy. "Offering Sanctuary," *Catholic Worker* 52, 1 (Jan./Feb. 1985): 1, 3.

Traces the story of one refugee from Guatemala, escaping the threat of murder by the paramilitary, her journey north, and the aid given her by the Sanctuary movement. Briefly examines the repressive and violent role of the U.S. government in Central America and the activity of the INS in prosecuting these Sanctuary people and deporting as many of the estimated 500,000 refugees that they can find. Catholics aiding these brothers and sisters do so in the spirit of solidarity urged by *Pacem in Terris.*

1453   Stengel, Richard. "Sanctuary Without Safety," *Time* (July 9 1984): 68.

On the beginnings of prosecutions of the Sanctuary people and the likelihood that the INS will become increasingly punitive toward both refugees and sanctuary workers.

1454   "Threat to Religious Liberty," *Christian Century* (Nov. 13, 1985): 1021.

Not seen.

1455   Tolan, Sandy, and Carol Ann Bassett. "Operation Sojourner; Informers in the Sanctuary Movement," *The Nation* 241, 2 (July 20/27, 1985): 40-44.

Examines the issues raised by Federal INA infiltration, not only of Sojourner meetings, but of Bible classes conducted by members of the movement, including Central American refugees. Begins to focus on the true conflict between God's law and human law posed by the movement.

1456   "Violating the Sanctuary," *America* (Feb. 9, 1985): 97.

INS efforts to infiltrate Sanctuary groups by spying of church and Bible-study sessions.

The Bishops and the Bomb

1457   Allen, John. "The Bishops' Letter: Challenge...What

Response?" *The Objector* 4, 1 (Sept. 1, 1983): 4.

Reviews the final draft of the bishops' letter and concludes that it will confront many Catholics for the first time with the morality of war. The letter uses both pacifist and just-war traditions, condemns attacks on population centers, first strikes, limited retaliation, questions deterrence and the morality of nuclear war at all. Allen stresses that after the pastoral Catholics seem to be left with only two choices: service to their country either in military defense or in nonviolent action, with the imperative that Catholics seek to define nonviolent methods of defense. He notes that we must avoid dehumanizing service people as instruments of war, and that the Department of Defense is now worried over the rise of pacifism. The letter stresses the rights of conscience and appears to approve selective conscientious objection.

1458   Benedictines for Peace. *Reflection Guide on the Challenge of Peace: God's Promise and Our Response. Pastoral Letter of U.S. Catholic Bishops.* Sr. Mary Lou Kownacki, O.S.B., ed. Chicago: Pax Christi, 1983.

The complete text of the pastoral interspersed with commentary. Each section of the pastoral is accompanied by appropriate questions for reflection. Attractively illustrated.

1459   Bernardin, J.L. "Pacem in Terris: Twenty Years Later," *Bulletin of Atomic Scientists* 40 (February 1984): 11-14.

Not seen.

1460 "Bishops: Catholic Personnel Must Look at Own Role in Nuclear Warfare," *The Objector* 3, 3 (December 1982): 5-6.

The military is becoming concerned about sections in the draft of the bishops' pastoral calling on personnel in the military and the defense industries to reexamine their roles in the light of Christian teaching and contemporary moral problems, and then to act on their consciences to leave such lives.

1461 Caplan, R. "People Who Are Deducting Defense," *The Nation* (April 6, 1985): 399-400.

A growing number of Americans, including many Catholics, are deducting that portion of their taxes that would otherwise go to fund defense spending. They do this out of the same logic that compels conscientious objectors to refuse military service.

1462 Castelli, Jim. *The Bishops and the Bomb*. Garden City, NY: Doubleday-Image, 1983.

On the three different drafts of the pastoral letter and the politics, both ecclesiastical and secular, behind the process. Prints text of **1479** on pp. 185-276.

1463 "Catholic Orders Sell G.E. Stock," *Fellowship* 50, 7-8 (July/August 1984): 35.

Twenty-six Roman Catholic orders sell 49,000 shares worth $2.4 million to protest G.E. involvement with nuclear and other weapons programs, after trying unsuccessfully to persuade the company to pull out of such war production.

1464   *The Church and the Arms Race.* Cambridge, MA: Pax
        Christi, 1977.

        Not seen.

1465   Clarke, T.E., "To Make Peace, Evangelize Culture,"
        America 150 (June 2, 1984): 413-17.

        The path to peace is not direct but involves a total
        conversion of individuals and our culture of violence and
        materialism.

1466   Cornell, Thomas. "War and Peace Pastoral," *Catholic
        Peace Fellowship Bulletin,* March 1983, 1-2.

        The second draft of the pastoral is far stronger than the
        first, giving more attention to the pacifist tradition,
        recognizing nonviolence as a principle, and using the just-
        war tradition to deny the morality of civil defense. Its
        parameters for nuclear war are so restrictive as to make it
        morally impossible. The letter will make a big difference
        in Catholic thought, not overnight, but it will cause more
        and more people to change their minds. It will form the
        will to make peace.

1467   Hehir, J. Bryan. "The Catholic Church and the Arms
        Race," *Worldview* 21 (July/August 1978): 13-18.

        Not seen.

1468   Hunthausen, Most Rev. Raymond. "Faith and Disarma-
        ment." See **1483**, 1-2.

        The bishop of Seattle, Washington, an area heavily
        dependent on the U.S. Trident submarine, shocked his
        diocese with his announcement in June 1981 that he would

withhold 50% of his taxes to protest nuclear arms. Such action is more terrifying to Americans than the thought of nuclear annihilation, for the alternative is the abandonment of America's privileged life-style and our terror over other peoples. This is our nation's great sin. Catholics must, therefore, abandon their passivity. Hiroshima and Nagasaki have sunk into our very souls and changed our Christianity. Our consent to the use of nuclear weapons is the taproot of all violence in our society. When such crimes are being prepared in our names, we must speak out against this new holocaust.

Politics are incapable of removing the despair of the nuclear age, we therefore need a deepening of faith and prayer to break the cycle. Yet such a gospel life is not easy. It requires Christians to take up their cross and to suffer persecution for their imitation of Christ. In this modern Catholics can imitate the lives of the early Christians under Rome who were punished for treason to the state. "Some would call what I am urging 'civil disobedience.' I prefer to see it as obedience to God."

1469   Kenny, Most. Rev. Michael. "The Way of Jesus." See **1483**, 4.

The bishop of Juneau, Alaska declares that he has always been a loyal citizen of the United States and still believes in its ideals and constitution and affirms that he accepts his responsibilities as a citizen, recognizing that many countries are far worse than the U.S. Yet over time the bishop has come to see nonviolence as the only course for Christians. His pacifism is personal, however. He will not condemn others who are engaged in what they honestly believe to be the legitimate defense of their country. He notes, however, that nonviolence, and the martyrdom it produced, was the seed of the church for its first 300 years.

1470   Kownacki, Sr. Mary Lou, O.S.B. *A Race to Nowhere:
        An Arms Race Primer for Catholics.* Chicago: Pax
        Christi, 1985.

        Well illustrated, with sectional bibliographies, this
        booklet discusses the general problem of armaments, the
        supposed Soviet threat, the cost of such military spending
        at home and around the world, the teachings of the
        Judaeo-Christian tradition on war and peace, pacifism and
        the just-war, and alternatives to the arms race.

1471   Matthiesen, Most Rev. Leroy T. "The Arms Race,
        Learning to Speak Out," *Catholic Worker* 51, 5
        (August 1984): 1-2, 8.

        Begins with a description of the activities of the Pantex
        nuclear arms factory in Amarillo, within his diocese, the
        final, and only, assembly plant for all U.S. nuclear
        weapons. Matthiesen, a native of this conservative city,
        began to question the morality of this center, preaching his
        first sermon on the justness of nuclear weapons on
        Christmas 1980. At first people gave only intellectual
        assent to the problem. He followed this with a written
        letter, then visited someone arrested for a demonstration
        outside the plant. He then received clandestine visits from
        Catholics troubled by their involvement with the pro-
        duction of nuclear weapons.
        Following statements by several bishops, including
        Raymond Hunthausen (See **1468**), Matthiesen himself
        wrote urging Catholics to reconsider their defense work.
        This finally caused an uproar, because it called on people
        to reexamine the very foundations of their lives and
        livelihoods. Gradually, however, the bishop is getting a
        lot of support, still clandestine, for his outspoken stance.

Gradually, the courage of others will make us all gather strength.

1472   ——."The Production and Stockpiling of the Neutron Bomb." See **1483**, 4.

This bishop caused a furor in Texas for his call for workers in nuclear-weapons industries to leave their jobs. He launched a fund to ease their transition to peace industries. Condemning the neutron bomb, he declared, "enough of this greater and greater destructive capability. Let us stop this madness."

1473   Murnion, Philip J. *Catholics and Nuclear War: A Commentary on The Challenge of Peace.* New York: Crossroad, 1983.

Prints text of **1479** on pages 245-38. Analyses by Gordon Zahn, J. Bryan Hehir, David O'Brien, James Finn, and other leading Catholic peacemakers. Articles examine the text from several points of view, however, including the pastoral's background, the Catholic peace tradition, the biblical roots of the letter, pacifism and just war, nuclear war and deterrence, world order, and the significance of the document for the life of the church in conscience, prayer, and penance.

1474   Newman, Judy. "CO, Nuclear Weapons, and the Bishops' Letter," *The Objector* 6, 3 (December 1985): 4. See also **1358**.

Focuses on some of the issues where the bishops have not been as clear as they could have been: deterrence, the role of Roman Catholics in the armed forces, the issues of individual conscience, and selective conscientious objection are among them.

1475   Ostling, Richard N., and others. "The Bishops and the
        Bomb," *Time* (Nov. 29, 1982): 68-77.

        Reviews the issues involved in the pastoral, outlines
        the debate among the bishops, and focuses on some of the
        leading personalities of the conference. The article also
        examines some of the changes within American
        Catholicism itself, from a defensive, immigrant church to a
        major social and religious force in the United States,
        briefly reviewing the change in tone of the bishops'
        previous pastoral letters and the historical roots of the
        church's stand on peace.

1476   "Peace Fund," *Christian Century,* March 3, 1982.

        On Bishop Leroy Mathiesen's fund to help Pantex
        nuclear-weapons employees transfer to peace-economy
        work.

1477   Quinn, Most Rev. John R. "The Very Survival of the
        Human Race Is At Stake." See **1483**, 3.

        The arms race has become the major cause of
        insecurity in our lives. The Catholic church clearly teaches
        that nuclear weapons are evil. What response is therefore
        necessary? Cooperation with peace movements like the
        Freeze, opposition to Department of Defense nuclear war
        plans, conversion of military technology, and work for
        bilateral disarmament. The arms race destroys the human
        race in human terms, robbing fully one-third of the world
        of basic livelihoods. "The billions of dollars presently
        being spent on arms each year throughout the world are
        surely an appalling form of theft in a world where so many
        persons die each day of starvation and privation." As

Einstein warned, we must change our ways of thinking to keep in step with the new destructive technologies that we have unleashed.

1478   Roth, R.J. "The Bishops' Pastoral and Individual Conscience," *America* 150 (March 31, 1984): 237-39.

Not seen.

1479   U.S. Conference of Catholic Bishops. *The Challenge of Peace: God's Promise and Our Response.* Washington, DC: U.S. Conference of Catholic Bishops, 1983.

The text of the controversial pastoral on war and peace. Part One discusses peace in the modern world, first from a historical perspective of peace theory and action from the Old and New Testaments, then from the developing theory of the just war. Part Two discusses the problem of war and peace in the modern world, religious leadership in the debate, and then carefully analyzes the use of nuclear weapons, examining their use against population centers, as first-strike weapons, and in the context of limited nuclear war. The bishops then go on to assess the moral worth of the theory of deterrence and venture tentatively into policy questions.

Part Three recommends specific policies for promoting peace through arms control, replacement of nuclear by conventional armaments, and civil defense. The bishops then take a hard look at nonviolent means of defense, recommending that these be given equal attention with military defense. They then discuss the role of conscience in making peace before reviewing the Catholic tradition of internationalism and world order, reviewing the present chaotic state of the world between the superpowers, and stressing the need for global interdependence.

Part Four lays bare the pastoral's theological heart: the church as a community of conscience, prayer and penance, not a hierarchical structure of law and obedience, and recommends certain forms of working for peace. These include educational programs to help form consciences, the reverence for life that underpins all peacemaking, the role of prayer, and finally of penance and conversion. Peace is finally defined as the challenge and the gift of Christ, and the future hope of Christians.

1480   ——.Daughters of St. Paul, eds. Boston, 1983.

Another edition.

1481   ——.Edited in *The Catholic Standard.* Washington, DC, 1983.

Another edition.

1482   ——.*To Live in Jesus Christ: A Pastoral Reflection on the Moral Life.* Washington, D.C., 1976.

The bishops' previous condemnation of nuclear arms, even as a deterrent.

1483   *U.S. Bishops Speak Against Nuclear Arms.* Catholic Peace Fellowship, Peace Education Supplement 4. New York: Catholic Peace Fellowship, 1981.

Includes **1468, 1469, 1472, 1477.**

1484   Wallis, Jim, ed. *Peacemakers. Christian Voices from the New Abolitionist Movement.* San Francisco: Harper & Row, 1983.

The varieties of modern responses to nuclear and conventional war.

1485 Zahn, Gordon. "On Not Writing a Dead Letter," *Commonweal* (March 8, 1985): 141-43.

Not seen.

* *
*

INDEX OF TITLES

523

INDEX OF AUTHORS, EDITORS, AND TRANSLATORS

563

INDEX OF PROPER NAMES

Composition of This Book Was Completed on
Easter Sunday, 1987 at Italica Press,
New York, New York
Deo Gratias

* *
*